Weapons of Mass Migration

A volume in the series

CORNELL STUDIES IN SECURITY AFFAIRS

edited by Robert J. Art, Robert Jervis, and Stephen M. Walt

A list of titles in this series is available at www.cornellpress.cornell.edu.

Weapons of Mass Migration

Forced Displacement, Coercion, and Foreign Policy

Kelly M. Greenhill

CORNELL UNIVERSITY PRESS
ITHACA AND LONDON

Cornell University Press gratefully acknowledges receipt of a
subvention from the Security Studies Program at the Massachusetts Institute of Technology, which aided in the publication of
this book.

First published 2010 by Cornell University Press
First printing, Cornell Paperbacks, 2016

Library of Congress Cataloging-in-Publication Data

Greenhill, Kelly M., 1970–
    Weapons of mass migration : forced displacement, coercion,
and foreign policy / Kelly M. Greenhill.
        p. cm. — (Cornell studies in security affairs)
    Includes bibliographical references and index.
    ISBN 978-0-8014-4871-3 (cloth : alk. paper)
    ISBN 978-1-5017-0436-9 (pbk. : alk. paper)
    1. Refugees—Case studies. 2. Forced migration—Political
aspects—Case studies. 3. Emigration and immigration—
Political aspects—Case studies. 4. International relations—
Case studies. I. Title. II. Series: Cornell studies in security
affairs.
    HV640.G73   2010
    325'.21—dc22   2009042857

To B. R. P. and L. J. G.

Contents

Acknowledgments

Writing a book can be likened to an athletic contest—sometimes a sprint, other times a marathon. This particular book has most resembled a triathlon, with a few obstacle courses thrown in for good measure. But like any challenge embraced and eventually surmounted, the satisfaction derived from crossing the finish line has put paid to all the pain that preceded it. To be sure, I would gladly have circumvented some of the obstacles along the way: most notably, the destruction of my desktop hard drive (and the broken limbs that preceded it), the theft of my external backup drive, and the disappearance of the manuscript en route to a reviewer (and the drama that followed). Nevertheless, the rough terrain traversed along the way resulted in greater learning and a far more rewarding journey than a short race would have yielded. I can only hope that it has also resulted in a stronger, better book. Yet I would never have made it past the first mile marker—much less finished the race—without the invaluable advice, support, and assistance of a great many individuals and organizations. My gratitude is both deep and immense.

This book literally could not have been written but for the mentoring and support I received in the Security Studies Program (SSP) at the Massachusetts Institute of Technology (MIT). I owe a special debt to Barry Posen, but for whom I probably would not even be a political scientist. As an advisor and as a friend, he has been without peer, relentlessly pushing me both by example and by design to make my research as good as it could be, while just as unerringly supporting and encouraging me on those occasions when my own faith and optimism flagged. Stephen Van Evera's input is visible in every chapter of this book. His role in sharpening both my writing and my arguments has been key, as has his support for this project. Kenneth Oye's contribution is likewise evident throughout. Ken's unique, personally informed knowledge of refugee policy and history, coupled with the excellent training in international relations theory and research design that he provided, has informed and improved this book in more ways than I can easily enumerate.

The editorial team in the Security Studies Series at Cornell—and most particularly, Robert Art and Roger Haydon—warrant special thanks as well. Any one of a myriad of obstacles could have sent this project off the rails. Yet the editors encouraged me to persevere and offered all manner of excellent advice along the way. The unwavering faith and support Bob provided throughout the process has been singularly and critically important. Roger's encouragement, assistance, and dry wit have likewise been instrumental. I offer my thanks as well to several anonymous reviewers for their very thoughtful assessments and detailed suggestions on how to improve this book.

Many friends and colleagues also read closely and offered valuable comments on written portions of this project in its various guises: Peter Andreas, Nikolaos Bizouras, Michael Boyle, Joshua Busby, Daniel Byman, Kanchan Chandra, Matthew Evangelista, Martha Finnemore, Peter Gourevitch, Robert Jervis, Dominic Johnson, Peter Katzenstein, Charles Keely, Alan Kuperman, Chappell Lawson, Roy Licklider, Jennifer Lind, Sarah Lischer, John Park, Michael Reynolds, Stephen Rosen, Robert Rotberg, Evan Schofer, Oxana Shevel, Jack Snyder, Elizabeth Stanley-Mitchell, Sharon Stanton-Russell, Sherrill Stroschein, and Benjamin Valentino. The roles played by David Art, Alexander Downes, Lincoln Greenhill, Jeremy Pressman, and Jacob Shapiro are worthy of particular note. As scholars, they graciously provided feedback on multiple versions of the chapters herein, served as sounding boards for my ideas, and shared terrific ideas of their own. As friends, they were likewise exceptional; among other things, they kept me sane and laughing throughout this sometimes profoundly unfunny process. I offer my sincere thanks to one and all and also offer apologies to anyone I may have inadvertently forgotten to mention. The comments I received improved this book immeasurably. The errors and shortcomings that remain are my own.

I received additional helpful feedback when presenting this work at various stages at the following institutions: SSP, MIT; the Olin Institute for Strategic Studies, Harvard University; the Center for Science and International Affairs (CISAC); Stanford University (with special thanks to Tonya Putnam and Todd Sechser); the University of California, Berkeley (where feedback from Thad Dunning was especially valuable); the

Patterson School, University of Kentucky (where incisive critiques by Michael Desch, Eugene Gholz, and Stuart Kaufman were particularly useful); Tufts University and the Intrastate Conflict Program at the Belfer Center for Science and International Affairs, Harvard University (where feedback from Robert Rotberg and Fotini Christia also warrants special mention).

Several institutions and organizations also deserve my thanks for their generous financial support of this research; this book would have been impossible without them. The MacArthur Foundation; the Mellon Foundation; the Eisenhower Foundation; the Johnson Library Foundation; SSP; and MIT all provided funding for fieldwork, archival study, and the project in general. I am also greatly indebted to the Social Science Research Council; the Olin Institute for Strategic Studies, Harvard University; CISAC, Stanford University; and the Belfer Center for Science and International Affairs, Harvard University for awarding me year-long fellowships, which freed me from other obligations and allowed me to concentrate my full energies on this project. I also thank CISAC for graciously hosting me each summer since my original stint as a fellow. I am especially grateful for all the advice, moral support, and encouragement provided by Lynn Eden, Scott Sagan, and Elizabeth Gardner as I went through the painstaking process of (re)constructing much of this book from scratch, as well as for granting me the opportunity to do that work in such a beautiful and intellectually stimulating environment. I also thank SSP for going far beyond the call of duty in providing funding for the book's "caboose."

Portions of chapter 2 were previously published in my article "Engineered Migration and the Use of Refugees as Political Weapons: A Case Study of the 1994 Cuban *Balseros* Crisis," *International Migration* 40, no. 4 (2002): 39–74. Parts of chapter 3 appeared in "The Use of Refugees as Political and Military Weapons in the Kosovo Conflict," in *Yugoslavia Unraveled: Sovereignty, Self-Determination, and Intervention,* edited by Raju G. C. Thomas, 205–42 (Lanham, Md.: Lexington Books, 2003). I thank Blackwell Publishers and Rowman and Littlefield for permission to adapt those materials herein.

Finally, I thank my *beshert*—my partner in everything that matters. He makes every day an adventure, and every adventure utterly unmissable. He has been by my side every inch, every foot, every mile of this contest, and to quote Robert Frost—a writer far more eloquent than I—"that has made all the difference."

Weapons of Mass Migration

Introduction

One refugee is a novelty, ten refugees are boring and a hundred refugees are a menace.

On October 11, 2004, the foreign ministers of the European Union met and agreed to lift all remaining sanctions on one-time international pariah state, Libya. This broad array of sanctions, which included a comprehensive arms embargo, had been in place since the 1980s following several high-profile Libyan-sponsored terrorist attacks within Western Europe. What catalyzed this dramatic shift in EU policy? Although relations between Libya and the European Union had been improving for some time, it was neither the Libyan decision to disband its weapons of mass destruction program nor its public repudiation of terrorism nor even its acceptance of responsibility for the bombing of Pan Am Flight 103 over Lockerbie, Scotland, that was ultimately decisive.[1] Instead, sanctions were lifted in exchange for a Libyan promise to help staunch a growing flow of North African migrants and asylum seekers across the Mediterranean and on to European soil. The prime instrument of influence? Not bullets or bombs, but human beings. Simply put, European fears of unfettered migration permitted Libyan leader Muammar al-Gaddafi to engage in a successful, if rather unconventional, form of coercion against the world's largest political and

Epigraph: An unattributed but oft-quoted phrase in refugee literature, found among other places, in D.P. Kent, *The Refugee Intellectual: The Americanization of the Immigrants of 1933–1941* (New York: Columbia University, 1953), 172; and A. J. Sherman, *Island Refuge: Britain and the Refugees from the Third Reich 1933–1939* (London: Elek Books, 1973), 13.

[1] But these developments undoubtedly helped make the EU decision easier to sell domestically and internationally.

economic union—a form of coercion predicated on the intentional creation, manipulation, and exploitation of migration and refugee crises.[2]

This book offers the first systematic theoretical and empirical exploration of this highly irregular method of persuasion. It examines three key questions, which serve three discrete analytical functions: How often does it happen (measurement of incidence), how often does it work (evaluation of success and failure), and how and why does it ever work (description of the phenomenon)? Much of the rest of the book is then devoted to testing the proposed theory and to exploring the theoretical and policy implications of its findings.

Using a combination of large-N and comparative case-study analyses, this book identifies more than fifty attempts at what I term *coercive engineered migration* (or migration-driven coercion) since the advent of the 1951 Refugee Convention alone—well over half of which succeeded in achieving at least some of their objectives. This is an impressive rate of success, given that the U.S. rate of success when engaged in coercive diplomacy, employing conventional military means, lies somewhere between 19 and 37.5 percent.[3] Given these relatively favorable odds, there are compelling incentives—particularly for relatively weak state and nonstate actors who lack recourse to traditional methods of influence—to create, manipulate, or simply exploit migration crises, at least in part, to influence the behavior of target states. A better understanding of the factors that make the use of this unconventional strategy attractive, the conditions under which it tends to succeed, and how it can be more effectively deterred and combated could therefore prove important from both a scholarly and a policy perspective. This is especially true because of the potentially devastating consequences that these unnatural disasters portend for the true victims— the displaced themselves. Given that many tens of millions have been driven from their homes since World War II alone, this is a matter of more than academic importance.

---

[2] EU officials, personal communication, Frankfurt, Germany, February 2005, and United Nations headquarters, New York, June 2005. See also Sara Hamood, "EU-Libya Cooperation on Migration: A Raw Deal for Refugees and Migrants?" *Journal of Refugee Studies* 21 (2008): 19–42; "EU Lifts Arms Embargo on Libya for Refugee Deal," *Afrol News*, October 11, 2004, http://www.afrol.com/articles/14503; "Immigration: EU to Assist Libya," *AKI* (Italy), June 3, 2005; the report from the *Third European Parliament/Libya Interparliamentary Meeting*, April 2005, www.europarl.eu.int/meetdocs/2004_2009/documents/cr/569/569969/569969en.pdf.

[3] Barry Blechman and Stephen Kaplan, in *Force without War: U.S. Armed Forces as a Political Instrument* (Washington, D.C.: Brookings Institution, 1978), posit a coercive diplomacy success rate of 19 percent; Alexander George and William Simons, *The Limits of Coercive Diplomacy* (Boulder: Westview Press, 1994), place it at 29 percent; Robert Art and Patrick Cronin, *The United States and Coercive Diplomacy* (Washington, D.C.: United States Institute of Peace, 2003), cite a figure of 31 percent; and Todd Sechser, in his 2007 Stanford doctoral dissertation, "Winning without a Fight: Power, Reputation, and Compellent Threats in International Crises," reports the highest rate of 37.5 percent.

I also propose an explanation as to how, why, and under what conditions this kind of coercion succeeds and fails. My central claim is that coercive engineered migration can be usefully conceived as a two-level, generally asymmetric, coercion by punishment strategy, in which challengers on the international level seek to influence the behavior of their targets by exploiting the existence of competing domestic interests within the target state(s) and by manipulating the costs or risks imposed on their civilian population(s).[4] In traditional coercion, these costs are inflicted through the threat and use of military force to achieve political goals "on the cheap." In coercive engineered migration, by contrast, costs are inflicted through the threat and use of human demographic bombs to achieve political goals that would be utterly unattainable through military means.[5]

As with terrorism and strategic bombing, those within the target state singled out for punishment (the civilian population) are not generally synonymous with the primary targets of coercion (the government).[6] As is likewise true of these other two instruments of influence, the (threatened) punishment may be imposed all at once or through gradual escalation and promises of future pain if concessions are not forthcoming. Regardless of how the punishment is meted out, however, challengers aim to impose costs on target populations that are higher than the stakes in dispute in the hope that target governments will be pressured, either directly or indirectly, to concede to the coercer's demands rather than incur the expected political costs of continued resistance.[7]

There are two nonmutually exclusive, yet independently sufficient, pathways by which would-be coercers can impose costs on targets: (1) through straightforward threats to overwhelm the physical or political capacity of a target state to accommodate an influx and (2) through a kind of norms-enhanced political blackmail predicated on exploitation of the heterogeneity of interests that frequently exists within polities.[8] Political heterogeneity becomes problematic in this context because migration crises tend to engender diverse and often quite divisive responses within the societies expected to bear or absorb their consequences. During most

---

[4] Robert A. Pape, *Bombing to Win: Air Power and Coercion in War* (Ithaca, N.Y.: Cornell University Press, 1996), 21.

[5] For instance, the idea that Albania could successfully coerce Italy or Greece via threats of military force is absurd. Yet its exploitation of mass migrations across the Adriatic Sea into Italy and through the Pindus Mountains into Greece resulted in a series of concessions by both Italy and Greece during the 1990s. See appendix for details.

[6] For instance, those targeted in strategic bombing raids are often not the leaders but, rather, noncombatants, who are expected to exert pressure on said leaders to remove the threat of further pain and escalating costs.

[7] Pape, *Bombing to Win*, 21.

[8] Robert Putnam, "Diplomacy and Domestic Politics: The Logic of Two-Level Games," *International Organization* 42 (1988): 427–60.

crises, for instance, some segment of society will strongly support offering protection, refuge, or asylum to the displaced, whereas another segment will be steadfastly opposed. For reasons I detail in chapter 2, an inability to simultaneously satisfy these competing and often highly mobilized (and politically potent) groups can make conceding to a coercer's demands—in the expectation that doing so will make a real or threatened crisis dissipate or disappear—a compelling proposition. To be sure, however, because this strategy depends on the existence of domestic discord and political contestation, not all states will be equally vulnerable. Nor will even particularly vulnerable states be vulnerable at all times and under all conditions.

I further contend that a key (norms-based) mechanism that can enhance the coercive power of the second pathway is the imposition of what I call *hypocrisy costs*—defined as those symbolic political costs that can be imposed when there exists a real or perceived disparity between a professed commitment to liberal values and norms and demonstrated actions that contravene such a commitment. Target states disposed to respond to a threatened influx with promises to forcibly repatriate unwelcome asylum seekers or simply turn migrants back at the border, for instance, may find themselves facing significant hypocrisy costs if they attempt to undertake such actions after having previously made rhetorical and/or juridical commitments to protect and defend those fleeing violence, persecution, or privation. Such moral contradictions are well recognized—and often quite deliberately exploited—by those who engage in this kind of coercion. Hypocrisy costs are not necessary for coercion to succeed; however, they can serve as effective force multipliers for weak challengers, allowing them to punch above their weight and to influence the behavior of actors normally outside their ambit.

For two distinct yet interrelated reasons, it follows that liberal democracies should be particularly vulnerable to the imposition of hypocrisy costs and to coercive engineered migration, more generally. First, the competitive, pluralistic, and largely transparent nature of policymaking within liberal democracies means that potential challengers can often readily measure the existence and extent of political contestation (or consensus) within a polity, calculate the likely reactions within that polity to a given influx, and, consequently, evaluate how broad or narrow a target state's set of possible policy responses to a crisis are likely to be. Second, because democracies are more likely than their illiberal counterparts to have codified juridical human rights and migration-related commitments, they are correspondingly more vulnerable to claims of hypocrisy if they seek to behave in ways that contravene such commitments. Not surprisingly, perhaps, evidence suggests liberal democracies have indeed been the most popular targets of this kind of coercion in the last half century. Nevertheless, for reasons I outline in chapter 2 and explore further in chapter 5 with specific reference to China, illiberal regimes have not been immune.[9]

Still, to be clear, coercive engineered migration is no superweapon. For one thing, for reasons both within and outside their control, challengers sometimes miscalculate. Targets that appear quite vulnerable at the outset may grow less so over time, as, for instance, Yugoslav president Slobodan Milosevic discovered in spring 1999 when his attempt to undermine North Atlantic Treaty Organization (NATO) unity with the threat of a massive outflow directed toward his southern European neighbors backfired (see chap. 4). For another, the weapons in migration-driven coercion are themselves sentient beings who may undermine coercive attempts by, among other things, moving in larger numbers and in different directions from those envisioned by would-be coercers. In short, due to the potential costs and the dangers associated with initiating mass migrations—including the possibility of political destabilization at home and military intervention from abroad—it is rarely an instrument of first resort.

Moreover, as is true of its conventional military counterpart, the circumstances under which migration-driven coercion will succeed are highly circumscribed; challengers will prevail only if targets deem the costs of concession lower than the costs of continued resistance. Nevertheless, although the limitations of this unconventional strategy are real, so are its potential merits—from a strategic standpoint, albeit not a moral one. This is particularly true for weak (and highly committed) state and nonstate actors with few other options at their disposal. The cases examined in detail in chapters 2–5 illustrate my theory in a variety of different geographic and temporal contexts and test it against plausible alternative explanations. The case-selection criteria and a discussion of the methodology employed in the case study analysis can be found at the conclusion of chapter 1. The appendix provides short synopses of all heretofore identified cases.

This analysis and findings offered in this book have clear policy implications in today's immigration anxiety–ridden environment. Long before September 11 galvanized a new preoccupation with border security, issues surrounding refugees and illegal migrants had transmuted in many countries from a matter of low politics to high politics, involving a shift in the definition of *national security threats* and in the practice of security policy. Indeed, migration-related fears can catalyze consequential political and military responses, even in cases in which coercion does not ultimately succeed. For instance, following repeated threats in 2002 and 2004 by Belarussian President Aleksandr Lukashenko to flood the European Union with asylum seekers if it failed to meet his demands, member states

[9] See also the appendix for additional cases in which illiberal states have been targeted.

pledged to spend more than half a billion euros to enhance their border security and deter future attempts at coercion.[10]

In fact, the popularity of radical right parties in many European countries can be directly linked with growing xenophobia and fears associated with being overrun. French and Dutch voters failed to adopt the European Constitution in spring 2005 at least in part because of such fears; recall, for instance, the mobilizing power of the proverbial, job-snatching Polish Plumber, who loomed large in the lead-up to the French vote.[11] Similarly, in the United States calls to increase the stringency of immigration policies—and to tighten access to social services—have proven to be effective campaign fodder, especially in states with large immigrant populations. Those opposed to inflows have gained further political traction since the attacks on the World Trade Center by stressing looming dangers associated with border porosity, asylum system abuses, and disaffected exiles turned terrorists.[12]

Moreover, the political and national security implications of engineered migrations extend far beyond the politically charged realms of immigration, asylum, and border security policy. Indeed, it has been suggested that the nonspontaneous "flood of refugees from East to West Germany in 1989...helped to bring down the Berlin Wall, expedited the unification of the two German states, and generated the most significant transformation in international relations since World War II."[13] Migration and refugee flows have likewise been identified as one of the most significant causes of armed conflict in the post–Cold War period.[14] Since 2004 alone, we have witnessed the consequences of coercive engineered migration in arenas as significant and diverse as economic sanctions and arms embargoes (in the aforementioned Libyan case); ethnic conflict, military intervention, and interstate war (between Sudan and Chad, over refugees from Darfur); and nuclear proliferation and regime change (in that China's fears of a mass influx of North Koreans have tempered its posture toward, and deal-

[10] "Will Belarus Flood Poland with 50,000 Migrants by Christmas?" *Wprost* (Warsaw), December 15, 2002; Robin Shepherd, "Belarus Issues Threat to EU Over Summit," *Times*, November 14, 2002; "EU Asked for Payment to Stop Refugees," *Irish Times*, May 27, 2004; Volker ter Haseborg, "Radioactive Refuge: Offering Asylum in Chernobyl's No Man's Land," *Der Spiegel On-Line*, October 14, 2005, http://www.spiegel.de/international/0,1518,379727,00.html.

[11] See "The Polish Plumber," *Newsweek International Edition*, October 17, 2005.

[12] The popularity of the private border patrol, known as the Minutemen, provides further evidence of apprehensions within the United States. See Deborah W. Meyers, "US Border Enforcement: From Horseback to High-Tech," *Migration Policy Institute Task Force Policy Brief*, November 7, 2005, www.migrationinformation.org/Feature/display.cfm?ID=370.

[13] Gil Loescher, "Refugee Movements and International Security," *Adelphi Paper* no. 268, London, International Institute for Strategic Studies, 1992, 3.

[14] Idean Salehyan and Kristian Gleditsch, "Refugees and the Spread of Civil War," *International Organization* 60 (2006): 335–66.

ings with, both North Korea and the United States over the North Korean nuclear program).[15]

In an effort to help decision makers become better prepared to address some of the more serious humanitarian and political-military issues to which real and threatened crises can give rise, this book also explores the contemporary policy implications of its empirical findings. Each case study chapter includes an analysis of the policy consequences of past actions, which in turn suggest lessons that may be applied in future. Further, the final chapter identifies a variety of policies that may reduce the susceptibility of target states to this kind of coercion. The implementation of these recommendations may leave potential targets better prepared to combat attempts to exploit their vulnerability; it may also help them better protect those most at risk by introducing effective disincentives to the creation and manipulation of migration crises.

Beyond presenting the first comprehensive analysis and accounting of this unique brand of nonmilitary coercion, this book also takes a small step toward plugging three holes in the international relations literature: on norms, on migration, and on coercion. In doing so, it also supplements the existing literatures on two-level games, audience costs, and the instrumental use of norms.

Numerous recent studies have explored how norms can be harnessed and used by states and nonstate actors that abide by them to improve the behavior of states that violate them.[16] To the best of my knowledge, however, this is the first book to conduct a systematic examination of the converse condition—how norms may be instrumentally violated and exploited by actors to influence the behavior of states that adhere to them. Correspondingly, that weak actors may use norms to help compensate for their relative deficiencies when seeking to influence more powerful counterparts is well understood. But the conditions under which the use

---

[15] Moreover, the *Economist* reported in August 2006 that Gaddafi, the Libyan leader, was probably again attempting to coerce the EU through the use of migrants. See "Sunk: More Boats, More Drownings—and Suspicions about Libya's Role," *Economist*, August 24, 2006. On Darfur, see "Chad: President Threatens to Expel Darfur Refugees as Attacks Surge in Lawless East," *IRIN*, April 14, 2006. On North Korea, see "Kim Jong Il Goes Ballistic," *Economist*, July 6, 2006; Jayshree Bajoria, "The China-North Korea Relationship," *Council on Foreign Relations Backgrounder*, June 18, 2008, www.cfr.org/publication/11097/chinanorth_korea_relationship.html.

[16] See, for instance, Margaret E. Keck and Kathryn Sikkink, *Activists beyond Borders: Advocacy in International Politics* (Ithaca, N.Y.: Cornell University Press, 1998); Thomas Risse, Stephen C. Ropp, and Kathryn Sikkink, eds., *The Power of Human Rights: International Norms and Domestic Change* (Cambridge, UK: Cambridge University Press, 1999); Daniel C. Thomas, *The Helsinki Effect: International Norms, Human Rights, and the Demise of Communism* (Princeton: Princeton University Press, 2001); Sanjeev Khagram James V. Riker, and Kathryn Sikkink, *Restructuring World Politics: Transnational Social Movements, Networks and Norms* (Minneapolis: University of Minnesota Press, 2003).

of norms-based sources of influence succeed and fail remain markedly less so; this book offers a model of one such set of conditions. It simultaneously addresses an often-levied criticism about scholarship on norms—that it tends to focus almost exclusively on "good" norms and their benefits, ignoring an entire subclass of actors whose goals are far less altruistic in intent or beneficent in consequence.[17] This book focuses squarely on those who self-consciously flout and deliberately exploit norms for self-serving, power-political objectives; its findings may materially enhance our understanding of the conditions under which the instrumental use of norms, for better and for worse, succeed and fail.

In a similar vein, a quarter century has now past since Myron Weiner first asserted that sending states exercise far more control over their out-migrations than was previously thought and may use them like a "'national resource' to be managed like any other."[18] Yet this issue has still received remarkably little attention. Refugee expert Michael Teitelbaum has deemed this omission "the most striking weakness in migration theories drawn from the social sciences"—one that is particularly regrettable because the aggregate number of such outflows has been steadily rising since the early 1970s.[19] (Indeed, 87 percent of the cases identified in this book transpired after 1970.) This book takes a step toward filling this theoretical void by proffering a testable theory of strategic outmigration; in the concluding chapter, it also offers a potential explanation for the steady rise in outflows witnessed in recent decades.

In part as a prescriptive tool to aid policymakers, this book also speaks to an analogous gap in the coercion literature, most of which grew out of the Cold War. Although some noteworthy exceptions do exist, the bulk of this literature continues to focus largely on interstate threats, usually involving territorial aggression or intergovernmental intimidation via the threat of military force. However, a nontrivial amount of contemporary coercion falls outside these traditional parameters. This book—which

[17] See, for instance, Paul Kowert and Jeffrey Legro, "Norms, Identity and Their Limits," in *The Culture of National Security: Norms and Identity in World Politics,* ed. Peter J. Katzenstein (New York: Columbia University Press, 1996). Works that *do* speak to this set of issues, however, include Fiona Adamson, "Global Liberalism vs. Political Islam: Competing Ideological Frameworks in International Politics," *International Studies Review* 7 (2005): 547–69; Jeffrey W. Legro, *Cooperation under Fire: Anglo-German Restraint during World War II* (Ithaca, N.Y.: Cornell University Press, 1995).

[18] Myron Weiner, "International Emigration: A Political and Economic Assessment," paper presented at the conference on Population Interactions between Poor and Rich Countries, Cambridge, Mass., October 6–7, 1983, quoted in Michael Teitelbaum, "Immigration, Refugees, and Foreign Policy," *International Organization* 38 (1984): 447.

[19] Michael Teitelbaum, "International Migration: Predicting the Unknowable," in *Demography and National Security,* ed. Myron Weiner and Sharon Stanton Russell (New York: Berghahn Books, 2001), 26. See also Alan Dowty, *Closed Borders: The Contemporary Assault on the Freedom of Movement* (New Haven: Yale University Press, 1987), chap. 5.

focuses on less conventional methods of coercion as well as coercion by *non-state* actors—could provide a useful complement to the existing literature, particularly in extending our understanding of the power of nonmaterial factors in influencing coercive outcomes. In particular, my findings complement recent research by Ivan Arreguín-Toft and Gil Merom, as well as a now-classic piece by Andrew Mack.[20] Although Mack's analysis focuses on traditional military force—whereas I focus on nonmilitary instruments of persuasion—we both find that stronger actors (1) tend to fare poorly against highly committed, weaker adversaries, and (2) may find themselves crippled by domestically imposed constraints on behavior.[21]

My argument directly relates to Merom's theory as to why democracies lose small wars. Merom and I concur, for instance, that states' room for policy maneuver can be undercut by the fact that domestic liberals may point out the gap between the rhetoric used by a government and its actual actions. However, whereas Merom's model assumes that the critical cleavage lies between the state and society as a whole, in coercive engineered migration, the lynchpin of coercive success lies in the fact that targets can find themselves trapped *between competing segments* of society. Similarly, for Merom, external actors simply present "an exogenous problem that magnifies the domestic challenge [democracies] face in small wars." However, in cases of migration-driven coercion, external actors—and their ability to foment and stoke domestic discord—are the fundamental and essential source of the problems facing targets.[22]

That some actors may exploit others' competing domestic interests for their own bargaining advantage has long been recognized, as has the significance of the dynamic, intertwined connections between what happens on the domestic and international levels during bargaining. Most previous two-level analyses, however, have treated as axiomatic the assumption that—at least on the international level—both parties are trying to reach a negotiated settlement, albeit one that is most beneficial to its side. Most also treat the domestic level as simply a ratification process, after the "real" international game has resulted in an agreement. In contrast, I show that under some conditions challengers on the international level may try

---

[20] Ivan Arreguín-Toft, *How the Weak Win Wars: A Theory of Asymmetric Conflict* (Cambridge, UK: Cambridge University Press, 2005); Gil Merom, *How Democracies Lose Small Wars* (Cambridge, UK: Cambridge University Press, 2003); Andrew Mack, "Why Big Nations Lose Small Wars: The Politics of Asymmetric Conflict," *World Politics* 27 (1975): 175–200. See also Stephen Biddle, *Military Power: Explaining Victory and Defeat in Modern Battle* (Princeton: Princeton University Press, 2006).

[21] The direct overlap with Arreguín-Toft's work, which focuses on interaction effects of adversaries' military strategies, is also noteworthy, if limited. Specifically, in both military and nonmilitary realms, raw-material capabilities appear to influence policy choices, but can be poor predictors of ultimate outcomes.

[22] Merom, *How Democracies Lose Small Wars*, 22.

to force or blackmail reluctant counterparts (targets) into negotiated settlements to which they are opposed ex ante. Moreover, although within the confines of conventional warfare punishment strategies may indeed be inferior to denial strategies, my findings suggest that—at least in this particular nonmilitary realm—punishment strategies can work relatively well, at least relative to the available alternatives.[23] This finding has implications for our understanding of both coercion and the instrumental use of norms, although further research is necessary to isolate the full scope and range of conditions under which it holds.

In addition, although hypocrisy costs might be construed as a special subset of reputation or audience costs, they function in ways that run counter to traditional understandings of audience costs.[24] Audience costs are supposed to make democracies more credible in crisis-bargaining situations because (so the argument goes) as they rise, the probability that actors facing them will back down declines. By extension, because democracies theoretically face the highest audience costs, they should rarely back down.[25] Conversely, the cases examined here suggest that, with respect to hypocrisy costs, the higher the (anticipated) costs targets face, the *more likely* it is that they will back down. As such, this book builds on research that finds that democracies may be hobbled by their very nature in crisis bargaining situations.[26]

Although our understanding of the precise role reputational costs play in target decision making is still in its infancy, existing research, as well as anecdotal evidence from the crisis management field, suggests that these costs are not only real but also affect the attitudes and behaviors of both leaders and the public.[27] Because migration scholars who have studied the "soft" political power of human rights norms have largely restricted their

---

[23] Mark Clodfelter, *The Limits of Air Power: The American Bombing of North Vietnam* (New York: Free Press, 1989); Pape, *Bombing to Win*. See also Allan C. Stam, *Win, Lose or Draw: Domestic Politics and the Crucible of War* (Ann Arbor: University of Michigan Press, 1996).

[24] On audience costs, see James Fearon, "Domestic Political Audiences and the Escalation of International Disputes," *American Political Science Review* 88 (1994): 577–92.

[25] Ibid.; Alastair Smith, "International Crises and Domestic Politics," *American Political Science Review* 92 (1998): 23–638; Kenneth A. Schultz, *Democracy and Coercive Diplomacy* (New York: Cambridge University Press, 2001); Alexandra Guisinger and Alastair Smith, "Honest Threats: The Interaction of Reputation and Political Institutions in International Crises," *Journal of Conflict Resolution* 46 (2002): 175–200; Bahar Leventoğlu and Ahmer Tarar, "Prenegotiation Public Commitment in Domestic and International Bargaining," *American Political Science Review* 99 (2005): 419–33.

[26] For instance, Bernard Finel and Kristen Lord, eds., *Power and Conflict in the Age of Transparency* (New York: Palgrave, 2000), 137–80.

[27] See, for instance, Michael Tomz, *Reputation and International Cooperation: Sovereign Debt across Three Centuries* (Princeton: Princeton University Press, 2007); Eric Dezenhall and John Weber, *Damage Control: Why Everything You Know about Crisis Management Is Wrong* (New York: Portfolio, 2007); Maureen Mancuso, et al., *A Question of Ethics: Canadians Speak Out*, 2nd ed. (Oxford: Oxford University Press, 2007).

empirical focus to the judicial realm, this analysis presents an important contribution toward a more systematic—and testable—theory of normative constraint.

Finally, although this book focuses principally on migration, the theory it develops regarding the leverage weak actors can exercise through skillful exploitation of political heterogeneity and normative inconsistencies (the instrumental use of norms) is more broadly generalizable. The theory may be applied to any issue area in which the rhetorical pronouncements and/or juridical and normative commitments of actors and governments come into conflict with their observed behavior.[28] Additional potential applications include humanitarian intervention; wartime rules of engagement; and policies regarding sanctions, embargoes, and other nonlethal instruments of persuasion. Furthermore, states and their leaderships are also not the only targets of hypocrisy-based political pressure.[29] Hence, although further research is necessary to better understand how, where, and how successfully this unconventional method of influence can be employed outside the migration realm, the significance of this kind of norms-driven, two-level coercion should be neither underestimated nor ignored.

[28] See, for instance, Jeffrey Taliaferro, "*A Pact with the Devil* Roundtable," H-Diplo/H-Net: Social Sciences On-line, 2007, www.h-net.org/~diplo/roundtables/PDF/APactWithThe Devil-Roundtable.pdf.
[29] For example, as I discuss in chapter 6, the avowedly "green" energy company British Petroleum (BP) has been a recurrent target of environmentalists because it very publicly embraces an environmentally friendly ethos while sometimes behaving in ways that belie this ethos. See, for instance, Darcy Frey, "How Green Is BP?" *New York Times Sunday Magazine*, December 8, 2002.

1

Understanding the Coercive Power of Mass Migrations

If aggression against another foreign country means that it strains
its social structure, that it ruins its finances, that it has to give up its
territory for sheltering refugees...what is the difference between that
kind of aggression and the other type, the more classical type, when
someone declares war, or something of that sort?
SAMAR SEN, India's ambassador to the United Nations

Coercion is generally understood to refer to the practice of inducing or
preventing changes in political behavior through the use of threats, intimidation, or some other form of pressure—most commonly, military force.
This book focuses on a very particular nonmilitary method of applying
coercive pressure—the use of migration and refugee crises as instruments
of persuasion. Conventional wisdom suggests this kind of coercion is
rare at best.[1] Traditional international relations theory avers that it should
rarely succeed. In fact, given the asymmetry in capabilities that tends to
exist between would-be coercers and their generally more powerful targets, it should rarely even be attempted.[2] However, in this book—which
offers the first systematic examination of this unconventional policy

---

Epigraph: United Nations Security Council Resolution, 1606th meeting, December 4,
1971, 15.
[1] In a recent volume that functions as a survey of state of the field of migration, for instance, it was not even mentioned as a possible driver of forced migration. See Heaven Craw-
ley, "Refugees, Asylum-Seekers and Internally Displaced: The Politics of Forced Migration,"
in *The Politics of Migration: A Survey,* ed. Barbara Marshall (London: Routledge, 2006), 60–62.
Likewise, at a conference in Chiang Mai, Thailand, in January 2003, an internationally known
migration scholar told me, "Your theory is all very logical, very persuasive and everything;
I just don't believe this ever happens."
[2] For a pithy discussion of traditional views on crisis initiation by weaker powers, see
T. V. Paul, *Asymmetric Conflicts: War Initiation by Weaker Powers* (Cambridge, UK: Cambridge
University Press, 1994), chaps. 1–2.

tool—I demonstrate that not only is this kind of coercion attempted far more frequently than the accepted wisdom would suggest but that it also tends to succeed far more often than capabilities-based theories would predict.

I begin by outlining the logic behind the coercive use of purposefully created migration and refugee crises. Concomitantly, I also demonstrate that, contrary to conventional wisdom, these unnatural disasters are relatively common. I also outline how such cases are isolated, identified, and coded.[3] In the second section, I describe the kind of actors who resort to the use of this unconventional weapon and why. I then highlight the diverse array of objectives sought by those who employ it. I also show that this kind of coercion has proven relatively successful, at least as compared to more traditional methods of persuasion, particularly against (generally more powerful) liberal democratic targets. I next propose an explanation for why democracies appear to have been most frequently (and most successfully) targeted. I also advance my broader theory about the nature of migration-driven coercion, including how, why, and under what conditions it can prove efficacious. I conclude with a discussion of case selection and the methodology employed in the case study chapters that follow.

Defining, Measuring, and Identifying Coercive Engineered Migration

I define *coercive engineered migrations* (or *migration-driven coercion*) as those cross-border population movements that are deliberately created or manipulated in order to induce political, military and/or economic concessions from a target state or states.[4] The instruments employed to effect this kind of coercion are myriad and diverse. They run the gamut from compulsory to permissive, from the employment of hostile threats and the use of military force (as were used during the 1967–1970 Biafran and 1992–1995 Bosnian civil wars) through the offer of positive inducements and provision of financial incentives (as were offered to North Vietnamese

---

[3] Because the accepted wisdom suggests this kind of coercion is rare at best, it serves as my operative null hypothesis.

[4] Because the focus is on strategically generated population movements, I have excluded from this definition externalities-driven inflows and outflows—that is, those inadvertently generated as a consequence of other policies (e.g., people displaced by the construction of the Three Gorges Dam in China) or of conflict (e.g., the Belgian and French refugees who fled the German offensive in World War I). Also excluded are migrations that result from policies of neglect (e.g., people fleeing the famine in Ethiopia in the early 1980s). Included, however, is strategic repatriation, and the unusual, but sometimes potent, situation in which the movement of people into a challenger's territory is encouraged for strategic reasons. (See the appendix for several coercion-related examples.)

by the United States in 1954–1955, following the First Indochina War) to the straightforward opening of normally sealed borders (as was done by President Erich Honecker of East Germany in the early 1980s).[5]

Coercive engineered migration is frequently, but not always, undertaken in the context of population outflows strategically generated for other reasons. In fact, it represents just one subset of a broader class of events that all rely on the creation and exploitation of such crises as means to political and military ends—a phenomenon I call strategic engineered migration. In addition to the coercive variant, these purposeful crises can be usefully divided by the objectives for which they are undertaken into three distinct categories: dispossessive, exportive, and militarized engineered migrations. *Dispossessive engineered migrations* are those in which the principal objective is the appropriation of the territory or property of another group or groups, or the elimination of said group(s) as a threat to the ethnopolitical or economic dominance of those engineering the (out-) migration; this includes what is commonly known as ethnic cleansing. *Exportive engineered migrations* are those migrations engineered either to fortify a domestic political position (by expelling political dissidents and other domestic adversaries) or to discomfit or destabilize foreign government(s). Finally, *militarized engineered migrations* are those conducted, usually during armed conflict, to gain military advantage against an adversary—via the disruption or destruction of an opponent's command and control, logistics, or movement capabilities—or to enhance one's own force structure, via the acquisition of additional personnel or resources.[6]

Coercive engineered migration is often embedded within mass migrations strategically engineered for dispossessive, exportive, or militarized reasons. It is likely, at least in part as a consequence of its embedded and often camouflaged nature, that its prevalence has also been generally underrecognized and its significance, underappreciated. Indeed, it is a phenomenon that for many observers has been hiding in plain sight. For instance, it is widely known that in 1972 Idi Amin expelled most Asians from Uganda in what has been commonly interpreted as a naked attempt at economic asset expropriation.[7] Far less well understood, however, is the fact that approximately 50,000 of those expelled were British passport-holders, and that these expulsions happened at the same time that Amin was trying to convince the British to halt their drawdown of military assistance to his country. In short, Amin announced his intention to foist

---

[5] See the appendix for the details of these cases.

[6] For a more detailed examination of the other categories and uses of strategic engineered migration, see Kelly M. Greenhill, Strategic Engineered Migration as a Weapon of War," *Civil Wars* 10 (2008): 6–21.

[7] At the time, Asians owned most of the big businesses in Uganda.

50,000 refugees on the British, but did so with a convenient ninety-day grace period to give the British an opportunity to rescind their decision regarding aid.[8] And Amin's actions are far from unique.

Measuring Incidence

In fact, well over forty groups of displaced people have been used as pawns in at least fifty-six discrete attempts at coercive engineered migration since the advent of the 1951 United Nations Refugee Convention alone. An additional eight cases are suggestive but inconclusive or "indeterminate" (see table 1.1). Employment of this kind of coercion predates the post–World War II era.[9] However, in this book I focus on the post-1951 period because it was only after World War II—and particularly after ratification of the 1951 Refugee Convention—that international rules and norms regarding the protection of those fleeing violence and persecution were codified.[10] It was likewise only then that migration and refugees "became a question of high politics" and that, for reasons discussed later in this chapter, the potential efficacy of this unconventional strategy really began to blossom.[11]

The numbers of migrants and refugees affected by these coercive attempts have been both large and small, ranging from several thousand (Polish asylum seekers in 1994—case 43 in table 1.1) to upward of 10 million (East Pakistanis in 1971—case 10). The displaced groups exploited have comprised both coercers' co-nationals (e.g., Cubans who left the island in 1965, 1980, and 1994—cases 6, 21, and 44, respectively) and migrants and asylum seekers from the other side of the globe (e.g., Tamils used by East Germany against West Germany in the mid-1980s—case 26). As table 1.1 also indicates, there have been dozens of distinct challengers and at least as many discrete targets. However, for reasons I explore

---

[8] Phares Mutibwa, *Uganda since Independence: A Story of Unfulfilled Hopes* (Trenton, N.J.: Africa World Press, 1992); Marc Curtis, *Unpeople: Britain's Secret Human Rights Abuses* (London: Vintage Books, 2004).

[9] During World War II, for instance, the Polish government-in-exile attempted to gain greater leverage over the postwar distribution of spoils by directing people fleeing the Nazi onslaught to England—obviously not the most direct path of escape—where they were enlisted in the Allied war effort. See, for instance, Anita Prazmowska, "Polish Refugees as Military Potential: Policy Objectives of the Polish Government in Exile," in *Refugees in the Age of Total War,* ed. Anna C. Bramwell (London: Unwin Hyman, 1988), 219–32. See also Michael R. Marrus, *The Unwanted: European Refugees from the First World War through the Cold War* (Philadelphia: Temple University Press, 2002), 284.

[10] I employ Legro's definition of *norms* as "collective understandings of the proper behavior of actors." Jeffrey Legro, "Which Norms Matter? Revisiting the 'Failure' of Internationalism in World War II," *International Organization* 51 (1997): 33.

[11] Arthur Helton, refugee and migration expert, quoted in Barbara Crossette, "The Century of Refugees Ends. And Continues," *New York Times,* December 31, 2000.

TABLE 1.1
Challengers, Targets, and Migrant/Refugee Groups, 1951–2006

	Year	Challenger(s)	Principal Target(s)	Migrant/Refugee Group
1	1953	West Germany	United States	East Germans
2	1954–1955	South Vietnam and United States	North Vietnam	North Vietnamese
3	1956	Austria	United States	Hungarians
4	1954–1960	Algerian insurgents	French allies, esp. the United States	Algerians
5	**1961**	**United States**	**Soviet Union**	**East Germans (Berlin)**
6	1965	Cuba	United States	Cubans
7	1967–1970	Biafran insurgents	Western Europe, United States	Biafrans
8	**1967**	**Israel**	**Jordan**	**Palestinians**
9	1967	Jordan	United States	Palestinians
10	1971	Pakistan	India	East Pakistanis
11	1972	Uganda	United Kingdom	British passport holders
12	1978–1982	Bangladesh	Burma	Rohingyas
13	1978–1982	ASEAN, Hong Kong	Western great powers, esp. the United States	Indochinese
14	**1979**	**Vietnam**	**EC, United States**	**Vietnamese**
15	1979–1980s	Thailand	United States; China	Cambodians
16	1979–1981	Haiti	United States	Haitians
17	1979–1981	NGO activists	United States; Haiti	Haitians
18	1980s	Pakistan	United States	Afghans
19	1980s	Soviet Union	Pakistan	Afghans
20	1979–1980s	Exiled Afghan insurgents	Pakistan	Afghans
21	1980	Cuba	United States	Cubans
22	1981–1982	Austria	Western Europe, United States	Poles
23	1982	Thailand	United States; France	Vietnamese
24	early 1980s	Honduras	United States	Nicaraguans, esp. Contras
25	**mid-1980s–1997**	**Bangladesh**	**India**	**Chittagong tribes/ Chakmas**
26	1983–1986	East Germany	West Germany	Mixed: South and Southwest Asians and North Africans
27	1984–85	East Germany	Sweden	Mixed: South and Southwest Asians and North Africans
28	**1985**	**Libya**	**Tunisia, Egypt, Mauritania (TEM)**	**Guestworkers**
29	Late 1980s	Hong Kong, ASEAN	United States; Western Europe	Vietnamese boatpeople
30	1989–early 1990s	Vietnam	EC/EU, United States	Vietnamese
31	1989–1992	Bangladesh	Burma	Rohingyas
32	1990–1992	Saudi Arabia	Yemen	Yemeni laborers

(TABLE 1.1—cont.)

	Year	Challenger(s)	Principal Target(s)	Migrant/Refugee Group
33	1990s	Israel	Palestinians	Soviet Jews
34	1991–1992	United States	Israel	Soviet Jews
35	1990–1991	Albania	Italy	Albanians
36	1991	Albania	Italy, EC	Albanians
37	1990–1994	Albania	Greece	Ethnic Greek Albanians
38	**1991**	**Poland**	**EC, United States**	**Poles; Mixed**
39	1991	Ethiopia	Israel	Falashas
40	1991	Turkey	United States	Iraqis
41	1992–1994	Jean-Bertrand Aristide	United States	Haitians
42	1992–1995	Bosnians	UN Security Council	Bosnians
43	1994	Poland	Germany	Poles
44	1994	Cuba	United States	Cubans
45	mid-1990s	Zaire	Largely United States, France, and Belgium	Rwandans
46	1995	Libya	Egypt	Palestinians
47	mid-1990s	North Korea	China	North Koreans
48	1997	Albania	Italy	Albanians
49	**1998**	**Turkey**	**Italy**	**Kurds**
50	Late 1990s	Kosovar Albanians	NATO	Kosovar Albanians
51	1998–1999	Federal Republic of Yugoslavia	NATO, esp. Germany, Greece, Italy	Kosovar Albanians
52	1999	Macedonia I	NATO	Kosovar Albanians
53	1999	Macedonia II	NATO	Kosovar Albanians
54	2001–2003	Nauru	Australia	Mixed: South Asians
55	2002	Belarus	EU	Mixed
56	2002–2005	Activists/ NGO network	China	North Koreans
57	2002–2005	Activists/ NGO network	South Korea	North Koreans
58	2002–2006+	North Korea	China	North Koreans
59	2004	Nauru	Australia	Mixed: South and Southwest Asians
60	2004	Haiti	United States	Haitians
61	2004	Belarus	EU	Mixed
62	2004	Libya	EU	Mixed: North Africans
63	**2004**	**Chad**	**UN Security Council**	**Darfurians**
64	2006	Libya	EU	Mixed: North Africans

Notes: I have conclusively identified fifty-six cases. An additional eight cases (in boldface) are suggestive, but at this point, inconclusive ("indeterminate"). See the appendix for details. ASEAN, Association of Southeast Asian Nations; EC, European Community; EU, European Union; NATO, North Atlantic Treaty Organization; NGO, nongovernmental organization.

in detail later in this chapter, advanced liberal democracies appear to be particularly attractive targets; indeed, the United States has been the most popular target of all, with its Western European liberal democratic counterparts coming in a strong second.[12]

But what shall we make of these numbers? To put the prevalence of coercive engineered migration in perspective, at a rate of at least 1.0 case per year (between 1951 and 2006), it is significantly less common than interstate territorial disputes (approximately 4.82 cases/year). But, at the same time, it appears to be markedly more prevalent than both intrastate wars (approximately 0.68 cases/year) and extended intermediate deterrence crises (approximately 0.58/year). At a minimum, this suggests that the conventional wisdom about the relative infrequency of coercive engineered migration (my operative null hypothesis) requires reconsideration. More ambitiously, it suggests that what we think we know about the size and nature of the policy toolbox available to, and used by, state and nonstate actors may too require reconsideration. A failure to appreciate the relative pervasiveness of a frequently employed policy weapon can actively impede the ability of both scholars and policymakers to understand, combat, and respond to potential threats, as well as to protect those victimized by its use.

The imperative to pay greater attention to this phenomenon is underlined by the recognition that the actual number of cases since 1951 may in fact be larger than the fifty-six to sixty-four identified in this book. In addition to the aforementioned fact that this kind of coercion is sometimes embedded within outflows also engineered for other reasons, identification of cases tends to be further impeded by two other mutually reinforcing tendencies. On one side of the equation, states that have been successfully targeted in the past are often reluctant to advertise that fact, even within their own foreign policy establishments. Consider, for instance, that the now infamous 1980 Mariel boatlift had been underway for close to ten days before Victor Palmieri, then U.S. coordinator for refugee affairs, discovered that 1980 was not the first time Cuban President Fidel Castro had attempted to use a mass migration to force concessions by the United States; nor, moreover, did it prove to be the last.[13] As the case study chapters that follow vividly illustrate, failing to share such critical information can prove highly problematic in the context of crisis decision making. Nevertheless, such reticence is not wholly surprising.

---

[12] It is possible that illiberal authoritarian states *are* being routinely targeted but that these cases remain hidden due to such societies' being significantly less transparent. Yet, in the known cases in which such states have been targeted, success has been rare, suggesting otherwise. See the discussion on data-acquisition difficulties.

[13] David Wells Engstrom, *Presidential Decision Making Adrift: The Carter Administration and the Mariel Boatlift* (New York: Rowman and Littlefield, 1998), 189.

Not only may publicizing past vulnerabilities make a target more susceptible to future predation, but it may also heighten the political costs to be paid within the state's own polity. After all, what leader wants to voluntarily admit having been forced to offer concessions to actors who are commonly portrayed in the media and public fora not as formidable adversaries but, rather, as pathetic foes worthy of derision—for instance, a "tin-pot dictator" like Fidel Castro or an "obsequious" "tyrant" like Erich Honecker?[14]

On the other side of the equation, some would-be coercers issue their threats and demands only privately. For virtually every obvious challenger, such as Belarussian President Lukashenko, who in 2002 and 2004 (cases 52 and 61 in table 1.1) publicly proclaimed that "if the Europeans don't pay, we will not protect Europe from these flows,"[15] we can identify a far less visible counterexample. After the 1967 War, for instance, King Hussein of Jordan privately made clear to U.S. diplomats that it was well within his power to turn the ongoing Palestinian refugee crisis into a major embarrassment for both the United States and Israel if the United States failed to exert sufficient diplomatic pressure on the Israelis to take back those displaced by the war (case 9)—a case I discovered simply by chance while in the archives perusing previously classified documents on Vietnam.[16] To go from the particular to the general, one can only wonder how many other such cases might remain unrecognized. In short, irrespective of whether coercion succeeds or fails, cases in which threats were issued only privately can be difficult to identify.

Moreover, issued threats may be not only private but also conspicuously ambiguous. Consider, for example, the suggestive reply of then Chinese Vice Premier Deng Xiaoping to U.S. President Jimmy Carter during their historic 1979 meeting. After Carter asserted that the United States could not trade freely with China until its record on human rights improved and Chinese were allowed to emigrate freely, Deng smilingly retorted, "Okay. Well then, exactly how many Chinese would you like, Mr. President? One

[14] See, for instance, Joe Klein, "Why Not Kill Dictators with Kindness?" *Time*, March 3, 2003; Stephen Kinzer, "Germans Remember Little Good of Honecker, and Much Evil," *New York Times*, May 31, 1994. The irony, of course, is that the failure of a target to take past behavior into account can materially undermine its ability to thwart or circumvent future coercion.

[15] Quoted in Robin Shepherd, "Belarus Issues Threat to EU over Summit," *Times*, November 14, 2002.

[16] Lyndon Baines Johnson Library (LBJL), National Security Files of the Special Committee of the National Security Council, Box 11, 12, 13, Refugees Folder: "(Secret) Telegram from Ambassador to Jordan, Burns to the Secretary of State," (circa) July 31, 1967. As the appendix illustrates, such cases are far from unusual. It is possible that I have by chance discovered all of them; however, the law of probability suggests this is unlikely.

million? Ten million? Thirty million?"[17] Whether Deng actually intended to influence U.S. behavior remains unclear, but, in point of fact, his rejoinder reportedly stopped Carter cold and summarily ended their discussion of human rights in China.[18]

Coding Cases and Alternative Explanations

The ambiguity of intent inherent in the Carter-Deng exchange—coupled with the fact that the migration crisis in question was merely hypothetical—effectively excludes it (and all similarly murky events) from inclusion in the accounting of cases presented here. But this raises several obvious questions: First, on what basis have I concluded that coercive engineered migration was attempted in the cases identified in table 1.1? Second, are there alternative explanations that might equally well, or better, explain the observed behavior?

Because the conventional wisdom suggests that coercive engineered migration is rare at best, no comprehensive alternative explanations exist. But specific alternatives have been put forward to explain particular cases. From these case-specific explanations, I have inductively derived three generalizable and testable alternative hypotheses:

1. An outflow may be the result of forces largely outside of the control of the principals. That is, because migrants and refugees themselves have agency, they themselves dictate when they leave and where they go.
2. An outflow may be the result of some non-rational, and certainly non-strategic, action that has little or nothing to do with coercion.
3. An outflow may be, in fact, strategic but not coercive in nature. In other words, an outflow may be driven by dispossessive, exportive, or militarized motivations, rather than coercive ones.

To test and evaluate the validity of the alternatives, three questions must be satisfactorily answered: (1) Was the (threatened) outflow (largely) controlled by the principals, (2) was it strategic, and (3) was it coercive? (See fig. 1.1.) Consequently, I deem a case to be a bona fide coercive attempt, and include it in the database if and only if there is evidence of (1) orchestration and/or overt control over the size, timing, and destination of a real or imminently threatened population movement; (2) strategic motivation; and (3) perception of coercive intent by the target. These are strict

---

[17] Quoted in George Borjas, *Heaven's Door: Immigration Policy and the American Economy* (Princeton: Princeton University Press, 1999), 3.

[18] Zbigniew Brzezinski, *Power and Principle: Memoirs of the National Security Adviser* (New York: Farrar, Straus, Giroux, 1983), 407.

(1) Was it (largely) orchestrated?

No. **Alternative 1:** The migration was driven by exogenous causes and controlled by the refugees or migrants themselves.

Relevant evidence includes, but is not limited to:
- *Testimony of and statements by the displaced.*
- *Timing, size, and destination(s) of population movements.*

Yes

If yes:
(2) Was it strategic?

No. **Alternative 2:** The migration was intentional (and controlled by the alleged challenger), but was driven by nonstrategic motivations, such as anger or a desire for revenge.

Relevant evidence includes, but is not limited to:
- *Challengers' statements about intent.*
- *Timing, size, and destination(s) of population movements.*

Yes

If yes:
(3) Was it coercive?

No. **Alternative 3:** The migration was strategic, but was not designed to induce concessions from the target.

Relevant evidence includes, but is not limited to:
- *Threats or demands issued?*
- *Challenger testimony.*
- *A congruence between the timing and execution of threats that appears related to targets' responses.*
- *Targets' testimony that indicates a belief that coercion was being attempted.*

Yes

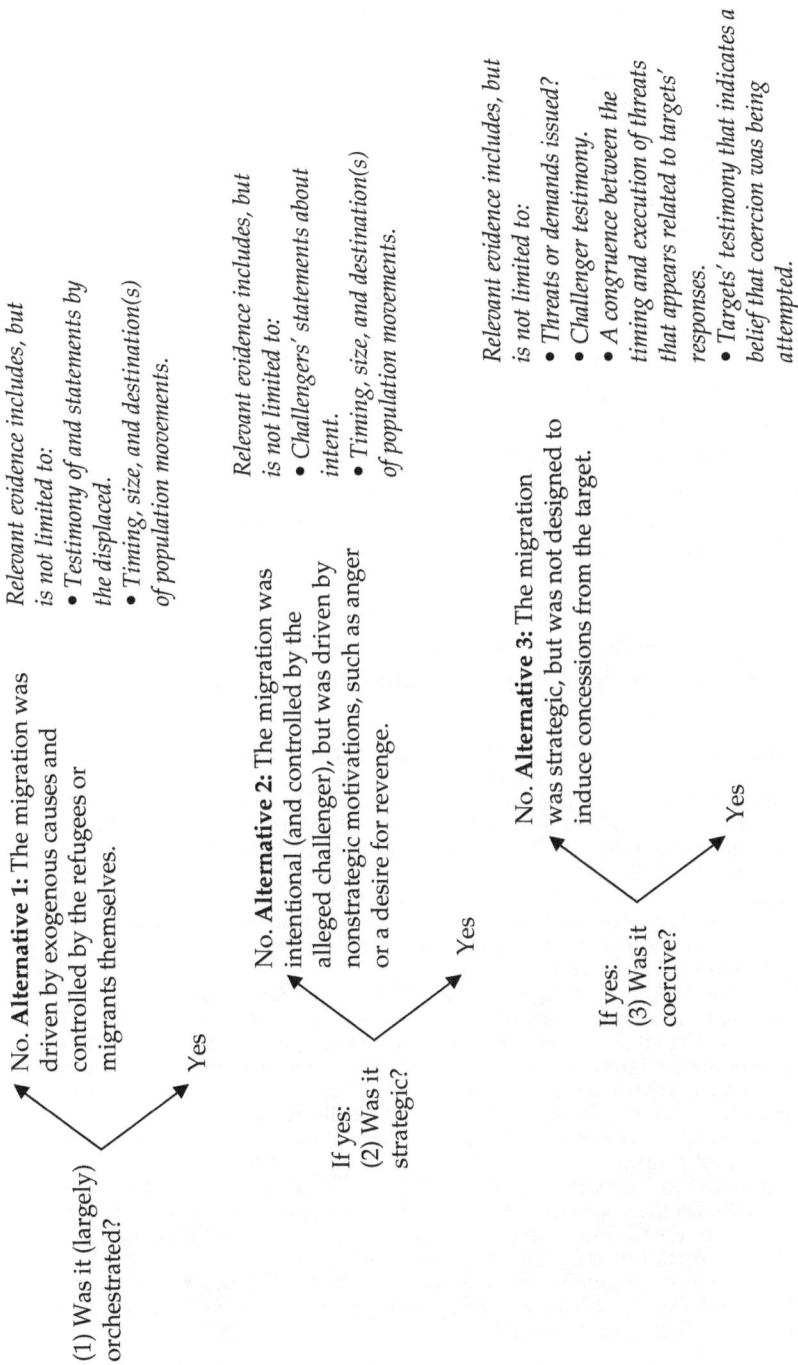

If the answer is yes to questions 1, 2, and 3, coercive engineered migration is deemed to have been attempted.

Figure 1.1. Competing explanations for mass migrations.

criteria and, to be clear, many real and threatened mass migrations do not meet them.[19]

Nevertheless, as the data in table 1.1 demonstrate, there has still been on average *at least* one attempt at coercive engineered migration per year since the Refugee Convention came into force. And although the potential significance of this phenomenon has been underappreciated by many migration scholars, the same cannot necessarily be said for potential target states.[20] For example, U.S. *National Intelligence Estimates* have included warnings of U.S. vulnerability to this kind of coercion and have recommended taking steps to guard against future predation.[21] Similarly, in 2007 Australia shut down the Pacific Solution in no small part to guard itself against future coercive attempts by the tiny island of Nauru. Likewise, in 2003 alone the European Union committed to spending 400 million euros to increase border security, at least in part to deter future migration-driven coercion; and in 2006, China constructed a fence along part of its border with North Korea to impede cross-border movements.[22] Some states have even conducted military exercises designed to leave them better prepared to respond to potential massive influxes across their borders.[23]

The bottom line is, whether publicly announced or privately implied, by threatening (or actually creating or catalyzing) migration crises oneself, or by pleading an inability or unwillingness to control crises generated by others, if conditions are right, these unnatural disasters can be effectively

[19] See, for instance, Susanne Schmeidl, "Conflict and Forced Migration: A Quantitative Review, 1964–1995," in *Global Migrants, Global Refugees: Problems and Solutions,* ed. Aristide Zolberg and Peter M. Benda (New York: Berghahn Books, 2001), 62–94.

[20] There have been a few noteworthy exceptions. See, for instance, Gil Loescher, "Refugee Movements and International Security," Adelphi Paper no. 268, London, International Institute for Strategic Studies, 1992; Michael Teitelbaum, "Immigration, Refugees, and Foreign Policy," *International Organization* 38 (1984): 429–50; Myron Weiner, *The Global Migration Crisis: Challenge to States and to Human Rights* (New York: Harper Collins, 1995). Nevertheless, no one has followed up or expanded on these important but largely descriptive works (and others like them published by these scholars).

[21] See, for instance, National Intelligence Council, "Growing Global Migration and Its Implications for the United States," National Intelligence Estimate 2001–02D, March 2001, which warns that the United States remains vulnerable to attempts by foreign governments to use the threat of mass migration as leverage in bilateral relations or to relieve domestic pressures. See also Central Intelligence Agency, *Long-Term Global Demographic Trends: Reshaping the Geopolitical Landscape* (Washington, D.C.: Central Intelligence Agency, 2001).

[22] On the Pacific Solution's demise, see Connie Levett, "Pacific Solution Cost $1 Billion," *Sydney Morning Herald,* August 25, 2007. On the European Union and Belarus, see Volker ter Haseborg, "Radioactive Refuge: Offering Asylum in Chernobyl's No Man's Land," *Der Spiegel,* October 14, 2005. On the Chinese border fence and North Korea, see Norimitsu Onishi, "Tension, Desperation: The China-North Korean Border," *New York Times,* October 22, 2006.

[23] James Brooke, "North Korea Lashes Out at Neighbors and US," *New York Times,* August 19, 2003; personal conversations with U.S. military officials, U.S. Southern Command (SOUTHCOM) Miami, Fla., April 2000, and MIT, Cambridge, Mass., October and November 2001; Sam Dillon, "US Tests Border Plan in Event of Mexico Crisis," *New York Times,* December 8, 1995.

exploited and manipulated in ways that allow a variety of would-be co-ercers to extract political and economic concessions from their targets. So what differentiates these actors? Exactly who employs this tool and why?

Who Engages in It?

Coercive engineered migration can be exercised by three distinct types of challengers: generators, *agents provocateurs*, and opportunists. As a rule, generators and *agents provocateurs* engage in the active creation and ma-nipulation of migration crises, whereas opportunists exploit crises initi-ated and created by others. I next describe the nature and motivations of all three types.

Active Manipulators: Generators and *Agents Provocateurs*

Generators are the most easily recognizable. They are actors, such as Idi Amin (case 11 in table 1.2) and Fidel Castro (cases 6, 21, and 44), who directly create or threaten to create cross-border population movements unless targets concede to their demands. Historically, the majority of gen-erators have been weak (at least relative to their targets), undemocratic actors, who, on the whole, lack effective recourse to more conventional methods of influence (see table 1.2).

As a rule, the same types of actors that are inclined to become generators—the weak, the illegitimate, and the disenfranchised—are also drawn to becoming *agents provocateurs.* These would-be coercers do not generally create crises directly, but rather deliberately act in ways de-signed to incite others to generate outflows. In contrast to the majority of generators, many *agents provocateurs* see themselves as engaging in a kind of altruistic Machiavellianism, whereby the ends (e.g., autonomy, independence, or the restoration of democracy) justify the employment of these rather unconventional means. Too weak to achieve their goals independently, such actors may aim to cultivate international political, economic, and/or military support for their causes. According to both scholars and practitioners, the more such actors are viewed as victims and the more they can provoke moral outrage on behalf of their group, the higher the probability that international assistance will be forthcoming.[24]

---

[24] See, for instance, Rory Braumann, "When Suffering Makes a Good Story," in *Life, Death and Aid: The Medecins Sans Frontieres Report on World Crisis Intervention,* ed. Medecins Sans Frontieres, 135–48 (London: Routledge, 1993); Clifford Bob, *The Marketing of Rebellion: Insur-gents, Media and International Activism* (Cambridge, UK: Cambridge University Press, 2005).

TABLE 1.2
Challenger Types, Nature of Challenger and Target Regimes, and Their Relative Strengths

	Year	Challenger and Type	Is the Challenger a Democracy?	Principal Target(s)	Is the Target a Democracy?	Power Distribution Favors Target or Challenger?
1	1953	West Germany (O)	Yes	United States	Yes	Target
2	1954–1955	South Vietnam and United States (G)	Flawed; Yes	North Vietnam	No	Challenger
3	1954–1960	Algerian insurgents (AP)	No	French Allies, esp. the United States	Yes	Target
4	1956	Austria (O)	Yes	United States	Yes	Target
5	**1961**	**United States (AP/O)**	**Yes**	**Soviet Union**	**No**	**Relatively even**
6	1965	Cuba (G)	No	United States	Yes	Target
7	1967–1970	Biafran insurgents (G)	No	United States and Western Europe	Yes	Target
8	**1967**	**Israel (G)**	**Yes**	**Jordan**	**No**	**Challenger**
9	1967	Jordan (O)	No	United States	Yes	Target
10	1971	Pakistan (G)	No	India	Yes	Target
11	1972	Uganda (G)	No	United Kingdom	Yes	Target
12	1978–1982	Bangladesh (G)	No	Burma	No	Issue-specific
13	1978–1982	ASEAN, Hong Kong (O)	Mixed	Western great powers, esp. United States	Yes	Targets
14	**1980–1990s**	**Vietnam (G/O)**	**No**	**EC, United States**	**Yes**	**Target**
15	1979–1980s	Thailand (O)	No	United States, China	Mixed	Targets
16	1980–1981	Haiti (G)	No	United States	Yes	Target
17	1979–81	NGO activists	No	United States, Haiti	Mixed	Targets
18	1980s	Pakistan (O)	No	United States	Yes	Target
19	1979–1980s	Soviet Union (G)	No	Pakistan	No	Challenger
20	1979–1980s	Exiled Afghan insurgents	No	Pakistan	No	Target
21	1980	Cuba (G)	No	United States	Yes	Target
22	1981–1982	Austria (O)	Yes	Western Europe, United States	Yes	Targets (largely)
23	1982	Thailand (O)	No	United States, France	Yes	Targets

No.	Date	Actor		Target actor		Type
24	early 1980s	Honduras (O)	Flawed (1982)	United States	Yes	Target
25	**mid 1980s–1997**	**Bangladesh (G)**	**Flawed (1990)**	**India**	**Yes**	**Target**
26	1983-86	East Germany (AP)	No	West Germany	Yes	Target
27	1984-85	East Germany (AP)	No	Sweden	Yes	Target
28	**1985**	**Libya (G)**	**No**	**Tunisia, Egypt, and Mauritania**	**No**	**Mixed**
29	late 1980s	Hong Kong, ASEAN (O)	Mixed	United States; Western Europe	Yes	Target
30	late 1980s–mid-1990s	Vietnam (O)	No	EC/EU, United States	Yes	Targets
31	1989–1992	Bangladesh (G)	No	Burma	No	Issue-specific
32	1990–1992	Saudi Arabia (G)	No	Yemen	No	Challenger
33	1990s	Israel (AP/O)	Yes	Palestinians	Yes	Challenger
34	1991–1992	United States (O)	Yes	Israel	Yes	Challenger
35	1990–1991	Albania (G)	Flawed	Italy	Yes	Target
36	1991	Albania (G)	Flawed	Italy, EC	Yes	Target
37	1990–1994	Albania (G)	Flawed	Greece	Yes	Target
38	**1991**	**Poland (G/AP)**	**Yes**	**EC, United States**	**Yes**	**Target**
39	May 1991	Ethiopia (G)	No	Israel	Yes	Target
40	1991	Turkey (O)	Flawed	United States	Yes	Target
41	1992–1994	Jean-Bertrand Aristide (AP)	No	United States	Yes	Target
42	1992–1995	Bosnians (G/AP)	No	UN Security Council	Mixed	Target
43	1994	Poland (O)	Yes	Germany	Yes	Target
44	1994	Cuba (G)	No	United States	Yes	Target
45	mid-1990s	Zaire (O)	No	Largely United States, France, Belgium	Yes	Target
46	1995	Libya (AP/O)	No	Egypt	No	Target
47	mid-1990s	North Korea (G)	No	China	No	Target
48	1997	Albania (G)	Flawed	Italy	Yes	Target
49	**1998**	**Turkey (G)**	**Yes**	**Italy**	**Yes**	**Target**
50	1998–1999	Kosovar Albanians (AP)	No	NATO	Yes	Target

(TABLE 1.2—cont.)

	Year	Challenger and Type	Is the Challenger a Democracy?	Principal Target(s)	Is the Target a Democracy?	Power Distribution Favors Target or Challenger?
51	1998–1999	Federal Republic of Yugoslavia (G)	Flawed	NATO, esp. Germany, Greece, and Italy	Yes	Target
52	1999	Macedonia I (O)	Flawed	NATO	Yes	Target
53	1999	Macedonia II (O)	Flawed	NATO	Yes	Target
54	2001–2003	Nauru (O)	No	Australia	Yes	Target
55	2002	Belarus (AP)	No	EU	Yes	Target
56	2002–2005	Activists/NGO network (AP)	No	China	No	Target
57	2002–2005	Activists/NGO network (AP)	No	South Korea	Yes	Target
58	2002–2006+	North Korea (G)	No	China	No	Target
59	2004	Nauru (O)	No	Australia	Yes	Target
60	2004	Haiti (G)	Flawed	United States	Yes	Target
61	2004	Belarus (AP)	No	EU	Yes	Target
62	2004	Libya (AP)	No	EU	Yes	Target
63	**2004–2005**	**Chad (G)**	**No**	**UN Security Council**	**Mixed**	**Target**
64	2006	Libya (AP/O)	No	EU	Yes	Target

Notes: Indeterminate cases are in boldface. *Flawed democracies* are those regimes that boast some, but not all, of the five characteristics generally viewed as characterizing a fully functioning democracy: a free and fair election process, civil liberties, a functioning government, political participation, and a political culture. AP, *agents provocateurs*; ASEAN, Association of Southeast Asian Nations; EC, European Community; EU, European Union; G, generators; NATO, North Atlantic Treaty Organization; NGO, nongovernmental organization; O, opportunists.

A relatively effective, if morally dubious, method of mobilizing such support is to behave in ways anticipated to stimulate repressive government responses that catalyze outmigration. One prominent historical example is the Algerian Front de Libération Nationale (FLN) insurgents, who during the 1954–1962 French-Algerian War undertook actions they fully anticipated would provoke brutal, and refugee generating, responses by the French military (case 3 in table 1.2).[25] In the late 1990s, the rebel Kosovo Liberation Army (KLA) adopted a similar strategy in its struggle for independence from the Federal Republic of Yugoslavia (case 50).[26] In both instances, the insurgents' operative premise was that the humanitarian catastrophes precipitated by their actions would persuade international actors to intervene on their behalf.[27] At the same time, of course, such instigated mass migrations may not only provoke outrage and evoke sympathy but also generate fear of their consequences within potential recipient states. Consequently, international decisions to intervene on behalf of victimized groups may be driven as much, if not more, by anxiety as by empathy. For instance, during the 1992–1995 war in Bosnia-Herzegovina, Bosniak forces reportedly did not defend the safe area of Gorazde in the express expectation that the humanitarian, and refugee-generating, consequences would catalyze greater NATO involvement in the conflict (one incident within case 42).[28]

Agents provocateurs may alternatively threaten and actively aim to turn small-scale extant outflows into full-scale crises via lobbying or publicizing emergencies. They may even encourage outflows to stimulate regime change. In the early 2000s, for instance, a loose network of activists and nongovernmental organizations (NGOs) adopted such a strategy as one

[25] See, for instance, Yahia H. Zoubir, "US and Soviet Policies towards France's Struggle with Anticolonial Nationalism in North Africa," *Canadian Journal of History* 30 (1995): 439–66.

[26] For instance, as Bill Frelick, then on the U.S. Committee on Refugees, argued, "the KLA which was not in a position to fight a straight out battle between standing armies, used their civilian population as part of its tactic to win international support and to really bring the international community as an ally in their struggle against the Serbs." Quoted in ADM Online, *Refugees as Weapons of War*, documentary produced by America's Defense Monitor, 1999, www.cdi.org/adm/1306/index.html. KLA leader Hasim Thaçi likewise acknowledged that the insurgents knew full well that "any armed action we undertook would bring retaliation against civilians. We knew we were endangering a great number of civilian lives." Quoted in *Moral Combat: NATO at War*, BBC2 special, broadcast March 12, 2000, http://news.bbc.co.uk/hi/english/static/events/panorama/transcripts/transcript_12_03_00.txt.

[27] As one Kosovar Albanian demonstrator said in March 1998—a year before the commencement of the NATO bombing campaign—"We are going to have to spill a lot more of our own blood before we can expect the outside world to risk getting heavily involved here.... But I can't see any other way that we can hope to give better lives to our people." Quoted in Geoff Kitney, "The Killing Fields Of Blackbirds," *Sydney Morning Herald*, March 21, 1998.

[28] See, for instance, Oliver Ramsbotham and Tom Woodhouse, *Humanitarian Intervention in Contemporary Conflict: A Reconceptualization* (Cambridge, UK: Polity, 1996), 186. See also the appendix.

piece of a larger project aimed at causing the collapse of North Korea (cases 56 and 57 in table 1.2; see chap. 5). As was the case in both Algeria and Bosnia, the *agents provocateurs* understood well that their actions could have significant human consequences, but believed that the ends made the potential costs acceptable. Of course, "some people will perish, but the majority will get out.... There will be a continuous flow until the end," was how the leader of one international NGO involved in this blatantly coercive attempt put it.[29] With humanitarian ends, if not means, in mind, NGOs and activists often play the role of *agents provocateurs*. Sometimes that role is as a primary challenger, as was the case in North Korea in the early 2000s, and sometimes the role is a supporting one, as during the Bosnian Civil War.

Why would relatively weak actors resort to the creation and exploitation of mass migrations as a method of influence? For one thing, in a wide variety of international arenas, weak actors view the generation of crises as a necessary precursor to negotiations with their more powerful counterparts.[30] Crisis generation represents one of the few areas in which weak actors may possess relative strength vis-à-vis their targets—and, in the case of migration crises, also vis-à-vis their even weaker victims. After intentionally generating crises, weak actors can offer to make them disappear in exchange for financial or political payoffs. Indeed, international negotiators routinely report recognizable patterns of "drama and catastrophe" when dealing with particular leaders and their subordinates.[31] In the face of such catastrophes, a shared bargaining space may develop rapidly where before there was none. Indeed, strong actors who were previously unwilling to even talk to, much less negotiate with, their weaker counterparts will often abruptly temper or reverse their positions in the face of clear and present crises.[32] As one migration scholar bluntly put it, "Sending nations can sometimes structure emigration so that receiving states are very likely to respond with inconsistent administrative action," which can then be used as a lever against those who had "in effect brushed [them] off" previously.[33]

[29] Quoted in Elisabeth Rosenthal, "More Koreans Give China the Slip, Invading Embassy School," *New York Times*, September 4, 2002.

[30] For an examination of an analogous phenomenon in the nuclear arena, see Scott Snyder, *Negotiating on the Edge: North Korean Negotiating Behavior* (Washington, D.C.: U.S. Institute of Peace, 1999), esp. chap. 3. See also Hans Binnendijk, *How Nations Negotiate* (Washington, D.C.: National Defense University, 1987); Paul, *Asymmetric Conflicts*.

[31] Mark Habeeb, *Power and Tactics in International Negotiation: How Weak Nations Bargain with Strong Nations* (Baltimore: Johns Hopkins University Press, 1988); Snyder, *Negotiating on the Edge*, 71, 43.

[32] Snyder, *Negotiating on the Edge*, 71.

[33] Christopher Mitchell "Implications," in *Western Hemisphere Immigration and United States Foreign Policy*, ed. Christopher Mitchell (University Park: Pennsylvania State University Press, 1992), 298.

Put another way, generating a crisis can help level the playing field, enhance the credibility of weak actors, increase the potency of their threats, and thereby improve their coercive capabilities in several distinct ways.[34] First, under certain conditions, migration crises may permit weak challengers to inflict punishment on targets that is disproportionate to the costs of compliance. Although targets may be understandably reluctant to concede ex ante, quite often demands that were unacceptable at the outset may begin to appear nominal when compared to the costs of managing sustained large-scale outflows into the indefinite future. Consider that, unlike a bombing sortie (which may be profoundly damaging, but is per force finite), a migration crisis can be, to borrow a well-known phrase, "a gift that keeps on giving." Second, because in-kind retaliation is rarely an option for targets—most of which tend to be advanced liberal democracies—challengers may even achieve a kind of escalation dominance over their targets.[35] For instance, whereas Deng could with relative ease have facilitated the departure of 30 million Chinese to the United States in 1979, President Carter would have been hard-pressed to reciprocate.[36]

Moreover, because of the widespread belief that liberal democracies possess particular characteristics that make them, and their leaders, behave differently than (actors within) other regime types, "fellow liberals benefit from a presumption of amity; non-liberals suffer from a presumption of enmity."[37] Hence, illiberal actors—already viewed with suspicion and contempt by the most powerful members of the international community— have little left to lose should they choose to abrogate the norms associated

[34] This can be particularly important because powerful actors tend to dismiss the threats of weaker actors for two reasons. First, they frequently have trouble believing their weaker counterparts will initiate crises or conflicts they seem destined to lose based on their relative capabilities. This tendency may be further exacerbated by the targets' also underestimating the magnitude of the threats facing weak challengers when the issues at stake seem trivial to the targets, thus leading them to further discount the probability of crisis initiation. Second, because the majority of targets would not themselves initiate migration crises, they tend to dismiss threats to do so as "irrational" and "crazy" and consequently also incredible. See Paul, *Asymmetric Conflicts*, 17; Alexander George and William Simons, *The Limits of Coercive Diplomacy* (Boulder: Westview Press, 1994).

[35] For instance, launching a war to counter a crisis is an option in certain circumstances, but often the expected costs associated with escalation to that level exceed the expected costs of conceding to challengers' demands in whole or in part. Likewise, if the challenger is already internationally isolated, the methods short of war that powerful states may employ in response may be slow-acting (e.g., sanctions) and thus inappropriate as a method of counter-coercion during a crisis. See Daniel Byman and Matthew Waxman, *The Dynamics of Coercion* (Oxford: Oxford University Press, 2002).

[36] Politics and absolute numbers aside, consider that between 1949 and 1979 the population of China *grew* by 430 million people.

[37] Michael W. Doyle, "Liberalism and World Politics," *American Political Science Review* 80 (1986): 1151–69; Bruce Russett, "Why Democratic Peace?" in *Debating the Democratic Peace*, ed. Michael Brown (Cambridge, Mass.: MIT Press, 1996), 93.

with the generation of migration crises. In short, nondemocratic "illegiti-mate" states and nonstate actors face a double whammy—few are strong enough to impel their strong counterparts to take them seriously under normal conditions, and still fewer are likely to be trusted to negotiate in an above-the-board manner. Therefore, not only are the reputational bar-riers to resorting to such norms-violating tactics lower, but the bargaining advantages of doing so are also far greater. Hence, the instrumental gen-eration or manipulation of migration crises can be an attractive method of influence for those with limited resources and few other options at their disposal.

In terms of the obvious exceptions—namely, cases in which strong or democratic actors have acted as generators or *agents provocateurs*—their goals have usually been the achievement of political goals at lower cost than they could possibly have achieved through military means. For ex-ample, a faction within the George W. Bush administration reportedly supported the aforementioned activist-driven attempt to bring down the North Korean regime via migration-driven coercion, because employ-ing military force to pursue the same objective would have been, to put it mildly, problematic at best.[38] Likewise, although the John F. Kennedy administration was understandably reluctant to use force to influence So-viet behavior vis-à-vis Berlin in the early 1960s, U.S. officials—at the very least—entertained the idea of using this kind of coercion to encourage greater cooperation from Moscow (case 5 in table 1.2).[39]

Passive Exploiters: Opportunists

In contrast to the active roles played by generators and *agents provocateurs*, opportunists tend to be more passive, albeit equally enterprising. Oppor-tunists play no direct role in the creation of migration crises, but simply exploit for their own gain the existence of outflows generated or catalyzed by others. For instance, opportunists might threaten to close their borders, thereby producing humanitarian emergencies, unless targets take desired actions or proffer side-payments. Such was the case in 1956, for instance, when Austria threatened to cease support for those fleeing the Hungarian

---

[38] James Dao, "U.S. Is Urged to Promote Flow of Refugees from North Korea," *New York Times*, December 11, 2002.
[39] See, for instance, the partially declassified "(Secret) US Department of State Telegram, from US Embassy Berlin (Deputy Commandant Allen Lightner) to US Secretary of State, 'Ref-ugee Problem May Deter Soviets from Going Ahead with Treaty,'" July 24, 1961, no. 87, Con-trol No. 15686; "(Secret) Memo 'Discontent in East Germany,'" July 18, 1961, 3. Both are avail-able through the Digital National Security Archive (DNSA), www.gwu.edu/~nsarchiv/.

Revolution unless broad-ranging assistance was forthcoming (case 4 in table 1.2).[40]

Conversely, opportunists sometimes offer to alleviate existing crises in exchange for political or monetary payoffs. One widely recognized example is the government of Thailand, which in the early 1980s used the existence of Cambodian refugees on its border to extract a wide variety of political and economic concessions from the United States (case 1 in table 1.2).[41] Likewise, Mobutu Sese Seko of Zaire in the early 1990s (case 45) and General Zia ul-Haq of Pakistan in the 1980s (case 18) both exploited refugee flows generated by others to transform themselves "from international pariahs into 'respectable' statesmen."[42] Indeed, as one scholar noted, "the Afghan refugees provided the best public relations Zia ul-Haq could have imagined for a regime created by a military coup and internationally marginalized after the hanging of [former Pakistani president and prime minister] Zulfikar Ali Bhutto." The crisis afforded Pakistan an opportunity to "compensate for its somewhat lean international reputation in the field of human rights."[43]

In sum, historically, opportunists have been both weak and strong, both democrats and demagogues. Actors who opt to become opportunists need only believe that they can manipulate an existing crisis to their advantage; sometimes they do so out of perceived necessity, sometimes just because they can. So, when challengers—be they opportunists, generators, or *agents provocateurs*—employ coercive engineered migration, what do they seek, and how effective have past attempts been in helping these challengers achieve their aims?

[40] See, for instance, Presidential Library of Dwight David Eisenhower (hereafter DDEL), Papers as President of the United States (Ann Whitman file), Dulles-Herter Series, Box 8, "Department of State, Memorandum of Conversation, December 26, 1956, Subject: Hungarian Refugees." Austrian diplomats also warned that, absent help, Hungarians might seek to "continue the fight" against the Soviets from Austrian soil, thus endangering the neutral country politically. Johanna Granville, "Of Spies, Refugees and Hostile Propaganda: How Austria Dealt with the Hungarian Crisis of 1956," *History* 91 (2006): 76.

[41] As Gil Loescher puts it, "Thailand became a frontline state against an expansionist Vietnam, kept the *Khmer* resistance going, and provided a safe haven for Indochinese refugees. In return, the United States supported the Thai military, and Bangkok became America's remaining ally on the Southeast Asian mainland." "Refugee Movements and International Security," 35.

[42] Fiona Terry, *Condemned to Repeat? The Paradox of Humanitarian Action (Ithaca, Cornell University Press, 2002)*, 66. See also Pierre Centlivres and Michelle Centrelives-Demont, "The Afghan Refugees in Pakistan: A Nation in Exile," *Current Sociology* 36 (1988): 73; DNSA, "Draft Memo to the (US) Secretary of Defense, Subject: Your Meeting with President Zia ul-Haq," October 1, 1986, 2.

[43] Frédéric Grare, "Afghan Refugees in Pakistan," in *Refugee Manipulation: War, Politics and the Abuse of Human Suffering*, ed. Stephen Stedman and Fred Tanner (Washington, D.C.: Brookings Institution, 2003), 78.

Coercion Objectives and Rates of Success

Just as is the case with traditional military coercion, the demands of challengers who engage in migration-driven coercion have been highly varied in scope, content, and magnitude. Demands have been both concrete and symbolic and have comprised entreaties both to undertake actions and to cease undertaking them. They have run the gamut from the simple provision of financial aid to the termination of insurgent funding to full-scale military intervention and even regime change (see table 1.3). And, despite the fact that the majority of challengers have been markedly weaker than their targets (in 54 of 64 total possible cases, and 49 of 56 determinate cases), they have been relatively successful; in fact, they have been more successful than their more powerful counterparts.

Success in this context is defined as persuading a target to change a previously articulated policy, stop or reverse an action already undertaken, or disburse side-payments, in line with a challenger's demands; in other words, most of a challenger's demands were met. A case is coded as a "Success" if the challenger achieved most or all of its known objectives and as a "Partial Success" if the challenger achieved a significant fraction, but not all, of its aims. A case is coded as a "Failure" if the challenger achieved few or none of its objectives, or achieved its objectives for what appear to be exogenous reasons. Finally, a case is coded as "Indeterminate" if (1) the challenger achieved at least some of its objectives but causality is unclear; (2) there is insufficient evidence to conclude that coercion was in the end actually attempted; or (3) threats were issued but a crisis never materialized, and it remains unclear, as of this writing, whether the challenger's demands were met. (Indeterminate cases are excluded from aggregate assessments of coercive success and failure.)

In the fifty-six determinate cases, challengers achieved at least some of their objectives approximately 73 percent of the time (in 41 cases). If one imposes a stricter measure of success and excludes partial successes, coercers got more or less everything they reportedly sought 57 percent of the time (in 32 cases). Although rather more modest, this more restrictive rate is comparable to some of the best-case estimates of deterrence success (also 57 percent) and substantially greater than best estimates of the success of economic sanctions (approximately 33 percent) or U.S. coercive diplomacy efforts (between 19 and 37.5 percent).[44] As table 1.3 also intimates, this kind of coercion has been attempted in all types of crises—humanitarian

[44]See Paul K. Huth, "Deterrence and International Conflict: Empirical Findings and Theoretical Debates," *Annual Review of Political Science* 2 (1999): 25–48; Gary Clyde Hufbauer, Jeffrey J. Schott, Kimberly Ann Elliott, and Barbara Oegg, *Economic Sanctions Reconsidered,* 3rd ed. (Washington, D.C.: Peterson Institute, 2008). See also the introduction, note 3.

TABLE 1.3
Challengers' Objectives, Relative Strengths, and Coercive Outcomes

	Year	Challenger/Coercer and Type	Principal Target(s)	Principal Objective(s)	Outcome
1	1953	West Germany (O)	**United States**	Financial aid, political support	Partial success
2	1954–1955	**South Vietnam and United States (G)**	North Vietnam	Defer/cancel reunification elections	Failure
3	1954–1960	Algerian insurgents (AP)	**French allies, esp. United States**	Convince allies to pressure France to relinquish Algeria; political-military intervention	Partial success
4	1956	Austria (O)	**United States**	Aid and resettlement	Success
5	1961	United States (AP/O)	Soviet Union	Deterrence re: Berlin	Indeterminate
6	1965	Cuba (G)	**United States**	Regularized immigration	Partial success
7	1967–1970	Biafran insurgents (G)	**United States**	Aid; intervention; political and diplomatic support	Partial success
8	1967	**Israel (G)**	Jordan	Bilateral negotiations/peace talks	Indeterminate
9	1967	Jordan (O)	**United States**	Pressure Israel re: Palestinian return	ST success; LT failure
10	1971	Pakistan (G)	India	Cease support for Bengali rebels	Failure
11	1972	Uganda (G)	**United Kingdom**	Rescind decision re: military assistance	Failure
12	1978–1982	Bangladesh (G/O)	Burma	Halt outflow of Burmese Muslims	Success
13	1978–1982	ASEAN, Hong Kong (O)	**Western great powers, esp. United States**	Resettlement and financial aid	Success
14	1979	Vietnam (G/O)	EC, **United States**	Aid, diplomatic recognition, credit	Indeterminate
15	1979–1980s	Thailand (O)	**United States**, China	An alliance; political-military support	Success
16	1979–1981	Haiti (G)	**United States**	Financial and military aid	Success
17	1979–1981	NGO activists	**United States**, Haiti	End support for regime; undermine it	Failure
18	1980s	Pakistan (O)	**United States**	Alliance; political-military support	Success
19	1979–1980s	**Soviet Union (G)**	Pakistan	Cease support for insurgents	Failure
20	1979–1980s	Exiled insurgents (O)	**Pakistan**	Control over peace settlement	Success
21	1980	Cuba (G)	**United States**	End hijacking; normalize migration, etc.	Partial success
22	1981–1982	Austria (O)	**Western Europe; United States**	Refugee resettlement and aid	Success
23	1982	Thailand (O)	**United States, France**	Financial aid	Success

(TABLE 1.3—cont.)

	Year	Challenger/Coercer and Type	Principal Target(s)	Principal Objective(s)	Outcome
24	early 1980s	Honduras (O)	**United States**	Military aid, training; security pact	Success
25	1980s–1997	Bangladesh (G)	India	End Shanti Bahini (insurgent) funding	Indeterminate
26	1983–1986	East Germany (AP)	**West Germany**	Aid; tech assistance; border fixity	Success
27	1984–1985	East Germany (AP)	**Sweden**	Financial aid	Success
28	1985	Libya (G)	Tunisia, Egypt, and Mauritania	Shift diplomatic alliances/positions	Indeterminate
29	late 1980s	Hong Kong, ASEAN (O)	**United States, Western Europe**	Aid and resettlement	Success
30	1989–1990s	Vietnam (O)	EC, **United States**	Political-diplomatic recognition; aid	Success
31	1989–1992	Bangladesh (G)	Burma	Halt outflow of Burmese Muslims	Success
32	1990–1992	**Saudi Arabia (G)**	Yemen	Change position on Gulf War/Iraq	Failure
33	1990s+	Israel **(AP/O)**	Palestinians	Relinquish claims on Jerusalem	Failure (so far)
34	1991–1992	**United States (O)**	Israel	Stop settlements in Occupied Territories	Partial success
35	1990–1991	Albania (G)	Italy	Food aid, financial credits, and other assistance	Success
36	1991	Albania (G)	Italy, EC	Financial aid	Success
37	1990–1994	Albania (G)	Greece	Financial aid	Success
38	1991	Poland (G/AP)	EC, **United States**	Debt relief; financial aid	Indeterminate
39	1990	Ethiopia (G)	Israel	Monetary payoff	Success
40	1991	Turkey (O)	**United States**	Humanitarian-military intervention	Success
41	1992–1994	Jean-Bertrand Aristide (AP)	**United States**	Return to power; U.S. military intervention	Success
42	1992–1995	Bosnians (G/AP)	**UN Security Council**	Troop presence; air evacuation	Partial success
43	1994	Poland (O)	**Germany**	Monetary payoff	Success
44	1994	Cuba (G)	**United States**	Regularized immigration, etc.	Success
45	mid-1990s	Zaire (O)	**Largely United States, France, and Belgium**	Political-diplomatic recognition; aid	Success
46	1995	Egypt	Lifting of sanctions; shift in policy toward Palestinians	Failure
47	mid-1990s	North Korea (G)	**China**	Financial aid; political support	Success
48	1997	Albania (G)	Italy	Military intervention	Success

49	1998	Turkey (G)	Italy	Support/punishment re: EU bid	Indeterminate
50	1998–1999	Kosovar Albanians (AP)	NATO	Military aid; intervention	Success
51	1998–1999	Federal Republic of Yugoslavia (G)	**NATO, esp. Germany, Greece, and Italy**	Deterrence, then compellence	Failure
52	1998–1999	Macedonia I (O)	NATO	Financial aid	Success
53	1999	Macedonia II (O)	NATO	Financial aid	Success
54	2001–2003	Nauru (O)	Australia	Financial aid	Success
55	2002	Belarus (AP)	EU	Diplomatic recognition; aid	Failure
56	2002–2005	Activists/NGO network (AP)	China	Policy shift on North Korea; regime collapse	Failure
57	2002–2005	Activists/NGO network (AP)	**South Korea**	Policy shift on North Korea; regime collapse	Failure
58	2002–2006+	North Korea (G)	China	Continued diplomatic support & aid	Success
59	2004	Nauru (O)	Australia	Financial aid	Success
60	2004	Haiti (G)	**United States**	Military assistance	Failure
61	2004	Belarus (AP)	EU	Financial aid	Failure
62	2004	Libya (AP)	EU	Lifting of sanctions	Success
63	2004–2005	Chad (G)	**UN Security Council**	Military/political intervention	Indeterminate
64	2006	Libya (AP/O)	EU	Financial aid	Partial Success

Notes: Where discernable, the more powerful actor (challenger v. target) is shown in boldface. AP, *agents provocateurs*; ASEAN, Association of Southeast Asian Nations; EC, European Community; EU, European Union; G, generators; LT, long-term; NATO, North Atlantic Treaty Organization; NGO, nongovernmental organization; O, opportunists; ST, short-term.

disasters, low-intensity conflicts, and full-scale wars—as well as in cases in which crises have been latent or only threatened.

This discussion notwithstanding, one might still conclude that selection effects–related issues mean that this kind of coercion is still a pretty poor method of persuasion, undertaken only by highly resolved challengers and only when they believe there is a relatively high probability of success.[45] This may indeed be true. To be sure, for a variety of reasons, coercive engineered migration is a blunt instrument that is rarely a weapon of first resort. First, challengers may ultimately catalyze larger crises than they anticipate or desire, and massive outflows can destabilize both states of origin and destination.[46] Fears of just such a collapse, for instance, led to the construction of the Berlin Wall in the early 1960s.[47]

Second, once crises have been initiated, challengers often lose (some degree of) control over them, in no small part because engineered migration–related "cleansing" operations may be carried out by irregulars, or even bands of thugs, who lack discipline and whose objectives may not be synonymous with those who instigated the outflows.[48] Likewise, once migrants and refugees find themselves outside their states of origin, they are often capable of autonomous actions—they might move in different directions and do so in smaller or larger numbers than challengers desire. When this happens, outflows can become more like unguided missiles than smart bombs, making coercing particular targets more difficult.

Third, as Thomas Schelling has argued, "the ideal compellent action would be one that, once initiated, causes minimal harm if compliance is forthcoming and great harm if compliance is not forthcoming."[49] Nevertheless, although migration and refugee movements, once initiated, can be stopped, under certain conditions they can be difficult to undo. As such, threats of further escalation can be quite persuasive, but promises of minimal harm in the face of compliance can be difficult to keep, thereby potentially reducing the value of concession for targets. Indeed, evidence suggests that both China and South Korea viewed concession to the activists trying to compel them to embrace and admit North Korean migrants

---

[45] See James Fearon, "Selection Effects and Deterrence," *International Interactions* 28 (2000): 5–29.

[46] Although just such an outcome will be as a good thing if the challenger is, for instance, an NGO trying to bring down a dictatorship, it is a highly undesirable outcome in most cases.

[47] "The Construction of the Berlin Wall," Berlin website, www.berlin.de/mauer/geschichte/index.en.html.

[48] As one Yugoslav journalist put it when discussing the 1999 Yugoslavian offensive in Kosovo: "there were differences between the police and the army. The police were in favour of expulsions because they could steal money from people. The intelligence guys were against it because they said it was bad for us." Quoted in Tim Judah, *Kosovo: War and Revenge* (New Haven: Yale University Press, 2000), 241–42. See also John Mueller, "The Banality of 'Ethnic War,'" *International Security* 25 (2000): 42–70.

[49] Thomas Schelling, *Arms and Influence* (New Haven: Yale University Press, 1966), 89.

as likely to stimulate *greater* future harm by encouraging more individuals to follow in their footsteps. Not surprisingly, coercion in this case failed (see chap. 5).

Fourth, the potential for blowback can be great and the intended consequences quite costly. For instance, not only did the U.S.-instigated mass migration of North Vietnamese southward following the First Indochina War fail to achieve its stated objective of deterring Ho Chi Minh from pushing for reunification elections, but it also inadvertently further weakened the sitting regime in South Vietnam while simultaneously increasing the U.S. commitment to propping it up (case 2 in table 1.3).[50] And although Mobutu Sese Seko of Zaire benefited significantly from the concessions he was granted in exchange for his agreement to host Rwandan refugees in the mid-1990s, the decision to allow said refugees to use the camps as bases to launch attacks back across the border provoked enough ire within Rwanda that its government subsequently helped engineer his ouster.[51]

Nevertheless, given its apparent success rate of 57–73 percent, for highly committed actors with few other options coercive engineered migration can still appear to be a strategy worth pursuing. This is particularly true for challengers seeking to influence the behavior of potentially vulnerable targets disinclined to accede to their demands under normal circumstances—powerful advanced liberal democracies. From the perspective of traditional international relations theory, this in and of itself represents something of a puzzle. Weak actors should only rarely challenge more powerful ones. So what makes the world's most powerful democracies such attractive marks? Why should they—and, particularly, the United States—be most often and most successfully targeted? And, more generally, how and why does using human beings as coercive weapons ever work?

How, When, and Why Does It Succeed and Fail?

Coercers typically employ a variety of overlapping mechanisms when trying to manipulate the decision making of their targets, including the following five most common mechanisms: (1) power-base erosion—threatening

---

[50] As one U.S. serviceman who helped transport Vietnamese south put it, "What would happen if southern Vietnam fell?... Be it right or wrong, we have declared ourselves to these people and to the world as encouraging their flight to freedom, and, participating in it. We have therefore, morally married a long-term responsibility. Even politically, we must not lose face in the Far East by selling these people short." Quoted in Ronald B. Frankum Jr., *Operation Passage to Freedom: The United States Navy in Vietnam, 1954–1955* (Lubbock: Texas Tech University Press, 2007), 207. See also Kathryn C. Statler, *Replacing France: The Origins of American Intervention in Vietnam* (Lexington: Kentucky University Press, 2007), 152.

[51] See Sarah Kenyon Lischer, *Dangerous Sanctuaries: Refugee Camps, Civil War and the Dilemmas of Humanitarian Aid* (Ithaca, N.Y.: Cornell University Press, 2005), chap. 4.

a regime's relationship with its core supporters; (2) unrest—creating popular dissatisfaction with a regime; (3) decapitation—jeopardizing the regime leadership's personal security; (4) weakening—debilitating a country as a whole; and (5) denial—preventing battlefield success (or political victories via military aggression).[52] Because coercive engineered migration relies on nonmilitary means of persuasion, the mechanisms of decapitation and denial are for all intents and purposes off the table. But such is not the case for power-base erosion, unrest, and weakening. Each of these mechanisms relies to varying degrees on affecting the behavior of a target's leadership by manipulating the opinions and attitudes of its civilian population. The success of each in turn is predicated on the effective manipulation of the costs or risks imposed on that same population. In other words, operationally speaking, these three mechanisms rely on what are commonly known as coercion by punishment strategies. Challengers aim to create domestic conflict or public dissatisfaction within a target state in an attempt to convince its leadership to concede to the demands of the challenger rather than incur the anticipated (domestic and/or international) political costs of resistance.[53] In short, challengers try to inflict costs on the population that are higher than the stakes in dispute.[54]

There are two distinct, but non-mutually exclusive, pathways by which migration-driven coercion can be effected using punishment strategies; loosely speaking, they might be thought of as "capacity swamping" and "political agitation." Simply put, capacity swamping focuses on manipulating the *ability* of targets to accept/accommodate/assimilate a given group of migrants or refugees, whereas political agitation focuses on manipulating the *willingness* of targets to do so. In both swamping and agitation, coercion is effectively a dynamic two-level game, in which the responses of the target on the international level to threats issued or actions taken by the challenger tend to be driven by simultaneous (or subsequent) actions taken by actors within the target state.[55]

Thus, as Daniel Byman and Matthew Waxman suggest, "although there is obvious analytic appeal to treating coercion as singular and discrete

[52] Byman and Waxman, *Dynamics of Coercion*, 50.

[53] For a compelling discussion of how a similar logic can lead states to resort to the targeting of noncombatants in wartime, see Alexander B. Downes, *Targeting Civilians in Wartime* (Ithaca, N.Y.: Cornell University Press, 2008).

[54] "The hope is that the government will concede or the population will revolt." Robert A. Pape, *Bombing to Win: Air Power and Coercion in War* (Ithaca, N.Y.: Cornell University Press, 1996), 21.

[55] See Robert Putnam, "Diplomacy and Domestic Politics: The Logic of Two-level Games," *International Organization* 42 (1988): 427–60; John S. Odell, "International Threats and Internal Politics: Brazil, the European Community and the United States, 1985–1987," in *Double Edged Diplomacy: International Bargaining and Domestic Politics*, ed. Peter B. Evans, Harold K. Jacobson, and Robert D. Putnam (Berkeley: University of California Press, 1993).

events that follow a straightforward, linear logic," coercive engineered migration is more appropriately viewed as "series of moves and countermoves in which each side acts not only based on and in anticipation of the other side's moves, but also based on other changes" in the prevailing environment.[56] Somewhat paradoxically, evidence suggests the objective dangers posed to targets tend to be greater in the case of swamping but that the probability of coercive success tends to be greater in the case of agitating.

In the developing world, coercive attempts most often focus on swamping and comprise threats to severely tax or overwhelm a target's physical and/or economic capacity to cope with an influx—thereby effectively debilitating it—if it fails to concede to the coercer's demands.[57] As previously suggested, although weakening is the primary coercive mechanism in play, such cases often also rely to some degree on the mechanisms of power-base erosion and/or general unrest. In locations where ethnic tensions may already be elevated, where the extension of central government control may be compromised even at the best of times, and where essential resources are limited and consensus on the legitimacy of the political regime is shaky at best, a large influx can present a real and persuasive threat.[58] Such was the case in late 1990, for instance, when Saudi Arabia expelled over 650,000 Yemenis in an attempt to compel the government of Yemen to rethink its "Saddam Hussein–friendly position" and policies in the lead-up to (and during) the First Gulf War (case 32 in table 1.3).[59] Because Yemeni citizens were highly dependent on remittances from guestworkers employed in Saudi Arabia, the Saudis believed the expulsions would engender sufficient dissatisfaction within the Yemeni population to impel them to pressure their government to shift allegiance.[60]

Capacity swamping can also be an effective strategy in the West. This is particularly true if the incipient crisis is large and sudden, because even highly industrialized states need time to gear up to effectively deal with disasters, be they natural or manufactured.[61] That said, advanced

[56] Byman and Waxman, *Dynamics of Coercion*, 37–38.

[57] See, for instance, Karen Jacobsen, "Factors Influencing the Policy Responses of Host Governments to Mass Refugee Influxes," *International Migration Review* 30 (1996): 655–78.

[58] Cheryl Benard, "Politics and the Refugee Experience," *Political Science Quarterly* 101 (1986): 623–24.

[59] William Drozdiak, "UN Force Resolution Dangerous, Yemen Says; Bush Urged to Send Envoy to Meet Iraqis," *Washington Post*, November 26, 1990.

[60] As one expellee reported, Saudi police asked: "Are you for or against us?'" When he replied that he did not know much about the Gulf crisis, they said, "Go to your country and, when you have found out which side you are on, come back and tell us." Patrick Cockburn, "Crisis in the Gulf: Immigrant Yemenis Incur Saudis' Wrath," *Independent*, November 24, 1990.

[61] Consider, for instance, the tragically underwhelming initial U.S. response to Hurricane Katrina.

industrial societies tend to have greater resources to bring to bear in a crisis, making threats to fundamentally overwhelm their physical ability to cope harder—although far from impossible—to accomplish. Furthermore, whereas in most cases migration-driven coercion consists of threats to initiate an outflow unless the coercer is assuaged, in the developed world threats not to allow people to leave may also be successfully employed. Under such conditions, however, capacity swamping is obviously a moot point.[62]

In the developed world, therefore, political agitation often supplants capacity swamping as the lynchpin of this kind of coercion. Specifically, challengers on the international level seek to influence target behavior on the domestic level by engaging in a kind of norms-enhanced political blackmail that relies on exploiting and exacerbating what Robert Putnam has called the "heterogeneity" of political and social interests within polities.[63] Exploitation of heterogeneity within Western states is possible because population influxes, such as those created in migration and refugee crises, tend to engender diverse and highly divisive responses within the societies expected to bear the brunt of their consequences. As Marc Rosenblum puts it: "efforts to bend immigration policy to the national interest compete with pluralistic policy demands originating at the party, sub-national (local and state), and sector- or class-specific levels."[64] Like immigration and refugee policy more generally, real and threatened migration crises tend to split societies into (at least) two mutually antagonistic and often highly mobilized groups: the pro-refugee/migrant camp and anti-refugee/migrant camp.

What it means to be pro- or anti-refugee/migrant varies depending on the target and the crisis. Pro-refugee/migrant camps may call for relatively limited, short-term responses, such as accepting financial responsibility for settling the migrant or refugee group in a third country, or far more significant (even permanent) commitments, such as offering the group asylum or citizenship. On the other side, anti-refugee/migrant groups may demand that requests for financial assistance be rejected. More radically, they may demand that migrants be interdicted, refugees be refused asylum, or, in extreme cases, that the displaced even be forcibly repatriated. The bottom line is that, because targets cannot simultaneous satisfy demands both to accept and reject a given group of migrants or refugees, leaders facing highly mobilized and highly polarized interests can find

---

[62] In one such example, Israel reportedly paid $2,000 for each of the 16,000 Falashas it evacuated from Ethiopia after the fall of Mengistu in 1991. See the appendix, case 39.

[63] Putnam, "Diplomacy and Domestic Politics," 444.

[64] Marc R. Rosenblum, "Immigration and U.S. National Interests," in *Immigration Policy and Security: U.S., European and Commonwealth Perspectives*, ed. Terry E. Givens, Gary P. Freeman, and David L. Leal (London: Routledge, 2008), 15.

themselves on the horns of a real dilemma—whereby it may be impossible to satisfy the demands of one camp without alienating the other.[65]

Thus, it is not heterogeneity per se that makes targets vulnerable. Instead, the crux of agitation-based coercion rests on the fact that pro- and anti-refugee/migrant camps tend to have mutually incompatible interests—which both groups are highly committed to defending—while at the same time target leaderships may have compelling political, legal, and moral reasons to avoid running afoul of either camp. Under such conditions, leaders may face strong domestic-level incentives to concede to coercers' international-level demands. This is particularly true in those cases when concession is likely to make a real or threatened migration crisis cease or disappear, thereby freeing a besieged leader from the proverbial trap between a rock and a hard place.

The existence of this two-level dynamic, and the potential vulnerability to which it can give rise, is to a certain extent not particularly surprising. Despite rhetorical pronouncements to the contrary, most Western liberal democracies have long had schizophrenic relationships with migrants and refugees. For instance, as Rogers Smith has noted, aside the liberal tradition of the United States and its self-identification as a "nation of immigrants," there has been an illiberal tradition of "ascriptive Americanism" that envisions an ethnic core of Protestant Anglo-Saxons that must be protected from "external dilution."[66] In other words, the U.S. "romance with the Statue of Liberty has always been a hot and cold affair."[67]

The situation is not markedly different in either Europe or Asia. Germany, for example, is officially a no-immigration country. Nevertheless, anti-immigration rhetoric has long "been counteracted by extensive rights and protections for foreigners granted by the legal system,...[which] tames sovereign state power with a catalogue of universal human rights."[68]

---

[65] This is consistent with Richard Ullman's view of a national security threat as any "action or sequence of events that 1) threatens dramatically and over a relatively brief span of time to degrade the quality of life for the inhabitants of the state, or 2) threatens to significantly narrow the range of policy choices available to the government of a state or to private non-state government entities (persons, groups, corporations) within the state." "Redefining Security," *International Security* 8 (1983): 19.

[66] See Rogers Smith, *Civic Ideals: Conflicting Visions of Citizenship in US History* (New Haven: Yale University Press, 1997), 101 and chap. 11.

[67] Victor H. Palmieri, former Ambassador-at-large and U.S. Coordinator for Refugee Affairs, quoted in Mary M. Kritz, ed., *US Immigration and Refugee Policy, Global and Domestic Issues* (Toronto: D. C. Heath and Company, 1983), xi.

[68] Christian Joppke, *Immigration and the Nation State: The United States, Germany and Great Britain* (Oxford: Oxford University Press, 1999), 64; see also, Hermann Kurthen, "Germany at the Crossroads: National Identity and the Challenges of Immigration," *International Migration Review* 29 (1995); Philip Martin, "Germany: Reluctant Land of Immigration," in *Controlling Immigration: A Global Perspective,* ed. Wayne Cornelius, Philip Martin, and James Hollifield, 189–226 (Stanford: Stanford University Press, 1994).

Likewise, although less than 2 percent of the Japanese population is made up of foreigners—none of whom is a Japanese citizen—the idea of a mono-ethnic Japan is somewhat farcical given that many Japanese, including the emperor, have Korean roots.[69] Nor is this Janus-faced attitude a new phenomenon. For example, as the authors of *Refugees in an Age of Genocide* note, "Of all the groups in the 20th century, refugees from Nazism are now widely and popularly perceived as 'genuine', but at the time German, Austrian and Czechoslovakian Jews were treated with ambivalence and outright hostility as well as sympathy."[70]

Moreover, although there are significant legal and normative distinctions that can be drawn among refugees, asylum seekers, and migrants, "Just as in spring 1940, when German Jews were interned on the Isle of Man, British newspapers blurred the distinctions between refugee, alien and enemy, so today, according to Alasdair Mackenzie, coordinator of [UK] Asylum Aid, 'There's general confusion in many newspapers between an asylum seeker and someone from abroad—everyone gets tarred with the same brush.'"[71]

In point of fact, the burden borne by Western liberal democracies represents but a small share of the world's total displaced population, yet flows into the West are considered disproportionately threatening relative to their size.[72] Within these states, pundits, politicians, and even some policymakers argue that migrants who are from different religious, linguistic, and ethnic backgrounds than the majority in their newly adopted homelands are a danger to societal security. Popular discourses that draw on traditional nationalistic sentiments and xenophobic assertions, such as Samuel Huntington's *Clash of Civilizations* and *Who Are We?* and Robert Kaplan's "The Coming Anarchy," assert that current waves of migrants and refugees reduce national living standards by siphoning away social resources from "real" citizens, taking employment away from more qualified applicants, bringing tensions from their home state with them, and committing a disproportionate amount of crime.[73]

---

[69] Doug Struck, "In Japan, U.S. Expat Fights the Yankee Way," *Washington Post,* July 5, 2003.

[70] Tony Kushner and Katherine Knox, *Refugees in an Age of Genocide: Global, National and Local Responses* (London: Routledge, 1999), 408. See also Rosenblum, "Immigration and U.S. National Interests," 16–18.

[71] Anne Karpf, "We've Been Here Before," *Guardian,* June 8, 2002, Weekend Pages.

[72] Mark Mazower, *The Dark Continent: Europe's Twentieth Century* (New York: Knopf, 1998), 346. See also Robert Mandel, "Perceived Security Threat and the Global Refugee Crisis," *Armed Forces and Society* 24 (1997): 77–103; Human Rights Watch, "Stemming the Flow: Abuses against Migrants, Asylum Seekers and Refugees," 2006, http://www.hrw.org/en/reports/2006/09/12/stemming-flow.

[73] Kyle Grayson and David Dewitt, "Global Demography and Foreign Policy: A Literature Brief and Call for Research," York Centre for International and Security Studies Working Paper no. 24, York University, Toronto, 2003, 9. See also Samuel Huntington, *The Clash of Civilizations and the Remaking of World Order* (New York: Simon and Schuster, 1996); Huntington,

Resistors and Restrictionists

Consequently, although most Western states are normatively, if not legally, bound to offer refuge and protection for those fleeing persecution, violence, and, in some cases, privation, at least some segment of most target states' populations is usually unwilling to bear the real or perceived domestic economic and social costs and security risks of doing so. This resistance offers coercers a potential wedge through which they can inflict pain that can endanger a leader's relationship with his or her core supporters or even stimulate general unrest within a target state. Indeed, in contrast to most foreign policy issues, refugees and immigration have engaged Western publics like few others, especially in regions that have been host to the largest numbers of illegal migrants and asylum seekers.[74]

In one 2004 survey, 52 percent of Americans polled claimed that the present level of immigration represented a "critical threat to the vital interests of the United States," and 76 percent favored "restricting immigration as a means of combating terrorism."[75] In a separate 2008 survey, 61 percent said that "controlling and reducing illegal immigration" should be a very important U.S. foreign policy goal, a larger percentage than believed "maintaining superior military power worldwide" was similarly critical (57 percent).[76] The situation is analogous in Western Europe, where an EU-wide survey uncovered a disturbing level of racism and xenophobia within its member states, with nearly 33 percent of those interviewed openly describing themselves as "quite racist" or "very racist."[77] More than 71 percent of those interviewed claimed, "There was a limit to the number of people of other races, religions, or cultures that a society can accept," and 65 percent of interviewees said that this limit had already been reached in their country.[78] In 2007, Europeans ranked immigration behind only fighting crime as the most important policy issue facing the EU in coming years.[79] Even the historically welcoming Swedes and Dutch

---

Who Are We? The Challenges to America's National Identity (New York: Simon and Schuster, 2004); Robert Kaplan, "The Coming Anarchy," *Atlantic Monthly* (February 1994).

[74] Ole Holsti, *Public Opinion and American Foreign Policy* (Ann Arbor: University of Michigan Press, 1996), 193–94; Joppke, *Immigration and the Nation State*, chaps. 5–7.

[75] Chicago Council on Foreign Relations "2004 Global Views Survey," Chicago, 2004, chap. 4, 49–50.

[76] Chicago Council on Global Affairs, "American Attitudes on US Foreign Policy," September 22, 2008, http://www.thechicagocouncil.org/UserFiles/File/POS_Topline%20Reports/POS%202008/2008%20Public%20Opinion_Foreign%20Policy.pdf.

[77] Eurobarometer, "Racism and Xenophobia in Europe," Opinion Poll 47.1, special report no. 113, Luxembourg, December 18–19, 1997, http://ec.europa.eu/public_opinion/archives/ebs/ebs_113_en.pdf.

[78] Ibid., 5–6.

[79] European Commission, "National Report, Executive Summary: Germany," Standard Eurobarometer 68, 2007, http://ec.europa.eu/public_opinion/archives/eb/eb68/eb68_de_exec.pdf.

have grown more restrictionist. In one 2003 poll, for example, 50 percent of Swedes polled said they were opposed to accepting large numbers of refugees, up from 44 percent in 2001; only 25 percent favored acceptance.[80] By 2007, a majority said they favored tighter restrictions on immigration as well.[81] In the Netherlands, 48 percent of the country's immigrants believe there are too many migrants in the country, an opinion shared by 65 percent of native Dutch.[82]

These sentiments are echoed throughout much of Asia. A 2007 Pew Global Attitudes survey found that 89 percent of Indonesians and Malaysians, 84 percent of Indians, 77 percent of Bangladeshis and Pakistanis, and 52 percent of Chinese agreed with the statement, "We should further restrict and control immigration."[83] Likewise, despite being the subject of repeated rounds of domestic and international opprobrium because of his government's treatment of would-be asylum seekers, Australian (Liberal Party) Prime Minister John Howard handily won reelection in fall 2004. Howard was eventually voted out of office in fall 2007, but few ascribe this loss to his tough stance on refugees and migrants.[84] In neighboring New Zealand, the (Labor Party) prime minister was able to retain power in October 2005 only *after* agreeing to name a politician who was openly hostile to refugees and migrants to the position of foreign minister.[85]

As Oliver Cromwell Cox sums it up, the "true democratic principle" is that the people "'shall not be made to do what [they do] not like.'... It is only necessary that the dominant group believes in the menace of the cultural tenets and practices of the other group; whether or not they are actually harmful or not is not the crucial circumstance."[86] Thus, whether refugees and migrants represent a real threat is beside the point; if they are *perceived* as fundamentally threatening to their country's security, culture,

[80] Tommy Grandell, "In Sweden, A Growing Tide against Admitting More Refugees," Associated Press, June 13, 2003.
[81] Pew Global Attitudes Project, "World Publics Welcome Global Trade—But Not Immigration," October 2007, http://pewglobal.org/reports/display.php?ReportID=258.
[82] "Even Migrants Say Netherlands Is Full," *Expatica*, October 24, 2003, www.expatica.com/index.asp?pad=2,18,&item_id=35222.
[83] Only South Koreans strongly disagreed (78 percent); Pew Global Attitudes Project, "World Publics Welcome Global Trade."
[84] In fact, for his own part, the former prime minister views his stringent migration and refugee policies as one of the things that made him popular and kept him in office for more than eleven years. Personal conversation with John Howard, former prime minister of Australia, March 2008.
[85] Winston Peters, the politician chosen, warned of an "immigrant invasion which would turn New Zealand into an 'Asian colony'" and "complained [that] Muslim extremists were being allowed in the country." "Peters Is NZ's New Foreign Minister," *Sydney Morning Herald*, October 17, 2005.
[86] Oliver Cromwell Cox, *Caste, Class, and Race: A Study in Social Dynamics* (Garden City, N.Y.: Doubleday, 1948), quoted in Andrew Bell-Fialkoff, *Ethnic Cleansing* (New York: St. Martin's Griffin Press, 1999), 48.

or livelihood, anxious and motivated individuals and groups will mobilize to oppose their acceptance.[87]

Depending on the location, composition, and magnitude of any given mass migration as well as, to a limited extent, the stage of the business cycle, the size and nature of the objecting group(s) will change. In general, the most vociferous opposition tends to follow a (Mancur) Olsonian logic—that is, groups that feel threatened by the (anticipated) magnitude, speed, or endurance of an inflow and anticipate having to bear concentrated costs associated with that inflow will be strongly motivated to raise vocal objections to accepting, assimilating, or simply shouldering the burdens associated with the migrants or refugees.[88] In contrast to those anticipating more diffuse costs, such individuals and groups will have intensely held interests and strong incentives to mobilize against the refugees or migrants in question. Directly affected populations are frequently joined by nationalistic groups that favor restrictive immigration policies more generally. They tend to represent segments of society that expect to lose some of their social, cultural or political dominance to the group in question. Sometimes, however, these actors are simply political entrepreneurs, trying to cash in on public hostility to immigrants (and thereby derive some personal benefit from opposing their admittance). Indeed, such groups have grown large and powerful enough within the European Union that they have created a formal caucus, which offers both more political clout and eligibility for EU funding.[89]

Whatever the complexion of the anti-refugee/migrant camp in a given crisis, if rejectionists mobilize against the group in question, pressure is likely to grow for the target's leadership to rebuff the group, close the state's border(s), engage in interdiction and repatriation, or even undertake military action to forestall or stop the outflow at its source. Therefore, ceteris paribus, as mobilization increases, so will pressure on the target leadership to take steps to reject or resist accepting responsibility for the relevant migrants or refugees.

---

[87] As Robert Jervis makes clear, what constitutes a threat lies in its perception. Even though what Klaus Knorr termed an "anticipation of harm" may or may not be warranted, the effects of a perception of threat may be the same. *Perception and Misperception in International Politics* (Princeton: Princeton University Press, 1976), 28–31, 372–78. For the definition of a threat as the "anticipation of harm," see Klaus Knorr ed., *Historical Dimensions of National Security Problems* (Lawrence, Kans).

[88] Mancur Olson, *The Logic of Collective Action: Public Good and the Theory of Groups* (Cambridge, Mass.: Harvard University Press, 1971). See also Jeannette Money, *Fences and Neighbors: The Political Geography of Immigration Control* (Ithaca, N.Y.: Cornell University Press, 2001); Deutsche Bank Research, "Rise in Anti-immigration Sentiments in the United States," Frankfurt Voice Demography Special, July 30, 2002, 1–8; Peter H. Schuck, "Immigration Law and the Problem of Community," in *Clamor at the Gates: The New American Immigration,* ed. Nathan Glazer (San Francisco: Institute for Contemporary Studies, 1985), 285–307.

[89] Jumana Farouky, "The Many Faces of Europe," *Time,* February 15, 2007.

That said, although leader(s) within target states may experience moral qualms about adopting rejectionist responses, such responses need pose no significant political problems for said leader(s) if the majority of the country's population concurs with them.[90] No significant unrest will result, and the leadership's support base will remain intact. Tragically, such was the case for European Jews trying to escape the Nazis by fleeing to the United States during the early part of World War II. Most would-be émigrés were rejected, and for a long time, few Americans objected.[91]

Protectors and Promoters

However, states hostile to migrants or refugees generally do not operate in a vacuum—nor do their leaderships. More commonly in societies marked by heterogeneous and competing interests, while the members of anti-refugee/migrant camps are lobbying for rejection, other equally motivated pro-refugee/migrant groups concomitantly labor to ensure that targets cannot eschew their normative and legal obligations to those seeking refuge from violence, persecution, or privation. As is true of their restrictionist counterparts, the composition, strength, and visibility of pro-refugee/migrant camps varies from crisis to crisis depending on the race and ethnicity of the refugees/migrants in question and the expected material and/or psychic benefits to be derived from supporting them.[92] Pro-camps tend to be smaller than anti-camps, however, their members also tend to be extremely vocal, publicly savvy, and rhetorically skillful actors such as lawyers and activists. Given their cohesion, focus, and intensely held preferences, pro-refugee/migrant camps may thus make up in political efficacy what they lack in numbers.

More importantly, the relative strength of pro-refugee/migrant camps tends to be bolstered by their members' connections with a variety of domestic and international NGOs and advocacy groups, whose *raison d'etre* is the protection and expansion of human rights generally and of migrant and refugee rights more specifically. Since the end of World War II, both

[90] Although legal challenges to such responses may be mounted.

[91] Kushner and Knox, *Refugees in an Age of Genocide;* Arthur D. Morse, *While Six Million Died: A Chronicle of American Apathy* (New York: Random House, 1967), 41; Herbert Druks, *The Failure to Rescue* (New York: Robert Speller and Sons, 1977), chap. 1.

[92] See, for instance, Martin Baldwin-Edwards and Martin A. Schain, "The Politics of Immigration in Western Europe: Introduction," *West European Politics* 17 (1994): 1–16; Loescher, "Refugee Movements and International Security"; Tony Smith, *Foreign Attachments: The Power of Ethnic Groups in the Making of American Foreign Policy* (Cambridge, Mass.: Harvard University Press, 2000); Joppke, *Immigration and the Nation State.* Joppke persuasively demonstrates how the differing "moral obligations" of states toward particular immigrant groups have profound and varying effects on their policies toward members of these and other groups.

refugee advocacy and human rights groups have increasingly joined hands with philanthropic organizations, concerned individuals, churches, concerned ethnic lobbies, and others to create transnational human rights networks that span the globe. As the Irish rock star and activist Bono has observed, "The administration isn't afraid of rock stars and activists—they are used to us. But they are nervous of soccer moms and church folk. Now when soccer moms and church folk start hanging around with rock stars and activists, then they really start paying attention."[93] Although these networks have been growing in strength since the signing of the 1948 Universal Declaration on Human Rights, they really began to blossom after 1961—with the founding of Amnesty International—and to proliferate, diversify, and grow in robustness after 1970.[94] Indeed, the number of human rights–related NGOs doubled between 1973 and 1983, and many of these organizations have been growing in size and efficacy ever since, in no small part due to an enhanced ability to identify causes with "well-institutionalized international norms."[95]

These networks and their allies—members of the media, academia, legislature, and ethnic and political interest groups—rely on two factors in particular to exercise domestic influence over leaders in support of international norms.[96] The first is leaders' desires to remain popular, either due to short-term electoral considerations or because of longer-term concerns about how they will appear in the context of history. The second is policy legitimacy.[97] Policies that prescribe strategies or tactics that violate norms can threaten policy legitimacy and thereby severely limit support for those policies in the legislature or parliament, in the media, or in the public at large.[98] Although the nature and scope of migration-related legal and normative commitments vary across states, generally speaking the human rights regime has put two major limits on state discretion as it pertains

[93] Quoted in Sheryl Gay Stolberg, "Getting Religion on AIDS," *New York Times*, February 2, 2003.

[94] See Margaret E. Keck and Kathryn Sikkink, *Activists beyond Borders: Advocacy in International Politics* (Ithaca, N.Y.: Cornell University Press, 1998), chap. 4.

[95] Darren Hawkins, "Human Rights Norms and Networks in Authoritarian Chile," in *Restructuring World Politics: Transnational Social Movements, Networks, and Norms*, ed. Sanjeev Khagram, James V. Riker, and Kathryn Sikkink (Minneapolis: University of Minnesota Press, 2002), 47.

[96] Robert W. McElroy, *Morality and American Foreign Policy* (Princeton: Princeton University Press, 1992).

[97] See William Quandt, "The Electoral Cycle and the Conduct of Foreign Policy," *Political Science Quarterly* 101 (1986): 826–37; John H. Aldrich and John L. Sullivan, "Foreign Affairs and Issue Voting: Do Presidential Candidates 'Waltz before a Blind Audience?'" *American Political Science Review* 83 (1989): 123–41; Alexander George, "Domestic Constraints on Regime Change in US Foreign Policy: The Need for Policy Legitimacy," in *Change in the International System*, ed. Ole Holsti (Boulder: Westview Press, 1980), 235.

[98] McElroy, *Morality and American Foreign Policy*, 44–45.

to policy legitimacy: the right of asylum and the principle of racial non-discrimination, both of which have matured into customary international law that is binding on states.[99]

The most broadly recognized manifestations of these norms can be found in the 1948 Human Rights Declaration, the 1951 United Nations Convention on Refugees, and the 1967 Protocol Relating to the Status of Refugees.[100] As legal scholar David Martin put it, "Before the development of these international instruments, opponents of a government practice might have been able to argue only that the measure was a bad idea. Since the adoption of such statements, those opponents are often able to wield a more powerful weapon in the debate, for they may then claim the government practice is not merely bad policy but rather violates international law."[101] The need for legitimacy, particularly when coupled with a desire to remain popular or get reelected, can create a conduit from norms to norms-adherent behavior.[102]

As mobilization within a pro-refugee/migrant camp grows, targets will be placed under greater pressure to admit, assimilate, or simply accept responsibility for a given group of refugees or migrants. To be clear, as is true of the converse (rejectionist) situation, if a particular group is relatively popular or viewed as innocuous—such as was the case during the first exodus of Cubans to the United States soon after Castro took power in 1959—such pressure may prove unproblematic for a potential target.[103] Public opinion may remain generally favorable, making admitting, assimilating, or simply assuming the financial burden for a particular group of migrants or refugees relatively costless. Domestic unrest will not be a significant issue, nor will the target's power base be threatened.

When Rejection Collides with Protection, Vulnerability Results

But in societies marked by disparate and competing interests and unevenly distributed costs and benefits—material, psychic, or both—associated with

---

[99] David Martin, "Effects of International Law on Migration Policy and Practice: The Uses of Hypocrisy," *International Migration Review* 23 (1989): 553–54.

[100] The right to seek and enjoy asylum from persecution is enshrined in Article 14 of the 1948 Universal Declaration of Human Rights. The 1951 Convention Relating to the Status of Refugees and the 1967 Protocol define who refugees are and establish their rights in their country of refuge. The strongest limit on state discretion is the principle of *nonrefoulement* (enshrined in Article 33 of the 1951 Convention), which stipulates that, save in certain limited and exceptional cases, refugees must not be returned in any manner whatsoever to territories where their "lives or freedom" might be endangered.

[101] Martin, "Effects of International Law," 554–55.

[102] McElroy, *Morality and American Foreign Policy,* 45.

[103] See, for instance, Silvia Pedraza, *Political Disaffection in Cuba's Revolution and Exodus* (New York: Cambridge University Press, 2007).

mass migrations, situations in which only one (either the pro- or anti-) camp mobilizes in the face of a crisis will tend to be the exception rather than the rule. This is especially true because of the existence of concomitant splits between elites and the general public. In fact, recent polls suggest that there is no other foreign policy–related issue, including controversial issues such as globalization and the importance of the UN, on which the U.S. public and its elites disagree more profoundly. For example, one Chicago Council on Foreign Relations poll found that 59 percent of the U.S. public identified reducing illegal immigration as a "very important" foreign policy goal, compared with only 21 percent of those in the elite.[104] Thus, in the face of an incipient or ongoing crisis, targets will find often themselves facing highly polarized factions with mutually incompatible interests.

Challengers who engage in this kind of coercion recognize the existence of these political conundrums and purposefully aim to exploit them for their own political ends; again, this is the crux of the political agitation strategy. In summer 1994, for instance, boats were "being prepared in nearly every village along the southern coast of Haiti" in an explicit attempt to "put more pressure on the US to hasten the return of Aristide." As one villager noted at the time: "We cannot get arms to fight.... *The only way to fight is to get the Americans to keep their promises. The only way to do that is to do what they fear most* [have us come to America]" (author's emphasis).[105] Likewise, when East German officials quipped in the mid-1980s that their West German counterparts "claim they have a liberal society over there. [We will] let them prove it!," they fully anticipated that loosing South Asian asylum seekers on West Germany would cause widespread discontent and persuade the previously reluctant West German government to concede to their demands.[106] And they were right.[107]

In fact, would-be coercers often do more than simply exploit extant heterogeneity within target states. They may also aim to increase target vulnerability over time by acting in ways designed to directly or indirectly catalyze greater mobilization, heighten the degree of polarization between groups, and thereby reduce the available policy options open to targets. They may do so by increasing the size, scale, and scope of an existing outflow, shifting

[104] Chicago Council on Foreign Relations "2004 Global Views Survey," chap., 49–50. See also MORI Social Research Institute for Migration Watch UK, "British Views on Immigration," report, February 10, 2003, www.mori.com/polls/2003/migration.shtml.

[105] "Incident at Baie du Mesle," *Time*, July 11, 1994.

[106] Frank Johnson, "East Germans' Refugee Ploy Upsets the West," *Times*, July 26, 1986; Rupert Cornwell, "Bonn Takes Steps to Stem Flood Of Refugees," *Financial Times*, August 28, 1986.

[107] "Bonn, Feeling Pressure of Voters, Is Trying to Curb Refugee Influx," *New York Times*, August 24, 1986. See also, the appendix, case 26.

its character (e.g., by adding more members of either "undesirable" or particularly sympathetic groups), making escalatory threats, or simply directly lobbying members of pro- and anti- refugee/migrant camps.

In short, challengers aim to influence targets by what is, in traditional coercion, known as *force majeure,* a choice dictated by overwhelming circumstances. Targets, of course, always have a choice, but one that is skewed if they believe the consequences of non-compliance will be a denial of future choice.[108] Thus, coercers seek to narrow a target's set of domestic policy responses to an outflow—in game theory terms, to narrow the target's win set—such that concession to their demands begins to appear more attractive, at least as compared to the possibility that the future will hold fewer, still less auspicious choices.[109] This is simply because, with fewer policy options available, the target's capacity to reconcile internal political conflicts and satisfy competing domestic interests becomes far more circumscribed.[110] As Andrew Mack puts it, costs may "steadily escalate without the 'light at the end of the tunnel' becoming more visible....[In which case], the divisions generated within the metropolis become in themselves one of the political costs for the leadership....Any attempt to resolve one contradiction will magnify the other."[111] This can create a particularly nettlesome dilemma for a target's leadership, as well as significantly narrow its room for maneuver.[112]

Under such conditions, concession—to avoid general unrest, to avoid power-base erosion, or to simply make a crisis disappear—can become increasingly appealing, which is of course exactly the coercer's intent. This is not to suggest that concession in such cases is cost-free, only that in the face of a threatened or mounting crisis the anticipation of future pain and mounting costs has to be weighted against the costs and opportunities associated with ending the crisis now, by conceding to the challenger's demands.

Predicting and Measuring Coercive Success and Failure

Consequently, targets will be most vulnerable not when their publics and/or elites are unified but rather when there is broad and intense

[108] Lawrence Freedman, "Strategic Coercion," in *Strategic Coercion: Concepts and Cases,* ed. Lawrence Freedman (Oxford: Oxford University Press, 1998), 29.

[109] See, for instance, Kenneth Shepsle and Barry Weingast, "Uncovered Sets and Sophisticated Voting Outcomes with Implications for Agenda Institutions," *American Journal of Political Science* 28 (1984): 49–74.

[110] See, for instance, Byman and Waxman, *Dynamics of Coercion.*

[111] Andrew Mack, "Why Big Nations Lose Small Wars: The Politics of Asymmetric Conflict," *World Politics* 27 (1975): 187.

[112] See, for instance, Judith Kelley, "Who Keeps International Commitments and Why? The International Criminal Court and Bilateral Nonsurrender Agreements," *American Political Science Review* 101 (2007): 573–89.

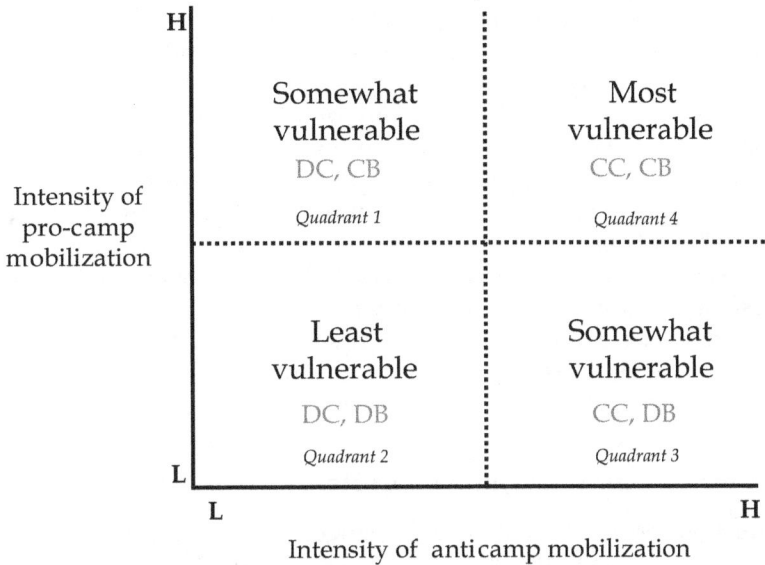

Figure 1.2. Vulnerability to coercion. CB, concentrated benefits; CC, concentrated costs; DB, diffuse benefits; DC, diffuse costs; H, high; L, low.

disagreement about the way in which a target should respond to an incipient or ongoing migration crisis. Again, in Olsonian terms, targets will be most vulnerable when a crisis is widely expected to engender both concentrated costs (CC) and concentrated benefits (CB)—albeit by different segments of society—leading to high levels of mobilization both by those in favor of the refugee/migrant group and those opposed to the same group (fig. 1.2, quadrant 4).[113] Conversely, in cases in which a crisis is anticipated to produce low or diffuse costs (DC) and only diffuse benefits (DB)—and, consequently, neither camp is mobilized and opinion is less polarized—targets will be least vulnerable, and coercion will be least likely to succeed (quadrant 2). Indeed, in most such cases, coercion is unlikely even to be attempted. In cases in which only the pro-refugee/migrant camp is highly mobilized (quadrant 1: DC, CB), target vulnerability will be relatively low because assimilating or accepting the group in question should be relatively easy. Likewise, in cases in which only the anti-refugee/migrant camp is mobilized (quadrant 3: CC, DB),

[113] Olson, *Logic of Collective Action*, chap. 1. See also (although it focuses on more long-term policymaking processes rather than crisis responses), Gary P. Freeman, "National Models, Policy Types, and the Politics of Immigration in Liberal Democracies," *West European Politics* 29 (2006): 227–47.

targets should also be relatively less vulnerable because the options of interdiction, border closure, or simple rejection should be easier to implement. That said, vulnerability in quadrants 1 and 3 will be greater than in quadrant 2 because, from those starting points, only one camp's expectations about the relative size and distribution of costs and benefits needs to shift upward to move the potential target into quadrant 4 (CC, CB).[114]

How can one effectively measure levels of pro- and anti-camp mobilization and political polarization within a target state? Pertinent evidence that I draw on to measure these levels includes, but is not limited to, public opinion data; the level and nature of media coverage, including editorials and op-ed pieces, before and during a crisis; the size and existence (or absence) of public protests; the quantity and content of constituent mail; and the nature of legislative discussion and action.[115]

The Force Multiplier of Hypocrisy Costs

A factor that can further enhance challengers' probability of coercive success is target susceptibility to a special class of political reputational (or audience) costs that I call hypocrisy costs. Political hypocrisy entails the exaggeration by political actors of their state's commitment to morality.[116] As I define them, therefore, hypocrisy costs are symbolic political costs that can be imposed when there exists a real (or perceived) disparity between a professed commitment to liberal values and/or international norms, and demonstrated state actions that contravene such a commitment. Hypocrisy costs are operationalized in a manner akin to what human rights network advocates call "accountability politics," which is to say "once a government has publicly committed itself to a principle...networks can use those positions, and their command of information, to expose the distance between discourse and practice. This is embarrassing to many governments, which may try to save face by closing that distance" or by making the gap disappear altogether by ending the crisis through concession.[117]

Political scientists and international legal scholars have traditionally focused on the normatively positive potential consequences of accountability politics.[118] But hypocrisy-exposing gaps between word and deed can equally well be exploited by actors driven by less benevolent

---

[114] Conversely, of course, in such cases only one camp needs to be assuaged to move the target into the relative security of quadrant 2.

[115] But, given geographical, temporal, and linguistic constraints and limitations, precisely the same kinds of data cannot be used in every case.

[116] Suzanne Dovi, "Making the World Safe for Hypocrisy," *Polity* 34 (2001): 10.

[117] Keck and Sikkink, *Activists beyond Borders*, 24.

[118] See, for instance, Martin, "Effects of International Law," 547–78; Keck and Sikkink, *Activists beyond Borders*; Frank Schimmelfennig, "The Community Trap: Norms, Rhetorical Action, and the Eastern Enlargement of the European Union," *International Organization* 55 (2001): 47–80.

motivations; in fact, the creation of such gaps can even be purposefully instigated or catalyzed by self-serving actors. In the context of this kind of unconventional coercion specifically, having failed to achieve their objectives through traditional channels of influence, challengers may resort to the creation or exploitation of refugee or migration crises. The existence of said crises may encourage targets to behave in norms-violating ways as they attempt to avoid bearing the burdens and incurring costs associated with running afoul of anti-refugee/migrant groups within their societies.

Then, if normative violations do in fact follow, hypocrisy costs can be imposed by domestic and international pro-refugee/migrant groups seeking to protect those under threat, or even by challengers themselves. For instance, in the middle of the aforementioned attempt by East Germany to coerce West Germany in the mid-1980s, an observer on the western side acknowledged, "As West Germans become angry and start to say rude things about all these black and brown abusers of the right of asylum, it enables West Germany to be depicted as 'racialist'"—and in violation of its own constitution.[119] Such charges, particularly when coupled with the threat of future and escalating costs, can make concession more attractive, which again is precisely the intent![120]

In other words, would-be coercers can effectively engage—with the (often unintentional) assistance of the pro-refugee/migrant camp—in a kind of norms-aided entrapment, whereby humanitarian norms are used as coercive cudgels by actors with selfish, self-serving motives as well as those with more altruistic aims, often simultaneously.[121] One might usefully conceive of this mechanism as a perverse manifestation of what Margaret Keck and Kathryn Sikkink call a boomerang pattern—but one that operates in reverse of the normatively positive mechanism Keck and Sikkink describe. Instead of costs being imposed by norms-adherent actors on those who routinely violate them, in the case of coercive engineered migration, norms-violating actors seek to impose costs on those who left to their own devices generally aim to adhere to them.[122]

[119] Quoted in Johnson, "East Germans' Ploy Upsets the West."

[120] In fact, leaders who anticipate vulnerability to claims of hypocrisy may make preemptive concessions to forestall crises before they arise. For example, soon after taking office in 1981, President Ronald Reagan—who had previously criticized Jimmy Carter's handling of uncontrolled migration from Haiti—offered concessions to Baby Doc Duvalier of Haiti to circumvent the possibility that similar criticisms might be levied against him (see chap. 4).

[121] *Entrapment* is traditionally defined as the act of a law enforcement agent that induces a person to commit an offense that the person would not have, or was *unlikely* to have, otherwise committed.

[122] This is because, if norms-violators block redress to domestic NGOs, these organizations can activate transnational networks, whose members then pressure their own states and (if relevant) third-party organizations, which in turn place pressure on targets. Keck and Sikkink, *Activists beyond Borders*, 13.

The susceptibility of targets to hypocrisy costs can also be self-inflicted. But why would leaders make rhetorical commitments that could come back to haunt them? One reason is to expand their political options at home. Actors may hope their words will generate votes or offer them other political advantages during a campaign or at some other moment. To quote Michael Ignatieff, academic, activist, and Canadian Liberal Party politician, in the midst of his own attempt to impose hypocrisy costs on the British government:

> That is exactly what makes this cooked up indignation about bogus asylum-seekers so absurdly hypocritical. For after manfully attempting to whip up xenophobia against the alien horde of liars and cheats at our gates, both the *Daily Mail* and the Home Secretary piously profess their attachment to our "liberal traditions" in relation to right of asylum. Come off it. Liberalism means something. It commits you to protecting the rights of asylum-seekers to a hearing, legal counsel and a right of appeal. Either you treat asylum-seekers as rights-bearing subjects, or as an alien horde. You can't have it both ways. When British liberal tradition has [Home Secretary Kenneth] Baker and the *Daily Mail* as its friends, it needs no enemies.[123]

As Ignatieff's invective suggests, potential targets can make themselves vulnerable by declaring certain groups of (actual or potential) migrants "victims" who are worthy of protection or refuge—for instance, by referring to members of a particular group as refugees whether or not they would appear to fit the legal definition—but then failing to uphold the normative and legal commitments such a normatively exalted designation engenders.[124]

Such norms-enhanced designations may be applied to a broad group for ideological reasons, as was the case when Western leaders promised to welcome all those "fleeing with their feet" from communism during the Cold War, all the while hoping few would come. According to Cheryl Benard, these states very much wanted to "contrast favorably with the communist countries" and to "present life in the West in the best possible light." On the other hand, they did "not want to encourage more refugees to come" because they "would never be genuinely welcomed."[125] In trying to have it both ways, Western countries routinely placed themselves in rhetorical and normative binds.

---

[123] Michael Ignatieff, "Mythical Hordes in a Lurid Fantasyland," *Observer*, October 13, 1991.

[124] On the political significance of defining groups as legitimate or illegitimate migrants, see Lina Newton, "'It's Not a Question of Being Anti-Immigration': Categories of Deservedness in Immigration Policy Making," in *Deserving and Entitled: Social Constructions and Public Policy*, ed. Anne L. Schneider and Helen M. Ingram (Albany: SUNY Press, 2005), esp. 147–67.

[125] Benard, "Politics and the Refugee Experience," 621.

These tendencies did not die with the end of the Cold War. As one British commentator put it, when calling the Germans on the carpet for their apparent hypocrisy in the midst of the crisis surrounding the 1998 influx of Kurds into Western Europe:

> In this particular case, the obvious villains are German politicians, outbidding each other on law and order in an election year, and barely veiling their ancestral prejudices against slapdash Italians who couldn't run a dog show, let alone a serious border control policy. In one breath they castigate Turkey for gross human rights violations against its Kurdish population—only to insist in the next that Kurds who do make it to Italy are simply in search of the economic good life, and should be sent home forthwith.[126]

Aspiring and incumbent political leaders sometimes also apply normatively privileged designations more narrowly to particular ethnic, religious, or national groups.[127] They may do so to broaden their popularity with new segments of their electorates, to shore up their traditional power bases, or—in the midst of active electoral competitions—to draw distinctions between themselves and their competitors, distinctions for which they may be later held to account.

Sometimes actors employ migration-related, normatively enhanced rhetoric with the aim of obtaining not just domestic but also international approval and praise—which may be of value in and of itself, especially for actors concerned about their status and reputation. For example, the 1997 Italian decision to launch Operation Alba was driven not solely by Albanian President Sali Berisha's promise that the flow of Albanians across the Adriatic would end if Italy delivered aid and military assistance (case 48 in table 1.3) but also by the Italian imperative "to take into account both Italian popular opinion regarding Albanians," which was, to put it mildly, not positive,[128] and "Italy's aspirations in joining the EMU." At the time, Romano Prodi's government justified the intervention "in terms of how the Europeans would see them" and "the impression on Europe that its politics would make."[129]

---

[126] Rupert Cornwell, "A Good Time Not to Say 'I Told You So,'" *Independent*, January 8, 1998.

[127] See, for instance, Lina Newton, *Illegal, Alien or Immigrant: The Politics of Immigration Reform* (New York: New York University Press, 2008); Frank R. Baumgartner and Bryan D. Jones, *Agendas and Instability in American Politics* (Chicago: University of Chicago Press, 1993).

[128] Jessika ter Wal. "Racism and Cultural Diversity in the Mass Media," 2002, http://eumc.eu.int/eumc/material/pub/media_report/MR-CH4-8-Italy.pdf.

[129] Ted Permutter, "The Politics of Proximity: The Italian Response to the Albanian Crisis," *International Migration Review* 32 (1998): 211, 203. See also John Morrison, *The Trafficking and Smuggling of Refugees: The Endgame of European Asylum Policy?* (Geneva: UNHCR Policy and Evaluation Unit, 2000), 31.

Even if individual politicians have not personally made rhetorically problematic statements, they may nevertheless find themselves vulnerable to hypocrisy costs based on the actions (or historical positions) of their predecessors and, in particular, as a result of long-standing national commitments to a specific group or groups. (The U.S. relationship with Cubans is but one obvious example.) As Arthur Schlesinger Jr. has quipped, "standards solemnly declared, even if unobserved, live on to supply ammunition to those who thereafter demand observance."[130] Whether leaders resort to the use of normatively exalted rhetoric for instrumental reasons or actually espouse the values they articulate is immaterial. In either case, leaders who employ such rhetoric may set the stage for having to make good on those rhetorical claims or face the political costs of failing to do so, if their actions fail to comport with their articulated commitments.[131]

EVIDENCE AND MEASUREMENT OF HYPOCRISY COSTS   Hypocrisy costs are a theoretical construct and are thus not directly observable; however, their consequences are. That leaders *perceived* the existence of hypocrisy costs can thus be inferred if and when there exists documentary evidence that target leaders or their advisors recognized the dangers of failing to undertake or to change behavior that make them appear hypocritical, incompetent, insensitive, or simply perfidious. For instance, cognizant of the fact that its "own extremely restrictive refugee policy would become the object of critical examination" if it were under the public spotlight, Canada resisted U.S. appeals that it host a 1943 meeting about how to deal with the ongoing European refugee problem.[132] Likewise, the British agreed not to return the Jewish refugees then languishing on the ship the *St. Louis* to Germany—after they had been refused entry to both Cuba and the United States—for "fear their liberal reputation might be tarnished after the example provided by Holland to take 200" of the displaced.[133] Similarly, as the more recent East German and Haitian examples suggest, evidence of the *attempted imposition* of hypocrisy costs can also be found

---

[130] Arthur Schlesinger Jr., "Human Rights and the American Tradition," in *The American Encounter: The United States and the Making of the Modern World*, ed. James F. Hoge and Fareed Zakaria (New York: Basic Books, 1997), 389.

[131] See, for instance, Gil Loescher, "The European Community and Refugees," *International Affairs* 65 (1989): 631. Such situations are analogous to the blowback that leaders sometimes face when they inflate the nature of security threats for the purposes of securing domestic support. Having aroused the passions of their domestic polities, they find that backing down can prove difficult at best. See also Brian Rathbun, *Partisan Interventions: European Party Politics and Peace Enforcement in the Balkans* (Ithaca, N.Y.: Cornell University Press, 2004), for a compelling set of examples of how European politicians and parties use their fellow politicians' rhetoric against them.

[132] Marrus, *Unwanted*, 284.

[133] Kushner and Knox, *Refugees in an Age of Genocide*, 145.

in documentation and testimony from would-be coercers and/or other actors who seek to impose them.

Some might retort that the evidence supporting the significance of hypocrisy costs is sometimes circumstantial at best. Such a criticism is fair but irrelevant, because the significance of these costs lies in their *perception*. Thus, offering definitive proof that challengers *actually* attempted to impose hypocrisy costs on targets is not necessary to demonstrate that they matter. Instead, what must be demonstrated is that targets *believe* that such costs exist and that they have the capacity to inflict tangible political harm—whether by eroding the power base of a target government, fomenting general unrest within the target state, or simply undermining the reputation of its leadership. Anyone skeptical that hypocrisy costs are *at least* perceived to exist and to matter materially must provide a plausible alternative answer to the question of why the Clinton administration studiously avoided using the word *genocide* to describe what was happening in Rwanda in spring 1994. As a *New York Times* piece put it at the time:

> Trying to avoid the rise of moral pressure to stop the mass killing in Rwanda, the Clinton Administration has instructed its spokesmen not to describe the deaths there as genocide.... "Genocide is a word that carries an enormous amount of responsibility," [according to a senior administration official]. If the United States joined in describing the killings as genocide, the official and others said, it would be natural—and unwelcome—for voters to expect that the response would include dispatching troops.[134]

Hence, even if only symbolic, hypocrisy costs can be a powerful motivator for besieged politicians to adopt positions, pursue policies, and concede to demands they were previously determined to eschew. As a senior official in the George H. W. Bush administration conceded when discussing the U.S. decision to take responsibility, reluctantly, for the displaced Kurds trapped on the Turkish border after the First Gulf War, "You have to put aside the medium-term problems and the long-term problems and deal with today and the fact that 1,000 people a day are dying and we are being held responsible"[135] (case 40 in table 1.3).

---

[134] Douglas Jehl, "Officials Told to Avoid Calling Rwanda Killings 'Genocide,'" *New York Times*, June 10, 1994.

[135] Unnamed Bush administration official, quoted in John Cassidy and Margaret Driscoll, "New Hope for Kurds as US Troops Fly In," *Times*, April 14, 1991. Just days before, while vacationing in Florida, President Bush had declared that the United States bore no responsibility for what was happening to the Kurds, saying, "I feel no reason to answer to anybody." Quoted in Martin Shaw, *Civil Society and Media in Global Crises: Representing Distant Violence* (London: Pinter, 1996), 22.

Norms need not be what Thomas Risse and Kathryn Sikkink call "socialized" to serve as effective cudgels; they need only be recognized as being important to a segment of society that can inflict costly punishment on the target.[136] Hence, to the extent that politically costly charges of hypocrisy can be leveled against a target, its vulnerability to coercion will increase.[137] That said, hypocrisy costs are not a necessary condition; polarized and mobilized interests can be independently sufficient to persuade leaders to concede. Neither is the imposition of hypocrisy costs a guarantee of coercive success.[138] Nevertheless, in the face of acute heterogeneity and high pro- and anti-camp mobilization, hypocrisy costs can serve as effective force multipliers that enhance the vulnerability of certain leaders and certain targets to migration-driven coercion.

Target Defenses and Evasive Actions

To be sure, coercion is not a one-sided game, and targets are not without recourse. Although, due to their generally liberal democratic nature, the majority of targets are constrained from responding in kind (by initiating outflows of their own), many do find ways to fight back and to resist, sometimes successfully. Three responses in particular warrant mention. First, under certain conditions, targets can externalize, outsource, or simply buck-pass the visible (and politically costly) consequences of migration crises onto others, thereby skirting successful coercion by persuading third parties to warehouse, host, or even assimilate an undesirable group.[139] Transferring responsibility is not always an option, however, particularly if the displaced are already inside the target state or if other potential host or asylum states themselves fear destabilizing consequences associated with an influx.

Second, some target governments manage to navigate the political shoals represented by their constituents' mutually incompatible interests,

---

[136] Thomas Risse and Kathryn Sikkink, "The Socialization of International Human Rights Norms into Domestic Practices: Introduction," in *The Power of Human Rights: International Norms and Domestic Change*, ed. Thomas Risse, Stephen C. Ropp, and Kathryn Sikkink (Cambridge, UK: Cambridge University Press, 1999). See also Ian Hurd, "Legitimacy and Authority in International Politics," *International Organization* 53 (1999): 379–408.

[137] For an argument that suggests leaders differ in their susceptibility to charges of hypocrisy, see Vaughn P. Shannon and Jonathan W. Keller, "Leadership Style and International Norm Violation: The Case of the Iraq War," *Foreign Policy Analysis* 3 (2007): 79–104.

[138] See, for instance, Human Rights Watch, *Stemming the Flow*, chap. 10, in which Human Rights Watch notes, "Despite rhetoric about making the 'extent and development' of cooperation on migration matters contingent on Libya's commitment to fundamental refugee and human rights, the EU is moving forward with Libya, particularly on migration enforcement."

[139] See, ibid. Nevertheless, as became clear in the midst of the Indochinese boatpeople crisis in the late 1970s, attempted buck-passing can also backfire, inadvertently permitting further—and more successful—coercion by enterprising opportunists. See the appendix, case 13.

by assuaging one or another camp through the use of side-payments or by changing mobilized actors' minds about the desirability of a given migrant or refugee group through issue redefinition. In other words, leaders may succeed in shifting domestic perceptions of the expected costs or benefits associated with a particular influx.[140]

Third, targets may successfully launch military action—or threaten to do so—to forestall or stop outflows at the source. Indeed, sometimes targets even use the threat of hypothetical outflows to justify military actions they wish to take for other reasons. In a 1982 speech before the National Governor's Association, for instance, former U.S. Secretary of State Alexander Haig sought to raise support for U.S. interventions in Latin America with reference to the potential migration-generating consequences of failing to act.[141] President Ronald Reagan used similarly inflammatory language in a speech the following year, claiming that a failure to forestall the installation of Marxist regimes in the region could result in "a tidal wave of refugees—and this time they'll be feet people, not boat people—swarming into our country seeking a safe haven from Communist repression to our south."[142] Sometimes targets simply convincingly threaten other actions that persuade challengers to back down or staunch an outflow. When evasion succeeds, coercion will fail, or at least be less successful than challengers may have hoped or anticipated.

Coercion can also fail because of miscalculations by challengers themselves. For instance, although such cases appear to be relatively unusual, attempted migration-driven coercion may—like strategic bombing—unify the target's population rather than polarize it. Similarly, if a group of migrants or refugees—previously viewed with skepticism or hostility—is effectively recast as the victim of gross human rights abuses and worthy of protection, mobilized opposition may evaporate and with it the possibility of successful coercion.[143] This is a key point that reinforces the fact of the dynamic nature of this coercive, two-level game. More broadly, whenever

---

[140] See H. Richard Friman, "Side-Payments versus Security Cards: Domestic Bargaining Tactics in International Economic Negotiations," *International Organization* 47 (1993): 387–409. On their specific application to the migration realm, see Marrus, *Unwanted.*

[141] Haig asked his audience to "just think what the level might be if the radicalization of this hemisphere continues.... why it would make the Cuban influx [referring to the Mariel boatlift of 125,000 people two years before] look like child's play." Quoted in "Haig Fears Exiles from Latin Areas May Flood the US," *New York Times,* February 23, 1982.

[142] Quoted in Teitelbaum, "Immigration, Refugees, and Policy," 435.

[143] See Friman, "Side-Payments versus Security Cards." Of course, the converse is also true should coercers aim to galvanize action within the pro-camp. That said, research suggests that, at least in the U.S. context, changing the prevailing frame in policy debates is a difficult task. See, for instance, Jeffrey M. Berry, Frank R. Baumgartner, Marie Hojnacki, David C. Kimball, and Beth L. Leech, "Washington: The Real No-Spin Zone," in *Lobbying and Policy Change: Who Wins, Who Loses, and Why,* ed. Frank R. Baumgartner, Jeffrey M. Berry, Marie Hojnacki, David C. Kimball, and Beth L. Leech (Chicago: University of Chicago Press, 2009).

there are significant downward shifts in the level of mobilization of (and degree of polarization between) pro- and anti-camps over time, coercion is likely to fail.

The ability to effect successful coercion in the migration realm is further inhibited, in part, by the fact that relatively few of these crises ever reach the desk of target state executive(s). Instead, most remain within quadrant 2 (fig. 1.2) and off the radar screen of the country's executive branch. As Morton Halperin, former National Security Council (NSC) member, has noted vis-à-vis the U.S. context, leaders "lack the time or inclination to concern themselves with such issues. A president might link a particular policy with a particular disaster, but the bottom line is that the president is just too busy to focus upon anything but the larger strategic issues."[144] Thus, whatever its normative repercussions, a migration crisis will become an issue of executive-level concern only when a failure to make it disappear promises to inflict tangible political costs on the target's leader(s)—in short, only when a crisis moves toward the danger zone of quadrant 4.

Nevertheless, as we have now seen, migration-driven coercive attempts happen at least once a year. Moreover, when attempted, coercive engineered migration has succeeded at least in part almost three-quarters of the time, most often against relatively powerful, advanced liberal democracies. In light of all we know about international politics, coupled with all the aforementioned potential obstacles to success, why should this be the case?

Why Liberal Democracies are Particularly Vulnerable

Advanced, industrial, liberal democracies are particularly susceptible to the imposition of hypocrisy costs (and to coercive engineered migration, more generally) for two interrelated and self-reinforcing reasons, each of which reflects a distinct conception of what are traditionally viewed as liberal values and virtues.[145] The first factor—a consequence of what is often referred to as *normative* or *embedded liberalism*—is that the majority of liberal democracies have codified commitments to human rights and refugee protection through instruments such as the 1948 Human Rights Declaration, the 1951 Convention, and the 1967 Protocol.[146] These international conventions and associated domestic laws not only provide a set of

---

[144] Morton Halperin, quoted in Joshua Rovner, "Pathologies of Intelligence-Policy Relations," unpublished paper (2005), 40.

[145] I thank an external reviewer for encouraging me to tease out this distinction.

[146] See, for instance, James Hollifield, "Migration and International Relations: Cooperation and Control in the European Community," *International Migration Review* 26 (1992): 568–95.

normative standards against which the actions of actors can be judged but also place certain legal obligations on states to meet the responsibilities they impose.

On the one hand, such codified commitments provide certain protections and guarantees for those forced to leave their home countries in times of crisis and under duress. On the other hand, however, these same safeguards constrain the ability of states to control their borders and so afford other actors bargaining leverage over signatory states through the employment of norms-enabled (political and legal) entrapment. As James Hampshire observes (albeit only with actors with beneficent intentions in mind), "International law plays a role, not so much as an external constraint upon national sovereignty...but as a source of liberal norms, which can be mobilized by domestic [and international] political actors including judiciaries and non-governmental organizations."[147] Simply put, norms do, as many argue, "provide incentives and disincentives for different kinds of actions" for those who embrace them. They also, however, provide incentives and disincentives for exploitation of these same norms—sometimes with the indirect assistance of well-meaning activists and jurists.[148] Hence, as the adoption and codification of relevant norms grow, and the extent to which individual rights are constitutionally protected increases—and, by extension, what we might refer to as normative liberalization rises—susceptibility to hypocrisy costs likewise grows, and vulnerability to coercion concomitantly increases.

The second source of particular liberal democratic vulnerability lies in the transparent and inherently conflictual nature of political decision making within these states. This *political liberalism* manifests itself, among other ways, in a wide variety of domestic political arrangements that provide access points for societal groups to influence governmental policy. As I discuss further later in this chapter, there is great variation in the nature and scope of these arrangements, as well as in their level of transparency. Thus, the degree to which this factor constrains the policy options available to target leaderships facing real or threatened crises varies significantly, even among liberal democracies. Nevertheless, politically liberal states share certain vulnerability-enhancing tendencies in common. For one thing, not only do opposition parties in democracies tend to have strong incentives to criticize and publicize missteps by sitting governments, but they also face powerful political incentives to adopt positions

---

[147]James Hampshire, "Disembedding Liberalism? Immigration Policies and Security in Britain since 9/11," in *Immigration Policy and Security: US, European and Commonwealth Perspectives*, ed. Terri E. Givens, Gary P. Freeman, and David L. Leal (London: Routledge, 2009), 116–17.

[148]Ward Thomas, *The Ethics of Destruction: Norms and Force in International Relations* (Ithaca, N.Y.: Cornell University Press, 2001), 195. See also Jeffery Legro, "Which Norms Matter?"

that run counter to those embraced by incumbents, whether or not those policies are currently viewed as problematic.[149] Thus, opposition leaders may add the handling of an ongoing migration or refugee crisis to their list of grievances, and the position adopted could be either in favor or opposed to the displaced. For instance, the opposition may contend that the government is "betraying a just cause and sabotaging the political rights" of a group of migrants or refugees or they may equally well claim the government "has sold out to the refugees [or migrants] at the expense of the nation itself."[150]

Consequently, bold assertions by the leaders of target states that they can withstand the competing, often intense domestic political pressures exerted by a migration or refugee crisis—and thus will not ultimately concede to coercers' demands—may ring hollow to challengers, who can readily observe the sometimes hostile and escalatory push and pull of democratic political battles.[151] In short, this particular (political liberalism-motivated) vulnerability arises from the fact that liberal democracies espouse what are supposed to be absolutist principles, but cross-cutting cleavages and the inherently conflictual nature of pluralistic politics make them anything but absolute. As Alexis de Tocqueville long ago observed:

> Foreign politics demand scarcely any of those qualities which are peculiar to a democracy; they require, on the contrary, the perfect use of almost all those in which it is deficient....a democracy can only with great difficulty regulate the details of an important undertaking, persevere in a fixed design, and work out its execution in spite of serious obstacles. It cannot combine its measures with secrecy or await their consequences with patience.[152]

In other words, just as credibility can be a major problem for weak actors trying to convince more powerful ones to comply with their demands, credibility can prove equally problematic for powerful states if they are liberal democracies.

Of course, states (liberal and otherwise) do differ significantly in their capacities to shape—and be shaped—by their societies. The structural position of a state in relation to its society can be viewed as varying along a continuum from decentralized and constrained by societal groups to

---

[149] See Kenneth A. Schultz, "Do Democratic Institutions Constrain or Inform? Contrasting Two Institutional Perspectives on Democracy and War," *International Organization* 53 (1999): 233–66.

[150] Benard, "Politics and the Refugee Experience," 624.

[151] For an analogous argument, see Bernard Finel and Kristen Lord, "The Surprising Logic of Transparency," in *Power and Conflict in the Age of Transparency*, ed. Bernard Finel and Kristen Lord (New York: Palgrave, 2000), 137–80. See also Amy Gutmann and Dennis Thompson, *Democracy and Disagreement* (Cambridge, Mass.: Harvard University Press, 1996).

[152] Alexis de Tocqueville, *Democracy in America*, ed. and trans. Harvey C. Mansfield and Delba Winthrop (Chicago, IL: University of Chicago Press, 2002), 219.

centralized and insulated from society. Analytically speaking, we can distinguish between "soft" (decentralized and constrained) and "hard" (centralized and autonomous) states.[153] "Soft" states tend to be characterized by a high number of policy inputs and actors and relatively low levels of policy autonomy. Because they are most exposed to the vagaries of pluralism, we consequently expect the most highly liberalized and decentralized soft states (such as the United States) to be the most vulnerable of all.[154] Although further research is necessary to confirm the preliminary findings offered here, the data in table 1.3, which demonstrate that the United States appears to have been the single most popular target of migration-driven coercion between 1951 and 2006, support this proposition.

In sum, codified commitments to protect human rights and pluralistic politics can interact in such a way as to offer would-be coercers powerful bargaining leverage via exploitation of what liberal targets rightly view as their virtues and, in effect, transform liberal democratic virtues into international bargaining vices.[155] To reiterate, this represents the converse of traditional two-level games logic: Whereas in traditional two-level games, domestic actors seek to convince their international counterparts that they face significant constraints on their autonomy, in the coercive context, they seek to convey the precisely the opposite impression. But due to the independent and joint effects of normative and political liberalism within liberal democracies, this can prove onerous at best.

Moving beyond Liberal Democracies

Although liberal democracies are particularly vulnerable to this unconventional brand of coercion, they are not equally vulnerable; nor are they exclusively so. For one thing, as previously noted, variation exists in levels of political and normative liberalization across liberal states. For another, many illiberal states possess some liberal characteristics and exhibit some measure of political and normative liberalization—sometimes more than their supposedly liberal counterparts.

We can conceptualize variation in the two sources of target vulnerability in a 2 × 2 matrix as a function of variation in the degree to which the

---

[153] Michael Mastanduno, David A. Lake, and John Ikenberry, "Towards a Realist Theory of Foreign Policy," *International Studies Quarterly* 33 (1989): 467–69.

[154] This proposition is consistent with an argument made by Myron Weiner and Michael Teitelbaum about variability in the abilities of states to restrict immigration. See *Political Demography, Demographic Engineering* (London: Berghahn Books, 2001), 101–2.

[155] Susan Peterson, *Crisis Bargaining and the State: The Domestic Politics of International Conflict* (Ann Arbor: University of Michigan Press, 1996); Ronald Rogowski, "Institutions as Constraints," in *Strategic Choice and International Relations*, ed. David A. Lake and Robert Powell (Princeton: Princeton University Press, 1999), 125–26.

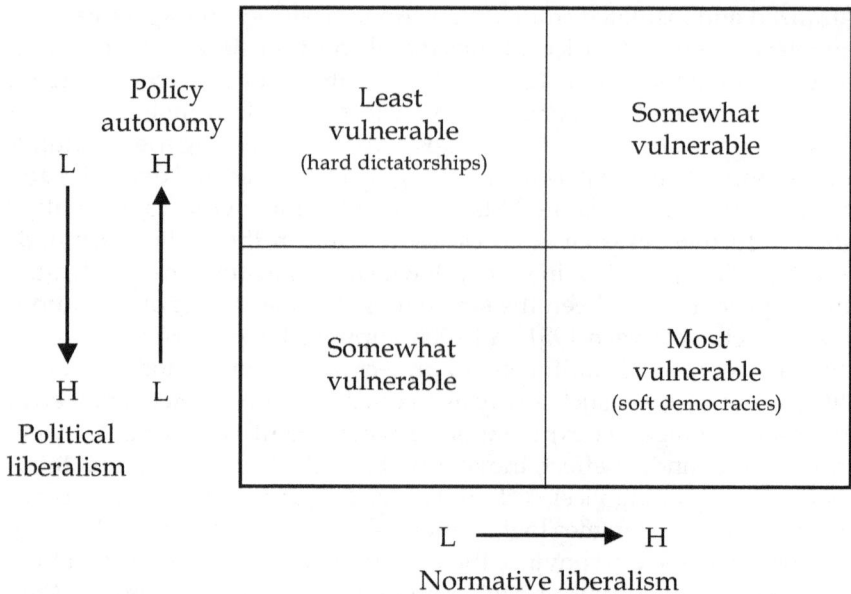

Figure 1.3. Vulnerability across regime types. H, high; L, low.

target has adopted and codified norms that provide rights and protections for refugees and migrants, specifically, and human rights, more generally (normative liberalism), and the level of decision-making and policymaking autonomy within the target state (political liberalism) (see fig. 1.3).[156]

Although both factors are significant, the existence of the hypocrisy cost force multiplier suggests the degree of normative liberalism might be ultimately more influential than the degree of policymaking autonomy (political liberalism) in determining target vulnerability ex ante. On the other hand, politicians naturally care more about domestic politics than international influences, so the degree of political liberalism might be expected to offer more predictive value in terms of ultimate outcomes. In any case, as levels of normative and political liberalism rise (and policy autonomy declines) the aggregate vulnerability of a state also rises—consequently making "soft" liberal democracies particularly vulnerable.

Conversely, ceteris paribus, personalistic authoritarian or totalitarian governments should be least vulnerable to this kind of coercion. By definition,

---

[156] The proposition that the level of domestic autonomy is a key variable comports with Idean Salehyan and Marc Rosenblum's empirical (U.S.-focused) findings with respect to asylum admissions. See "International Relations, Domestic Politics and Asylum Admissions in the United States," *Policy Research Quarterly* 61 (2008): 104–21.

such states are less politically liberalized than their democratic counterparts. They are consequently also "harder", more centralized, and characterized by relatively high degrees of policy autonomy, thereby granting their leaderships greater latitude in responding to potential migration crises. In the aggregate, illiberal, authoritarian states tend to be less normatively liberalized than their democratic counterparts and correspondingly subject to fewer constraints on this dimension, too. As table 1.3 illustrates, few such states appear to have been targeted since 1951, and still fewer successfully so.

That said, only rarely are all other things equal. For one thing, not all autocracies are alike. Like democracies, they too differ in the level, degree, and scope of policy autonomy afforded to their leaderships.[157] Moreover, few leaders, even in illiberal states, can operate for long without the consent of at least a significant subset of their people. The size of the so-called selectorate—the group of individuals formally responsible for determining the fate of the leadership of a state—also varies across states.[158] What is key, however, is that illiberal leaders too must answer to some subset of their constituents, so domestic discord can exercise some (albeit weaker) effects within these states, too.

Moreover, in an era of increasing globalization, it is widely assumed that most states (illiberal or otherwise) want to be a part of what is often referred to as the "international community of states" and to reap the political and economic benefits enjoyed by its members. As Victor Cha puts it, illiberal regimes in the post–Cold War era have no choice but to open up simply in order to survive.[159] (Although the global economic crisis that began in 2008 may have dampened the enthusiasm of some for the global project, the sentiment largely remains.) Thus, although their domestic constraints are fewer, the behavior of most illiberal states is still subject to potentially costly, external scrutiny (see, for instance, chap. 5, which explores the Chinese response to an engineered influx of North Koreans). Non-democracies are therefore also vulnerable to the imposition of hypocrisy costs by other states and by international and domestic political actors, albeit rather less so than their liberal democratic counterparts.

Alternative Explanations

Might there be other explanations that can better account for or explain the decisions of targets—liberal or otherwise—to concede or resist? Three

[157] Brandon J. Kinne, "Decision Making in Autocratic Regimes: A Poliheuristic Perspective," *International Studies Perspectives* 6 (2005): 114–28.

[158] Bruce Bueno de Mesquita, Alastair Smith, Randolph M. Siverson, and James D. Morrow, *The Logic of Political Survival* (Cambridge, Mass.: MIT Press, 2003).

[159] Victor D. Cha, "Korea's Place in the Axis," *Foreign Affairs* 81 (2002): 79–92.

obvious alternatives are worth considering: (1) geographic proximity, (2) size of a (threatened) mass migration, and (3) prior target affinity or hostility toward a particular migrant/refugee group (as manifested in part by preexisting policies directed at relevant migrant/refugee groups).

The first two alternatives are premised on the idea that a target's propensity to resist or concede is predicated on its ability to stop or to absorb an influx. By extension, the smaller the distance from the source of the outflow and/or the larger the size of the outflow, the lower the probability that a target can independently combat or absorb the group in question, the higher the credibility of the threat to inflict the promised punishment on the target, and thus the greater the probability of coercive success.

Although geographic proximity between the source of an outflow and the target undoubtedly increases the vulnerability of that target, propinquity is neither a necessary nor a sufficient condition for success. As the data in table 1.4 and figure 1.4 illustrate, history has been characterized by myriad non-proximate successes and by numerous proximate failures. In short, geography has been far less important than the degree to which targets are held responsible for, and thus are compelled to respond to, particular crises—whether for historical, domestic constituency-driven, or geopolitical reasons.[160] For example, given the root culpability of the United States for what ultimately became known as the Vietnamese boat-people crises, the United States twice found itself vulnerable to coercion from afar by Hong Kong and a core group of ASEAN member states.[161]

In terms of evaluating the second alternative explanation—real or threatened migrant outflow size—obtaining reliable numbers on the precise size of outflows is difficult at best. Nonetheless, it is reasonably easy to distinguish among orders of magnitude, from hundreds to millions. Again, although larger outflows assuredly place greater stress on the carrying capacities of states and affect their susceptibility to both swamping and agitation, the data in table 1.4 demonstrate that overall outcomes are not correlated with the scale of the unnatural disasters in question (see fig. 1.4). For example, both Ethiopia and Poland successfully convinced Israel and Germany, respectively, to make concessions over groups that were small (even by per capita standards), whereas India did not alter its behavior to comport with Pakistani desires, despite an inflow of 10 million

---

[160] For instance, Ruth Wolf, an Israeli Foreign Ministry official involved in a project designed to encourage Palestinian refugees to emigrate to West Germany in the 1960s, suggested, "perhaps it is necessary to hint to the Germans that they bear a special 'guilt' for the establishment of Israel, because of the Holocaust. Here they have a chance to resettle refugees whose problem resulted from the creation of the State of Israel." Quoted in Tom Segev, *1967* (New York: Metropolitan Books, 2005), 532.

[161] See, for instance, W. Courtland Robinson, *Terms of Refuge: The Indochinese Exodus and the International Response* (London: Zed Books, 1998). See also cases 13 and 29 in the appendix.

TABLE 1.4
Examining Alternatives: Threatened Outflow Size and Geographical Proximity

	Challenger(s)	Migrant/Refugee Group	Principal Target(s)	Outcome	Expected Size of the Migration?[a]	Is Target Geographically Proximate to Source?[b]
1	West Germany	East Germans	United States	Partial success	Medium	No
2	South Vietnam and the United States	North Vietnamese	North Vietnam	Failure	Large	Yes
3	Algerian insurgents	Algerians	French allies, esp. United States	Partial success	Large	No
4	Austria	Hungarians	United States	Success	Medium	No
5	United States	East Germans (Berlin)	Soviet Union	Indeterminate	Medium–large	No
6	Cuba	Cubans	United States	Partial success	Small	Yes
7	Biafran insurgents	Biafrans	Western Europe, United States	Partial success	Large	Yes
8	Israel	Palestinians	Jordan	Indeterminate	Large	Yes
9	Jordan	Palestinians	United States	ST success; LT failure	Large	No
10	Pakistan	East Pakistanis	India	Failure	Large	Yes
11	Uganda	British passport holders	United Kingdom	Failure	Medium	No
12	Bangladesh	Rohingyas	Burma	Success	Medium	Yes
13	ASEAN, Hong Kong	Indochinese	Western great powers, esp. United States	Success	Large	Yes
14	Vietnam	Vietnamese	EC, United States	Indeterminate	Medium	No
15	Thailand	Cambodians	United States; China	Success	Large	No; yes
16	Haiti	Haitians	United States	Success	Medium	Yes
17	NGO activists	Haitians	United States; Haiti	Failure	Medium	Yes
18	Pakistan	Afghans	United States	Success	Large	No
19	Soviet Union	Afghans	Pakistan	Failure	Large	Yes
20	Afghan insurgents	Afghans	Pakistan	Success	Large	Yes
21	Cuba	Cubans	United States	Partial success	Medium	Yes
22	Austria	Poles	Western Europe, United States	Success	Medium	No

(TABLE 1.4—cont.)

	Challenger(s)	Migrant/Refugee Group	Principal Target(s)	Outcome	Expected Size of the Migration?[a]	Is Target Geographically Proximate to Source?[b]
23	Thailand	Vietnamese	United States, France	Success	Medium	No
24	Honduras	Mostly Nicaraguan Contras	United States	Success	Medium	No
25	Bangladesh	Chittagong tribes/Chakmas	India	Indeterminate	Medium	Yes
26	East Germany	Mixed	West Germany	Success	Medium	Yes
27	East Germany	Mixed	Sweden	Success	Medium	No
28	Libya	Guest workers	Tunisia, Egypt, and Mauritania	Indeterminate	Medium–large	Yes; yes; no
29	Hong Kong, ASEAN	Vietnamese boatpeople	Western great powers, esp. United States	Success	Large	No
30	Vietnam	Vietnamese	EC/EU, United States	Success	Large	No
31	Bangladesh	Rohingyas	Burma	Success	Medium	Yes
32	Saudi Arabia	Yemeni laborers	Yemen	Failure	Large	Yes
33	Israel	Soviet Jews	Palestinians	Failure (so far)	Small–medium	Yes
34	United States	Soviet Jews	Israel	Partial success	Small–medium	No
35	Albania	Albanians	Italy	Success	Medium	Yes
36	Albania	Albanians	Italy, EC	Success	Medium	Yes
37	Albania	Greek Albanians	Greece	Success	Medium	Yes
38	Poland	Poles; mixed	EC, United States	Indeterminate	Large	Yes; no
39	Ethiopia	Falashas	Israel	Success	Small–medium	No
40	Turkey	Iraqis	United States	Success	Large	No
41	Aristide	Haitians	United States	Success	Medium	Yes
42	Bosnians	Bosnians	UN Security Council	Partial success	Large	Mixed
43	Poland	Poles	Germany	Success	Small–medium	Yes

44	Cuba	Cubans	United States	Success	Medium	Yes
45	Zaire	Rwandans	Largely United States, France, and Belgium	Success	Large	No
46	Libya	Palestinians	Egypt	Failure	Small	Yes
47	North Korea	North Koreans	China	Success	Large	Yes
48	Albania	Albanians	Italy	Success	Medium	Yes
49	Turkey	Kurds	Italy	Indeterminate	Small	Yes
50	Kosovo Liberation Army	Kosovar Albanians	NATO	Success	Large	Mixed
51	Federal Republic of Yugoslavia	Kosovar Albanians	NATO, esp. Germany, Greece, and Italy	Failure	Large	Mixed
52	Macedonia I	Kosovar Albanians	NATO	Success	Large	Mixed
53	Macedonia II	Kosovar Albanians	NATO	Success	Large	Mixed
54	Nauru	Mixed: South Asians	Australia	Success	Small	No
55	Belarus	Mixed	EU	Failure	Large	Yes
56	Activists/NGO network	North Koreans	China	Failure	Small–medium	Yes
57	Activists/NGO network	North Koreans	South Korea	Failure	Small–medium	Yes
58	North Korea	North Koreans	China	Success	Large	Yes
59	Nauru	Mixed	Australia	Success	Small	No
60	Haiti	Haitians	United States	Failure	Medium–large	Yes
61	Belarus	Mixed	EU	Failure	Large	Yes
62	Libya	Mixed: North Africans	EU	Success	Medium	Yes
63	Chad	Darfurians	UN Security Council	Indeterminate	Medium	Mostly no
64	Libya	Mixed: North Africans	EU	Partial success	Medium	Yes

Notes: ASEAN, Association of Southeast Asian Nations; EC, European Community; EU, European Union; LT, long-term; NATO, North Atlantic Treaty Organization; NGO, nongovernmental organization; ST, short-term.

[a] Small outflows: <15,000; medium outflows: 15,000–500,000; large outflows: >500,000.

[b] *Geographically proximate* states are directly adjacent to, or have borders that lie within several hundred miles of, the source of the outflow.

Geographically proximate?

		Successes		Failures		Number of cases
		Yes	No	Yes	No	(total = 56)
Flow size	Small	1	3	0	3	7
	Medium	14	7	2	1	24
	Large	9	8	8	0	25

Figure 1.4. Why alternative explanations are insufficient. Large flow, >500,000; medium flow, 15,000–500,000; small flow, <15,000.

Bengalis who were relatively unwelcome for reasons other than pure numbers.[162]

This leaves us with the final alternative, prior affinity or hostility toward a particular refugee/migrant group. It has been hypothesized that a prior affinity or historical (e.g., colonial) relationship with a particular group might affect the response of a target to attempted coercion.[163] But in which direction? In favor of the group or against it? On the one hand, it is widely understood that target countries in which particular immigrant communities have become well established can have significant influence over their leaders, which would lead to enhanced support and heightened mobilization within the pro-refugee/migrant camp.[164] And it is certainly true that asylum burdens are strongly (positively) correlated with historical links between countries of origin and countries of destination.[165]

---

[162] See, for instance, the provocative statement of India's ambassador to the UN at the start of this chapter and in the appendix, case 10. Regarding the Israeli and German examples, see cases 39 and 43 in the appendix.

[163] I thank an anonymous reviewer for raising this important issue.

[164] See, for instance, Smith, *Foreign Attachments*.

[165] Eiko Thielemann, "Towards a Common European Asylum Policy: Forced Migration, Collective Security and Burden Sharing," in *Immigration Policy and Security: U.S., European and Commonwealth Perspectives*, ed. Terry E. Givens, Gary P. Freeman, and David L. Leal (London: Routledge, 2008), 173.

On the other hand, however, research has also shown that, historically, hostility and envy have not been highest vis-à-vis entirely foreign groups but, rather, groups "who have some ethnic or other affinity to that host country—such as Algerian *pied noirs* forced to return to France in the 1960s after the war of independence, displaced Germans resettling in West Germany after World War II, Ugandan Asians with British passports admitted to England, and Afghan Pathans moving into ethnically-related areas of Pakistan."[166] Thus, it could equally well be true that prior relationships with migrant groups enhance the strength and size of the anti-refugee/migrant camp.[167]

Likewise, both situations—highly developed affinity in one segment of society and highly developed hostility in another—could simultaneously obtain, making coercive success still more likely. As Robert Art rightly noted, "previous immigration into a target state and its immigration policies [toward that group can] play an important role, [however] that role only has significant effects for its disruptive (as opposed to absorptive) effects for democracies."[168] In short, existing relationships with particular migrant/refugee groups can and often do play a measurable role in determining outcomes, but whether those effects make coercive success more or less probable is case-specific, rather than systematically correlated (either directly or inversely) with the nature of the preexisting relationship or policies.

More to the point, prior relationships will indeed heighten potential effects in cases in which crises become salient to pro- or anti-camps (or to both). However, neither the existence of previous policies nor the nature of extant relationships is independently determinative, that is, neither one is a necessary nor a sufficient condition for determining outcomes. For instance, despite the fact that West Germany had no significant prior relationships with Sri Lankans and other South Asians in the early to mid-1980s, it was still vulnerable to East German coercive attempts that relied largely on exploitation of these selfsame migrant groups during that period.[169]

Likewise, despite the fact that Cubans were a generally well-regarded migrant group within much of the United States, wielded significant lobbying power before and during the 1980 Mariel and 1994 *balseros* crises, and benefited from the existence of special legislation designed specifically to protect them, the U.S. government still found itself vulnerable to

---

[166] Benard, "Politics and the Refugee Experience," 622.

[167] See, for instance, Noora Lori, "The Institutionalization of Un-assimilation: Second-Generation North African Immigrants in France," *Columbia University Journal of Politics and Society* 17 (2006): 95–116.

[168] E-mail communication with author, March 2009.

[169] See case 26 in the appendix.

coercion by Castro and the Cuban government in both 1980 and 1994.[170] Conversely, despite the fact that Haitians as a migrant group did not possess any of the aforementioned political advantages in the periods leading up to the 1979–1981 and 1992–1994 crises, the U.S. government nevertheless still found itself vulnerable to migration-driven coercion.[171] Put another way, crises involving groups with which targets have preexisting relationships, and for which they have preexisting policies, are unlikely to ever commence in quadrant 2 (fig. 1.2). Rather, they are likely to originate either in quadrant 1, if in the main the relationships have been perceived as positive ones; in quadrant 3, if they have been perceived as largely negative; and in quadrant 4, if history and previous migration patterns have left the target state(s) in question with well-developed, competing, and polarized attitudes toward the relevant group(s).

Consequently, I am not arguing that liberal democracies are, simply by their nature, equally vulnerable to coercion by any given challenger in any given crisis. Real or potential crises in which neither the pro-refugee/migrant camp nor the anti-refugee/migrant camp is likely to mobilize tend to be dubious candidates for coercion, a calculation that, as strategic, rational actors, would-be coercers are also capable of making. That does not mean would-be coercers never make mistakes, only that we should see few cases in which would-be coercers target seemingly invulnerable targets, as indeed (it at least appears that) we do.

Case Selection and Methodology

As stated at the outset, this book is animated by three key questions, each of which serves a distinct purpose: (1) how often does coercive engineered migration happen (measurement of incidence), (2) how often does it work (evaluation of success and failure), and (3) how and why does it work (description of the phenomenon)? Having demonstrated its prevalence, evaluated its efficacy, and proposed an explanation of the conditions under which it is likely to succeed and to fail, the next step is to examine whether the proposed causal mechanism is empirically valid. To that end, in the following four chapters, I conduct a series of qualitative case studies using the qualitative methods of structured, focused comparison and process-tracing.[172] In doing so, I employ a wide variety of primary and secondary sources, including data gathered from fieldwork, interviews, and

---

[170] See chap. 2 and cases 21 and 44 in the appendix.

[171] See chap. 4 and case 16 and 41 in the appendix.

[172] See Alexander L. George and Andrew Bennett, *Case Studies and Theory Development in the Social Sciences* (Cambridge, Mass.: MIT Press, 2005), chaps. 3, 10.

government archives. I test the proposed theory on its own terms (against the null hypothesis) and against the plausible alternatives. Although the large-N analysis makes clear that none of the proposed alternatives is sufficient on its own, it is nevertheless worth exploring the relative weight of each in specific cases.

In the chapters that follow, I examine the following specific attempts at (what I argue is) migration-driven coercion:

- Cuba (using Cubans) against the United States, in three separate incidents—1965, 1980, and 1994—against three different U.S. administrations.
- The Federal Republic of Yugoslavia (using Kosovar Albanians) against NATO and, particularly, against three frontline states, Germany, Greece, and Italy, from 1998 to 1999 in the lead-up to and during the 1999 Kosovo campaign.
- Haiti and a deposed Haitian leader (using Haitians) against the United States in three distinct contexts: (1) Haiti in 1979–1981, (2) Haitian President Jean-Bertrand Aristide (as an *agent provocateur*) while in exile in 1991–1994, and (3) Aristide (as a generator) while in office in 2004.
- A loose international network of activists and NGOs (using North Koreans) against both China and South Korea from 2002 to 2005, an attempt that transpired concomitantly with Kim Jong Il's own opportunistic coercive exploitation of Chinese fears of a mass influx of North Koreans.

Every good theory, in addition to positing a relationship between two variables, contains a causal logic that explains why the hypothesized relationship exists.[173] Therefore, if my theory is correct, in the individual cases examined in this book we should find that both challengers and targets behave in ways consistent with what the causal logic predicts. The criteria I used to select cases for closer analysis should permit me to make relatively robust claims about causality. First, I chose cases that exhibit variation on the key independent variables—level of pro- and anti-camp mobilization and degree of polarity. I also chose cases in which hypocrisy costs appeared to play a role and others in which they did not. Second, to avoid biases associated with selecting on the dependent variable, I chose cases of both coercive success and failure.[174] Third, because a number of the cases examined extend over several years, I was able to include cases that looked like they might succeed at the outset but in the end failed

[173] Jon Elster, *Nuts and Bolts for the Social Sciences* (Cambridge, UK: Cambridge University Press, 1989), 3–10.

[174] Barbara Geddes, "How the Cases You Choose Affect the Answers You Get: Selection Bias in Comparative Politics," *Political Analysis* 2 (1990): 149.

and cases that looked likely to fail ex ante yet ultimately succeeded (that is, cases for which there is within-case variation in terms of mobilization and polarization, on one hand, and in terms of coercive outcomes, on the other). As such, it is possible to evaluate whether a shift in the independent variable generated a corresponding change in the dependent variable—an application of what Alexander George and Andrew Bennett call a "before-after design."[175]

Finally, to test the spatial and temporal generalizability of my proposed explanation, I selected cases from three different regions—North America, Europe, and Northeast Asia—during the latter half of the twentieth century. Some of the coercive attempts examined were undertaken by states, whereas others were undertaken by nonstate actors. Some attempts were driven by objectives as simple as financial aid, whereas others were driven by objectives as complex and far-reaching as regime change. Some involved using the coercers' own co-nationals; others did not. Some escalated into wars and military action; others ended preemptively with targets conceding even before an outflow commenced. As the chapters that follow demonstrate, however, what these cases share—both in terms of how coercion was attempted and why (and when) it succeeded or failed—far exceeds the differences that divide and distinguish them.

[175] George and Bennett, *Case Studies and Theory Development*, 166–67.

2

The 1994 Cuban *Balseros* Crisis and Its Historical Antecedents

[Castro] is using people like bullets aimed at this country.
JACK WATSON, White House aide in the administration of U.S. President James Earl Carter

In August 1994, in the wake of some of the worst civil unrest Cuba had witnessed in decades, President Fidel Castro reversed his long-standing policy of arresting anyone who tried to escape the island by sea. Castro laid the blame for Cuba's domestic turmoil on the United States, claiming the riots were caused by rumors of a U.S.-sponsored boatlift to Miami. Castro then demanded that "either the US take serious measures to guard their coasts, or we will stop putting obstacles in the way of people who want to leave the country, and we will stop putting obstacles in the way of people in the United States who want to come and look for their relatives here."[1] This invitation, coupled with a threat, marked the beginning of a major, although short-lived, migration crisis, during which tens of thousands fled the island and headed north toward Florida. The outflow ended after about a month, following the announcement of a new immigration accord between the United States and the Caribbean island nation. This agreement presaged the beginning of the end of a three-decade-long

---

Quoted in Rivera, *Decision and Structure*, 7. Such sentiments were echoed in discussions at the Cuban-Haitian Task Force, the Cuban Desk, and the Bureau of Refugee Programs. See, for instance, Rivera, *Decision and Structure*, 23.

[1] Fidel Castro, "La Razon Es Nuestra: Comparencia de Fidel Castro en la TV Cubana y las Ondas Internacionales de Radio Habana Cuba" (televised speech), Havana: Editora Politica, 1994. See also Felix Masud-Piloto, *From Welcomed Exiles to Illegal Immigrants: Cuban Migration to the US, 1959–1995* (London: Rowman and Littlefield, 1996), chap. 9, esp. 137–44.

U.S. policy of welcoming all Cubans into the United States as de facto refugees and the advent of their being treated (at least on paper) like other groups trying to gain entry to the country; a follow-up accord eight months later solidified this historic policy shift.[2]

In this chapter, I present a longitudinal case study of the August 1994 crisis as well as two previous Cuban migration crises: the little-known 1965 Camarioca crisis and the infamous 1980 Mariel boatlift. These three cases offer particularly good tests of my proposed theory for several distinct reasons. First, unlike many cases of coercive engineered migration, these three are straightforward bilateral cases. They are thus not complicated by the analytical difficulties associated with cases in which generators and *agents provocateurs* (and even opportunists) are operating at cross-purposes.[3] Nor are they complicated by the difficulties associated with analyzing cases in which there are multiple targets.[4] Second, because Castro's Cuba represents the only known set of three documented cases of coercive engineered migration exercised by the same challenger, these cases offer a rich collection of data that amply illustrates recurrent patterns in Castro's behavior. Third, the fact that these patterns persisted across three distinct target administrations provides a strong test of my theory, in that they demonstrate that particular outcomes are not specific to particular leaders or specific time frames (e.g., Cold War vs. post–Cold War) but, rather, may be more widely generalizable.[5]

To briefly summarize my findings: The 1994 *balseros* crisis represented Castro's third known application of migration-driven coercion against

---

[2] Research materials for this chapter comprise archival sources (in particular, documents from the John F. Kennedy Library, JFKL; Lyndon Baines Johnson Library, LBJL; and James Earl Carter Library, JECL; the U.S. State Department Archives; the National Archives; and the University of Miami Cuba archives) and more contemporary U.S. and Florida state government documents. I also consulted a variety of secondary scholarly sources, in particular the myriad interviews conducted by David Wells Engstrom for his valuable examination of the Mariel crisis, *Presidential Decision Making Adrift: The Carter Administration and the Mariel Boatlift* (Lanham: Rowman and Littlefield, 1998), and a wide array of U.S. and Cuban newspaper and magazine articles. For additional perspective, I conducted interviews with former Carter and Clinton administration officials; a European diplomat whose country maintains diplomatic relations with Cuba; a variety of Cuba experts; U.S. military officers who participated in Haitian and Cuban-related operations; U.S. military officers responsible for Caribbean immigration enforcement at SOUTHCOM and U.S. Coast Guard, Miami; officials from the administration of former Florida governor Lawton Chiles; employees of the Miami District Office of the U.S. Immigration and Naturalization Service (INS); and representatives of the Cuban American community in south Florida.

[3] As happened, for instance, in Kosovo from 1998–1999.

[4] As was the case, for instance, in North Korea from 2002 to (at least) 2005.

[5] See also Christopher Mitchell, "The Political Costs of State Power: US Border Control in South Florida," in *The Wall around the West: State Borders and Immigration Control in North America and Europe*, ed. Peter Andreas and Timothy Snyder, 81–97 (Lanham: Rowman and Littlefield, 2000).

the United States.[6] As he had done twice before—most famously in 1980 but also to a lesser degree in the mid-1960s—Castro successfully used a mass migration to pressure the United States to the negotiating table on immigration and a wider array of issues. Castro's gambit was moreover relatively successful in each of the three cases. This was largely because he thrice succeeded at internationalizing what had on each occasion commenced as a domestic economic and political crisis, and at effectively transforming each into a U.S. foreign and domestic policy crisis. Furthermore, in each instance, Castro was aided in his coercive efforts by U.S. rhetorical grandstanding and reactive policy responses, responses which had to be abandoned each time the outflows began in earnest. In particular, Castro was able to play on the discord that existed within the United States between a general public growing less tolerant of refugees and immigration and a state government in Florida reluctant to pay the costs of what it viewed as a federal problem, on the one hand, and a Cuban American community that was (largely but not universally) deeply committed to the protection of fleeing Cubans and to the further political isolation of Fidel Castro, on the other.[7] Nevertheless, as will become clear, not all three of Castro's attempts were equally successful, and these disparities offer lessons and implications of their own.

In this chapter, I first examine Castro's possible motivations for and objectives in launching the 1994 crisis. Then, I move backward in time to examine the two earlier attempts to use his own people as weapons and, in doing so, offer additional evidence as to why Castro thought he would succeed in 1994. Next, I trace the chronology of the crisis and highlight its consequences and outline what Castro did and did not achieve in 1994. Finally, I evaluate my hypotheses in light of the evidence presented in all three cases and offer a few additional thoughts and possible implications of these cases.

Castro's Motivations: Why the Conventional Explanations Do Not Suffice

Some observers have suggested that Castro's decision to open the island's borders in 1994 was simply an act of desperation, aimed at defusing tensions on the ground in Havana and propping up his regime in the face

[6] Whether additional, still classified, preempted attempts occurred is unknown. My pending Freedom of Information Act (FOIA) requests for documents from the late 1960s through the early 1980s may uncover additional data on this front.

[7] See, for instance, Mario Antonio Rivera, *Decision and Structure: US Refugee Policy in the Mariel Crisis* (New York: University Press of America, 1991), chap. 1, on the divisions within the Cuban American community, at least by the end of the Mariel crisis.

of a major economic downturn and growing social unrest.[8] Those who
advance this explanation usually argue that Castro's regime was close to
collapse during this period.[9] However, most analysts—inside and outside the U.S. government—discount this assessment, noting that "Cuba's
repressive apparatus [was] still efficient and loyal, and the ruling group
remain[ed] unified."[10] As Jorge Dominguez, a Cuba expert, observed at the
time, "Any policy based on the idea that Castro is about to fall in the next
few weeks is misguided.... Bill Clinton could very easily reach the end of
his presidency still waiting [for Castro to topple]"—as of course he did.[11]
And Jerrold Post, a political psychologist, noted, "This may not be a man
who will be willing to go quietly into that good night....[he retains] an
electrifying chemical connection with his people."[12]

At the same time, it is true that the prevailing strife on the ground in
Havana did serve as the *proximate* cause of the 1994 crisis and influenced
its timing. Due in no small part to the collapse of the Soviet Union a few
years before, by the summer of 1994 Cuba was an economic mess. Its gross
domestic product had declined a precipitous 35 percent between 1989 and
1993, following termination of the Soviet subsidies and preferential trade
arrangements Cuba had relied on for decades. In addition, the country
had just experienced one of its worst sugar harvests in decades. By escalating tensions in U.S.-Cuban relations through a rafters' crisis—thereby
reminding the Cuban population of U.S. hostility to the Cuban Revolution and diverting public attention from the economic situation—Castro
was naturally able to boost his popularity during a period of heightened
domestic turmoil.

Nevertheless, were it the case that Castro was simply and primarily
using the 1994 outflow as a political pressure-release valve, we should
have seen two things happen that did not and we should not have seen
two things happen that did. First, Castro should have opened the borders without first warning the United States that he was considering
such a move; that is, he should not have issued an explicit threat or set

---

[8] In short, the theory is that Castro chose to open an internal pressure-release valve in
response to growing dissent and economic pressure. See, for instance, Susan Eckstein and
Lorena Barberia, "Cuba-American Cuba Visits: Public Policy, Private Practices," Report of
the Mellon MIT Inter-University Program on NGOs and Forced Migration, Cambridge,
Mass., January 2001.

[9] See, for instance, *El Nuevo Herald*, August 6, 1994. See also, the CNN interview with Jorge
Dominguez, July 30, 1994; David LaGesse, "'Castro's No Pipsqueak,' Never Was: 'Relic' of
the Cold War Still Gets America's Goat," *Arizona Republic*, September 6, 1994.

[10] U.S. Congress, "Testimony of Gillian Gunn," Capitol Hill hearing testimony before the
House International Relations Committee, February 23, 1995.

[11] Quoted in Dick Kirschten, "What Next for Cuba? Stay Tuned," *National Journal* 26, September 3, 1994.

[12] Quoted in Bill Lambrecht, "A Policy Adrift: Suddenly It's Cuba Demanding Action, and
Clinton Facing Another Dilemma," *St. Louis Post-Dispatch*, August 28, 1994.

of demands to the United States, but he did. Second, he should have opened the borders as soon as it became clear that the prevailing political discontent would spill over into serious violence. Yet when Castro held a news conference on August 5—*after* riots had been in full swing for several days—he publicly warned that he might *consider* opening the border if the United States did not shift policy or change its behavior. He then waited an entire week before authorizing the initial departures by sea. Moreover, he did not publicly declare Cuba's borders open until August 20, right on the heels of the announcement that U.S. sanctions on Cuba would be tightened. Third, Castro should *not* have publicly demanded a shift in U.S. policy as a precondition for staunching the flow, yet he did. In each of his pronouncements on the crisis, Castro asserted that negotiations on U.S. immigration policy were a necessary precondition for ending the crisis.[13] Finally, he should have re-closed Cuba's borders exactly when it suited him—the timing of which would presumably *not* have coincided exactly with the conclusion of a new immigration accord with Washington. More specifically, since, as many argue, Castro liked nothing better than to embarrass the United States, had he not been engaged in a tit-for-tat bargaining game with Washington, he would have surely closed the island's borders at any time *other* than just after he had concluded an accord with the United States.[14] Yet it was only after the Clinton administration conceded to negotiations that the exodus was brought to an end.[15] Thus, the evidence suggests Castro's actions were indeed coercive in nature.

Moreover, evidence further suggests that Castro's actions were designed to influence the behavior of the U.S. government as much as that of dissidents in Cuba.[16] Many analysts and government officials who spent time in Cuba and have dealt personally with the Cuban leadership share this view. During the crisis itself, both U.S. Attorney General Janet Reno and Undersecretary of State Peter Tarnoff publicly acknowledged that Castro deliberately caused the crisis in "an effort to force a dialogue with the United States."[17] "He has been doing this for a living for 35 years, and realizes he only has one card to play, the weapon of refugees. He needs the breathing space and knows that the only way to get it is to force the

---

[13] See, for instance, Fidel Castro, televised speech, CNN, August 24, 1994.

[14] See, for instance, Leon Gordenker, *Refugees and International Relations* (New York: Columbia University Press, 1987).

[15] Engstrom, *Presidential Decision Making Adrift*, 190.

[16] See, for instance, Walter Pincus and Robert Suro, "Ripple in Florida Straits Overturned US Policy," *Washington Post*, September 1, 1994; Holly Ackerman, "Transition in Cuba: Terms of Change, Pt. 2," *Peace Magazine*, March–April 1997, http://archive.peacemagazine.org/v13n2p08.htm.

[17] Norman Kempster, "Clinton Rejects Castro's Call for Top-Level Talks," *Los Angeles Times*, August 26, 1994.

Americans into a dialogue."[18] Richard Nuccio, former special advisor on Cuba to the Clinton administration, acknowledged, "the Cuban government exacted changes in the policy of the Clinton Administration towards Cuba by threatening and by carrying out those threats.... Most of our Cuba policy is a result of those kinds of threats."[19] And as former Florida governor and U.S. Senator Bob Graham (D-Fla.)—a man whose career path provided a variety of direct and indirect dealings with the Castro regime—conceded: "Castro, over and over in the last 35 years, has used his own people as a means of accomplishing his foreign policy objectives."[20]

Castro's Objectives

So if Castro intended to use the August 1994 migration surge to force a shift in U.S. policy, exactly what did he hope to accomplish? For some time before the crisis erupted, Castro had been complaining that the United States was failing to hold up its end of a 1984 agreement the Cubans had negotiated with the Reagan administration. This agreement promised 20,000 visas per year for Cubans in exchange for Castro's willingness to take back a number of "undesirables" from the 1980 Mariel crisis.[21] As the Cubans understood the 1984 accord, 160,000 visas should have been granted in a period during which only 11,000 had been forthcoming.[22] In this same period, however, more than 13,200 illegal migrants had been welcomed into the United States, many of whom reached U.S. shores on vessels hijacked in Cuba.[23] This state of affairs reinforced Castro's long-standing claim that for thirty-five years it had been U.S. policy to encourage people to leave Cuba illegally, even if that meant stealing and hijacking boats

[18] Tad Szulc, Castro biographer, quoted in Larry Rohter, "Castro Plays His Cards with Cunning," *St. Petersburg Times*, September 4, 1994; see also Ackerman, "Transition in Cuba."
[19] Telephone interview with Nuccio, May 2000. See also the transcript of a National Public Radio (NPR) interview as part of "What's Next in the Elian Gonzalez Story," *Talk of the Nation*, April 24, 2000, in which the same sentiments were expressed.
[20] "Helm's Bill Could Push More Cubans to Leave for US," CNN News, April 12, 1995.
[21] Masud-Piloto, *From Welcomed Exiles to Illegal Immigrants*, 134.
[22] Ibid., 135, table 9.1. See also "News Briefing with Former Presidential Candidate and Senator George McGovern," Major Leader Special Transcript, Federal News Service, September 15, 1994, www.fednews.com.
[23] Castro, "La Razon Es Nuestra." Interestingly, Castro's claims were consistent with a report generated by the U.S. Interest Section (USINT) in January 1994. In a top-secret memorandum to the State Department, Central Intelligence Agency (CIA), and INS, visa officers in the USINT discussed the problems they were facing in trying to identify applicants with legitimate human rights cases, in that "most people apply more because of the deteriorating economic situation than a real fear of persecution." Masud-Piloto, *From Welcomed Exiles to Illegal Immigrants*, 34–35.

and airplanes.[24] In a sign that he was fully aware of the hypocrisy of the U.S. position, Castro further argued that even people who used violent means of escape were welcomed as "heroes in Miami." Yet "whenever he interfered with these illegal departures, he was accused of human rights violations; while each time he let people leave, he was accused of trying to embarrass the US."[25]

Castro's frustration apparently deepened in summer 1994 as it became clear that the reception rafters were being afforded in July and early August 1994 was "specially warm,...(even) after stealing boats, using violence, endangering the lives of people who did not wish to emigrate, and even committing murder." Rafters arriving during this period were further reassured and "encouraged by the US government's pledge *not to change its immigration policy under any circumstances.*"[26] Such reassurances, coupled with discontent on the ground in Havana, probably served as the tipping point that led Castro to consider initiating a new crisis. As one Latin American scholar has put it, Castro relaxed the strictures against emigration because he was "greatly (and understandably) amazed by US officials' welcome to Cuban refugees who had hijacked ferry boats in Havana."[27]

In short, Castro's principal objective appears to have been a quick end to the irregular and destabilizing pattern of immigration between Cuba and the United States. First and foremost, Castro desired a normalization of U.S.-Cuban immigration and an end to the hijackings that were generating instability inside Cuba.[28] It appears that he would have also welcomed a loosening of the embargo, although the available evidence suggests he did not expect such a relaxation to be immediately forthcoming.[29] As noted at the outset, Castro clearly also benefited from the domestic popularity boost he garnered from going toe-to-toe with the U.S. behemoth; however, evidence suggests this boost was a side-benefit rather than a principal objective.

---

[24] This is essentially an argument (in my view, correct) that the United States, too, was using refugees as a political weapon.

[25] See "News Briefing with Former Presidential Candidate."

[26] Ernesto Rodriguez Chavez, "La Crisis Migratoria Estados Unidos-Cuba en el Verano de 1994," *Cuadernos de Nuestra America* 11 (1994): 24–25.

[27] Peter H. Smith, *Talons of the Eagle: Dynamics of U.S.-Latin American Relations*, 2nd ed. (Oxford: Oxford University Press, 1999), 394n4. On July 26 and August 3 and 4, the ferry that had transported passengers from Havana to Regla for nearly one hundred years was hijacked to Miami. Violence was used in each of the hijackings, and, in one case, a Cuban policeman was killed. Masud-Piloto, *From Welcomed Exiles to Illegal Immigrants;* Chavez, "Crisis Migratoria."

[28] This claim was echoed to me during a conversation I had with a European diplomat (who asked that even his country not be identified), November 1998, Westchester County, N.Y.

[29] Similar impressions were expressed to me in interviews with former Clinton administration officials, July 2000 and May 2001, Washington, D.C.

Why Did Castro Anticipate Success? A Compelling
Track Record of Two for Two

Castro likely believed the migration gambit was worth trying, in part, because it had worked at least twice before: in a quiet way in 1965 and dramatically and very visibly in 1980. By engaging in the use of coercive engineered migration—purposefully designed to create political conflict within the United States—Castro succeeded in dictating the course and pace of events while officials in Washington, working with far more resources at their disposal, struggled to respond.[30]

Recall that, as outlined in chapter 1, the difficulty for leaders of target states lies in the fact that moves that may be rational on the international level may prove untenable on the domestic level, or vice versa. Castro—who was known to be a keen observer of U.S. politics—understood well the dilemmas facing U.S. policymakers who were simultaneously seeking to satisfy competing domestic constituencies without sacrificing international credibility and to solve international crises without creating domestic ones.[31] Although Castro himself was hardly immune from such concerns, the nature and stability of his military dictatorship allowed him to undertake potentially risky moves internationally with considerably less concern about the possibility of domestic backlash, making coercive engineered migration a potentially potent asymmetric weapon against the United States.[32]

---

[30] For a different application of Putnamesque logic to U.S.-Cuban relations, see William LeoGrande, "From Havana to Miami: US Cuba Policy as a Two-Level Game," *Journal of Interamerican Studies and World Affairs* 40 (1998): 67–87.

[31] A September 1994 report by the U.S. Commission on Immigration Reform clearly articulates the dilemma facing policymakers trying to meet both their international normative obligations and their domestic political imperatives: "US policy has tried to balance a number of competing interests and concerns: preserving its international and domestic commitments to provide asylum to those fleeing persecution or a well-founded fear of persecution and providing protection to aliens who would otherwise face return to dangerous conditions in a home country; deterring illegal immigrants who abuse the asylum system as a backdoor to entry; responding to domestic ethnic and political constituencies; ensuring that US policy does not serve as a magnet for otherwise avoidable mass migration; upholding foreign policy commitments; and helping states and localities faced with the costs and other impacts of dealing with immigration emergencies." U.S. Commission on Immigration Reform, *US Immigration Policy: Restoring Credibility* (Washington, D.C.: Government Printing Office, 1994), 164.

[32] Of course, overall, the United States remained immeasurably stronger. So, if a refugee crisis had been really major—say, involving many hundreds of thousands or more—the United States might have entertained an invasion of Cuba rather than conceding to Castro. Nevertheless, the predicted material and political costs of invasion would still have been seen as significant, even though the Cuban military had become a shadow of its Cold War self. For an analysis of Castro's post–Cold War capabilities, see Walker, "Cuba's Revolutionary Armed Forces." See also Jorge Dominguez, "U.S.-Cuban Relations: From the Cold War to the Colder War." *Journal of Interamerican Studies and World Affairs* 39, no. 3 (1997): 49–75.

In each of the three cases, the course of events more or less followed the same five-step pattern. First, Cuba experienced a significant economic downturn. Second, Castro sought a *rapprochement* and/or negotiations with Washington. These overtures took place publicly via a U.S. journalist or public figure as well as privately via a Cuban (or Cuban American) businessman or political envoy. Such overtures were usually rebuffed outright or (at best) received a lukewarm noncommittal response from Washington. Third, within a short period of time, Castro threatened to unleash a crisis by opening his borders, a move to which the United States (in all three cases) responded with contempt. Fourth, within days or weeks Castro opened the Cuban border.[33] Each time, the incumbent U.S. government initially (and very vocally and publicly) welcomed those fleeing from Cuba but was later forced to quickly shift position—often several times in quick succession—as the numbers of migrants rapidly grew and the seriousness of the crisis increased. Finally, initially secret and then public bilateral negotiations resulted and a new policy was announced. Although the course of events could have transpired differently in each crisis, the path of decision making followed a remarkably similar trajectory in each case.

The Camarioca Boatlift

On September 28, 1965, following a period of economic turmoil[34] and several years of unsuccessful, if halting and erratic,[35] attempts at achieving a rapprochement with the United States,[36] Castro surprised the government in Washington and the exile community in Miami with the announcement that any Cuban who had relatives living in the United States would be allowed to leave the island via the port of Camarioca, located on the

---

[33] The exception is the 1965 case, in which Castro opened the border almost simultaneously with the issuance of his threat.

[34] Jorge Dominguez, *Cuba: Order and Revolution* (Cambridge, Mass.: Belknap Press, 1978), 161.

[35] Note, for instance, the stark contrast between the conciliatory position taken by Castro in July 1964 interviews and those taken with C. L. Sulzberger in late October and published in early November of that same year. See, for instance, "Fidel Castro, interview with C. L. Sulzberger," *New York Times*, November 7, 1964. Some of this might be attributable to an escalation in U.S.-supported covert actions against Castro that fall.

[36] In addition to the much debated attempts before John F. Kennedy's death in November 1963 and a few thereafter, in a memo from Bill Moyers to the president, Moyers reports that Edwin Tetlow, the president of the Foreign Press Association and UN correspondent—who interviewed Castro in summer 1965—said, "Castro wants a rapprochement with the U.S. and is willing to agree to give up his ambitions to export his revolution" as he is "depressed" due to the "loss of sugar income." LBJL, "Memorandum to the President from Bill Moyers," August 10, 1965, WHCF EX CO 55, 3/1/64–11/3/66.

Cuban northern shore.[37] Castro also invited exiles to come by sea to pick up family members who had been stranded on the island following the suspension of commercial flights between the two countries during the Cuban Missile Crisis three years earlier. To erase any doubts that he was serious, two days later Castro began offering two flights daily from Havana to Miami.[38]

At the time, many alleged (rightly, I believe) that Castro opened the border largely to rid the island of remaining political dissidents with close ties to the exile community in Miami—that is, that he was engaged in an explicit use of exportive (not coercive) engineered migration.[39] As one observer puts it, "in one clean sweep, he release(d) the internal pressure of 'closet counter-revolutionaries' who stood ready to undermine his regime."[40] At the same time, Castro also effectively demonstrated to the U.S. government—and to himself and his advisors—how easily he could disrupt U.S. immigration policy. Thus, the opening of the port at Camarioca carried with it a "lightly-veiled" threat, namely that it was Havana, not Washington, that controlled the coastal borders of Florida.[41] Almost overnight, and with little warning, the Cuban government presented the administration of Lyndon Baines Johnson with a major migration crisis.

A WARY WELCOME EXTENDED   Having failed to contemplate the possibility that Castro might open his borders, in fall 1965 the Johnson administration found itself at sixes and sevens as to how to respond. U.S. officials were greatly concerned with the potential political, logistical, and economic problems associated with a massive influx of Cubans arriving in small boats in a short period of time. They also worried that this spectacle would "make the US look powerless." Nevertheless, Johnson and his advisors felt they had little choice but to react with contempt and call what they assumed was a bluff by Castro.[42] Thus, in a calculated political move, on October 3 during a prescheduled speech before the Statue of Liberty[43] to announce landmark U.S. immigration-reform

[37] See, for instance, "Castro Tells Rally Cubans Are Free to Leave Country," *New York Times*, September 30, 1965; "US Thinks Over Castro's Offer, but Exiles Skeptical," *Miami Herald*, September 30, 1965.

[38] "Castro Offer Weighed; Castro Offers Two Daily Flights," *New York Times*, October 1, 1965; "Castro Says Exits Open to All," *New York Times*, October 2, 1965.

[39] See, for instance, the text of Castro's speech in *Granma*, October 1, 1965.

[40] Miguel Gonzalez-Pando, *The Cuban Americans* (Westport, Conn.: Greenwood Press, 1998), 44.

[41] Ibid.

[42] Engstrom, *Presidential Decision Making Adrift*, 20.

[43] Ever attuned to domestic politics, Jack Rosenthal, LBJ's director of public information, before settling on the signing's being conducted on Liberty Island with the Statue of Liberty as a backdrop, indicated that the administration had "given thought to some other possibilities: [but] Jamestown or Plymouth would give too much of a DAR [Daughters of the

legislation, Johnson took the opportunity to publicly proclaim that the United States would continue to welcome Cubans "who seek refuge here in America.... The dedication of America to our tradition as an asylum for the oppressed is going to be upheld."[44] Furthermore, with this statement, Johnson signaled that the United States was willing to take as many Cubans as Castro would permit to leave, even though few would probably have qualified for legal refugee status.[45]

In what can only be viewed as a tacit acknowledgement of the power of hypocrisy costs, officials in the Johnson administration admitted that they felt—whatever the negative consequences of *accepting* the Cubans—they had no choice, even though to allow the boats to come would mean that the United States had to "dance to Cuba's tune."[46] Consider the admission made in the following Memorandum for the President:

> There is unanimity that we should make clear our readiness to accept Cuban refugees. They will pose problems of screening and welfare, and there is also a problem of sentiment in Florida where the bulk of the burden has fallen in the past. *But these difficulties are wholly outweighed by the fact that neither at home nor abroad can we accept the notion that our interest in refugees is a bluff and that we really don't want them.*[47]

Because the United States had long used Cuban emigration barriers as proof of the bankruptcy of Castro's regime—the idea being that Cuba could keep its people only by preventing them from leaving—after Castro opened the port at Camarioca, the United States could maintain its integrity only by accepting all those Cubans who wished to leave. As George Smathers, former U.S. senator and advisor to President Johnson, put it, "[After everything we'd done,] we could not all of the sudden say

---

American Revolution]-type cast, quite the wrong emphasis, [while] a place associated with the Golden Gate, might, by looking to the Orient, have a favorable diplomatic aspect. But the only feature is the bridge—not particularly appealing." LBJL, "Memorandum for Bill Moyers from Jack Rosenthal," August 31, 1965, WHCF, EX IM 11/23/63, File: IM 8/1/65–8/31/67.

[44] Lyndon B. Johnson, "Remarks at the Signing of the Immigration Bill," Liberty Island, New York, October 3, 1965, in *Public Papers of the Presidents, Lyndon B. Johnson, 1965*, vol. 2 (Washington, D.C.: Government Printing Office, 1966), 1040.

[45] A 1964 intelligence report had suggested that most of those who would wish to emigrate from Cuba by the mid-1960s would be seeking to escape economic deprivation rather than political repression; Masud-Piloto, *From Welcomed Exiles to Illegal Immigrants*, 60. See also LBJL, Central Intelligence Agency, *Survey of Latin America*, vol. 1 (Washington, D.C.: Government Printing Office, 1964), 77–78.

[46] Engstrom, *Presidential Decision Making Adrift*, 20.

[47] LBJL, National Security Files of McGeorge Bundy (hereafter NSFMcB), CHRON FILE Oct 1–20, 1965 [3 of 3], "Memorandum for the President, Subject: Cuba and Cuban Refugees," October 2, 1965.

we are not going to let you come."[48] Johnson administration officials also feared that, if they attempted to stop the boatlift, Castro would exploit the shift in policy by highlighting the hypocrisy of the U.S. policy flip-flop. Wayne Smith, the former head of the U.S. Interests Section (USINT) in Cuba has noted, "We assumed that Castro wanted us—indeed, was trying to force us—to close off the sealift and to announce that we would accept no more refugees. The onus would then have been squarely on us, and from that point forward Castro could have crowed that not he but the United States refused to permit emigration."[49] At the same time, as frequently happens in cases of migration-driven coercion, there were those who doubted the credibility of Castro's threats.[50] His credibility was in question for three distinct reasons: (1) too little attention was being paid by those in Washington to what was happening on the ground in Havana for a realistic assessment to be made about Castro's willingness to open the floodgates;[51] (2) Castro had made similar, albeit vague, promises once before;[52] and (3) it was widely, although mistakenly, believed that Castro would view an outflow as too potentially destabilizing and threatening to his regime.[53] As a *New York Times* editorial put it at the time, "It is difficult to believe that Premier Castro really will risk a mass exodus. But Mr. Johnson's imaginative and magnanimous response is designed to find out."[54] And find out he did.

A SUDDEN POLICY SHIFT AVERTS A POLITICAL DISASTER   Within a week, it became increasingly clear that, much to the chagrin of U.S. immigration authorities, "hundreds, if not thousands" of Cuban Americans were responding to Castro's offer and planning to travel to Cuba and bring their relatives back to the United States. In the wake of Johnson's welcoming speech, telephone calls between Miami and Havana increased

[48] Quoted in Engstrom, *Presidential Decision Making Adrift*, 21n52.

[49] Wayne Smith, *The Closest of Enemies: A Personal and Diplomatic Account of US-Cuban Relations since 1957* (New York: W. W. Norton, 1987), 91.

[50] See, for instance, LBJL, NSFMcB, CHRON FILE Oct 1–20, 1965 [3 of 3], "Memorandum for the President from McGeorge Bundy, Subject: Cuba and Cuban Refugees," October 2, 1965, in which Bundy notes "the first time we said it [Castro's] was a vague offer, and we would need to know whether he was serious."

[51] John H. Crimmins, coordinator of Cuban Affairs at the State Department, acknowledged that Castro's announcement caught the United States totally flat-footed. In contrast with later crises, no one in the U.S. government had any prior knowledge that Cuba intended to start the exodus in 1965. Engstrom, *Presidential Decision Making Adrift*, 20n47.

[52] See, for instance, "US Thinks Over Castro's Offer."

[53] Ibid.

[54] "Responding to Castro," *New York Times*, October 5, 1965, cited in Engstrom, *Presidential Decision Making Adrift*, 37n72.

by 800 percent and teletype traffic grew by 300 percent.[55] By October 9, Cuban American exiles had organized a flotilla of small boats and set out for Camarioca, eager to arrive by the following day when the port would be officially opened. Those who did not own boats "scoured the marinas of south Florida to buy or rent one."[56] At the same time, *Time* magazine reported: "newspapers and broadcasting stations had received hundreds of letters and phone calls objecting to the new influx of immigrants."[57] Suddenly faced with a potentially much larger than anticipated (and imminent) influx—coupled with growing anxiety among the public in Florida—the very next day, the administration quickly changed tack and began a series of secret negotiations with Castro to normalize the outflow.[58] The result, announced the following month, was a formal Memorandum of Understanding that established procedures and means for the movement of Cuban refugees to the United States.[59] On the same day (i.e., once the ink was dry on the memorandum), Castro closed the port of Camarioca.[60] This was followed in December 1965 by the establishment of an open-ended airlift, which continued until 1973.[61]

Because the Johnson administration—preoccupied with Vietnam and fearing a tragedy in the Straits of Florida—was so quick to propose an acceptable solution to the crisis, Castro swiftly acquiesced and the crisis ended with little immediate political cost to either side.[62] The administration

[55] U.S. Congress, "Cuban Refugee Problem, Hearings before the Subcommittee to Investigate Problems Connected with Refugees and Escapees," 2nd session, U.S. Senate Judiciary Committee, Washington, D.C., 1966, 4.

[56] Engstrom, *Presidential Decision Making Adrift*, 25.

[57] *Time*, November 12, 1965, quoted in Masud-Piloto, *From Welcomed Exiles to Illegal Immigrants*, 69n28.

[58] As an October 14 memo to the president noted, "The negative attitude expressed by the Governor of Florida and what appears to be mounting apprehension among Miami area residents, present a potentially serious situation. We are planning additional measures to keep the net increase of Cuban refugees in southern Florida to a minimum. [But] the Governor and the Mayor are protecting their flanks. The *Miami Herald* is not helping either." LBJL, NSFMcB, CHRON FILE Oct 1–20, 1965 [2 of 3],"Memorandum for the President from McGeorge Bundy, Subject: Latin American Developments," October 14, 1965. Note as well Bundy's recognition of the power of negative press coverage to undermine the administration's policies in Florida.

[59] The memorandum did not, however, constitute a formal normalization of U.S.-Cuban immigration policy; steps in that direction would have to wait until the next crisis fifteen years later. See Masud-Piloto, *From Welcomed Exiles to Illegal Immigrants*, 61–68; Engstrom, *Presidential Decision Making Adrift*, 26–28; Gonzalez-Pando, *Cuban Americans*.

[60] LBJL, NSFMcB, CHRON FILE Nov 1–12, 1965 [2 of 2], "Memorandum for the President from McGeorge Bundy, Subject: Latin American Developments," November 3, 1965.

[61] The airlift resulted in the relocation of 270,000 Cubans by the time it ended in 1973. Rivera, *Decision and Structure*, 4.

[62] An examination of the correspondence from the affected constituencies and their congressional representatives strongly suggests that, had the crisis engendered a less rapid and financially lucrative response from the administration, a domestic political crisis was imminent. LBJL, White House Central Files—National Security-Defense (EXND 19/Korean War),

also helped itself combat potential costs by exhibiting domestic political forethought. Cognizant of potential opposition in Florida—where the population was hostile to a new influx of Cubans—the new airlift was designed so that most Cubans would be settled outside of the state.[63] Likewise, the federal government not only arranged to pick up the entire resettlement tab, but also acted early enough—only four days after Castro announced he would open Camarioca—that the necessary supplemental spending bill had been passed and funds appropriated long before the true costs of the outflow became evident to the host communities.[64] As McGeorge Bundy wrote to President Johnson on the day the Memorandum of Understanding was finalized, "[HEW] Secretary Gardner and Governor [of Florida] Ellington went on Monday to Miami to explain to State and local officials and community leaders what the Federal Government was planning to do to keep the impact of the new refugee movement to the Miami area to a minimum. *They report pretty good success in calming those troubled waters.*"[65]

The Johnson administration acted quickly to staunch the outflow before the crisis escalated further, which limited the potential domestic damage. At the same time, however, Castro also learned a valuable lesson from

---

ND 19–2/c0, "Memorandum to George Culberson, From Seymour Samet, Subject: Growing Negro-Cuban Tensions, Miami Florida," October 19, 1965; LBJL, "Letter from A. C. Adams to Lyndon B. Johnson," October 26, 1965, Folder: File: National Security-Defense; LBJL, White House Central Files—National Security-Defense (EXND 19/Korean War), ND 19–2/ c0, "Memorandum to George Culberson, From Harold T. Hunton, Subject: Growing Negro-Cuban Tensions, Miami Florida," October 19, 1965, in which Hunton reports (among many other troubling trends) that "we have a very tense situation here; a potentially dangerous one. Unless a major effort is launched immediately Miami may have had it.... There are indications that tensions will continue to mount. Since the Federal Government is being cast as 'the villain' in the eyes of the community, efforts should be made to deal appropriately with the situation or severe consequences may result." Luckily, perhaps such efforts were implemented almost immediately thereafter. By January 1966, the potential for crisis had passed. Bill Bowdler reported, "The Negro-Cuban problem is under careful review—and control. The first month of the new refugee airlift brought in about 3,500 (*sic*) persons, of which approximately 60% were promptly resettled outside the Miami area." LBJL, White House Central Files—National Security-Defense (EXND 19/Korean War), ND 19–2/c0, "Memorandum for Mr. Califano (from William G. Bowdler)," January 4, 1966.

[63] See "Memorandum for Mr. Califano"; interview with Smathers, 1988, cited in Engstrom, *Presidential Decision Making Adrift*, 36n64.

[64] Engstrom, *Presidential Decision Making Adrift, 196.* See also LBJL, NSFMcB, CHRON FILE Oct 21–31, 1965 [2 of 2], "Memorandum for the President from McGeorge Bundy, Subject: Latin American Developments," October 21, 1965, in which Bundy reiterates that "as soon as the supplemental appropriation is passed, State and HEW [Health, Education, and Welfare] will issue a general statement making clear that we plan to do everything possible to minimize the burden of additional refugees in the south Florida area and announcing the visit to Florida of a high level team to discuss the refugee program with State and local officials and community representatives."

[65] LBJL, NSFMcB, CHRON FILE Oct 21–31, 1965 [2 of 2], "Memorandum for the President from McGeorge Bundy, Subject: Latin American Developments," November 3, 1965, 4:30 p.m.

the Camarioca dress rehearsal, namely that the appearance of a loss of control over U.S. borders—coupled with the perception inside the United States that Florida might be overrun—would be viewed by U.S. leaders as politically costlier than the alternative of dealing with him.[66] Thus if Castro could transform his own domestic problems into U.S. problems via the exploitation of outflows, he could coerce U.S. leaders into helping him solve them. In other words, Castro quickly learned that he was effectively able to "manufacture negotiating leverage for [Cuba] as a result of [his country's] own weakness by negotiating its own options and relying on the 'goodwill' of the United States, while simultaneously retaining the capacity to threaten his counterpart's interests."[67] The most impressive part of this exercise was that (weak actor) Castro was able to negotiate this outcome with his superpower target after fewer than 681 Cubans had entered the United States.[68]

The 1980 Mariel Boatlift: Castro's Second Migration Gambit

In early 1980, portents of another mass outflow began to emerge.[69] The Cuban economy stood at a five-year nadir, its GDP having shrunk by 5 percent since the previous year as world sugar prices plummeted.[70] Castro himself candidly admitted, in a December 1979 speech before the National People's Assembly, that Cuba was "sailing in a sea of [economic] difficulties."[71] Meanwhile, visits by exiles living in the United States, which had begun in late 1978, were making painfully plain what might be

[66] Interview with a European diplomat, formerly stationed in Havana, who had a close and long-standing relationship with the regime, November 1999, Westchester County, N.Y.

[67] For an analogous argument vis-à-vis North Korea, see Scott Snyder, *Negotiating on the Edge: North Korean Negotiating Behavior* (Washington, D.C.: United States Institute of Peace, 1999), 86.

[68] LBJL, NSFMcB, CHRON FILE Oct 21–31, 1965 [2 of 2], "Memorandum for the President from McGeorge Bundy, Subject: Latin American Developments," October 21, 1965.

[69] Numerous attempts at a *rapprochement* were attempted between 1977 and 1980, including through (1) meetings between Castro and Senator Frank Church (D-Utah), chairman of the U.S. Senate Foreign Relations Committee, in August 1977 (JECL, WHCF, CO 20, Box C0–20, File CO 38 [1/20/77–1/20/78]); (2) the use of private intermediaries such as Bernardo Benes and Charles Dascal, businessmen, in March 1978 (DM ZB Geographic File, Box 10, File [Cuba 2/78–4/78]); and (3) additional congressional visits, including by Senators George McGovern (D-S.D.), Claiborne Pell (D-R.I.), and James Abourezk (D-S.D.). Meetings were also held in New York in June 1978 between mid-level U.S. and Cuban officials; JECL, DM ZB, Box 10, File [Cuban 5/78–8/78]. Also, early in spring 1980, some low-level discussions took place in Washington and Havana on the applicability of the 1980 Refugee Act to Cuban emigration. Rivera, *Decision and Structure*, 5, 192–94; Masud-Piloto, *From Welcomed Exiles to Illegal Immigrants*, 74–78.

[70] Juan Tamayo, editorial, *El Nuevo Herald*, April 23, 2000.

[71] "Admite Fidel Castro la Existencia de una Crisis General en el Seno del Partido Comunista de Cuba," *Diario Las Americas*, December 7, 1979.

politely described as "the contrast" between life in Cuba and in the United States.[72] Further discord was arising from the fact that, since late October 1979, a growing number of Cubans had been forcibly hijacking Cuban vessels to the United States. In violation of the 1973 Hijacking Treaty, the U.S. response was to immediately parole the hijackers and to make little or no effort to prosecute them, which greatly angered the Cuban government.[73] After each hijacking, Cuba issued a diplomatic note of protest, which the U.S. government promptly ignored.[74]

WARNINGS ISSUED, DEMANDS ARTICULATED   Then, on February 19, 1980, in a meeting between Rafael Rodriguez, Cuban vice president, and Wayne Smith, head of the United States Interests Section (USINT) in Havana, Rodriguez proclaimed that the Cuban government was distressed over the welcome extended to Cubans illegally leaving the island and over the unwillingness of the United States to admit more Cubans under its immigration programs.[75] According to Smith, Rodriguez said:

> You turn people away everyday at the Interest Section when they apply for entry documents, but if they enter illegally you greet them with open arms....As you are not applying your laws, we may well stop applying ours. We are considering [an] announcement that any Cuban who wishes to leave will be given [an] exit permit and can go to...Camarioca to be picked up by relatives or friends from [the] US.[76]

Smith viewed the Cuban vice president's threats as credible and requested guidance from Washington as to how to proceed. "I believe Cubans are serious in expressed intention to reopen Camarioca....It seems to me we are faced with a basic decision: Do we wish to dissuade Cubans

---

[72] This perception was made worse by the fact that exiles returned bearing lavish gifts and stories of "streets paved with gold."

[73] Engstrom, *Presidential Decision Making Adrift*, 48; Masud-Piloto, *From Welcomed Exiles to Illegal Immigrants*, 96–97. An August 1980 *Miami Herald* editorial noted that this is an issue "the Cuban government resents deeply....Americans logically cannot condone a crime of violence when its perpetrator is headed North, but condemn it when the criminal wants to go South." *Miami Herald*, August 19, 1980, cited in Masud-Piloto, *From Welcomed Exiles to Illegal Immigrants*, 97.

[74] Masud-Piloto, *From Welcomed Exiles to Illegal Immigrants*.

[75] Some media reports suggest that the issue had been raised at several previous, secret, meetings in the late 1970s. See, for instance, Guillermo Martinez and Helga Silva, "Carter Aides, Cubans Met Secretly," *Miami Herald*, October 12, 1981.

[76] U.S. Department of State, "Cuban Intention to Reopen Camarioca," telegram 1681, USINT, Havana to Secretary of State Vance, Washington, D.C., February 21, 1980.

from going back to [the] Camarioca syndrome, and if so, how?"[77] However, according to Smith, no such guidance was forthcoming.[78]

Two weeks later, the Cuban government repeated its threat. This time, however, the warning came directly from Fidel Castro, who, in a speech on March 8, declared that:

> We hope [the United States] will adopt measures so they will not encourage the illegal departures from the country because we might also have to take our own measures. We did it once.... We were forced to take measures in this regard once. We have also warned them of this. We once had to open the Camarioca port.... We feel it is proof of the lack of maturity of the US government to again create similar situations.[79]

Castro issued another similar threat several weeks later in the April 1 issue of the state-run newspaper, *Granma*, in which he declared that Cuba would be forced to open its borders if the U.S. government did not stop giving asylum to Cubans who commandeered ships to reach the United States.[80]

There were further warnings. In February 1980, the Central Intelligence Agency's (CIA) Cuba Analytic Center issued a report warning that Castro might again unleash large-scale emigration.[81] Throughout this period Cuban exiles in Miami also repeatedly warned federal officials that the Cuban government had made plans to open Camarioca or the Barlovento Yacht Basin in Havana.[82] In addition, on March 27, 1980, Ramon Sanchez-Parodi, chief of Cuba's Interests Section, reportedly told U.S. State Department officials point blank that Castro's government was seriously considering another Camarioca but that, although the threat was "real," *"it would be exercised only as a last resort if [the] US did nothing to accelerate intake of Cubans to [the] US or deter hijacking of Cuban vessels."*[83] In short, the Carter administration had concrete and multisourced intelligence on

---

[77] Ibid.

[78] Interview with Wayne Smith, 1988, quoted in Engstrom, *Presidential Decision Making Adrift*, 57n28.

[79] Fidel Castro, quoted in U.S. Congress, "The Cuban Émigrés: Was There a U.S. Intelligence Failure? Staff Report of the Subcommittee Oversight," 2nd session, House Permanent Select Committee on Intelligence, June 1980, 3; also quoted in *Granma Weekly Summary*, March 16, 1980, 4.

[80] See also Naomi Flink Zucker and Norman L. Zucker, *The Guarded Gate: The Reality of the American Refugee Policy* (San Diego: Harcourt Brace Jovanovich, 1987), 60–61; Rivera, *Decision and Structure*, 196.

[81] See U.S. Congress, "Cuban Émigrés." JECL, "Bloomfield memo—April 23, 1980."

[82] Interview with Manuelo Gomez, director of the Cuban-American Committee, 1986, quoted in Engstrom, *Presidential Decision Making Adrift*, 50.

[83] U.S. Department of State, "Camarioca," telegram 85959 to Secretary of State Vance, Washington, D.C., to USINT, Havana April 1, 1980; emphasis added.

the conditions on the ground and clear warnings of Cuban intentions. But no policy guidance was forthcoming, no diplomatic overtures were made, and no preparatory actions were taken.

"CRY HAVOC, AND LET SLIP" THE DEMOGRAPHIC BOMBS OF WAR?   On April 1, 1980, six Cubans crashed a bus through the front gate of the Peruvian Embassy, amid a hail of gunfire that resulted in the death of a Cuban guard. Much to the annoyance of the Castro government, the Peruvians granted the gatecrashers political asylum and rebuffed repeated requests that the six be returned. In response, Castro announced that he would remove the security forces and the barricades that surrounded the Peruvian Embassy.[84] He further announced that anyone who wanted to leave the country should show up at the embassy, and he would permit them to go to any country that would take them.[85] Within three days, 10,000 Cubans had crowded into the embassy complex, creating a major embarrassment for Castro[86] and a big political headache for those ostensibly committed to the "free emigration of peoples."[87] The UN High Commissioner for Refugees (UNHCR) offered no assistance, claiming that "the problem was not in his jurisdiction because 'scrammers' were not refugees, they were just people wanting to emigrate."[88] Nor did many in the international community offer aid, since most were "relieved that the Mariel formula put the onus on [the] US [and removed it from them]."[89] For its part, Peru agreed to grant asylum to only 1,000 of the embassy crashers. It appeared, however, that the crisis would be averted when Costa Rica offered to take all 10,000 on a temporary basis and to serve as a processing center while Cuban asylum claims were processed.[90] Nevertheless, this respite was to be very brief indeed.

Having made threats to reopen the borders of his country, Castro decided the time was ripe to follow through on these threats. Via editorials published in *Granma* between April 19 and 21, Castro publicly invited

[84] See, for instance, Gonzalez-Pando, *Cuban Americans*, 65–66.

[85] U.S. Department of State, "Peruvian Embassy Situation—What the Cuban Press Does Not Say," Telegram 3971, USINT, Havana to Secretary of State, Washington, D.C., April 24, 1980.

[86] According to former Castro-regime insider, Jose Luis Llovio-Menendez, "Fidel devoted himself body and soul to this crisis from its outset. He set up what was called his 'war headquarters' in a house near the Embassy and from there directed a three-part strategy aimed at containing the embarrassment of events and, if possible, taking advantage of them." Jose Luis Llovio-Menendez, *Insider: My Hidden Life as a Revolutionary in Cuba*, trans. Edith Grossman (London: Bantam Books, 1988), 384.

[87] U.S. Department of State, "Cuba Refugee Problem," telegram 98652, Secretary of State, Washington, D.C., to American Embassy, Lima, April 15, 1980.

[88] Masud-Piloto, *From Welcomed Exiles to Illegal Immigrants*, 81.

[89] U.S. Department of State, "Cubans Push Small Boat Departures as a Solution," telegram 3998, USINT, Havana to Secretary of State Vance, Washington, D.C., April 25, 1980.

[90] Masud-Piloto, *From Welcomed Exiles to Illegal Immigrants*, 82.

Cuban exiles to come by sea to the island and pick up not just the refugees who had originally sought asylum at the embassy but anyone who wanted to leave.[91] He also contacted the Cuban American community directly to encourage its members to come and pick up their relatives.[92] Any doubts about the seriousness of Castro's offer had dissipated by April 21, when the first forty Cubans landed in Florida. Within three days, over 1,000 boats had sailed for Cuba. A week later, Castro announced, "Camarioca was nothing compared to Mariel. We really have an open road. Now let us see how [the United States] can close it."[93] Unfortunately, it could not.

The 1965 Camarioca boatlift had plainly demonstrated the limited political—if not physical—capacity the United States had to prevent boats from sailing to Cuba. If anything, exercising control had gotten significantly harder in the intervening fourteen years.[94] Thus, when the editorials in *Granma* called on Cuban Americans to act, they were ready. Within three days of the first arrivals in Miami, over 1,000 boats had sailed from Florida to Mariel Harbor.[95] Within a month, more than 75,000 Cubans—including a nontrivial number of criminals, the mentally ill, and the chronically infirm—had been transported to the United States, despite the Carter administration's earnest attempts to stop them. By the time the crisis ended in late September, more than 125,000 Cubans had arrived. Castro once again transformed what had begun as a domestic Cuban crisis into an international and U.S. domestic crisis, and he did so via what Victor Palmieri, then U.S. coordinator for refugee affairs, characterized as "a form of guerrilla warfare."[96]

In a clear indication that nonmilitary coercion was exactly what Castro had in mind—as well as that Castro had a clear appreciation of the power of hypocrisy costs—Jose Luis Llovio-Menendez, former Castro regime insider, has noted:

> Fidel had a hidden motive, too, for provoking the mass exodus. His scheme was conceived at the very beginning of the crisis *in response to the United States' contradictions and vacillations....* On the one hand, President Carter had

[91] See editorials published in *Granma* during this period, available at www.granma.cu/index.html.

[92] "On Fidel's orders, Cuban agents and exiles with whom the Cuban government maintained contacts were told to spread the story in Miami that any boat that reached Cuba would be allowed to take relatives out." Llovio-Menendez, *Insider*, 385.

[93] Quoted in Stephen Webbe, "Flight from Cuba," *Christian Science Monitor*, May 8, 1980.

[94] Two changes in the Cuban American community since Camarioca promised to make Mariel a different ballgame entirely. First, the community had almost doubled in size since 1965, meaning more could participate. Second, the community's financial and political resources had grown substantially. Engstrom, *Presidential Decision Making Adrift*, 62.

[95] Robert L. Scheina, *Coast Guard Operations during the Cuban Exodus* (Washington, D.C.: USCG, 1980), 4.

[96] Quoted in Rivera, *Decision and Structure*, 7.

proclaimed that the United States would receive them with "open arms"; on the other hand, the authorities in Miami had threatened to confiscate the boats that returned from Cuba with refugees on board so that the boats could not go back to Mariel to pick up more Cubans.[97]

Further evidence is suggested by Castro's decision to include so-called "undesirables" as part of the outflow. ("I'll fill his arms with sh-t!," Castro reportedly said at the time.[98]) Doing so had the virtue of demonstrating that indeed many of those leaving were the "criminals, *lumpen,* and antisocial elements, loafers and parasites" Castro had said wanted to leave.[99] But including such people was also bound to generate the kind of additional fear and outrage, and raise the perceived costs of the influx, among segments of the target public on which two-level, agitation-centered coercion depends. Moreover, the inclusion of undersirables further strengthened Castro's hand because—as soon became clear—the administration found it nearly impossible to return them without the Cuban leader's assistance.[100]

THE RESPONSE OF THE UNITED STATES AS TARGET—A NEARLY UNMITI-GATED FAILURE   By 1980, public opposition to refugees—particularly in Florida—was acute.[101] At least as early as May 3 (in this case, in the *Miami Herald*), editorials calling on the Carter administration to exercise greater control over Cuban emigration, contending that south Florida could not handle the influx, started to appear.[102] Although rates of immigration had been low during the Richard Nixon and Gerald Ford years, between 1976 and 1980 almost 2.5 million immigrants had arrived in the United States, along with several hundred thousand Indochinese refugees. By 1979, a variety of public opinion surveys revealed that between 57 and 66 percent of the U.S. public was opposed to additional inflows,[103] and a 1980 Gallup Poll found that 66 percent of those queried favored an immigration freeze

[97] Llovio-Menendez, *Insider,* 387.

[98] Ibid.

[99] Quoted in the editorial, "Cuba's Position," *Granma,* April 19, 1980. See also Smith, *Closest of Enemies,* 214.

[100] As indeed it did. See JECL, Staff Office Counsel Files Lloyd Cutler, Box 70; Cuban Refugees, "Memorandum for the President, from Lloyd Cutler, 6/3/80; Subject—"Criminal Statutes and Cuban Parolees"; JECL, Domestic Policy Staff Files, Eizenstat, Box 178, File: Cuban Refugees [C/f, O/a 703] [1], "Memorandum from Stu Eizenstat, From Frank White, Subject: Your 2:30 meeting re return of undesirable Cubans." See also Office of the U.S. Coordinator for Refugee Affairs, text of speech given to UNHCR, October 6, 1980; Rivera, *Decision and Structure,* 12.

[101] Mitchell, "Political Costs of State Power."

[102] See also "Most in Poll Concerned Over Influx of Cubans," *New York Times,* May 18, 1980.

[103] See, for instance, Gallup Poll, "Boat People," Survey #135-G, data collected August 3–6, 1979; CBS News/*New York Times* poll, "Boat People," data collected July 9–11, 1979.

until the unemployment rate fell.[104] In short, the general public in Florida wanted the boatlift stopped—and fast. (For instance, one May 5 memo to the president noted that the Florida congressional delegation "has been besieged by its constituents" about the refugee influx in Florida.[105]) At the same time, the majority of the Cuban American community—widely recognized by those in Washington as a "potent swing-voting bloc in a state with a rich cache of electoral votes"—was committed to keeping it going.[106] Meanwhile, the occupant of the White House was the human rights President, James Earl Carter—whose administration had declared that "by emphasizing human rights America could make itself the carrier of human hope, the wave of the future."[107] As such, Carter was particularly vulnerable to accusations of bad faith and hypocrisy in the migration and refugee realm. It was in this complex and highly contentious political environment that Castro launched his boatlift.

Faced with these competing and—at times, irreconcilable—political pressures, the Carter administration floundered its way through the crisis, trying to please everyone, and, in the end, pleasing no one. Indeed, as Castro had anticipated, the Carter administration found itself trapped between two sets of competing, highly committed, and seemingly incompatible interests: the would-be Cuban refugees and their supporters, and those opposed to their reception and assimilation. As one memo noted:

> Our heritage as a nation of immigrants and your human rights policy compels us to respond in a compassionate and humanitarian way to the current and potential flow of Cubans and Haitians (and others)...[yet] there is also an undercurrent of concern that these new arrivals will compete for limited health and social services and that there ought to be a limit to the ability and willingness of the United States to take refugees."[108]

The scope, magnitude, and seeming intractability of the problems the administration was facing were made clear in another memo, this one from Jack Watson to President Carter:

> Based on my one week's submersion in this problem, I have painfully concluded that the government's current posture and policies towards refugees

[104] Gallup Poll, Survey #155-G, data collected May 16–19, 1980.

[105] JECL, CR&J-White Files, Refugees, Cubans and Haitians [6], "Meeting with the Florida Congressional Delegation," May 6, 1980.

[106] Mitchell, "Political Costs of State Power," 90.

[107] Zbigniew Brzezinski, *Power and Principle: Memoirs of the National Security Adviser, 1977–1981* (New York: Farrar, Straus and Giroux, 1983), 53.

[108] JECL, CR&J, White Files, Refugees, Cubans and Haitians [6], "Undated Draft Memorandum for the President, from James T. McIntyre, Jack Watson, and Stu Eizenstat; Subject: Strategy for Dealing with Status and Benefits of Cubans and Haitian Arrivals."

are filled with contradictions, implausibilities, unrealistic assumptions, and impractical answers. The extraordinary circumstances posed by the current Cuban and Haitian emergency simply illuminate very starkly some of the underlying inconsistencies and problems in our laws that must be addressed with the Congress.[109]

Basically, according to Watson, the administration was trapped.

Another memo further highlighted some of the political dangers inherent in the fact that competing domestic interests were at play—as well as the administration's lack control over them—and the potential hypocrisy costs they entailed:

> The normal administrative machinery is inappropriate to cope with the special problems posed by the Cuban refugee situation.... The Cuban community in Florida is taking matters into its own hands. The Coast Guard reports 600 boats enroute to Cuba to bring refugees to Florida. These issues are compounded by growing resentment in the national black leadership that we are treating Cubans preferentially as compared to Haitians.[110]

In the same vein, at an April 26 meeting, the administration made a crucial decision regarding interdicting Cuban nationals once they had embarked. Noting that the United States had opposed Thai and Malaysian policies of pushing boats loaded with Vietnamese refugees back to sea, Vice President Walter Mondale stated that the administration could not do what it had criticized other countries for doing.[111] "Such a policy would have also undercut efforts to co-opt the Cuban-Americans. Victor Palmieri observed, 'All you needed was one news copter overhead while you were pushing them out to sea. The Cuban community in Miami would have gone crazy.'"[112] In short, the administration was, almost from the outset, acutely conscious of the competing domestic interests in play, the dangers of having to navigate in a sea of self-contradictory refugee policies, and the potentially large hypocrisy costs it was facing.[113] At the same time,

---

[109] JECL, "Memorandum for the President, From: Jack Watson, Subject: Cuban Refugees—A Status Report," May 2, 1980, DPS Eizenstat, Box 178, File Cuban Refugees [C/f, O/A 730] [1].

[110] JECL, DPS Eizenstat, Box 178, File Cuban Refugees [CF, O/A, 730] [2], "Memorandum for the President, From Stu Eizenstat, Jim McIntyre, Jack Watson, and Anne Wexler, Subject: Caribbean Refugee Issues—Zbig's Memo of April 23," April 24, 1980.

[111] JECL, Notes of Stuart Eizenstat, Cuban/Haitian Refugee Situation File, April 26, 1980.

[112] Interview with Victor Palmieri, 1988, quoted in Engstrom, *Presidential Decision Making Adrift*, 74.

[113] There is also evidence to suggest that Carter was well aware of the potential risks and political costs associated with going public with expansive promises. Carter himself composed a handwritten note on a memo to Secretary of State Cyrus Vance, in preparation for a 1977 meeting that Richard Holbrooke was to have with the Vietnamese in Paris, declaring

officials appear to have been at a loss as to how to respond to these dilemmas.[114] The possibility of cutting a deal with Castro was not an option under consideration.

THE HYPOCRISY COST TRAP: THE UNITED STATES MEETS THREATS WITH DEFIANCE   Instead of making overtures to Castro, like Johnson before him, President Carter issued a defiant speech as his first public pronouncement on the boatlift; in it, he reaffirmed the U.S. "open-arms" policy toward Cubans fleeing Castro's regime, proclaiming "we'll continue to provide an open heart and open arms to refugees seeking freedom from Communist domination."[115] And like Johnson, Carter immediately found himself in political hot water as a consequence of his remarks.[116] Although the focus of Carter's comments had been directed at a growing public backlash, especially in Florida, against the Mariel Cubans, when positioned against previous administration statements, Carter's words were interpreted as explicit encouragement to those wishing to leave Cuba and to those helping them.[117] The situation was complicated further by Carter's use of the word *refugee* to describe those fleeing Cuba; calling the Marielitos refugees suggested the President had unilaterally decided the status issue, which he had not.[118] (Other administration officials had intentionally used the term *"asylum seekers,"* rather than "refugees," precisely to avoid this incorrect conclusion.)

That the administration was puzzled as to how to deal with the prevailing domestic discord is clear from the following reflective and telling memo, written by Stu Eizenstat soon after Carter's speech:

The Problem: We don't have an acceptable policy. Until the President's statements on Monday, our public posture was: (1) We were opposed to the boat

---

he was to "minimize press statements—[to] avoid excessive expectations." JECL, "Memorandum for the President, From: Cyrus Vance, Subject: US-Vietnamese Talks in Paris; copy signed and annotated by the President" National Security Affairs Files, Zbig Brzezinski Material, Box 55, File Vietnam 1/77–12/78.

[114]See "Cubans at the Peruvian Embassy in Havana: Policy Options," JECL, Staff Office Files, Special Assistant to the President—Torres, Box 17 File [Cuba 12/7/79–2/14/80].

[115]James Earl Carter, "League of Women Voters, Remarks and a Question-and-Answer Session at the League's Biennial National Convention," May 5, 1980, *Public Papers of the Presidents, Jimmy Carter, 1980–81,* vol. 1 (Washington, D.C.: Government Printing Office, 1981), 834.

[116]Martin Schram and Charles R. Babcock, "President Moves to Halt Illegal Cuban Boatlift; Carter's Ad Lib Affected Policy; Policy on Refugees Affected by Ad Lib," *Washington Post,* May 15, 1980.

[117]See, for instance, a memo from Esteban Torres to Jack Watson, in which Torres admits their "meeting with community leaders on Saturday left much to be desired. Frankly, we lost control." Misfiled in JECL, Staff Office Files, Special Assistant to the President—Torres, Box 17 File [Cuba 12/7/79–2/14/80].

[118]JECL, DPS Eizenstat, Box 178, File: Cuban Refugees [C/F, O/A 730], "Undated Memo, Title: Notes for 12:00 Meeting" (written by Stu Eizenstat).

flotilla and would enforce our laws. (Enforcement was half-hearted and did not include stopping [*sic*] boats from leaving to make the trip.) (2) However, we would not return anyone who reached our shores.... *This initial half-in half-out policy alienated everyone. The Cuban community was angry since we were not providing any assurance that their relatives could come; the alleged enforcement policy offended those who believed it was contrary to our traditions; persons opposed to massive refugee intake believed our enforcement efforts to be ineffective.*

The overall impression was of indecisiveness and that the U.S. was once again the victim of Castro's most recent machinations.... The President's statements served both to clarify but complicate the problem. The clear thrust of his answer was that the U.S. would receive and welcome this most recent group fleeing Cuba.... His statements further confused the situation in a number of ways: (1) The mood of Congress (and perhaps the country) is generally restrictive at the moment and there appears to be some negative fall-out... (2) We should have done some consultation on the Hill before taking an "open arms" posture. (There is *both* resentment and relief up there that we did not.) Resentment by the people who oppose the policy. Relief by those who realize the difficulty of the decisions and are eager to have the President take the heat. (3) The President was not adequately briefed on the entire subject. He continually uses the word "refugees" when the rest of the government is deliberately using "asylum-applicant" and this has led to confusion about whether we have unilaterally decided the status question.

Our attempts to narrow the President's remarks have reintroduced confusion, suggesting that we are back in the twilight zone again.[119]

FROM TWILIGHT ZONE TO PANIC ZONE   In a clear sign that Eizenstat's fears were not misplaced, only one day after his "open hearts and open arms speech" Carter declared a state of emergency in Florida. A mere eight days after that, Carter was compelled to reverse his welcoming stance and take actions to halt the boatlift. Basically, after three weeks of trying to juggle the problems—and the Cubans—piling up daily at Key West while it stalled for time hoping that the flow of Cuban exiles would slow or that Castro would stop the outflow, the administration decided a change in tack was unavoidable.

On May 14, Carter made a new formal declaration of U.S. policy. Unfortunately, the new one looked to observers exactly like an abrupt reversal of his "apparently heartfelt but ill prepared 'open heart and open arms' statement" nine days before.[120] The administration in turn appealed to the exile community for assistance with the implementation of its new policy.

---

[119] Ibid.
[120] Schram and Babcock, "President Moves to Halt Illegal Cuban Boatlift."

It threatened arrests, heavy fines, and vessel confiscation for those who continued to bring refugees into the United States, while promising that it would replace the boatlift with an orderly sea- or airlift. The administration's offer was summarily rejected by the Cuban American community, and its threats of sanctions were ignored or deemed incredible. As Palmieri put it, "I have always thought this is one of the greatest jokes that this group of highly ranked government officials would sit there for a week...thinking they were going to co-opt these crazed Cuban freedom fighters who came up to the State Department to say 'get lost, we are not going to call off the boatlift.'"[121]

The administration's already abundant problems were further aggravated by the fact that both the Cuban American community and the U.S. national media—both of which had praised Carter's "open hearts and open arms" statement—lambasted the administration for its rapid "policy turnabout."[122] Within the administration itself, there was rightful concern about the mixed message its policy flip-flop had sent. In an internal memo to Lloyd Cutler, White House counsel, one staffer mused, "It is extremely confusing to the public to hear on the evening news generous expressions of welcome for the refugees who arrive by private boats juxtaposed with threats of executions and fines on these very boats."[123] And as Jack Watson put it, *"We did not want to say we were going to do something and then be seen by the community...as not doing it. That did not help us."*[124] Meanwhile, in Havana, the May 15 issue of *Granma* lampooned in cartoons and editorials the Carter administration's "foundering attempts" to take control of the crisis and proclaimed, "Carter governs in Florida, but in Mariel, Cuba governs."[125]

"HE NEEDS US MORE THAN WE NEED HIM"   Yet, faced with competing and seemingly irreconcilable domestic interests, many within the administration still remained steadfastly opposed to approaching Castro directly.

---

[121] Interview with Palmieri, quoted in Engstrom, *Presidential Decision Making Adrift*, 80. As one Cuban American put it at the time, "I want to see them arrest these hundreds of Cubans. I want to see them arrest me for going to get my parents. I want to see them arrest me and keep me from feeding my children." Quoted in "Hundreds in Boats, Defying US Sail for Cuba to Pick Up Refugees," *New York Times*, April 24, 1980. Another said, "If they fine us, they'll end up with a lot of boats on their hands, because we can't afford to pay. They'd have to put me in jail and feed me for the rest of my life." Quoted in Margot Hornblower and Charles R. Babcock, "Cuba to Disregard U.S. Effort to Halt Refugee Boatlift; Flotilla Is Unfazed By Stiffer Policies; Refugee Boatlift Unfazed," *Washington Post*, May 16, 1980.

[122] Rivera, *Decision and Structure*, 7.

[123] JECL, Files of Lloyd Cutler, Box 70; Cuban Refugees, "Memo to LC from Philip Bobbitt," May 13, 1980.

[124] Interview with Jack Watson, 1988, quoted in Engstrom, *Presidential Decision Making Adrift*, 101.

[125] Ibid., 116.

They held fast to the view that the United States retained the upper hand, and Cuba would soon crack. As late as May 9—more than three weeks into the crisis—Robert Pastor, NSC Latin America director, claimed, "our international strategy has been quite successful in maximizing international pressure on Castro, and he is clearly feeling it. . . . In summary, our policy is to continue to take all who arrive, to marginally deter additional arrivals, and to await Castro's decision to work out a reasonable solution."[126] On the same day, Pastor's colleague, David Aaron, sent a similarly minded memo to the president:

> Our information on events in Cuba is admittedly spotty, but there is an increasing body of evidence suggesting that the exodus to the Peruvian Embassy and to Mariel has unleashed powerful human forces in Cuba, which Castro is having a difficult time trying to contain. . . . He can no more control his population than we can control the Cuban/American community right now. But he is faced with a much more serious problem than we. Our major concern is how to cope with the dislocations of a new refugee population. He is dealing with a revolution—*his revolution*—which may be unraveling. Unquestionably, he will stop the emigration and the violence before it goes too far. . . . But he is feeling the pressure, and he is trying to get us to scream first.[127]

Still, as weeks went by, the number of arriving Cubans grew from several thousand to one hundred thousand, and still Castro did not back down. By early June, even the hard-liners were willing to concede that they had a real crisis on their hands. Not only was the administration facing a hostile public reaction and growing unrest among the Cuban migrants, but they were also under increased media scrutiny. The U.S. press had started asking hard questions, including if and when the CIA had warned the president that Castro might unleash a mass exodus and whether any actions had been taken in response.[128]

Moreover, the administration was confronted with an antagonistic and resentful response from some quarters of the government itself, as an excerpt from an early June 1 memo makes clear:

> Here are some random thoughts regarding the meeting [about how to deal with the return of undesirable Cubans]: State Department and military people approached the discussion as if the President had an unfortunate "domestic"

---

[126] JECL, DPS Eizenstat, Box 178, File: Cuban Refugees [C/F, O/A 730], "Memorandum for ZB, SE/FW, and JW, from Robert Pastor," May 9, 1980.

[127] JECL, David Aaron/MH ZB; 71–81 (9/78–12/78); File: Weekly Reports to President 136–150 [4/80–8/80].

[128] JECL, CR&J, White File, Refugees, Cubans and Haitians [3], Box 22, "Transcript of News Conference with Jody Powell," June 2, 1980.

political problem in which their help was sought. Their attitude was almost that "there are some limits beyond which you should not ask us to go to solve your political problem."...Every discussion is laced with (a) dire predictions of what Castro will or won't do, and (b) all the reasons in the world why we cannot take effective counter actions.[129]

The same memo also noted that "The tone of events has become even more negative in the last 10–14 days. Even if Castro were *now* to accept our offer of pre-screening in Cuba in order to send more here, I would strongly question whether Congress or the public would let us negotiate for another 100,000."[130]

THE ROLE OF THE AFRICAN AMERICAN COMMUNITY   The prevailing po- litical crisis was further exacerbated by the apparent differential treatment afforded asylum seekers from Cuba and from Haiti. Two weeks into the Cuban crisis, the president's advisors were warning that the Cuban prob- lem was being "compounded by growing resentment in the national black leadership" that the administration was treating Cubans preferentially compared to Haitians.[131] Administration officials were right to be con- cerned. In mid-May, a scathing telegram arrived from the Congressional Black Caucus, in which the administration was excoriated for "the legal, moral, and political implications" of their position, which were "devastat- ing" and "indefensible in the black community and [would] not [be] soon forgotten."[132] In an April 18 White House memo, it was noted:

While initial support for the Haitians came mainly from the Black Caucus, there is evidence that a broader consensus may be emerging....critics argue that most of the Cubans who want to leave to find a better life and not be- cause of political involvement and, in that respect, are just like the Haitians. Louis Martin [special assistant to the president] believes [this disparity of treatment] is a serious political problem for the President and that we need to better explain our policy or change it....No one is entirely comfortable with our existing practices and all agree that the Cuban decision—even if correct standing alone—makes our Haitian policies suspect.[133]

[129] JECL, CR&J, White File, Refugees, Cubans and Haitians [3], Box 22, "Memorandum for the President, from Frank Moore, Bob Schule, and Terry Straub," June 6, 1980.
[130] Ibid.
[131] JECL, CR&J, White Files, Refugees, Cubans and Haitians [7], Box 23, "Memorandum to the President," April 24, 1980.
[132] JECL, CR&J, White Files, Refugees, Cubans and Haitians [4], "Telegram to the President from the CBC," May 15, 1980.
[133] JECL, DPS Eizenstat, Box 178, File Cuban Refugees [CF, O/A, 730] [2], "Memorandum for Stu Eizenstat, From Frank White, Subject: Haitian Refugees," April 18, 1980.

Pressure was growing in other quarters as well (i.e., the size and scope of the pro-camp was growing), as others joined with the caucus to criticize the apparent hypocrisy of the U.S. position; supporters included a variety of celebrities, national religious leaders, and congressional representatives. Before Congress, Representative Walter E. Fauntroy (D-D.C.) criticized the Carter administration in the strongest terms, proclaiming that:

> We, as black people, want to make it clear that we understand the connection between treatment of the Haitian refugees and the regard which [sic] this administration may have for black people here at home. For the administration to fail to address this issue immediately and in a humane and rational way by granting political refugee status by May 15, 1980, when the President's power to grant refugee status on a group basis to the Haitian boat people already in the United States expires, would condemn this administration as one of gross hypocrisy and racism.[134]

In a further sign of the political damage this perceived hypocrisy could cause, the Reverend Jesse Jackson explicitly threatened that, if Carter did not change his policy toward Haitians in short order, Jackson would instruct the black community to stay home on Election Day rather than turn out and vote for Carter.[135] As he later put it, "Whites are greeted by the Statue of Liberty and blacks are deleted by the statute of limitations."[136]

WHEN ALL ELSE FAILS, DO AN ABOUT-FACE—TWICE   Confronted with more than 100,000 Cuban boatpeople, an increasingly hostile public (both within the pro- and the anti-refugee/migrant camps), riots in the migrant detention centers, buck-passing government officials, and mounting criticism and charges of racism and hypocrisy from the African American community, the Carter administration finally decided to abandon the idea of waiting for Castro to make a conciliatory move and approached the Cubans for help in ending the crisis.

Astonishingly, however, even at this point no one inside the administration—barring perhaps a few people at the State Department and in Havana—yet recognized that Castro was trying to accomplish anything strategic with the outflow.[137] As one Cuban representative later put it, "the

---

[134] U.S. Congress, "The Caribbean Refugee Crisis: Cubans and Haitians," 2nd session, U.S. Senate Committee on the Judiciary, May 12, 1980, 16.

[135] To avoid further discrimination charges and defuse the crisis, Carter was compelled to create a new classification—Cuban-Haitian Entrant (status pending)—which promised equal treatment for all those Haitians who had arrived prior to and during the Mariel crisis.

[136] Jackson, quoted in Masud-Piloto, *From Welcomed Exiles to Illegal Immigrants*, 118.

[137] JECL, Files of Lloyd Cutler, Box 70, Cuban Refugees, "Memorandum for the President, From Warren Christopher, Subject: Hijacking of Cuban Vessels," June 26, 1980; Tarnoff memo and interview. See also Smith, *Closest of Enemies*; Engstrom, *Presidential Decision Making Adrift*.

miscalculation was on your side. . . . Someone in Washington should have answered our notes on maritime hijacking."[138] Hence, when U.S. officials showed up in Havana to meet with Cuban authorities in mid-June, reportedly they did not come to negotiate but rather to dictate. The meeting was, according to one participant, "a disaster." U.S. officials offered the Cubans nothing; they simply demanded a suspension of the boatlift.[139] Not surprisingly, the Cubans promptly rejected the U.S. proposal. According to Wayne Smith, head of the U.S. Interests Section in Havana, "As soon as the Cubans realized that we had come only to demand suspension of the sealift, they turned us out."[140] "The Cubans came in waiting to hear us say that this would be the first step in a process. *That* was the key, the *sine qua non*. When we didn't say it, the talks were finished."[141] As Ricardo Alarcon, Cuban representative and then vice-minister of foreign relations, responded at the time, "if we ever get back to negotiating anything, it will have to be on the basis of a step-by-step process based on reciprocity. . . . We aren't going to sit down with you to talk about stopping the Mariel operation and then have that be the end of it."[142]

In the end, more than three additional months passed—during which U.S. opinion on the Cuban/Haitian situation reached "70–80 percent negative," with 75 percent of the American people saying the Cuban refugee situation is "bad for our country"—before the United States made the kind of proposal the NSC had rejected as too placatory the previous spring, namely that the migration talks would be linked to a future, broader agenda.[143] Shortly thereafter, on September 26, 1980, the Cubans "unilaterally" closed the port at Mariel. Wayne Smith; Peter Tarnoff, State Department envoy; and others believe this same conclusion would have been reached much earlier had a more conciliatory proposal been forwarded the previous spring and that, consequently, 100,000 fewer Cubans would have come to the United States.[144]

---

[138] This was reported by Wayne Smith, head of the USINT in Havana, who held private meetings with the Cubans throughout summer 1980. Smith, *Closest of Enemies*, 180.

[139] Smith claims that an earlier, more conciliatory offer was rejected by Pastor (and the NSC). According to Smith, Pastor said, "We thought the other approach was too soft." Ibid., 216.

[140] Ibid.

[141] Wayne Smith, quoted in Engstrom, *Presidential Decision Making Adrift*, 121.

[142] Quoted in ibid.

[143] JECL, Public Affairs Files, Press Clippings 5/4–5/20-/81, File PA: State Department, Box 27, "Memorandum to Christian Holmes, from Arthur Brill, Director of Public Affairs, Subject: Negative public reaction," August 22, 1980; Engstrom, *Presidential Decision Making Adrift*, 135n115, contains details of a relevant interview with Peter Tarnoff, U.S. State Department negotiator. See also Smith, *Closest of Enemies*; Alex Larzelere, *The 1980 Cuban Boatlift: Castro's Ploy—America's Dilemma* (Washington, D.C.: National Defense University Press, 1988).

[144] Smith, *Closest of Enemies*, 216; Engstrom, *Presidential Decision Making Adrift*, 120; Larzelere, *1980 Cuban Boatlift*, 254. A recently declassified memo from Brzezinski to President Carter leaves some small room for doubt, however: "ZB claims that Tarnoff 'is not entirely trustworthy. He cooked up his trip to see Fidel Castro, claiming that the Cubans wanted to talk to us but, in fact, when Castro met with Tarnoff and Pastor, Castro made clear the entire

ASLEEP AT THE SWITCH   Arguably a still greater failure occurred before
the boatlift even began—namely, that the administration had failed to even
recognize that a crisis was afoot. Even though myriad warnings about
Cuba had been issued, they were not received by actors with either the
political power or the acuity to respond to them. There were four reasons
for this. First, in a period fraught with a variety of foreign policy crises
from Iran to Afghanistan, Cuba did not become a front-burner issue until
mass outflows commenced.[145] As Charles Renfrew, former assistant U.S.
attorney general, put it, "You are fighting so many firefights at the same
time. When you look back, all you can see is the scorched earth. Mariel
really deserved a lot of time [that it didn't get] and a policy established
[which didn't happen]."[146] This was even true within that part of the Carter
policymaking apparatus devoted to making and managing refugee policy.
Distracted by their need to handle ongoing Cambodian, Vietnamese, Afghan, and Somali refugee crises, while also putting the finishing touches
on the Refugee Act of 1980, "Cuba was not on the radar screen."[147]

Second, because relatively few in the Carter administration had fore-
knowledge of the Camarioca crisis, they ignored repeated warnings that
Castro was considering reopening his borders. As David Engstrom puts it,
"The word 'Camarioca' had no meaning for them. It set off no alarms."[148]
And as Palmieri later put it, "The amazing thing was that we spent a week
in the Situation Room worrying about what to do about [stopping the
boatlift] before I heard the word Camarioca. I walked out of there and
I remember saying you mean this has happened before?"[149]

Third, those within the government who *were* cognizant of the Camarioca precedent made two assumptions that soon turned out to be dead
wrong: (1) that Cuba would not follow through on its threats, and (2) if it
did, any uncontrolled migration event could be managed under the new
1980 Refugee Act.[150] The officials in question naïvely decided that—even

meeting was at the State Department's initiative.'" JECL, ZB Files, Meetings—Muskie/
Brown/Brzezinski, [5/80–6/80], "Memorandum for the President, from ZB; Subject: Unity
and the New Foreign Policy Team," May 1, 1980. For his part, Engstrom believes that the
failed June negotiations meant fewer Cubans came than otherwise would have had the talks
succeeded. Engstrom, *Presidential Decision Making Adrift,* 121.

[145] Consider that in a meeting held at the White House on April 23 (two days after Mariel
was opened)—in which the topic on the agenda was Carter policy toward *Haitian* refugees—
the Cuban situation was covered only tangentially. JECL, Bloomfield Haiti memo, April 23,
1980.

[146] Quoted in Engstrom, *Presidential Decision Making Adrift,* 92–93n46.

[147] Victor Palmieri, U.S. Coordinator for Refugee Affairs, quoted in ibid, 51.

[148] Ibid., 189.

[149] Quoted in ibid., 58.

[150] From interviews with Myles Frechette, director of the Cuba Desk at the U.S. State Department, 1980, quoted in Rivera, *Decision and Structure,* chap. 1; author interview with Lincoln Bloomfield, Carter Administration NSC staff member, April 2001, Cohasset, Mass.

after Castro had made repeated threats and the Cuban government had made concrete statements directly linking the issue of hijackings with the possibility of another Camarioca—simply admitting several thousand additional Cuban refugees would somehow satisfy the Cuban government, and threats of a crisis would soon evaporate.

Finally, the failure to respond appropriately was a consequence, at least in part, of the fact that a number of those who were given the task of dealing with Cuba felt the issue was beneath them and/or was not within their purview, and therefore the problem of some other department. Whereas McGeorge Bundy, national security advisor to President Johnson, had taken a leading role in managing the Camarioca crisis, no one of equal stature steered the response to the (much larger and more significant) Mariel problem. For instance, Stuart Eizenstat, Carter's assistant for domestic policy affairs, and Zbigniew Brzezinski, his national security advisor, had "officially" assumed responsibility for developing immediate and long-term options to respond to the boatlift.[151] But Brzezinski balked at having to spend time on what he considered a domestic issue and left his deputies, David Aaron and Robert Pastor, as the primary NSC players.[152] Thus, the task of monitoring Cuba was left to junior policymakers who lacked the power and the gravitas to respond in any significant way.[153] At the same time, Eizenstat's domestic policy staff—which was occupied with the disastrous state of the economy and other domestic problems in the lead-up to the fall 1980 election—viewed Mariel "as a foreign policy issue" and "to the extent to which it was a domestic issue,... viewed [it] as a state and local issue," which is to say, it was not *their* policy issue.[154]

This lack of attention and the administration's unwillingness to consider earlier negotiations likely prolonged and exacerbated what might

[151] JECL, DPS Eizenstat, Box 178, File Cuban Refugees [CF, O/A, 730] [2], "Memorandum for the President, From Stu Eizenstat, Jim McIntyre, Jack Watson, and Anne Wexler, Subject: Caribbean Refugee Issues—Zbig's Memo of April 23," April 24, 1980.

[152] As Brzezinski told Watson at the time, "The problem is not one that I'm equipped to deal with or my job requires me to deal with. It has become a domestic crisis.... That is all clearly outside my purview as NSC advisor and it is clearly within your purview." Quoted in Engstrom, *Presidential Decision Making Adrift*, 69.

[153] Ibid., 194.

[154] As Eizenstat put it, "We were really on overload, I mean just unbelievable overload even for the White House which is always on overload. We were on extra circuits. We had the primary election campaign. We had the hostage crisis. We had a deteriorating economy and we had to just redo our budget.... We had gas lines and a new energy policy. It was an almost unbelievable time." Quoted in ibid., 70. It is worth remembering that the United States was in the midst of a recession during this period. Unemployment had risen 1.3 percent over the previous year, overall inflation was at 13.5 percent with energy inflation was nearly 38 percent, and GNP was in decline while trade deficits were rising.

otherwise have been a rather short-lived crisis. As Smith notes in his memoir:

> I had been on the Cuban deck back in 1965 when we had convinced Castro to replace the Camarioca sealift with an orderly departure process. In some ways, prospects were better in 1980 than they had been in 1965. Castro had initiated Camarioca without any prior expression of interest in establishing a normal flow of emigration. Yet, he had quickly closed down the sealift in return for a normal emigration process. This time, Cuban officials had been urging such a process long before the Mariel operation began.[155]

Castro, for his part, made a similar claim. In a speech before the Cuban people on May 1, after castigating the "Yankees" for "welcoming as heroes, dissidents, [and] patriots" those who had hijacked boats and taken hostages, Castro pointedly noted:

> We warned them—repeatedly—through diplomatic channels [that such welcomes would have to stop or else]. We also warned them publicly, because I spoke of this on March 8 [1980], International Women's Day, in the final session of the [Federation of Cuban] Women's Congress. We used every means to warn them of the consequences this could have and of the fact that Camarioca could be reopened.[156]

Even so, it is worth noting that Castro too softened his position over time, probably for two reasons: (1) it became increasingly clear that by embarrassing Jimmy Carter, he had increased the chances that Ronald Reagan would soon become the U.S. president,[157] and (2) as often happens, Castro had generated a larger outflow than he envisioned or desired. According to Llovio-Menendez, "Fidel had been interested in getting rid of a few thousand, perhaps 20,000 to 30,000 of the disaffected, but he had never suspected the volume of 'delinquents' would be so great."[158]

How 1980 Differed from 1965

It is instructive to note the disparity in the speed within which the Johnson and Carter administrations developed policy responses to their Cuban

[155] Smith, *Closest of Enemies*, 215.
[156] Fidel Castro, "Speech to the Fighting People," given before a rally in Havana on May 1, 1980, printed in *Granma*, May 11, 1980, reprinted in "Fidel Castro Speeches," in *War and Crisis in the Americas: Speeches 1984–85*, ed. Michael Taber (New York: Pathfinder Press, 1985), 276. See also Castro's March 8 speech, cited in n. 79
[157] Smith, *Closest of Enemies*, 233–34.
[158] Llovio-Menendez, *Insider*, 387.

migration crises, as well as the differences in their approaches. First, be-cause the policymakers in the Johnson administration figured out quickly the potential scale and negative domestic salience of the problem, they developed a response within days after Castro announced the opening of the port at Camarioca.[159] Within a month, officials in the Johnson admin-istration managed to provide states and localities with mollifying side-payments and financial relief for the costs associated with the boatlift.[160] In contrast, even with considerable forewarning that Castro was consider-ing reopening his borders, the Carter administration made no precaution-ary arrangements and took more than three weeks to generate a policy response, one that never adequately dealt with the crisis. In short, whereas the Johnson administration moved quickly to quash domestic discord and mollify those who might mobilize against the government, the Carter ad-ministration moved haltingly and in self-contradictory ways, which not only did not placate competing domestic interests but also actually exac-erbated them. Moreover, as Engstrom notes, for Carter officials to have stopped or slowed the boatlift, the administration needed to have acted immediately and dramatically to the news of the first boats headed to-ward Cuba—or even better, I suggest, to the myriad articulated threats of Castro's government before the crisis even commenced. Instead, the administration chose "a course of confusing policies that attempted both to oppose and welcome the arrival of Cuban nationals. In effect, the poli-cies it developed tried closing the barn door after the horse was out. As Palmieri put it: 'Once the boats were gone, the game was over.'"[161]

Second, whereas the Johnson administration provided affected com-munities with 100 percent reimbursement of their absorption costs, the Carter administration—much to its later regret—reimbursed states and localities at a rate of only 75 percent.[162] This was at least in part because Carter officials viewed the exile community in Miami as culpable in what became for the president a political fiasco.[163]

---

[159] For instance, during the period when the Memo of Understanding between the United States and Cuba was still being negotiated, Representative Claude Pepper (D-Fla.) wrote to LBJ, "Your sending Secretary Gardner and former Governor Ellington, with many other gov-ernment representatives, down here for a conference with our people about the Cuban refu-gee problem *gave great assurance to our people that the Federal Government is going to protect our people as far as possible from bearing a disproportionate part of the burden of the national policy which gave our traditional sanctuary to the persecuted Cubans.*" LBJL, "Letter to the President from Con-gressman Claude Pepper, FL (third district)," November 16, 1965, WHCF, National Security-Defense (GEN ND 19-2/CO), Box 419, Folder: ND 19-2/CO 55, 10/20/65–12/10/65.

[160] Engstrom, *Presidential Decision Making Adrift*, 196.

[161] Quoted in ibid., 89.

[162] *Public Papers of the Presidents of the United States: Jimmy Carter, 1980*, vol. 3 (Washington, D.C.: Government Printing Office, 1981); Engstrom, *Presidential Decision Making Adrift*, 199.

[163] As Rivera puts it, "Ironically, 'la Comunidad,' as it came to be called during the period of exile visits, had found it necessary to cooperate with Fidel Castro in order to pursue the

Third, it took the Carter administration nearly two months to even approach the Cuban government about talks to normalize immigration, and then the subsequent accord was not signed until after the boatlift was ended nearly six months later. As previously noted, this was in large part a consequence of the NSC belief that concession would be politically costly and would send the wrong message—that the United States was bowing to Castro's demands. As Pastor put it, "The moment that Castro was threatening you with human life is not exactly the time you stand up and say, 'I surrender, send me more.' That is not the kind of approach that you take to a little country that is illegally beating you over the head. You don't respond by saying, 'I surrender.'"[164] Finally, it was Congress, not the Carter administration, that (six months later) generated a policy to deal with the tremendous costs that Mariel posed to affected states and localities.[165]

In the end, it is clear that, because the crisis occurred in the midst of the 1980 presidential campaign, Carter absorbed the full backlash of voter indignation. He was blamed for his ineptitude in handling the crisis and for indecisive leadership, and Ronald Wilson Reagan, his Republican challenger, enthusiastically exploited this issue to his advantage. He took Carter to task both for losing control of the security situation and for failing those Cubans that the United States had an ideological obligation to help.[166] In light of the other tribulations that Carter was facing in the lead-up to the November 1980 election—including the Iran hostage crisis, the Soviet invasion of Afghanistan, and a floundering economy—it would be an exaggeration to claim that Mariel alone produced Carter's defeat.[167] Nevertheless, the crisis provided effective campaign fodder for Reagan and affected the psyche of the U.S. public, including the psyche of one particular American, future U.S. President William Jefferson Clin-

---

urgent [to its members] goal of family reunification. This peculiar cooperation continued long after it became obvious that the Cuban government was controlling the exodus entirely to its own advantage." Rivera, *Decision and Structure*, 8. Rivera notes that Palmieri, Frechette, and others in the Carter administration shared this view.

[164] Interview with Robert Pastor, quoted in Engstrom, *Presidential Decision Making Adrift*, 107.

[165] Ibid., 196.

[166] See, for instance, *Dallas Times Herald*, April 10, 1980, in which Reagan was quoted as saying that, if no other country would take the Cubans trapped in the Peruvian Embassy, then the United States should take them all. (Of course, at that point "them all" was only 10,000.) Later, Reagan made much of the presence of "the undesirables" and of the incumbent administration's failure to manage the crisis effectively.

[167] Carter himself, however, believed that Mariel was an important component in his defeat. Immediately after the election, he said, "the refugee question has hurt us badly. It wasn't just in Florida, but it was throughout the country. It was a burning issue. It made us look impotent when we received these refugees from Cuba." *Public Papers of the Presidents of the United States: Jimmy Carter, 1980*, vol. 3 (Washington, D.C.: Government Printing Office, 1981), 2693.

ton, who would himself be at the helm during the next U.S.-Cuban migration crisis.

The August 1994 *Balseros* Crisis

The Situation Heats Up: Castro Issues a Threat

On the streets of Havana, spring 1994 brought scenes reminiscent of those that presaged Mariel fourteen years earlier. After another series of aborted attempts at *rapprochement* with the United States, and in the midst of another economic crisis, between May and early August of 1994, Cuba became the site of an increasing number of embassy crashings and violent boat hijackings.[168] This violence culminated in a series of street riots in early August, after thirty-two Cubans were killed after they were swept overboard by water cannons when the Cuban military intercepted a tugboat bound for Miami.[169]

Reading the signs of restiveness on the ground, and by now familiar with Castro's modus operandi, at least some in the United States believed Castro might try to initiate another migration crisis.[170] Robert Gelbard, principal deputy assistant secretary of state for inter-American affairs, publicly warned Castro on July 30 that the "consequences of launching another Mariel boatlift would be quite grave."[171] But such threats surely had little resonance for Castro, who had twice played this same game with an initially defiant—but later compliant—U.S. government.[172]

Despite the cavalier assertions by the United States to the contrary, Castro probably recognized that the U.S. leadership stood to lose more from an uncontrolled outflow than he did. Moreover, evidence suggests he viewed threatening or even launching an outflow as a risk worth taking. Castro was again keen to engage the United States in negotiations,

---

[168] For instance, on May 28, more than one hundred people forced their way into the Belgian ambassador's residence, and during the week of July 13, twenty-one people crashed the German Embassy and another nine entered the Chilean Consulate. Although the embassy crashings were resolved without incident, many of the hijackings involved violence, and both civilians and Cuban police officers were killed. For details of the hijackings during this period, see *El Nuevo Herald*, July 14 to August 12, 1994; Masud-Piloto, *From Welcomed Exiles to Illegal Immigrants*, 137.

[169] Masud-Piloto, *From Welcomed Exiles to Illegal Immigrants*, 137.

[170] Executive Office of the Governor (Florida) and the Florida Advisory Council on Intergovernmental Relations, "The Unfair Burden: Immigration's Impact on Florida," Tallahassee, Fla., March 1994.

[171] CNN, July 30, 1993; John Zarrella, "Cuban-Americans, Officials Doubt Another Cuban Boatlift," CNN, August 11, 1994.

[172] Engstrom, *Presidential Decision Making Adrift*, 188. My interview with a former Clinton administration NSC official, May 2000, confirmed that [as in 1980] Cuba was not "on the radar screen." "My office was busy dealing with the Haiti 'problem.'"

and history had shown that only through the use of this kind of unconventional coercion were his objectives likely to be met.[173]

Frustrated by the rise in hijackings and escalating illegal departures[174]—and undeterred by U.S. threats—on August 5 Castro held an internationally televised news conference in which he asserted that the rioting was being triggered by rumors of a "US sponsored boatlift to Miami."[175] He also announced that Cuba could no longer afford to be "the guardian of the North Americans' coasts" if Washington "continued to strangle the faltering Cuban economy."[176]

The United States Thumbs Its Nose at Havana, Castro Escalates, and the United States Turns Defiant

Immediately following Castro's pronouncement, the United States responded with clear signs of encouragement for those who wanted to escape. Officials also announced the existence of a classified contingency plan, Operation Distant Shore,[177] which was designed to thwart Castro's ability to launch another Mariel.[178] Although the precise details of Distant Shore were classified, it was officially announced that the plan included responsibilities for forty different federal agencies that would respond to an immigration crisis, a blockade of the Florida Straits, and the arrest of any migrant caught trying to enter the United States through that route.[179]

---

[173] Christopher Mitchell "Implications," in *Western Hemisphere Immigration and United States Foreign Policy,* ed. Christopher Mitchell (University Park: Pennsylvania State University Press, 1992), 287.

[174] Martinez and Silva, "Carter Aides, Cubans Met Secretly"; Wayne S. Smith, "US-Cuban Relations: Twenty-Five Years of Hostility," in *Cuba: Twenty-Five Years of Revolution, 1959–1984,* ed. Sandor Halebsky and John M. Kirk (New York: Praeger, 1985), 347–48. The US-Cuban Anti-hijacking Agreement was signed in 1973. But it was abrogated by Cuba in 1976 after one of its airliners was destroyed in a terrorist bombing in which the Cubans suspected U.S. complicity. Nevertheless, the Cubans continued to try to negotiate with the United States to prevent hijackings because Castro viewed them as dangerous and potentially destabilizing. See Smith, *Closest of Enemies;* James Rowles, "Dialogue or Denial: The Uses of International Law in US-Cuban Relations," in *US-Cuban Relations in the 1990s,* ed. Jorge I. Dominguez and Rafael Hernandez (Boulder: Westview Press, 1989), 290; JECL, "Memorandum for the President, From Warren Christopher."

[175] "Protesters Battle Police in Havana; Castro Warns US," *New York Times,* August 6, 1994.

[176] Larry Rohter, "Flight from Cuba: The Overview," *New York Times,* August 25, 1994.

[177] Operation Distant Shore was developed early in the first Clinton administration. It was designed to deal with another Mariel-like exodus by redistributing Cubans to forts and other federal facilities around the nation to alleviate the concentrated burden on Florida. Interview with senior INS official, Cambridge, Mass., March 2000; follow-up phone interview during which the interviewee was in Miami, Fla.

[178] Ibid. Also immediately after Castro's August 5 statement, the United States claimed that it had the situation under control and that Castro would back down. See "State Department Regular Briefing," Federal News Service, August 8, 1994.

[179] See "US Maps Plan to Counter Cuban Threat of New Boat Lift; Castro Issues Warning after Violent Demonstration in Havana," *Miami Herald,* August 7, 1994; "Bracing for Potential Cuban Refugee Influx," *Miami Herald,* August 7, 1994.

Whatever the contents of the plan, the public announcement of its existence represented an explicit attempt to simultaneously deter Castro from launching an outflow—by trying to convince him that this time the United States was prepared and would not need to concede to his demands—and to reassure anxious Floridians that they would not soon find themselves victims of another Mariel.[180]

Nevertheless, those intent on fleeing were not deterred, and neither was Castro.[181] In fact, on August 12 he took two steps toward crisis escalation. First, he announced that he would view any attempt by the United States to institute a blockade as an act of war, and second, he quietly started allowing people to leave the island unharrassed.[182]

That same day, U.S. State Department officials announced that there were no signs that Castro had opened his coastline to unrestricted exits, but conceded that the Cuban coastal and land police were letting small groups leave without incident.[183] To those with an ear to the ground, Castro's move was a clear sign that he both could and would control the volume of the outflows as he saw fit. To those on the frontline in Florida, this was a portentous signal.[184] But to most of the principals in Washington, it registered as little more than a blip.

A Domestic Spoiler Catalyzes a Policy Shift

However, less than a week later, the administration view of the situation quickly and unexpectedly shifted. "In a matter of twelve hours . . . the Clinton Administration's view of the influx of Cuban refugees changed from a manageable, orderly flow to a crisis demanding a reversal of 28 years of immigration policy."[185] Significantly, this shift did not result from a move taken in Havana, Cuba, but rather from one taken in Tallahassee, Florida. Facing a tough reelection campaign in a state where immigration was an especially highly charged issue, Florida Governor Lawton Chiles decided

[180] Interview with senior INS official, March 2000, Cambridge, Mass.

[181] Nor were those in Florida particularly reassured, as will become clear later in this chapter.

[182] Reportedly, Castro made the decision in a meeting on August 12 not to interfere with those trying to leave the island, although he did not publicly declare the port open until a week and a half later. See Pincus and Suro, "Ripple in Florida Straits"; David Williams, "After 35 Years, Castro Still Annoys Washington," *Washington Post*, August 13, 1994. In the interim period, he had representatives at the USINT in Cuba simply announce, "the US is simply reaping what it sows by its own policy." William Booth, "Mixed Signals at Sea: US Opening Lures Desperate Cubans to Boats," *Washington Post*, August 18, 1994.

[183] See again the articles cited in previous note.

[184] On the ambivalence that south Floridians feel toward Caribbean migrants and refugees, see Mitchell, "Political Costs of State Power," 81–97.

[185] Paul Anderson, "Miscues, Awakenings Helped Spur Policy Reversal," *Miami Herald*, August 21, 1994. See also Rafael Lorente, Paul Anderson, and Andres Viglucci, "Dade Makes Plea for Help," *Miami Herald*, August 18, 1994.

he would not acquiesce to a repeat of the 1980 Mariel fiasco without a fight. Despite administration claims to the contrary, Chiles believed the trickle of Cubans would soon blossom into a flood and demanded that the federal government take action. On August 18, Chiles went public with his criticism and an implicit demand:

> Well, I think your numbers showed that we've had 2,200 [Cuban asylum seekers] already this year. But the interesting thing is this month. The interesting thing is 565 yesterday, 360 today. As we speak, they are still getting off the boat down there [in Key West]. I think we might well have 500 again today. In spite of the Coast Guard captain's statement, the most we ever had in a day in Mariel was about 856. So we're already up to 500 a day. Florida could die from a thousand small cuts and that's what Castro is doing to us. This is an emergency down here. We know that, all the citizens of south Florida know that and we're waiting for the administration to know that.[186]

By accident or design, Castro's modest outflow had generated a massive domestic political headache for the Clinton administration. Why did this happen? Governor Chiles had concluded that an anti-Cuban migrant position would help him in his re-election bid, and polling data from the period suggest this was a wise surmise. September 1994 Gallup data reveal that 79 percent of those surveyed did not believe that Cuban migrants should be allowed into the United States and 91 percent felt that Cubans should be treated just like Haitians trying to enter the country.[187] The majority of Floridians were opposed to the influx, and those who were not—namely the Cuban American community—were widely expected to vote for Chiles's Republican challenger, Jeb Bush, in any case.

The situation was further complicated by the fact that a key component of the Distant Shore contingency plan had just been rejected out of hand by Clinton, leaving Florida potentially even more exposed.[188] Specifically, on August 16, when Clinton discovered the nature of the State Department proposed resettlement plan (under which Cuban asylum seekers would be distributed at military bases throughout the country), he reportedly "went ballistic," yelling "Are you nuts? Do you think I am going

[186] Wolf Blitzer, "Chiles Says Feds Need to Toughen Immigration Policies," CNN, August 18, 1994.
[187] *The Gallup Poll, 1994* (New York: Random House, 1994), 228–33. Another poll conducted the following May, shortly after the accords were signed, indicated that 73 percent of Floridians supported banning illegal immigrants from access to government services. David Adams, "Protests of Cuba Policy Draw Little Support," *St. Petersburg Times*, May 13, 1995.
[188] Robert Greenberger, "Clinton Faces Pressure from All Sides, Even His Family, in Fight to Shape Policy on Cuba," *Wall Street Journal*, September 2, 1994. This assessment was confirmed in my interviews with former administration officials, July–August 2000, Washington, DC and Pentagon City, Va.

to do th[at] again?"[189] Other White House insiders confirm that Clinton's thinking on the August 1994 crisis was guided by two mottos: "No More Mariels" and "Remember Fort Chaffee."[190]

What Clinton feared most intensely was a repetition of the personal humiliation and defeat he had suffered while governor of Arkansas after the last massive Cuban refugee resettlement in 1980.[191] Dissatisfied with their long-term detainment, Marielitos had sparked riots at several of the military bases where they were being held, including Fort Chaffee.[192] Shortly thereafter, then Arkansas Governor Clinton lost his bid for re-election. Although there are reasons to believe that Clinton, like Carter before him, might have lost his 1980 election even in the absence of the Cuban crisis, Clinton clearly laid blame for his loss on the Chaffee riots. As Dick Morris, Clinton advisor and confidant, has made plain, his defeat in 1980 "was really the seminal experience in (Clinton's) career."[193]

Thus, on August 18, by which time it had become clear to Chiles that the administration was willing neither to recognize the escalating crisis as an emergency nor to implement Distant Shore's proposed resettlement plan, he decided to force Washington's hand.[194] In a domestically driven political move that led to a further escalation of the crisis internationally, Chiles declared a state of emergency in Florida. This move gave him the right to mobilize the Florida National Guard and to temporarily detain those refugees released by the INS. Chiles then announced that he would not permit Cubans transported from detention camps in Key West to get

---

[189] Interviews cited in previous note. This is consistent with press reports as well.

[190] Steven Greenhouse, "Freewheeling Ways Pay Off for the White House," *New York Times*, September 11, 1994; interview with former Clinton NSC official, July 2000, Lenox, Mass.; Elizabeth Drew, *On the Edge: The Clinton Presidency* (New York: Simon and Schuster, 1994).

[191] JECL, Records of the Cuban-Haitian Task Force—RG 220, Box 27, "Cuban Refugees and Security at Fort," *Arkansas Gazette*, September 14, 1980.

[192] Fort Chaffee housed more than 20,000 Cuban refugees by June 1980. On June 1, a group of about three hundred tried to escape. After most were captured, the detainees began rioting, which led to Clinton's decision to call out the Arkansas National Guard. Although few were injured and those involved were prosecuted, the perception that Clinton had lost control adversely affected his bid for reelection. He lost to Frank White, the head of a small savings and loan, who became the first Republican to serve as Arkansas governor in a century.

[193] William Degregorio, *The Complete Book of Presidents: From George Washington to Bill Clinton* (New York: Wing Books, 1993), 714. Also, notably several of Clinton's key foreign policy advisors had also served in the Carter administration during the Mariel crisis, including Anthony Lake, Warren Christopher, and Peter Tarnoff.

[194] Chiles argued that Washington was in a state of denial and that, if it would not respond, he would. Chiles declared, it "was not a manageable situation. Not for Florida....If we do not get a response from the federal government, we will open our own facilities." Robert Rankin, Tim Nickens, and Lizette Alvarez, "Rescued Rafters Will Be Sent to Guantanamo Base Camps," *Miami Herald*, August 19, 1994.

off the busses when they reached Miami; instead, he would have the rafters arrested and quarantined.

Suddenly and acutely aware that they were facing a potential political
train wreck less than three months before the fall congressional elections,
that same afternoon a principals-only meeting of many of Clinton's top
foreign policy advisors was held. Although it was a last-minute meeting, its consequences were momentous. With little analysis and still less
contingency planning, a decision was made to end the twenty-eight-year
U.S. policy of unequivocally welcoming all refugees fleeing from Cuba.
The general consensus was that the time had to come to "demagnetize"
the United States to avoid a continuous flow of refugees. According to
one participant, "the change was necessary to protect a basic fundamental policy of no massive influx that looked like Mariel" while also
avoiding any accusations that Cubans and Haitians were being treated
differently.[195]

Hence, even though Attorney General Janet Reno had publicly insisted
on the morning of August 18 that Governor Chiles was overreacting, and
that no change in policy was under consideration, that very evening a new
and radically different policy was announced.[196] In the wake of Chiles's
emergency declaration, a meeting had been held among Clinton, Chiles,
and Jorge Mas Canosa of the Cuban American National Foundation
(CANF), after which Clinton announced the new policy. Thenceforth, no
Cubans seeking to enter the United States illegally would be allowed to
enter U.S. territory. Instead, Cubans would be rescued at sea and detained
at the U.S. naval base at Guantanamo Bay, Cuba, indefinitely. Clinton further claimed that the policy shift was necessary because "we have gone
through [this before], when . . . we had 120,000 people sent to this country
as a deliberate attempt, not because they themselves wanted to flee—they
were encouraged to flee, they were pushed out."[197] This statement reads
like a bald attempt to forestall further charges of hypocrisy by providing a
rationalization for the administration's decision to no longer admit those
formerly treated as refugees. That is, because those fleeing were being
"pushed out" by Castro, they were not legitimate refugees, but rather

---

[195] Quoted in Pincus and Suro, "Ripple in Florida Straits." See also, Jonathan C. Smith,
"Foreign policy for Sale? Interest Group Influence on President Clinton's Cuba Policy," *Presidential Studies Quarterly* 28 (1998): 207–20; Drew, *On the Edge*, 430. Reportedly, neither Clinton, Secretary of State Warren Christopher, nor Deputy Secretary Strobe Talbott attended this
"principals" meeting. Nor was any State Department staffer consulted about the proposed
policy shift, including Assistant Secretary of State Alexander Watson—ostensibly in charge
of the State Department Bureau of Inter-American Affairs. Robert Novak, "Focus on Immigration Is a Victory for Castro," *Chicago Sun-Times*, August 29, 1994.

[196] Pincus and Suro, "Ripple in Florida Straits."

[197] John Aloysius Farrell, "Clinton Rips Castro on Refugees; Charges Ploy to Press US,
Defends Policy," *Boston Globe*, August 20, 1994.

"illegal refugees" who could be detained.[198] This, of course, begs the question of why the United States had a standing policy of welcoming these "illegal refugees" for the better part of the previous three decades.

The Aggravating Role of Mobilized Domestic Discord

In the end, although Clinton and his advisors were themselves disinclined to permit a repeat of Mariel, it was Governor Chiles's initiatives—coupled with Clinton's steadfast opposition to a domestic relocation scheme—that forced the U.S. policy shift.[199] This step satisfied the government of Florida and removed one source of political discord. But in making such a dramatic policy change, Clinton knew that he would have to contend with further political fallout: first, from the Cuban exile community, whose members would be furious that the United States would now consider returning the fleeing Cubans; and second, from congressional critics eager to make political hay out of Clinton's policy flip-flop.[200]

But, even at the time, risking the policy shift probably seemed like a good gamble for a number of reasons. For one thing, Clinton realized that the vast majority of Floridians, and Americans more generally, were opposed to accepting more refugees, whatever their origin.[201] Basically, "the new calculus [was] that Clinton need[ed] to worry more about immigration (and the highly mobilized anti-refugee/migrant camp) than about Cuban-American votes."[202]

For another thing, the Clinton administration had a plan to placate the mobilized and agitated CANF and the rest of the exile community—an offer to tighten restrictions on Cuba.[203] According to those present at their August meeting: "Mas thumped and slapped the table as he spoke, demanding that the President punish Fidel Castro for the refugee crisis.

[198] As Reno put it, those fleeing Cuba should know that "the odds of ending up in Guantanamo are going to be very, very great. The odds of ending up in the United States are going to be very, very small." Quoted in ibid.

[199] Burt Solomon, "Clinton's Fast Break on Cuba...or Foreign Policy on the Fly," *National Journal*, September 3, 1994.

[200] For instance, congressional Republicans used the opportunity to criticize Clinton on both Cuba and Haiti. "Fidel Castro has done more to harm American interests than any Haitian," said Senate Minority Leader Bob Dole (R-Kans.), whereas Senator Connie Mack (R-Fla.) asserted, "the policy seems to be to punish the rafters, as opposed to punishing Fidel." Quoted in ibid.

[201] As Robert Pastor put it, "to judge when and how to response to foreign policy crises, the administration employed a domestic political calculus." Pastor, "The Clinton Administration and the Americas: The Postwar Rhythm and Blues," *Journal of Interamerican Studies & World Affairs* 38, no. 4 (1996–1997): 98. See also Smith, "Foreign Policy for Sale?"

[202] Peter Hakim, president of the Washington think tank, Inter-American Dialogue, quoted in Dick Kirschten, "Guantanamo, Si; Otherwise, No," *National Journal*, May 13, 1995.

[203] Bruce Stokes, "The Cuban Conundrum," *National Journal*, September 17, 1994.

'You must kick out the last leg of the stool,' he insisted. According to Mas [in a later interview], he had bellowed at Clinton: 'No tengo piedad!—do not have any pity.''[204] Hence, on August 20 Clinton announced that visits to Cuba would thereafter be restricted to humanitarian cases and remittances would be suspended. As one observer put it at the time, Clinton "is responding to a growing anti-immigrant climate and at the same time he's trying assuage right-wing Cuban-Americans by tightening the economic screws on Castro."[205] As Richard Haass put it, there seemed to be a fundamental "inconsistency in simultaneously intensifying the pressures inside Cuba while making it harder for the discontented to flee... 'Clinton seems more interested in balancing the various interests than deciding between them.'"[206] In the end, although this compromise temporarily satisfied Clinton's competing domestic constituencies, it did nothing to bring the international crisis closer to a resolution. In fact, it led Castro to escalate further.

Castro Ups the Ante

While undoubtedly pleased that illegal rafters would finally be detained and returned, Castro was far less enamored of the measures taken to conciliate the Cuban exile community. So the following day, August 21, Castro announced that he was officially opening the borders to anyone who wanted to leave. Moreover, because the Cuban public remained unmoved by—and doubtful of—the claim that the three-decade-old U.S. policy of welcoming all Cubans really had changed overnight, the announced U.S. policy shift did not slow the flow. Indeed, three days later, in the largest one-day total ever, 2,886 rafters were intercepted at sea; the day before, 2,338 were rescued. And in the two weeks between August 13 and 25, the Coast Guard intercepted 13,084 rafters—a significantly larger number than the 9,340 who had arrived during the first twelve days of Mariel.[207]

Thus, the administration's gamble that Cubans would stop fleeing to the United States once it had been announced that they would not be allowed

[204] Quoted in Ann Bardach, "Mas Canosa: Mobster and Megalomaniac, Part I: Our Man in Miami," *New Republic*, October 3, 1994.

[205] Deborah Anker, immigration and refugee coordinator at Harvard Law School, quoted in Maria Puente, "Crazy Quilt Policy/Refugee Law 'Very, Very Complicated,'" *USA Today*, August 25, 1994.

[206] Solomon, "Clinton's Fast Break on Cuba." Pastor echoes Haass's sentiment, noting that "on issues concerning Central America and Cuba, US policy seemed to be driven by the interest groups with the greatest leverage and determination, whether in the Congress or in Miami. These issues were not priorities." Pastor, "Clinton Administration and the Americas," 108.

[207] Daniel de Vise and Elaine de Valle, "Rafters' Desperate Journeys Reshaped the Exile Experience," *Miami Herald*, August 22, 2004.

to enter had proven a serious miscalculation—one which Castro promptly exploited. On August 24, Castro gave an internationally televised speech on CNN announcing that the "new [U.S.] policy measures only [made] the problem more complicated...[and]...these measures [compelled] the massive exodus." During the same speech, Castro also officially announced that he had ordered the Cuban Coast Guard to stop impeding those who wanted to leave the island and to stop using force to prevent Americans from picking people up.[208]

At the same time, however, Castro also intimated that he might stop the exodus if the Clinton administration agreed to direct talks on a range of issues, including the embargo.[209] This position was reaffirmed the next morning when Cuban representatives in New York announced their willingness to end the flow "only if the United States agreed to broad talks on a full range of bilateral matters."[210] Meanwhile Cuba's ambassador to the United Nations turned the rhetorical heat up even higher, warning that the new U.S. strategy would lead to disaster, both for Cubans and Americans: "The US has devised a whole policy...to try to choke our country to hunger and allow an internal subversion that would lead to a blood bath, and *then how many millions of illegal immigrants will come?*"[211]

U.S. Defiance Soon Replaced with Willingness to Negotiate

By the following day (August 26), increasing (and very vocal) bipartisan opposition in Congress to the administration's unwillingness to negotiate with Castro was emerging. A growing number of news commentaries and newspaper editorials calling for negotiations also began to appear.[212] Moreover, that same day the *New York Times* ran a story announcing that the camps housing Cubans at Guantanamo would be filled to overflowing within two weeks if the exodus continued. Thus, Clinton's attempt to satisfy his competing domestic constituencies and reject Castro's entreaties had given rise to a bigger (and far more visible) international-level dilemma, one that did not suggest an easy unilateral

---

[208] Fidel Castro, Televised speech, CNN, August 24, 1994.

[209] Steve Greenhouse, "Flight from Cuba: US Rejects Castro's Proposals for Talks," *New York Times*, August 26, 1994.

[210] Larry Rohter, "Castro Rules Out Any Move to Halt Flow of Refugees," *New York Times*, August 25, 1994.

[211] "Castro Blasts U.S. Policy, Calls Base a 'Concentration Camp,'" *Los Angeles Times*, August 25, 1994.

[212] See national newspaper coverage of the *balseros* crisis in, for instance, the *New York Times*, *Washington Post*, and *Christian Science Monitor*, as well as TV coverage on CNN, from August 25 to 31, 1994.

(read negotiation-free) solution.[213] Despite the fact that the administration approached thirteen Caribbean and Central American states with offers of side-payments in exchange for housing Cubans, with the exception of Panama, few agreed.[214]

In the end, because the rafters kept coming, the only way to end the crisis was to once again rely on the Cuban government to resume its policy of blocking emigration.[215] But the U.S. imposition of new sanctions and staunch unwillingness to negotiate proved powerful disincentives for Castro to do so.[216] Thus, a mere two days later, with no indication that the flows might soon abate, the Clinton administration again abruptly changed position and agreed to negotiate with the Cuban government. A series of bilateral talks were held between September 1 and 10, which resulted in the announcement of a new immigration accord and plans for a series of additional meetings.[217] In exchange, Castro retracted some of his own demands (e.g., that the accord be linked to a softening of the embargo and/or to the shutdown of Radio Marti).

The *Balseros* Crisis, Part II: April–May 1995

In early April 1995, the Cuban government again began making vague threats to reopen its borders—a rumor that was privately leaked but publicly denied.[218] U.S. officials believed these renewed threats were a response to the proposed Helms-Burton legislation and to the fact that a large number of Cubans were still languishing at Guantanamo and being denied entrance into the United States. One Cuban official told the *Washington Post*, "last year, there were 30,000 rafters. Next time you might see a million."[219] At the same time, following a trip to Guantanamo in March–April 1995, then Senator Bob Graham (D-Fla.) and Representative Porter J. Goss (R-Fla.) warned the administration that another crisis was in the

---

[213] This was made even clearer by the fact that not all Cuban Americans supported tightening strictures on Havana; some were more concerned about the possible effects on their relatives' quality of life than with the pain it would inflict on Castro. See Jon Nordheimer, "Cuban Group Forges Link to Clinton," *New York Times*, August 26, 1994.

[214] St. Lucia offered to shelter Cubans in exchange for new water pipelines and roads, and the Turks and Caicos offered to take up to 2,000 people for short-term stays of up to four weeks. "And Still They Come on Risky Rafts," *Baltimore Sun*, August 25, 1994.

[215] Mitchell, "Political Costs of State Power"; Mitchell, "Implications."

[216] LeoGrande, "From Havana to Miami," 78.

[217] Ray Sanchez, "Exodus' End? U.S., Cuba Reach Pact on Refugees," *Newsday*, September 10, 1994.

[218] "Helm's Bill."

[219] Quoted in Scott Armstrong and Saul Landau, "Adrift off Cuba: Who's Making Clinton's Policy," April 2, 1995.

making, since the thousands of Cubans still being detained were "living in a tinderbox that could explode into rioting."[220]

These warnings set off what officials called "serious alarm bells" in the White House, in part because the administration was "poised to enter a critical and enormously tricky domestic policy stretch—a summer of high-stakes battles with Republicans over the size, shape and cost of government that could well define the 1996 presidential race." The last thing Clinton officials needed was a migration crisis. Top aides quickly concluded that another round of serious talks with the Cuban government was in order. In clear recognition of the potentially damaging political costs associated with another crisis, one official admitted, "We were facing a double whammy when all we want is to keep foreign policy problems off the screen....The word was: Solve it. Make it go away with the least amount of turmoil."[221]

Like Johnson and Carter before him, faced with the dilemma of choosing between absorbing the domestic political costs associated with another migration crisis and those associated with further negotiations with Castro to avoid one, the Clinton administration chose the latter. Two weeks later, on the anniversary of the Bay of Pigs debacle, Ricardo Alarcon and Under Secretary of State Peter Tarnoff met in secret—probably to shield themselves from domestic political pressure—and a new accord was announced on May 2, 1995.[222] As a result, eight months after initially refusing admission to those at Guantanamo, the administration again changed course and agreed to admit them on a case-by-case basis.[223] With this policy shift came the first official U.S. reference—by Attorney General Janet Reno—to the Cuban migrants as "illegal immigrants" rather than "political refugees."[224] In addition, on the heels of this new accord came word that the Clinton administration would oppose the

[220] During this period, the flow of rafters also began to rise again and reached the highest monthly total (190) since the end of the August 1994 crisis. Barbara Crossette, "Cuban Rallies Will Oppose a US Bill," *New York Times*, April 16, 1995. It is also worth keeping in mind that housing the refugees at Guantanamo and in Panama for the previous six months had already cost more than $400 million and that the Pentagon was planning to spend $100 million more to make the camps permanent.

[221] Ann Devroy and Daniel Williams, "'Serious Alarm Bells' Led to Talks with Cuba; Congressmen Warned of Exodus, Riots at Camp," *Washington Post*, May 5, 1995.

[222] For his part, Tarnoff claimed that negotiations were held in secret to preempt a massive exodus that might transpire in anticipation of any new immigration accord. See "Congressional Testimony of Peter Tarnoff," from U.S. House of Representatives Committee on International Relations, hearing: *The Clinton Administration's Reversal of U.S. Immigration Policy toward Cuba*, 104th Congress, May 18, 1995. See also LeoGrande, "From Havana to Miami"; "Guantanamo, Si; Otherwise, No."

[223] "Testimony of Gillian Gunn."

[224] "Janet Reno Wins Schneider's Play of the Week," CNN–Inside Politics, transcript no. 828-5, May 5, 1995.

embargo-tightening Helms-Burton legislation and that this new policy "could be followed by engagement on other areas of mutual interest, like the fight against narcotics or environmental problems."[225] According to a White House paper, "[The United States was] prepared to reduce sanctions in carefully calibrated ways, in response to significant, irreversible changes in Cuba."[226] For its part, the CANF called the policy shift "a second Bay of Pigs."[227]

Was Castro's 1994 Migration Gambit a Success?

Without a doubt, the *balseros* crisis was a coercive success for Castro.[228] As in 1965 and in 1980, initial resistance gave way to a willingness to negotiate, once the potential domestic political consequences of continued intransigence became clear. Moreover, Castro accomplished what were widely regarded as his primary objectives, although progress vis-à-vis his purported long-term goals—ending the embargo and shutting down Radio Marti—was far more modest, at least explicitly.

Primary Objectives Obtained

As one observer put it at the time, "through blackmail Castro has (again) been able to change US policy."[229] As a consequence of the crisis, Castro achieved what analysts regard as his key aims: a U.S.-backed halt to illegal emigration and the prosecution of Cuban hijackers.[230] The agreement provided that the United States would accept 20,000 Cubans per year plus an unspecified number of family members, and the 4,000–6,000 Cubans on the waiting list for visas would be permitted entry to the country.[231]

---

[225] Steven Greenhouse, "A First Step on Cuba? Americans Say the Accord on Immigration Might Be Followed by Other Agreements," *New York Times,* May 3, 1995.

[226] Paper written by Assistant Secretary of State Wendy Sherman, cited in George Moffett, "To Befriend or Not to Befriend Cuba? The US Takes Up a Loaded Question," *Christian Science Monitor,* May 19, 1995.

[227] Quoted in Bob Deans, "Showdown Looms on Cuba Policy," *Tampa Tribune,* May 4, 1995.

[228] A "stunning success," in fact, according to Masud-Piloto, personal conversation, July 2004, Miami.

[229] Frank Calzon, Washington director of the New York–based Freedom House, quoted in Peter Grier, "Raft Crisis Points Out Need for Long-Term Cuba Policy," *Christian Science Monitor,* September 12, 1994.

[230] See Castro's CNN speech on August 24, 1994; Martin Fletcher, "Clinton Offers to Increase Visas if Cuba Halts Exodus," *Times,* Overseas News Section, August 31, 1994.

[231] U.S. Department of State, "US-Cuba Joint Communiqué on Migration," *Dispatch* 5 (September 12, 1994). This provision gave Castro a guaranteed safety valve by which he could jettison tens of thousands of malcontents per year.

This marked—albeit imperfectly—the official end of illegal immigration between the United States and Cuba and was in essence a reaffirmation of the promises made to Castro by the Reagan administration a decade earlier.

Second, the United States agreed to extradite or prosecute those who hijacked or stole boats and aircraft to flee Cuba, thus expediting a "safer, legal and more orderly process" of immigration.[232] As noted previously, Castro had been pressing the United States for years to concede these two points.[233] In exchange, Cuba promised to end the boatlift, using "mainly persuasive measures" to crack down on those who tried to emigrate illegally and to take back 226 Cuban boatpeople being held at Guantanamo who had asked to be repatriated.[234]

Secondary Objectives: No Movement on the Embargo or Radio Marti, but Was Any Expected?

Castro made no explicit gains with respect to ending the embargo or silencing Radio Marti, two things his representatives began calling for publicly in the days leading up to the September meetings.[235] Nevertheless, it can be argued that the reason Castro agreed to shelve these issues was that, while he anticipated that he could achieve his objectives vis-à-vis immigration issues in the short run because of the visibility of the crisis, the more substantive issues of the embargo would require more time and wider support, particularly given that it was late in an election year. Consider, for instance, that shortly after the crisis ended, Castro met with George McGovern, former senator and U.S. presidential candidate, who concluded, "You would be impressed with his knowledge of American politics. He knows all the American players, and he knows the pressures that play on them. He knows all about the health care debate and the crime bill and Whitewater and everything else that's going on here and showed real sensitivity to the political squeeze that the President's going through now."[236]

McGovern also indicated that Castro acknowledged explicitly that Clinton "was politically incapable of tackling anything as controversial as lifting the embargo in the short run, particularly in the wake of the

---

[232] Daniel Williams, "Cuba Deal Depends on Castro Dropping Trade Demands," *Washington Post*, September 9, 1994.

[233] Chris Marquis and Mimi Whitefield, "Cuban Accord Favors Clinton," *Times-Picayune*, September 11, 1994.

[234] Ibid.

[235] Stanley Meisler, "US, Cuba Sign Accord to End Migrant Exodus," *Los Angeles Times*, September 10, 1994.

[236] "News Briefing with Former Presidential Candidate."

refugee crisis which was a matter of enormous embarrassment and anxiety to the US administration."[237] As a former Cuban official, who had spent seventeen years in the revolutionary elite, has noted, "Fidel is a shrewd student of United States society, institutions and government."[238] In the end, despite Cuban officials' eleventh-hour calls for discussions on issues wider than immigration, it appears Castro got everything that he expected to achieve in the short run.[239] This is not to suggest that he did not actively float trial balloons on the bigger issues in the hope that they might produce results, only that he probably had low expectations that they would.[240]

At the same time, Castro may have expected more dialogue and further positive developments down the road; otherwise, it seems unlikely that he would have agreed to end the crisis so quickly. As one Cuba analyst put it, "It's unthinkable that this was a rare moment of Castro charity at work....He had such leverage over Washington. He was in the position of either saving Clinton's political neck or causing him endless problems."[241] In addition, circumstantial evidence supports the existence of a tacit agreement that future negotiations would occur. Shortly after the September accords were announced, Secretary of State Warren Christopher appeared on *Face the Nation* and said of Castro, "If he moves toward democracy in a tangible, significant way, we'll respond in a carefully calibrated way.... Washington is 'to be prepared to reduce the sanctions in carefully calibrated ways in response to positive developments in Cuba.'"[242] Although Christopher declined to specify what either these developments or responses might be, State Department officials indicated that the administration "might ease—but not eliminate—economic or travel restrictions against Cuba if Castro allowed more freedom of expression or free elections."[243]

---

[237] Ibid.

[238] Rohter, "Castro Plays His Cards with Cunning."

[239] See "Tide of Cuban Boat People Eases; U.S. Officials Say Change in Immigration Policy May Have Stemmed Exodus," *Buffalo News*, August 29, 1994, which quotes experts whose views are consistent with this analysis; that is, although Castro has used the crisis to renew his demand for lifting the trade embargo, experts said they believed his real objectives were far more modest: easier legal migration, U.S. prosecution of Cubans who make it to Florida in stolen aircraft or boats, and restoration of remittances.

[240] Ibid.; interviews, May and July 2000, Washington, D.C.

[241] Larry Birns, director of the Council on Hemispheric Affairs, quoted in "Tide of Cuban Boat People Eases."

[242] Secretary of State, Warren Christopher (in an appearance on *Face the Nation*), quoted in Daniel Williams and Roberto Suro, "Upcoming Talks with Cuba on Immigration Issues Could Foster Deeper Dialogue," *Washington Post*, August 30, 1994.

[243] Steven Greenhouse, "Flight from Cuba: U.S. Policy; U.S. Promises to Respond If Castro Offers Reforms," *New York Times*, August 29, 1994.

More concretely, and tellingly, Richard Nuccio, then special advisor to the Clinton administration on Cuba, reports that following the migration crisis in 1994 and the subsequent May 1995 accords,

> a weak, and I'd emphasize weak, conditional engagement policy was added to the prior unconditional engagement policy towards Cuba. By this conditional engagement policy, an explicit understanding was arrived at between senior US and Cuban officials that Cuba's implementation of the May 1995 migration accords and its reaction to the US efforts to engage Cuba's emerging civil society could form the basis for further progress in US-Cuban relations.[244]

Following the May 1995 accords, administration envoys were reportedly so encouraged that they approached members of the Spanish Socialist Party to help mediate further talks with Castro. And in late 1995, in a meeting with Representative Esteban Torres (D-Calif.), Castro reportedly agreed to call for free elections, permit the creation of opposition political parties, and free political prisoners. In exchange, the United States was to lift the embargo and help Cuba obtain international development bank loans, according to congressional sources.[245]

However, the size of the Republican congressional victory in November 1994 may well have prevented some of the anticipated diplomatic openings from materializing. For example, it was reported that in mid-1994 National Security Advisor Anthony Lake said privately that he was prepared to recommend that Clinton lift the embargo and accept the political consequences. But the midterm election results put that "tightly held strategy on ice," according to a senior Clinton administration official.[246] Further, in March 1995, when NSC officials told reporters that they were about to recommend dropping the additional sanctions that Clinton had imposed during the height of the August 1994 crisis (the prohibitions on remittances and family visitations) the proposal was immediately attacked in Congress as a "capitulation to Castro" and promptly abandoned.[247] Finally, the Republican victory installed Senator Jesse Helms (R-N.C.) as

---

[244] "Dealing with the States Formerly Known as Rogues," Brookings press briefing, July 13, 2000, Brookings Institution, http://www.brookings.edu/events/2001/0713diplomacy.aspx. This assessment was confirmed by an unidentified former Clinton administration NSC official in an interview, May 2001, Washington, D.C.

[245] Lula Rodriguez, "Trying to Reconcile: US Quietly Questioning Policies That Have Led to 40 Years of Cold Relations with Cuba," Cuba in Evolution, September 7, 1998, http://www.lularodriguez.com/cuba-in-evolution/. In June 1997, Torres filed a bill to end trade restrictions on food and medicine, a bill that had more than ninety co-sponsors in the House, although none from Florida.

[246] "Adrift off Cuba."

[247] Ibid.

chairman of the Senate Foreign Relations Committee and Representative Dan Burton (R-Ind.) as chairman of the House Subcommittee on Western Hemisphere Affairs. With support from Helms and Burton, Cuban lobbies mobilized to tighten economic sanctions on Cuba; the resulting Helms-Burton legislation was designed to stop foreign investment in Cuba and, if possible, to damage Cuban trade.[248]

In any event, progress came to a screeching halt—if only temporarily—in February 1996 when Castro ordered his military to shoot down two unarmed planes flown by Brothers to the Rescue, a Cuban American exile group.[249] In Washington, the shoot-down outraged conservatives and panicked the Clinton administration, which was in the midst of its 1996 re-election campaign. Clinton responded by quickly throwing his support behind the Helms-Burton legislation, which, as noted previously, he had theretofore opposed.[250]

Case Evaluation

The three cases examined in this chapter represent the one set of cases that nearly all observers agree represents a strategic use of mass migration.[251] Thus, the operative question is not whether these outflows were strategic but whether they were coercive in nature. Some have suggested that exportive engineered migration alone can explain Castro's behavior. Mario Antonio Rivera, for instance, argues that Castro turned these incidents "into an opportunity for a purge of many Cubans considered socially or politically inimical to the regime."[252] Coercion, in other words, was not the objective. But, although it is undoubtedly true that engineered outflows from Cuba have served other purposes, exportive explanations alone are insufficient to explain either their causes or their consequences. As outlined at the outset of this chapter, Castro's behavior in August 1994 is consistent with the proposition that he was engaged in attempted coercion when he decided to unleash the *balseros* crisis. Castro issued explicit threats and demands and exercised control over the size and scope of the outflows. Moreover, his subsequent behavior was not only consistent with his own rhetoric regarding his ex ante demands but also shifted in

[248] Dominguez, "US-Cuban Relations," 60–65.

[249] It has been argued that Castro used the shoot-down to reaffirm his credibility and launched "a preemptive strike to signal to all political opponents, in Cuba and elsewhere, that he was prepared to use force to remain in power." Ackerman, "Transition in Cuba."

[250] Phil Willon, "Embargo against Cuba Scrutinized," *Tampa Tribune*, January 12, 1998.

[251] Some, however, ignore the little known Camarioca case.

[252] Rivera, *Decision and Structure*, 6.

response to changes in U.S. behavior (e.g., when the United States agreed to a deal, Castro closed the Cuban border).

The same holds true vis-à-vis the 1980 Mariel crisis. Although some observers have characterized this crisis as being driven by little more than a desire to embarrass the United States, evidence suggests otherwise.[253] For example, according to Tad Szulc, Castro biographer, Castro ordered Mariel "as a gesture of supreme personal rage" out of anger over President Carter's unguarded claim that the United States awaited Cuban political refugees with "open arms."[254] It is undoubtedly true that Castro had a bad temper and was subject to fits of pique; indeed, his "most senior associates" were known to fear what became known as "Fidel furies."[255] The problem with this explanation is that Castro opened the port at Mariel on April 21, two weeks *before* Carter made his "open hearts and open arms" speech.

Moreover, as in 1994, in the lead-up to the 1980 crisis Castro issued explicit threats and made specific demands, and his subsequent behavior was consistent with both. He also controlled the timing and the volume of the flows, starting and stopping them in response to U.S. actions. Thus, although the timing of the crisis was undoubtedly influenced by events on the ground, neither the dynamic and interactive nature of the give and take between the United States and Cuba nor the ultimate outcome of the crisis can be adequately explained without ascribing to Castro at least some degree of coercive intent.

The 1965 Camarioca crisis was likely a different, but very telling, story. In that case, evidence suggests that Castro did open the border in early October largely to rid himself of many of the remaining dissidents in Cuba. Nevertheless, this migration dress rehearsal provided Castro with clear evidence of the power of outflows to influence the behavior of the U.S. government. His two subsequent uses of coercive engineered migration bear this out.

Likewise evidence indicates that, as a relatively weak actor with limited policy options at his disposal, Castro relied on coercive engineered migration as a kind of asymmetric weapon that he could use to help level the playing field between his own regime and his immensely more powerful international adversary. Nevertheless, as predicted, it was not his strategy of first resort. In both 1980 and in 1994, Castro tried to induce the United States to negotiate *before* loosing outflows. As Castro himself asserted in a televised speech in December 1984—four years after the Mariel crisis

---

[253] See, for instance, Leon Gordenker, *Refugees in International Politics* (New York: Columbia University Press, 1987).

[254] Tad Szulc, *Fidel: A Critical Portrait* (New York: William Morrow, 1986), 42, 645.

[255] Ibid., 42.

ended—the United States brought Mariel on itself by leaving Cuba no other option:

> The policy of encouraging people to leave the country illegally continued. We warned them many, many times that this policy was being used as a political weapon and that antisocial elements were doing all kinds of things—murdering people to steal boats, hijacking boats—and, when they reached the US, they went unpunished. We warned them many, many times that measures had to be taken against that policy, that something had to be done to stop this situation and that it was going to lead to trouble, until finally it led to the Mariel episode.[256]

Castro's reluctance to resort to migration-driven coercion may be due to the fact that, when he did employ it, he sometimes generated larger outflows than he anticipated or desired. In 1965, for instance, "the Cuban government found that once the boatlift had started, it too had difficulties controlling it."[257] "Too many Cubans were taking him [Castro] at his word by simply walking off their jobs and heading for Camarioca."[258] Nevertheless, Castro was not deterred from using the strategy again and yet again. In 1980, Fidel had been "interested in getting rid of perhaps 20,000 to 30,000 disaffected Cubans," but in the end 125,000 left the island.[259] In 1994, by contrast however, the exodus was ended with sufficient alacrity that there is little reason to believe Castro was expecting a significantly smaller outflow.

In addition, Castro took advantage of anticipated discord within the United States in each of the cases; that is, he employed an agitation-based strategy. Former regime insiders, international diplomats, and U.S. officials have all observed that Castro was a keen observer of U.S. domestic politics and understood "the limitations on a president's power to act in many critical circumstances. This knowledge informs his every strategic maneuver."[260] Castro also acknowledged that he recognized the conflict-generating value of including undesirables in the migrant stream. Indeed,

---

[256] Fidel Castro, "The US-Cuba Accord on Migratory Relations," in *War and Crisis in the Americas: Speeches 1984–85*, ed. Michael Taber (New York: Pathfinder Press, 1985), 49.

[257] Engstrom, *Presidential Decision Making Adrift*, 27. In an October 21 memo to the president, Bundy noted that "the British and Canadian Embassies in Havana report that the response of Cubans wishing to leave is much greater than anticipated" and that "the Cuban Government has ordered the expulsion of American newsmen who went to Cuba from Florida without visas to cover the departure of refugees from Camarioca because their work is 'done.'" LBJL, NSFMcB, CHRON FILE Oct 21–31, 1965 [2 of 2], "Memorandum for the President from McGeorge Bundy, Subject: Latin American Developments," October 21, 1965.

[258] Smith, *Closest of Enemies*, 91.

[259] Llovio-Menendez, *Insider*, 387.

[260] Rohter, "Castro Plays His Cards with Cunning."

even two years before Mariel, "during his first interview with reporters from the Cuban Community, Castro had said, 'They [the United States] do not want common criminals to go [there].'"[261]

Furthermore, Castro took actions that appear—at least in retrospect— custom-designed to impose hypocrisy costs on the United States, both directly and indirectly. As noted previously, according to Llovio-Menendez, a former Castro confidante, Castro had "a hidden motive" in initiating a mass exodus, formulated in direct "response to the United States' contradictions and vacillations" regarding the Peruvian Embassy incident.[262] In short, Castro was fully aware that exploitation of such contradictions would create political conflicts within the United States, conflicts only he would be in a position to resolve.

Additional evidence of Castro's awareness of, and desire to impose, hypocrisy costs on the United States can be found in Cuban behavior toward Haitian boatpeople in spring and summer 1980. Not only did *Granma* carried editorial accusations of the differential treatment of Cubans and Haitians, but also the Cuban government sent to the United States more than 1,000 shipwrecked Haitians who had been stranded in eastern Cuba,[263] as well as provided food and water to Haitians trying to reach the United States.[264] As the coverage in *Granma* suggests, Castro quite intentionally transported Haitians to the United States because he knew full well that, on arrival, they would be immediately incarcerated at Krome Detention Center. Castro knew that he could score a propaganda coup by publicizing this fact and by pointing out the clear disparity between his own humane treatment of the Haitians and the repressive response of the United States.[265]

Nevertheless, the outcomes in the three cases were not precisely the same. For one thing, the Johnson administration's response was the swiftest and most effective. Which is to say, the crisis was solved at a low political—but not financial—cost and with little domestic turmoil. In contrast, the Carter administration fared particularly poorly on all three of these fronts. (The level of domestic turmoil was high, as were both the financial and political costs.) This may have been an artifact of Carter's own leadership style. Observers note that Carter was particularly poorly equipped to handle crisis situations due to his "determination to make detailed decisions himself without reference to any overarching

---

[261] Llovio-Menendez, *Insider*, 387.

[262] Ibid.

[263] Rivera, *Decision and Structure*, 6. *Granma* also provided "gleeful" coverage of the riots of Mariel refugee riots in June 1980. Ibid., 10.

[264] Brian Weinstein and Aaron Segal, *Haiti: Political Failures, Cultural Successes* (New York: Praeger, 1984), 124–25.

[265] Ibid.

strategy—and his willingness to make and remake them."[266] Or it may have been—as former Assistant Attorney General Renfrew suggests—an unavoidable consequence of the fact that the Carter administration simply had too many crises on its plate in spring 1980 to give Mariel the attention it deserved.[267] We might even argue that the fact that 1965 was settled so quickly actually contributed to the failed U.S. response in 1980—that is, because the 1965 crisis came and went so quickly, even though Castro learned a powerful lesson about the U.S. vulnerability to coercion, the United States learned no lessons at all. For his part, Castro succeeded to a greater or lesser extent in all three cases.

Although Camarioca ended before significant mobilization had occurred in the anti-migrant/refugee camp, mail from constituents and feedback from Johnson officials who traveled to Florida suggest that the situation would have rapidly escalated and become very damaging had the Johnson administration failed to act as quickly as it did. Although Castro appears to have gotten much of what he wanted, the United States likewise appears to have dodged a political bullet. In 1980, by contrast, the shift was dramatic and imposed devastating political costs on the Carter administration. The Cuban American community remained deeply committed to admitting Cuban migrants throughout the crisis. Its level of commitment declined somewhat over the course of the crisis, however, particularly as the magnitude of the monetary and social costs associated with assimilating more than 125,000 of their brethren— some of whom were Castro's undesirables—became clear. Finally, in 1994, even at the outset of the crisis the concentration of interest in the pro-migrant/refugee camp in favor of admitting Cubans was markedly lower than it had been at the start of Mariel. But those still dedicated to admitting Cubans—like Mas Canosa's CANF—were still intensely committed; their support did not waver as the crisis heated up. At the same time, having witnessed firsthand what the Mariel crisis had wrought, the concentration of interests opposed to admitting Cubans started at a high level and grew still higher, and it did so with great alacrity. Thus, consistent with the predictions made in chapter 1, the Clinton administration was somewhat vulnerable to coercion at the outset of the crisis and grew only steadily more so over time. (This analysis is summarized in fig. 2.1.[268])

[266] I. M. Destler, Leslie H. Gelb, and Anthony Lake, *Our Own Worst Enemy* (New York: Simon and Schuster, 1984), 250.

[267] Interview with Charles Renfrew, 1988, quoted in Engstrom, *Presidential Decision Making Adrift*, 92–93n46.

[268] Note in this figure that the location of the starting and ending points of the arrows is not significant; what matters is shifts in levels—and, hence, vulnerability—over time.

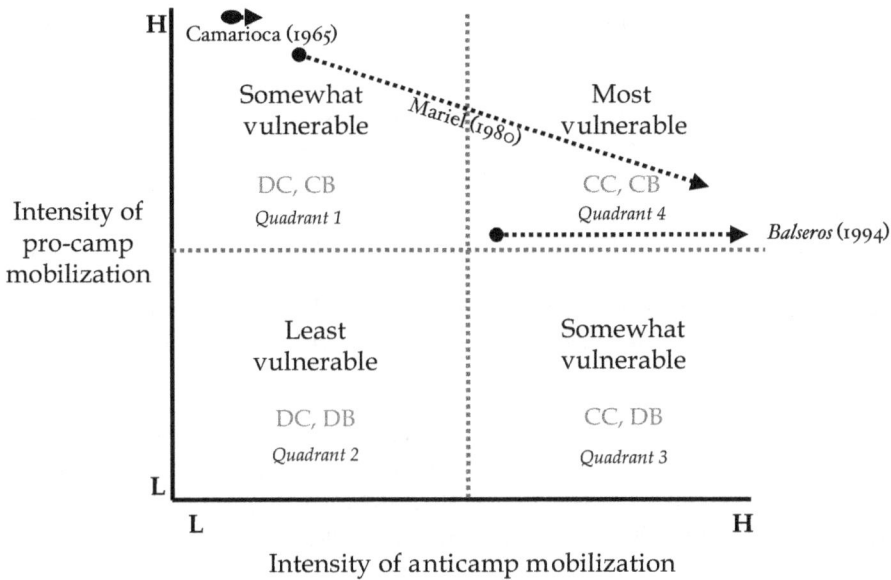

Figure 2.1. Why Castro thrice succeeded: Camarioca (1965), Mariel (1980), Balseros (1994). CB, concentrated benefits; CC, concentrated costs; DB, diffuse benefits; DC, diffuse costs; H, high; L, low.

A Few Final Thoughts

There is some irony in the fact that the 1980 and 1994 crises probably could have been avoided if the United States had not flatly rejected Castro's initial calls for negotiations. As observers have noted previously, the kind of immigration escape valve preferred by Castro is one "that is orderly and drawn out and not very splashy."[269] In both cases, orderly and splashless negotiations might well have generated little more than blips on the public's radar screen, thereby avoiding both domestic and international crises.

However, choosing to concede to Castro's threats as soon as he made them would obviously have generated its own costs, in reputation and credibility. This could in turn have encouraged Castro to threaten the United States more frequently and with increasing demands. Nevertheless, more careful monitoring of the prevailing economic and social

[269] Lisandro Perez, director of the Cuba Research Institute at Florida International University, quoted in Larry Rohter, "Best of Enemies; Castro, the Man with Few Cards, Always Winds Up the Dealer," *New York Times*, August 28, 1994.

conditions on the ground in Cuba could have led to earlier diplomatic intervention and staved off unnecessary humiliation and domestic political turmoil, both in 1980 and in 1994. As Christopher Mitchell has noted in his analysis of the Cuban and Haitian cases in the early 1980s, diplomatic contacts offer one of the few available options for preventing the manipulation of population outflows. "Through state-to-state dialogue, where other bilateral stakes are customarily available, interstate agreements may be reached that bring migration within the ambit of regular US legislation on the subject."[270] Moreover, history shows that, "each and every president [from Dwight Eisenhower to Bill Clinton] came to the conclusion that an important aspect of his Castro crisis [in the end] required negotiations."[271]

Furthermore, it is worth noting that with few recognized exceptions—including the one in April 1995 discussed herein—Castro usually followed through on his publicly articulated threats to open the Cuban borders. In other words, his threats were rarely idle. As Engstrom notes in his analysis of the Carter administration response to Mariel:

> The ahistorical approach of policy makers in the Carter Administration is particularly telling because the Camarioca boatlift provided tailor-made examples of the conditions that contributed to an earlier boatlift and the policies employed by the Johnson Administration to deal with it. The Camarioca boatlift offered relevant lessons that the Carter Administration did not explore. Had policy makers examined the dynamics of the Camarioca boatlift either before or during the Mariel boatlift, they may well have learned from history and developed better policies.[272]

This assessment remained equally valid in 1994 and, for that matter, may remain equally valid today as the country continues to be run by a fellow named Castro.

[270] Mitchell, "Implications," 298.
[271] Rohter, "Castro Plays His Cards with Cunning."
[272] Engstrom, *Presidential Decision Making Adrift,* 198.

3

"Now the Refugees *Are* the War"

NATO and the Kosovo Conflict

> As the numbers of refugees languishing in the muddy stinking fields to which they are confined grows with sickening speed, NATO countries have closed their doors. We don't mind images of them on the television screens but the people themselves are not welcome. That would make the story entirely too personal.... Let them stay in the Balkans, we say. We'll send a cheque.
> **ISABEL HILTON, British journalist**

On March 24, 1999, the North Atlantic Treaty Organization (NATO) commenced the first military campaign in its fifty-year history—a bombing war over the tiny Yugoslav province of Kosovo.[1] Although NATO had been conceived as a defensive alliance, its first mission turned out to be an offensive one whose stated objectives were three: "to demonstrate the

---

Epigraph: Isabel Hilton, "We Imagine War as a Hollywood Film," *Guardian,* April 5, 1999.

[1] Research materials for this chapter have been drawn from a wide variety of primary and secondary sources. These include government (e.g., U.S., British, German, and EU) documents and transcripts; international organizational reports and documents, particularly, *Kosovo/Kosova: As Seen, As Told,* an analysis of the human rights findings of the Organization for Security and Co-operation in Europe (OSCE) Kosovo Verification Mission (www.asylumlaw.org/docs/kosovo/osce99_kosovo_asseenastold.pdf); a variety of scholarly sources, including a statistical analysis of the population outflows; and a wide array of U.S., Eastern European, and Western European (and especially Yugoslav) newspaper and magazine articles, in particular the state-run TANJUG News Service (hereafter TANJUG), at www.serbia-info.com/news. I drew heavily on the extensive interviews conducted by Alan Little in conjunction with the British Broadcasting Company (BBC2) documentary, *Moral Combat: NATO at War,* broadcast on March 12, 2000; a transcript is available at http://news.bbc.co.uk/hi/english/static/events/panorama/transcripts/transcript_12_03_00.txt. I also conducted interviews of my own in immediately after the conflict (June–August 1999) with European government officials, aid agency representatives and officials, international military observers, and Kosovar refugees in Western Europe and in the Balkans. Between April 2000 and May 2004, I conducted additional interviews with former Clinton administration officials, U.S. Department of Defense analysts and planners, U.S. and French military officers, and former Albanian government officials.

seriousness of NATO's purpose so that the Serbian leaders understand the imperative of reversing course," "to deter an even bloodier offensive against innocent civilians in Kosovo," and "if necessary to seriously damage the Serbian military's capacity to harm the people of Kosovo."[2] It was also an operation that failed—at least at its outset—to accomplish a single one of these goals and, tragically and ironically, actually stimulated the largest strategic engineered population movement in Europe since World War II, in which more than 800,000 Kosovars fled or were driven from their homes in less than two months.

In this chapter, I tackle the question of why then Yugoslav President Slobodan Milosevic engineered a massive migration crisis in spring 1999 and what he hoped to gain by doing so. I also tackle the underlying questions of why Milosevic was undeterred by the NATO threat of a bombing campaign and why the alliance felt compelled to launch it. This case provides an instructive counterpoint to the Cuban crises examined in the previous chapter. In both instances, a weak, somewhat internationally isolated state actor attempted to alter the behavior of a vastly more powerful target via the use of migration-driven coercion. Likewise, in both cases, the challenger hoped to facilitate successful coercion by engaging in activities designed to foment conflict within the target state(s) while also using the outflows to accomplish other policy goals. But, whereas the Cuban cases were bilateral and relatively successful, the Kosovo crisis was multilateral—between the Federal Republic of Yugoslavia (FRY) and NATO members—and in the end, largely a failure.

To summarize the argument, the most widely promulgated history of the conflict suggests that Milosevic's cleansing campaign—purportedly dubbed Operation Horseshoe by the Serbs—was a premeditated plan designed to empty the province of its Albanian majority[3] and reestablish Serb dominance over the territory, irrespective of NATO actions.[4] The

[2] U.S. President Bill Clinton, quoted in *Moral Combat*.
[3] It has been argued that NATO needed to cling tightly to such an interpretation to justify its actions. Timothy Garton Ash, for instance, claims "western European leaders stressed the motive of averting 'humanitarian disaster' so strongly because this was the only way in which taking military action without the sanction of a UN Security Council resolution—something they had recoiled from doing for the best part of a year—might possibly be justified in international law. This legal expedient had been suggested by a British foreign office memorandum circulated to Britain's NATO allies as early as October 1998." "The War We Almost Lost: Was NATO's Kosovo Campaign a Legitimate Response to a Humanitarian Catastrophe—Or Did It Cause One?" *Guardian*, September 4, 2000.
[4] See, for instance, the statement of General Klaus Naumann, chairman of the NATO Military Committee, to the U.S. Senate, *Lessons Learned from the Military Operations Conducted as Part of Operation Allied Force*, Senate Armed Services Committee, November 3, 1999, 2, cited in Ivo Daalder and Michael O'Hanlon, *Winning Ugly: NATO's War to Save Kosovo* (Washington, D.C.: Brookings Institution, 2000), 292n137. Surprisingly this version of events persists, even after a retired general in the German Army (among others) admitted "claims of a plan

available evidence, however, simply does not support this interpretation of events. Instead, it suggests that the primary objective of the campaign was not a wholesale cleansing of the province but the destruction of the separatist Kosovo Liberation Army (KLA). Moreover, even though the evidence is not wholly conclusive, it suggests that Milosevic's preferred strategy for achieving this aim was a two-pronged coercive effort designed to simultaneously crush the KLA and deter NATO from interfering with this endeavor. Thus, while NATO was actively seeking to deter and then to compel Milosevic to cease his offensive through the use of air strikes, evidence suggests Milosevic was engaged in his own intensive game of counter-coercion against NATO and its allies. But, for Milosevic, refugees, rather than bombs, were the political and military weapons of choice.[5]

Politically, Milosevic initially attempted to deter a NATO attack by raising the specter of the destabilizing consequences of massive outflows, and he did so at least as early as February 1999, following the collapse of talks at Rambouillet. Already visible fissures in the façade of NATO unity gave Milosevic reason to believe that he might succeed.[6] After deterrence failed, he persisted in trying to fracture the alliance and cultivate fears of massive refugee influxes within those neighboring states supporting the war effort. He did so in an attempt to convince NATO to end its bombing campaign and to do so on terms more favorable than those offered at Rambouillet.[7]

[i.e., Operation Horseshoe] were faked from a vague intelligence report in order to deflect criticism in Germany of the bombing." Quoted in Human Rights Watch (HRW), *Under Orders: War Crimes in Kosovo* (New York: HRW, 2001), 59. See also John Goetz and Tom Walker, "Serbian Ethnic Cleansing Scare Was a Fake, Says General," *Sunday Times,* April 2, 2000. (It was the Germans who announced the existence of Operation Horseshoe.)

[5] This proposition has been echoed by others, including by Bill Frelick of the U.S. Committee on Refugees. See, for instance, the program transcript for the Center for Defense Information documentary *Refugees as Weapons of War,* September 7, 1999, www.cdi.org/adm/1306/Frelick.html. Frelick said," Initially in 1998 I think that the Serbian strategy was a counter-insurgency strategy. They were provoked by the KLA. At various points the KLA was seeking independence. They were trying a sort of Boston Tea Party, or to provoke the Redcoats, so to speak. And the Yugoslav army and the Serbian police overreacted, hitting civilian populations. But essentially it was directed at the KLA at that time. I don't think that the strategy, at that time was ethnic cleansing per se. That changed dramatically with the bombing campaign that NATO embarked upon on March 24, 1999....Once NATO bombing commenced, the Serbs saw an opportunity to cleanse the province and set about doing it." See also, Joseph Lelyveld, "The Defendant," *New Yorker,* May 27, 2002, 85.

[6] See, for instance, *Moral Combat;* Tim Judah, *Kosovo: War and Revenge* (New Haven: Yale University Press, 2002), chap. 8; Brian C. Rathbun, *Partisan Interventions: European Party Politics and Peace Enforcement in the Balkans* (Ithaca, N.Y.: Cornell University Press, 2004); Rosa Balfour, Roberto Menotti, and Ghita Micieli de Biase, "Italy's Crisis Diplomacy in Kosovo, March–June 1999," *International Spectator* 36 (1999): 67–81.

[7] The stipulations of the Rambouillet Accords would have allowed NATO unimpeded access to all of FRY—not just Kosovo—which many on both sides of the political spectrum acknowledge no sovereign country would willingly accept. See, for instance, Henry Kissinger, "The Wrong Invasion," *Ottawa Citizen,* February 22, 1999; William E. Ratliff, "Madeline's War and the Costs of Intervention," *Harvard International Review* 22 (2001): 70–76. The British

Militarily, it appears Milosevic sought to use engineered migration both to gain tactical advantage against the KLA and to impede NATO combat operations within the beleaguered province itself as well as in staging areas in adjacent states. Because population displacement—designed to sever rebel supply and communications lines and to reduce insurgents' capacity to hide among civilians—is a common tactic in counterinsurgency operations, some displacement would inevitably have occurred, even in the absence of NATO action.[8] Once bombing commenced, however, any restraint based on the fear of NATO reprisals vanished, leading Milosevic to pursue a larger and more destructive cleansing campaign than originally planned.[9] With respect to disrupting NATO operations, the intent of flooding neighboring countries appears to have been designed, in part, to directly undermine the ability of NATO to launch offensive operations and, in part, to overwhelm the logistical capabilities of the alliance (and of recipient states).[10]

Given the benefit of hindsight, Milosevic's reliance on engineered migration as part of his spring offensive may appear foolhardy, particularly given that he was ousted from power eighteen months later and soon thereafter found himself in The Hague facing war crimes charges. But, as many observers concede, Milosevic had few attractive policy options from which to choose.[11] He was by that point an international pariah in many

---

House of Commons Foreign Affairs Committee likewise concluded, "Whatever the actual impact of the Military Annex, NATO was guilty of a serious blunder in allowing a Status of Forces Agreement into the package which would never have been acceptable to the Yugoslav side, since it was a significant infringement of its sovereignty." House of Commons Select Committee on Foreign Affairs, "Fourth Report," May 23, 2000.

[8] In the midst of counterinsurgency operations, displacement frequently occurs even when the forces involved are less disposed to brutality than the Serbs. Consider, for instance, that the U.S. search-and-destroy tactics in Vietnam during spring 1965 alone generated over 400,000 refugees. Robert B. Asprey, *War in the Shadows: The Guerrilla in History* (New York: William Morrow and Company, 1994), 832. The Serbs' history and reputation for brutality would have likely encouraged some to flee preemptively as well.

[9] Greek diplomats predicted as much a month before the bombing began. Paul Wood, "Regional Tensions: Greece Fears the Balkans Could Ignite and Drag Her into Conflicts of the Past," *Independent*, February 21, 1999.

[10] It has been argued, for instance, that to "protect their forces on the ground and confound targeting, Serb units intentionally operated among civilian refugees, in villages, and near prohibited targets such as churches." William Arkin, "Operation Allied Force: 'The Most Precise Application of Air Power in History,'" in *War over Kosovo: Politics and Strategy in a Global Age*, ed. Andrew J. Bacevich and Eliot A. Cohen (New York: Columbia University Press, 2001), 15. See also U.S. Department of Defense (DOD), "Joint Statement on the Kosovo After Action Review," October 14, 1999, http://www.defenselink.mil/releases/release.aspx?releaseid=2220.

[11] It is worth keeping in mind that NATO aggregate GDP was approximately nine hundred times that of the FRY, its aggregate defense budget was three hundred times greater than the FRY, and its aggregate population was approximately seventy times greater than the FRY. Barry R. Posen, "The War for Kosovo: Serbia's Political-Military Strategy," *International Security* 24 (2000): 49.

circles, facing both a mounting insurgency by KLA rebels and a diktat-like ultimatum from the most powerful military alliance in the world, compliance with which would have made combating the KLA impossible.[12] Under these circumstances, counter-coercion via coercive engineered migration probably appeared a worthwhile gamble, particularly because for a time it appeared that it might succeed.[13]

In the course of examining Milosevic's failed gambit (as a generator), I also explore two other, rather more successful, attempts at coercive engineered migration underway during this same period: one by the independence-seeking KLA (acting as *agents provocateurs*) and another by neighboring Macedonia (in the role of opportunist). The KLA and its supporters were aided in their endeavor by the hypocrisy cost–generating behavior of some NATO members, whose rhetoric and poor track record in Bosnia a few years before drove the alliance inexorably toward an intervention that inadvertently precipitated a far greater humanitarian disaster than almost anyone anticipated at the outset.[14]

In this chapter I first provide a brief stage-setting narrative of the events leading up to the conflict. Then, I present evidence in support of the argument that Milosevic initially attempted to deter NATO from attacking by actively exploiting the refugee-related anxieties of frontline states, gambling that these fears would help undermine NATO cohesion and cultivate fear and discord within those neighboring countries supporting the war effort. Next, I explore how and why, after failing to deter NATO from attacking—and while moving ahead with his campaign to crush the KLA—Milosevic upped the ante and sought to compel NATO to stop its bombing campaign by using refugees as weapons. Finally, I offer an explanation as to why Milosevic's gambit was largely a failure, whereas simultaneous attempts by Macedonia and the KLA were successful.

Background

The proximate cause of the 1999 Kosovo conflict was the rise of the KLA in the mid-1990s. Its ascension followed the perceived failures of the

---

[12] As Henry Kissinger—while simultaneously highlighting U.S. hypocrisy—put it, "Rambouillet was not a negotiation—as is often claimed—but an ultimatum. This marked an astounding departure for an administration that had entered office proclaiming its devotion to the U.N. Charter and multilateral procedures." "New World Disorder," *Newsweek*, May 31, 1999, 41.

[13] This is not to suggest that engineered migration was Milosevic's only tool in the spring 1999 offensive.

[14] See, for instance, Samantha Power, *A Problem from Hell: America and the Age of Genocide* (New York: Basic Books, 2002), on the power of the Bosnia precedent in driving behavior in Kosovo.

non-violent activism of Ibrahim Rugova and his Democratic League of Kosovo (LDK) to improve the plight of the oppressed Albanian Kosovars. Frustrated with the trifling results of Rugova's efforts, the previously nascent KLA began actively targeting ethnic Serb officials and police, prominent Serb civilians, and Kosovar Albanians perceived to be Yugoslav loyalists.[15] The economic and political collapse of Albania in 1997—in the wake of the notorious failed pyramid investment schemes—further catalyzed KLA development because large quantities of Albanian army weaponry found their way over the border.[16] As the KLA became better armed and equipped, the number and efficacy of its attacks increased. In response, Serb security forces cracked down on suspected KLA members and, as the spiral of attacks and reprisals swelled, the situation within the province grew more violent. Then, on January 4, 1998, the KLA proclaimed itself "the armed forces of the Kosovar Albanians and that the armed struggle for the independence of Kosovo and its unification had begun."[17]

By late winter, the KLA reportedly controlled about half of the province. In an attempt to crush the expanding insurgency, FRY forces launched a massive and brutal counteroffensive, which by March 1998 had achieved considerable success.[18] But the cost for the Kosovar Albanians was high; many villages were razed and civilian casualties mounted. In response, the European Union and the United States publicly condemned the Serb offensive and stepped in to mediate. But Western diplomatic efforts resulted in little progress. Because the mediators were unwilling or unable to augment their diplomatic efforts with credible threats of military action, they likewise failed to persuade the Serbs they were serious about protecting the Kosovar Albanians. Shortly thereafter, the Serbs renewed their offensive, and by September 1998, the KLA had been largely—albeit temporarily—neutralized as a military force.

The renewed Serb offensive generated several hundred thousand additional refugees and internally displaced persons (IDPs), many of whom

---

[15] Although the KLA claims to have launched its first attack in 1993, most observers focus on the period between 1996 and 1998 as the key to understanding Serb fears regarding the growing strength, scope, and scale of their operations. Consider that there were thirty-one documented KLA attacks in 1996, fifty-five in 1997, and sixty-six in just the first two months of 1998. Chris Hedges, "In New Balkan Tinderbox, Ethnic Albanians Rebel against Serbs," *New York Times*, March 2, 1998; HRW, *Under Orders*, chap. 2.

[16] See, for instance, Judah, *Kosovo*, 128–29.

[17] Quoted in William Hayden, "The Kosovo Conflict and Forced Migration: The Strategic Use of Displacement and the Obstacles to International Protection," *Journal of Humanitarian Assistance* February 14, 1998, http://jha.ac/tag/kosovo/?PHPSESSID=c33ff4902f41f664037 21259ea0ba1f9.

[18] On February 23, 1998, during a visit to Pristina, Robert Gelbard, U.S. special envoy, announced that the United States "condemned very strongly terrorist actions in Kosovo. The UCK [KLA] is, without any question, a terrorist group." Quoted in Judah, *Kosovo*, 138. It is widely acknowledged that Milosevic interpreted this statement as a green light to act against the KLA.

fled to Western Europe seeking asylum. Alarmed by this turn of events, NATO intervened diplomatically in an attempt to curb Serb military attacks in Kosovo, this time with the threat of air strikes. After a series of meetings that October, Richard Holbrooke, the U.S. Balkan envoy, and President Milosevic came to terms, thus averting air strikes on Serbia and permitting the vast majority of those displaced during the Serb offensive to return to their homes. In exchange, the Serbs agreed to a ceasefire and were enjoined to reduce their forces in Kosovo to pre–March 1998 levels.[19] They also agreed to the presence of Organization for Security and Cooperation in Europe (OSCE) ceasefire monitors. Holbrooke promised that, for its part, NATO would secure KLA compliance with the ceasefire, even though it was not party to the agreement—a shortcoming that likely crippled the agreement from the outset.[20]

The partial withdrawal of Serb forces was met not by compliance but by immediate KLA advances and a concomitant rise in terrorist attacks, which were well documented by the OSCE and Kosovo Diplomatic Observation Mission (KDOM) monitors on the ground.[21] As KLA General Agim Ceku put it, "The cease-fire was very useful for us, it helped us to get organized, to consolidate and grow.... We aimed to spread our units over as much territory as possible, we wanted KLA units and cells across the whole of Kosovo."[22] By early 1999, large areas of Kosovo were again occupied by KLA forces. The Serbs witnessed a return to the situation they had faced prior to their offensive a year before.[23] Now convinced that

[19] According to General Naumann, Milosevic "really did what we asked him to do. He withdrew within 48 hours some 6,000 police officers and the military back into the barracks." Quoted in *Moral Combat*. (Members of the OSCE Verification Mission confirmed Naumann's assessment.) On the terms of the 1998 agreement, see Daalder and O'Hanlon, *Winning Ugly*, 45–62; General Wesley Clark, *Waging Modern War* (New York: Public Affairs, 2001), 131–36; Judah, *Kosovo*, 183–89.

[20] As Major General John Drewienkiewicz put it when discussing the Serb reaction to KLA advances in late 1998 to early 1999, "The Serbs said to us, well hang on, the deal was that we withdraw from these things, and you were going to police the agreement. So can you just get these [sic] Kosovo Liberation Army out of the trenches that we were in a month ago?" Quoted in *Moral Combat*. See also Daalder and O'Hanlon, *Winning Ugly*, 57–59; Timothy W. Crawford, *Hard Bargains, Fragile Peace: Pivotal Deterrence in World Politics* (Ithaca, N.Y.: Cornell University Press, 2003).

[21] OSCE and KDOM monitors on the ground verified that the KLA undermined the ceasefire almost as soon as it was signed. See *Kosovo/Kosova*, 1:26–30, chap. 5 (The Municipalities), 163–401, which contains information about the security situation and levels of violence in each of the Kosovo municipalities. See also *KDOM Daily Report*, October 31, 1998, in which monitors noted that "KLA [UCK] presence is growing in those areas where Serb troops and police have departed, having established its own checkpoints on secondary roads in the Drenica, Podujevo, and Malisevo areas." Quoted in Daalder and O'Hanlon, *Winning Ugly*, 292n. 133.

[22] Quoted in *Moral Combat*.

[23] According to Wolfgang Petritsch, EU special envoy to Kosovo, "They were really growing ever stronger from day to day, and there was nobody to really stop them....The KLA basically came back into its old positions that they held before the summer offensive." Ibid.

Western mediators were unable or unwilling to hold up their end of the bargain, the Serbs responded brutally and effectively.

Yugoslav and Serb security forces seized the initiative in mid-December, attacking suspected KLA strongholds, including the village of Racak, where the apparent massacre of forty-five civilians in mid-January 1999 regalvanized international efforts to mediate the conflict.[24] Peace plans were offered up at Rambouillet and in Paris, but as many (even within NATO) acknowledge, these agreements were understandably unpalatable to the Serbs.[25] It rapidly became clear there was no longer a peace for OSCE monitors to verify, and they withdrew.[26] Shortly thereafter, the FRY renewed offensive began apace, NATO air strikes commenced, and ethnic cleansing began in earnest.

Why Did Milosevic Think He Could Succeed?
Know Thine Enemy

In his seminal work on coercion, Thomas Schelling argues, "the coercive use of the power to hurt is the very exploitation of enemy wants and fears."[27] For their part, leaders within the most powerful NATO members had decided that what Milosevic probably "needed" was a little bombing before he could "justify acquiescence" and concede Kosovo without losing face.[28] As Secretary of State Madelaine Albright put it on the first day

---

[24] Although Hashim Thaci, KLA leader, acknowledges that a "key KLA unit was based in the area" around Racak, most believe that some—if not all—of those killed at Racak were innocent civilians. Ibid.

[25] See Judah, *Kosovo*; Posen, "War for Kosovo." For his part, James Rubin, then U.S. State Department spokesman, now acknowledges, "obviously, publicly we had to make clear we were seeking an agreement, but privately we knew the chances of the Serbs agreeing were quite small." Quoted in *Moral Combat*.

[26] There had been a total of 1,000–2,000 conflict-related deaths between the start of the first Serb offensive in March 1998 and the withdrawal of the OSCE observers in mid-March 1999. In this same period, perhaps 200,000–300,000 people had been displaced from their homes, most victims of what was "essentially a temporary rural displacement resulting from government operations against villages suspected of sympathizing with guerrillas...many of (whom) returned to their damaged homes over the course of the year." Michael Barutciski, "Western Diplomacy and the Kosovo Refugee Crisis," *Forced Migration Review* no. 5 (1999), 9. Daalder and O'Hanlon note that after the October agreement was signed "all displaced persons inside Kosovo had either returned to their villages or had found temporary shelter elsewhere." *Winning Ugly*, 49; see also 289n93. Some fled again once the ceasefire broke down, but as Fernando Del Mundo, UNHCR spokesman, put it, "last summer people were fleeing for their lives. Now they are being displaced because of fear." Thus, in early 1999 civilians were not being pushed out, but were fleeing preemptively. "Make-or-Break Time for Kosovo," *Christian Science Monitor*, February 25, 1999.

[27] Thomas Schelling, *Arms and Influence* (New Haven: Yale University Press, 1966), chap. 1.

[28] Thomas Lippman, "Albright Misjudged Milosevic on Kosovo," *Washington Post*, April 7, 1999. See also Carnes Lord, "What Milosevic Really Wants," *Boston Globe*, April 4, 1999; Jim Hoagland, "Misreading Milosevic," *Washington Post*, April 29, 1999.

of bombing, "I don't see this is a long term operation. I think this is something that is achievable within a relatively short space of time."[29] Key decision makers within NATO ignored the signals coming from Belgrade that
indicated Milosevic would not give up without a fight. In short, NATO
miscalculated the true nature of its adversary's "wants and fears" and underestimated the credibility of his counter-threats.[30]

In the month between the failure at Rambouillet (February 22) and the
start of NATO bombing (March 24), Milosevic received numerous representatives from the United States, the European Union, the OSCE, and
NATO. Throughout this period, Milosevic expressed a willingness to
grant autonomy to the Kosovar Albanians and to take part in further negotiations; whether he was in earnest or not, however, remains unclear.[31]
Nevertheless, Milosevic had strong motivations to avoid resorting to violence. As Michael Salla concluded long before the conflict erupted, "The
Serbian government [is] intent upon avoiding violent confrontation in
Kosovo that could trigger further international sanctions, the destabilization of Macedonia, some form of intervention by Albania, and a wider
Balkan war."[32] In short, it can be reasonably inferred that Milosevic's preferred strategy—both domestically against the Kosovar Albanians and
internationally against NATO—was deterrence rather than conflict.[33]

However, now confronted with an internal adversary that was no longer deterred (the KLA), due in large part to the rhetoric and actions of
an external potential adversary (NATO), it became evident to Milosevic
that his preferred strategy was no longer a viable option. This is due to
the fact that—even if Milosevic were willing to consider autonomy—he
was unwilling to accept NATO military provisions or to entertain independence for Kosovo, as mandated during the Rambouillet and Paris con-
ferences.[34] Milosevic made clear that he understood the consequences of

[29] "Kosovo, the Untold Story: How the War Was Won," *Observer*, July 18, 1999.
[30] Although, to be clear, there were some actors within these states who did hear them,
such as Anthony Lake, former national security advisor (and mediator).
[31] See TANJUG coverage for the month of March for more on the FRY view of the diplomacy between Rambouillet and the start of the war.
[32] Michael Salla, "Kosovo, Non-Violence and the Break-Up of Yugoslavia," *Security Dialogue* 26 (1995), 432.
[33] See Hayden, "Kosovo Conflict and Forced Migration" on Milosevic's reluctance to
engage in ethnic cleansing in the prebombing period for fear of provoking international
recriminations.
[34] Christopher Hill, Balkan envoy, believed Milosevic was open to a political deal but opposed to the military provisions because "he felt that the true intention of the force was to
eliminate him and/or detach Kosovo from Serbia. In fact there was nothing in the political
agreement, which was unsellable to Serbs." Judah, *Kosovo*, 220. This view was echoed by Ra-
dovan Radinovic, retired Yugoslav army general (and former chief strategist): "We believed
NATO was using the KLA as its invasion force." Quoted in Daniel Pearl and Robert Block,
"Body Count: War in Kosovo Was Cruel, Bitter, Savage; Genocide It Wasn't," *Wall Street
Journal*, December 31, 1999. This version of events is largely—but not wholly—consistent

failing to comply with NATO demands and that he was willing to absorb them.[35] Nevertheless, in evaluating his willingness to absorb these costs, it is worth noting that Milosevic had compelling reasons to believe that the NATO bombing campaign would be short-lived and, thus, that the costs to be absorbed not especially significant.[36] As one British official put it, "they thought five cruise missiles would come floating down the road, and that was it. Even when I spoke to the Yugoslav Minister in London to reiterate the threat, he still had not taken it on board. He said: 'Two cruise missiles will not make us bow.'"[37] Lieutenant General Mike Short, U.S. Air Force—who directed the air campaign—likewise reported, "I was being told, again quote, 'Mike you're only going to bomb for two or three nights, that's all the Alliance can stand, that's all Washington can stand.'"[38]

Milosevic's Clarity—Magnified by Western Transparency

Recognition of Widespread Fears of Outflows

In stark contrast to NATO's self-acknowledged "dysfunction of imagination," Milosevic understood exactly what the West feared most—large-scale refugee flows and regional destabilization—because its key representatives had told him.[39] When queried about whether bombing might simply accelerate the rate of engineered migration in Kosovo, Richard Holbrooke responded, "That is our greatest fear by far."[40]

---

with remarks made to me during interviews conducted with former Clinton administration officials (one of whom maintained that the Serbs were implacably opposed to reaching an agreement) in July 2000 and May 2001, with an external member of the U.S. negotiating team in December 2000, and with German officials in July 1999.

[35] As Holbrooke himself recounts their last meeting on March 23, Milosevic knew he would be bombed. "There was no question in his mind what we would do." Quoted in Doyle McManus, "Debate Turns to Fingerpointing on Kosovo Policy," *Los Angeles Times,* April 11, 1999.

[36] Not only did Milosevic have reasons to believe the Europeans would not tolerate a protracted campaign, but he also may have had intelligence from French (and possibly Russian) sources that indicated that the target set would be narrow. See ibid.; Paul Beaver and David Montgomery, "Mystery Still Shrouds Downing of F-117A Fighter," *Janes' Defense Weekly,* September 1, 1999; Paul Beaver and David Montgomery, "Belgrade Got NATO Attack Plans from a Russian Spy," *Scotsman,* August 27, 1999; *Moral Combat.* As further evidence of intelligence leaks, consider that in a July 2000 interview, a U.S. Air Force colonel confirmed to me that such leaks probably played a material role in the downing of a F-117 during the bombing campaign.

[37] "Kosovo, the Untold Story."

[38] Quoted in *Moral Combat.*

[39] Ibid.; author interviews with German government officials in Sarajevo, Bosnia-Herzegovina, July 1999.

[40] Bronwen Maddox, Michael Evans, Anthony Lloyd, Tom Walker, and Daniel McGrory, "The 80 Days War," *Times,* July 15, 1999.

Moreover, Holbrooke's statement was hardly the first inkling Milosevic had gotten of Western apprehension over population outflows.[41] As outlined in chapter 1—and as Milosevic was no doubt aware—refugees had come to be most unwelcome sights in Western Europe since the numbers of asylum applicants had begun a steep and prolonged ascent in the mid-1980s. Fear and distrust of foreigners more generally had grown since then as well.[42] A review of seven *Eurobarometer* surveys reveals that the number of Europeans who believed there were too many "non-EU foreigners in their country" rose dramatically during the 1980s and 1990s, with clear majorities in Italy and Germany.[43] As early as 1992, even before outflows from the wars of Yugoslav dissolution began in earnest, public opinion polls indicated that 78 percent of Germans thought that immigration was the most pressing problem in their country.[44] Similarly, a 1992 study concluded that Greeks were more hostile to immigrants than other Europeans, a result bolstered by the 1997 *Eurobarometer,* which found that that 72 percent of Greeks "tended to agree" with the statement that "all illegals should be sent back to their country of origin without exception"—the highest percentage in all fifteen of the countries surveyed.[45]

Additional inflows from the Balkans were likely viewed as particularly unwelcome.[46] One British study found that 80 percent of the Kosovar refugees who fled to the United Kingdom between 1997 and 1999 were subject to hostility from sections of the British public and the press—and the United Kingdom is not even in the neighborhood.[47] In countries on

[41] Western fears about the consequences of Kosovar refugee flows had been appearing in the press since at least the start of the March 1998 offensive, when Strobe Talbott said, "one of the greatest fears in Washington about Serbian brutality against ethnic Albanians in the province of Kosovo is that violence could spread into Albania and neighboring Macedonia." Quoted in Jane Perlez, "US Official Asks Restraint by Albanians," *New York Times,* March 17, 1998.

[42] See, for instance, "Austria, Switzerland, and the Politics of Nationalism," *Global Intelligence Update: Weekly Analysis,* November 1, 1999, www.stratfor.com. See also, Jeanette Money, *Fences and Neighbors: The Political Geography of Immigration Control* (Ithaca, N.Y.: Cornell University Press, 1999). Consider as well the recent rise in popularity of anti-immigration parties throughout Western Europe.

[43] See Thomas F. Pettigrew, "Intergroup Contact Theory," *Annual Review of Psychology* 49 (1998): 65–85.

[44] This same poll indicated that over 60 percent of Germans wanted immigration reduced or stopped altogether. Philip L. Martin, "Germany: Reluctant Land of Immigration," in *Controlling Immigration: A Global Perspective,* ed. Wayne Cornelius, Philip L. Martin and James Hollifield (Stanford: Stanford University Press, 1994), 189.

[45] "Xenophobia and Racism in Greece, 1988–1992: A Comparative Approach and Some Hypotheses Based on *Eurobarometer* Data," unpublished manuscript, 1992, 321, cited in Katerina Linos, "Understanding Greek Immigration Policy," www.hks.harvard.edu/kokkalis/GSW3/Katerina_Linos.pdf.

[46] See, for instance, Jessika ter Wal, "Racism and Cultural Diversity in the Mass Media," 2002, http://eumc.eu.int/eumc/material/pub/media_report/MR-CH4-8-Italy.pdf.

[47] One national tabloid featured an article about migrants from Slovakia and Kosovo seeking asylum to exploit British welfare provisions and displaying threatening behavior when

the frontline, fear and hostility were, in some corners, particularly acute. As Marcello Foa, foreign editor of Italian newspaper *Il Giornale*, put it, "People are scared to see hundreds of thousands of people coming from Albania, where they are right now, into Italy. So in one way, Italy wants to fight against Milosevic. In the other way, the other public opinion [*sic*] wants to have some guarantees that these people will not come all to our country."[48]

The existence of this antipathy—particularly among Germans, Italians, and Greeks—would not have been lost on Milosevic, nor would its potential effects on the political fortunes of European leaders. Both sides were aware of the potential dangers of large-scale refugee flows, particularly since they had already begun to affect, albeit in a limited way, the political makeup of the continent.

Milosevic also recognized that many Western European leaders viewed outflows as a danger from a security as well as a political standpoint. With this in mind, he appears to have gambled that he could exploit the fears of those countries likely to suffer more acutely than others, as well as fears of those certain to suffer if the crisis spread beyond the Balkans.[49] Three NATO countries in particular appear to have been targeted, both because they were the likely recipients of refugees in the event of a mass outmigration and because of their publicly acknowledged domestic discomfort with, and discord over, the military tack NATO was taking.

Given their geographical propinquity, the Greeks were particularly alarmed about the prospect of NATO bombing. As one official presciently stated in late February 1999, "up to now, the Serbs have held back for fear of provoking a NATO attack. 'Once bombing starts, they could lose all restraint.'"[50] Moreover, Greek concerns about Balkan refugees did not commence with the Kosovo crisis. In fact, such anxieties manifested

---

good housing was not available. Alice Bloch, "Kosovan Refugees in the UK: The Rolls Royce or Rickshaw Reception?" *Forced Migration Review* no. 5 (1999).

[48] Quoted in Public Broadcasting Service, "Views from Abroad," *News Hour with Jim Lehrer*, April 8, 1999, http://www.pbs.org/newshour/bb/europe/jan-june99/international_40-8.html.

[49] As British Prime Minister Tony Blair proclaimed in the midst of the Kosovo conflict, "when oppression produces massive flows of refugees which unsettle neighboring countries then they can properly be described as 'threats to international peace and security.'" "Doctrine of the International Community," transcript of a speech given before the Chicago Council of Economists, April 24, 1999, www.number10.gov.uk/Page1297.

[50] See Wood, "Regional Tensions," 20. The article goes on to note that the Greeks believed that bombing "would send refugees into Macedonia and Albania, filling camps with dispossessed ethnic Albanians bent on revenge. Albania is already highly unstable. Problems there, especially given the availability of weapons, would add to a separatist campaign by ethnic Albanians in Macedonia. Diplomats fear that such a conflict could see neighbouring states revive territorial claims: the Greeks to southern Albania, the Serbs to northern Macedonia and the Bulgarians to western Macedonia. It is not simply Kosovo which is at stake" (20).

themselves even before the Yugoslav wars of dissolution erupted. In 1991, in response to a sudden influx of (mostly Albanian) migrants, the sitting conservative government passed a highly restrictive law regulating the entry and exit, presence, work, and expulsion of foreigners.[51] But measures that could (at least in principle) keep out illegal immigrants could not be readily deployed against those seeking refuge and asylum. As Margarita Kondopoulou has observed:

> A large share of the [Greek] media at the time of the Kosovo crisis did not conceal their apparent concern about the influx of Albanians from Kosovo into Greece and Albania. And this concern at certain points reached the level of hysteria.
> Hostility toward Albanians in general was obvious in several news articles, particularly in right-wing newspapers, which, as mentioned above, warned about the "influx" of massive numbers of Albanians into the country, with whom the Greeks would have to deal for an indefinite period of time. Also, the presence of refugees in Albania would, according to some nationalistic voices, lead to disturbances in many Greek-dominated villages.[52]

In short, its extant anti-immigrant measures would be of little help to Greece in combating a sudden and massive influx and of no assistance at all should the conflict in Kosovo spark a wider and potentially destabilizing regional conflict. This was a refrain that was common among Greek politicians and diplomats in the period leading up to the bombing campaign, and it was a fear that the Serbs were happy to stoke.[53]

Germany, after having taken in 350,000 Bosnians during the last Yugoslav war—more than all other EU member states combined—likewise feared it would bear the brunt of a full-scale crisis in Kosovo. As one diplomat described the situation, "Germany feels that the rest of Europe is not pulling its weight. It wants its partners to see this as a European problem, not as a German problem."[54] Thus, while the talks at Rambouillet talks were foundering, Germany was hosting its own unsuccessful summit, a futile attempt to generate support for European refugee burden-sharing initiatives.[55] Indeed, as Brian Rathbun (quoting former German Deputy

[51] Linos, "Understanding Greek Immigration Policy."
[52] Margarita Kondopoulou, "The Greek Media and the Kosovo Crisis," *Conflict & Communication Online 1* (2002), 7, www.cco.regener-online.de/2002_2/pdf_2002_2/kondopoulou.pdf.
[53] See, for instance, Wood, "Regional Tensions."
[54] Ibid. Unfortunately for Germany, its "partners" did not share its view.
[55] European Commission burden-sharing proposals were rejected by France, the United Kingdom, and Spain. Emma Tucker, "Bonn Fears It May Be Left to Shoulder Burden of Refugees," *Financial Times*, February 16, 1999.

Foreign Minister Ludger Volmer) has noted, "Milosevic had set his sights on Germany from the beginning as a potential weak link" in the alliance. For one thing, "Germany, by virtue of its geographic position, was likely to be more tangibly affected by the conflict."[56] For another, there was tremendous concern that a bombing campaign could split the sitting coalition government. As one party conference report put it, "It is not the fate of Kosovo that will be decided in Kosovo, but the fate of the Greens."[57] There was, moreover, "another factor—the refugees," according to Joachim Falenski, advisor to the Christian Democratic Union (CDU) defense minister.[58] As Hanns Maull put it, after their experience during the Bosnian War, German authorities were especially "alarmed at the possibility of another influx of refugees." "Clearly, this was where most Kosovars would have wanted to go if they were unable to return. Many had relatives in Germany, and many more saw Germany as their destination of choice."[59]

Milosevic also appears to have bargained that Italy too might try to forestall a NATO bombing campaign. This may have seemed especially likely in the wake of the mass migration of Albanians across the Adriatic in 1997, following the collapse of Albania in the wake of the pyramid-scheme debacle. Memories of that recent crisis—and the Italian public's hostile response to it (the influx was often referred to in the press as "an invasion"[60])—would have been sharpened by reflection on the weak support provided by its allies during that crisis.[61] As Oswaldo Croci puts it:

> More precisely, [Italian Prime Minister Massimo] D'Alema confronted the following difficulties. First, [there was] the heterogeneous composition of his coalition government.... Within his own party, moreover, there was a left wing still sceptical of NATO and susceptible to anti-American rhetoric. Second, the existence of a traditional pacificist movement linked to the Church and Catholic associations. Third, public opinion that in the long run was likely to be negatively influenced by the proximity of the war. Some Italians

---

[56] Rathbun, *Partisan Interventions*, 117.

[57] Report cited in Jeffrey Lantis, "The Moral Imperative of Force: The Evolution of German Strategic Culture in Kosovo," *Comparative Strategy* 21 (2002): 33.

[58] Rathbun, *Partisan Interventions*, 118.

[59] Hanns W. Maull, "Germany and the Use of Force: Still a Civilian Power?" *Trierer Arbeitspapiere zur Internationalen Politik* 2 (November 1999), 19.

[60] Guilio Perrone, "Racism without Races: Stereotypes and Prejudice in the Immigration towards the Puglia Region," *L'Emigrato* 95(1998): 11–12.

[61] Ter Wal, "Racism and Cultural Diversity"; Jason Lee, "Portrait of a Young Italy: Asylum Practice and Public Opinion," *Contemporary Topics in Forced Migration* 4 (2005), 2–9, http://www.ccis-ucsd.org/fml/wrkg4_fml.pdf. As noted in chapter 1, the Italian government was forced to unilaterally launch Operation Alba to help staunch the outflow because Britain and Germany vetoed their own involvement and that of the European Union as a whole. See, for instance, Andrew Gumbel, "Italy Ready for Mission Impossible; Intervention in Albania Could Bring Instability to Rome," *Independent*, April 7, 1997.

could, after all, literally see and hear the war, since most of the sorties were taking off from bases in Italy.[62]

With that background in mind, D'Alema met with President Clinton in early March 1999 and reportedly asked skeptically about contingencies if NATO air strikes failed to subdue Milosevic. "The result, Mr. D'Alema said, would be 300,000 to 400,000 refugees passing into Albania and cross-ing the Adriatic into Italy. 'What will happen then?'" Reportedly, the only Clinton administration answer was, "'We'll keep on bombing.'"[63] Such an answer provided small comfort to the Italian leader, who then reiterated his concern publicly on March 24, requesting that his "European partners 'not leave Italy alone in the face of a possible humanitarian catastrophe.' Even if 'the refugee emergency' was going to be a problem primarily for Italy, it should be treated as a European problem."[64]

In short, the general belief of the leaders in all three of these frontline states was that escalating the crisis in Kosovo promised each of them concentrated costs—including the possibility of an end to their political tenures—and few, if any benefits.

Manipulating and Exploiting the Existence of Discord

Milosevic was aware of the underlying disagreements within NATO about the right tack to pursue in Kosovo,[65] both because they were regu-larly noted in the press during the lead-up to the conflict[66] and because the

[62] Oswaldo Croci, "Forced Ally? Italy and 'Operation Allied Force,'" in *Italian Politics: The Faltering Transition* (London: Berghahn Books, 2000), 42.

[63] Elaine Sciolino and Ethan Bronner, "The Road to War: How a President, Distracted by Scandal, Entered Balkan War," *New York Times*, April 18, 1999.

[64] Croci, Forced Ally?" 41.

[65] That Milosevic played close attention to what appeared in the Western press is clear. Consider, for instance, that in an April interview Milosevic noted that Kissinger had declared Rambouillet "a mechanism for the permanent creation of problems and confrontations" and suggested, "President Clinton should have listened to this wise geopolitical expert rather than some of his own less knowledgeable advisers." Arnaud de Borchgrave, "We Are nei-ther Angels nor Devils: An Interview with Slobodan Milosevic," United Press International, April 30, 1999. It is likewise known that the Serbs engaged in textual analysis of documents and therefore could have expected the West would do the same, thereby actually getting the messages it seems that Belgrade attempted to send. For instance, one article in the Serbian state-run paper attempts to deconstruct the NATO joint statement about operations in Ko-sovo and notes, "It is interesting in this unusually long statement, they permanently speak about 'innocent Kosovo civilians.' In previous NATO documents, in each sentence they used the term 'ethnic Albanians.'" "NATO Ministers Free Themselves of a Responsibility by Lies," *TANJUG*, April 13, 1999.

[66] See, for instance, Lucio Caracciolo's commentary in *La Repubblica*, October 12, 1998, in which—writing from the "front-line European country into which Albanian refugees will pour"—he notes that NATO was about to enter a war against Yugoslavia "without anybody, on either side of the Atlantic, having clear ideas about the objectives or the consequences of

Yugoslavs had "friends" within the alliance.[67] Milosevic appears to have attempted to intensify intra-alliance discord by fueling the unease that existed within some European countries about the militant stance taken by the United States. As the Serbian state-run TANJUG News Service reported of Rambouillet, "it could be clearly seen that 'the Americans and the English' stick fast, and completely to a military, militant option, while, on the other hand, considerable wavering has arisen, above all, among the Italians. But it was observable also with the Frenchmen and Germans."[68] In addition, as a further indication that Milosevic might have viewed Italy as particularly vulnerable to these tactics, in the first weeks of the war— during Milosevic's self-declared ceasefire—an open letter to the Italian government was published in the state-run newspaper, entreating the Italians to "show they were better than fascists" and renounce the "military aggression" being pursued by "American-NATO."[69] Public opinion data, gathered between March 25 and 28, 1999, support this surmise—at the outset of the bombing campaign, only 27 percent of Italians and 56 percent of Germans said the "airstrikes were justified," whereas Greeks simply condemned the bombing outright.[70] Pro-Serb Greek media also provided "frequently-live broadcast coverage of numerous protest marches and concerts jointly organized by political parties (mainly opposition parties), workers' unions, other activists and groups, as well as the Greek Orthodox Church, [which] demonstrated a united Greek opposition front."[71]

Exacerbating Fears

It appears that Belgrade also sought to sow cross-Atlantic divisions by reiterating the suggestion that the Europeans had a better appreciation of the possible refugee-generating consequences of NATO action than did the Americans. The West had broadcast its fears about the consequences of refugee flows to Milosevic, and he, members of his government, and his press representatives responded with vague and not-so-vague promises to realize them. An open letter by a Serb columnist, published in a

---

a military intervention unprecedented in Europe in this second half of the century." Quoted in Alexander Chancellor, "Fear of Bombing," *Slate*, October 14, 1998, http://www.slate.com/id/4101/. See also Arkin, "Operation Allied Force."

[67] As one well-placed NATO source put it, "Milosevic knew more about our thinking than we wanted [him] to. In a coalition war, more people get told things than they should. We don't think there was an agent, it could just have been clever Serbian intelligence, but he knew more than he should, put it that way." Quoted in Peter Beaumont and Patrick Wintour, "Leaks in NATO—and Plan Bravo Minus," *Observer*, July 18, 1999.

[68] "Seselj: Contact Group's Goals Not Reached," *TANJUG*, February 28, 1999.

[69] "Open letter to Scalfaro, D'Alema, and Dini," *TANJUG*, April 9, 1999.

[70] Public opinion data from Ispo/Cra Neilsen (Italy); *Sueddeutche Zeitung* (Germany); and Institute V-PRC, ALKO (Greece).

[71] Kondopoulou, "Greek Media," 6.

state-owned newspaper in early March, is illustrative.[72] The letter began by noting that, "there are not only cracks in the Contact Group but fundamental differences in opinion on the crisis and the possible solution" and proceeded to argue that:

> The perspective on Albanians can't be the same from Washington where they arrive with pockets full of dollars intended for certain senators and other individuals, and the perspective from let's say Rome where you can see boats full of desperate and aggressive Albanian immigrants along with Shiptar mafia, which is according to the documentation of Italian authorities already overpowering some Sicilian clans. The situation is similar in Germany, France and even Great Britain where...*The Economist* reports under the alarming headline "Tirana on Thames" that Albanians organized by their narco-bosses are flooding the "Proud Albion" under the pretext of political asylum.[73]

The columnist took aim at the more proximate FRY neighbors as well, noting that Europeans should be "concerned because Americans support Albanians and their extreme demands thus *creating grounds for a permanent crisis that could easily spread to Macedonia, Greece and trigger Turkish involvement in the Balkan boiling pot.*"[74] A day earlier, another columnist in another state-run newspaper, offered similar warnings:

> It's not a question of ordinary local conflicts or instability that they are provoking in Yugoslavia. It's about *a real possibility of expanding the war beyond Yugoslav borders.* In this conflict between ethnic groups and religious elements, the essential part have political games in the process which are also included [sic] NATO, so-called Contact Group (France, Great Britain, Italy, Germany, Russia) and one actor in the group that is acting for its own benefit: USA....Within all that, what is noticeable is that a military disposing [sic] is underway, and somebody will have to pay for it one day....[The] failure of the discussion in Rambouillet is *an introduction to the new migration wave, which benefits to regional disintegration as well as to stimulating xenophobic elements present in the conflict.*[75]

The columnist continued by warning that "Kosovo represents a strategic zone of terrorism and drug trade....It is well known that this

---

[72] I make a logical jump here in assuming that a column in the state-run press can reasonably be expected to reflect the views and attitudes of the government.

[73] Dusko Vojnovic, "American and European View on Kosovo and Metohia—Reasons for Differences and Disputes," *TANJUG*, March 5, 1999.

[74] Ibid.

[75] Juan Pablo Cordoba Elias, "The Reform: US Political Games on Kosovo and Metohia," *Politika*, March 4, 1999.

terroristic internal structure was supported by Albanian communist leader Enver Hoxha...(and) if we add to all this the fact that the terrorists are mostly Moslems, it seams [sic] that things are getting to quite another dimension."[76] This was a masterful piece of fear mongering, custom-tailored to push the buttons of anxious western European politicians: the threat from Kosovo is not only refugees, but communist, drug-trading, Islamic, terrorist refugees.

The federal government in Belgrade also offered more direct warnings of impending humanitarian disaster and of the potential spreadability of the conflict. On March 20—the day OSCE observers withdrew from Kosovo—the government published an open letter in the state-run press indicating that "all those threatening to use force against our country must face the responsibility for the consequences of humanitarian problems, which might arise as a result of the use of such force." The letter further suggested that the "build-up of foreign troops on the border of the FRY as well as the public threats of NATO aggression against our country...could pose a threat to peace and security in the wider region of South Eastern Europe," a fear that had been publicly enunciated and was widely shared in the West.[77] A day earlier, a letter from the FRY foreign minister prevailed on the then president of the UN Security Council to call for the withdrawal of NATO troops from the borders of the FRY, which would "contribute to the reduction of tensions and the elimination of unforeseen threats to peace and security in the region."[78]

Milosevic himself issued some warnings and threats, particularly to Germany, Italy, Greece, and neighboring Macedonia. For instance, he told German Foreign Minister Joschka Fischer in early March 1999 "that he could empty Kosovo within a week."[79] Similar warnings were issued to Italian Foreign Minister Lamberto Dini.[80] The day before the bombing started, Milosevic also threatened in an open letter that "anyone who tries to impose solutions by force will have to take the responsibility for actions against the policy of peace and face the ensuing consequences."[81] But it was Vojislav Seselj, "the rabidly nationalist" Serb deputy prime minister, who was clearest about what the Serbs were prepared to do in the event of a NATO attack. Speaking at a rally, Seselj warned that any bombs would be met by a Serb attack on Kosovo and that "not a single Albanian would remain if NATO bombed." And just four days prior, Lieutenant General Nebojsa Pavkovic,

[76] Ibid.
[77] "Yugoslav Government Condemns NATO Threats of Aggression," *TANJUG*, March 20, 1999. See Perlez, "US Official Asks Restraint by Albanians."
[78] "Minister Jovanovic Writes to Security Council and OSCE," *TANJUG*, March 19, 1999.
[79] Lara Marlowe, "War and Peace Revisited," *Irish Times*, March 25, 2000.
[80] "Minister Jovanovic."
[81] "Milosevic Receives Holbrooke, Hill, Petritsch, and Mayorsky," *TANJUG*, March 23, 1999.

commander of the Third Army in Kosovo, warned that if they were attacked, "Yugoslavia will deal with the remaining terrorists in Kosovo."[82]

Thus, it is reasonable to conclude that, between the end of the Rambouillet Conference on February 22 and the start of NATO bombing on March 24, Belgrade attempted to signal to the West that it would respond with force if provoked and would do so in a way designed to create fear and provoke panic in potential refugee-receiving states. Granted, some of the threats issued were vague, and others could have been easily construed as swagger or domestic propaganda. But it is also true that Milosevic realized that such threats would have real resonance in certain NATO capitals and neighboring countries.[83] Moreover, it is clear that some leaders *did* understand these signals. In addition to the concerns voiced by the Greeks and Italians, both President Milan Kučan of Slovenia and President Kiro Gligorov of Macedonia warned NATO that Milosevic might resort to mass expulsions.[84]

Even the independent Yugoslav media understood that Milosevic had an appreciation for the influential power of strategic expulsions. Three days after the bombings started, Belgrade-based journalist Braca Grubacic wrote in his column, "Milosevic will try to destabilize the entire southern Balkans and expand the conflict to Macedonia, Bosnia, and Albania in order to scare his adversaries in NATO. He intends to expel a large number of Albanians from Kosovo in order to provoke a reaction from Western Europe, which already does not know what to do what the masses of Albanian refugees and fake asylum seekers."[85] In addition, General Wesley Clark—at least after the fact—claimed that by Rambouillet those in Washington began to ask "the right questions," including, "What if the Serbs follow through on threats to take revenge on Albanian civilians?"[86] This statement by Clark implies two important things: first, that Milosevic and/or his proxies had articulated threats to launch outflows in a transparent enough manner that at least some in Washington recognized that he was trying to influence their behavior; and second, that at the end of February 1998, civilian-directed attacks had not yet begun in a systematic way, despite later claims to the contrary.

Signals Sent, but Not Received?

Despite the variety of threats and admonitions from Belgrade, worried queries from potential receiving states, and direct warnings from Yugoslav neighboring states, NATO nevertheless failed to prepare for the possibility

---

[82] "Kosovo, the Untold Story."
[83] See again Rathbun, *Partisan Interventions*, 118.
[84] Garton Ash, "The War We Almost Lost."
[85] Quoted in Judah, *Kosovo*, 242.
[86] Clark, *Waging Modern War*, 164.

that Milosevic might resort to the use of refugees as asymmetric weapons in any concerted fashion. Nicholas Morris, UNHCR special envoy, notes,

> Like almost every Western decision maker and commentator, and indeed like most Kosovan Albanians, UNHCR did not predict the mass expulsion of the majority of the ethnic Albanian population of Kosovo. That we were in such company is no excuse. However, in the days before the exodus began, the international community, particularly the Western governments, were banking on peace, and urging UNHCR to get prepared to the early implementation of the Rambouillet Accords.[87]

"There were a lot of Milosevic watchers who said a few bombs might do it [lead him to capitulate]. . . . What was not assumed, and not postulated was that he would try to empty the country of its ethnic majority," acknowledged another senior NATO official.[88] And the forewarned Joschka Fischer later said that "he regretted not having taken Milosevic seriously" when the Yugoslav leader said he could empty Kosovo in short order.[89] As French Foreign Minister Hubert Vedrine admitted, "What we had expected was the Serb army to attack all KLA positions, and for the KLA to launch a guerrilla war. That's what we thought. And most experts thought the KLA would have held out for longer. What most experts underestimated was that the collective memory of massacres in the Balkans was such as to unleash mass migrations."[90]

More significantly, however, NATO's failure to comprehend that Milosevic was engaged in coercive engineered migration demonstrates one reason why Milosevic's attempt to deter the alliance was destined to fail. As Schelling notes, "one needs the adversary to understand what behavior of his will cause the violence to be inflicted and what will cause it to be withheld. The victim has to know what is wanted, and he may have to be assured of what is not wanted."[91] Because NATO had crafted but one scenario—in which Milosevic's diplomatic intransigence would give way to retreat and deal-cutting once the stakes were raised—there was no room for bargaining, a key feature of successful coercion.[92]

---

[87] Nicholas Morris, "UNHCR and Kosovo: A Personal View from within UNHCR," *Forced Migration Review* no. 5 (1999) This view of events is supported by the fact that only one week into the bombing the alliance was running short of cruise missiles and had found that its stockpiled food aid in Kosovo was now behind enemy lines. See, for instance, Mary Dejevsky, "Will America Crack? While the US Stands High in Military Might, on the Human Front It Is Finitely Vulnerable," *Independent*, April 2, 1999.

[88] Quoted in Elaine Sciolino and Ethan Bronner, "The Road to War: How a President, Distracted by Scandal, Entered Balkan War," *New York Times*, April 18, 1999.

[89] Marlowe, "War and Peace Revisited."

[90] Vedrine, quoted in "Kosovo, the Untold Story."

[91] Schelling, *Arms and Influence*, 3.

[92] Even a month into the conflict, NATO leaders were unwilling to acknowledge that events might have gone differently if they had been willing to negotiate. At the NATO

In the end, although Milosevic got little of what he desired, he did receive a better deal than the one on offer at Rambouillet.[93] The question is,
if NATO had listened to the signals emanating from Belgrade and more
realistically evaluated its foe, would it have been better able to assess ex
ante what the final deal would cost? Evidence suggests the answer is yes.[94]
As Kevin Tebbit, the permanent under secretary at the British Ministry of
Defense, acknowledged: "The aim was to persuade him that he had miscalculated. It was designed as a deterrent—a coercive use of bombing. It
was never intended as straight war fighting. The speed with which he unleashed the ethnic cleansing took us all by surprise. We did not foresee he
would move so thoroughly and so fast. I have asked myself since whether
we should have predicted more precisely."[95] And again, although he may
have been playing Monday morning quarterback, General Clark suggests
some did exactly that. In recounting a prewar discussion with Madeleine
Albright, Clark says that he told the Secretary of State point blank that, if
NATO bombed, the Serbs would attack the civilian population because
that is "what they are promising to do....It will just be a race, our air
strikes and the damage we cause them against what they can do on the
ground. But in the short term, they can win the race."[96]

Deterrence Begets Compellence: Why the Campaign
Expanded after Bombing Commenced

Milosevic Ups the Ante

Despite claims to the contrary at the time, most now agree that the NATO
bombing campaign provided motivation and opportunity for wider and
more savage operations by Yugoslav forces than were originally envi-

---

summit in Washington, reporter Jim Hoagland asked the foreign ministers of Britain, France,
and Germany what they would change or do differently in Kosovo with the benefit of hindsight. "Their separate answers were terrifyingly uniform: They could think of nothing that
the international community could have done to change the course of events." Joschka Fischer went farther and said, "It was only in going through the experience of discovering
that Milosevic was capable of this...that we have arrived at the support we have in our
democratic societies for what we are doing now. I don't accept that it was a miscalculation."
Quoted in Hoagland, "Misreading Milosevic."
[93] Notably, in the end Milosevic got an agreement policed by the UN (not NATO) only in
Kosovo (not throughout the FRY), and the (impending) referendum was then taken off the
table for the indefinite future. See Posen, "War for Kosovo"; Judah, *Kosovo.*
[94] See, for instance, Barutciski, "Western Diplomacy," for a discussion of how the West
failed to exhaust the possible diplomatic options before resorting to force and the high costs
of doing so. See also House of Commons Select Committee on Foreign Affairs, "Fourth
Report."
[95] "Kosovo, the Untold Story."
[96] Clark, *Waging Modern War,* 171.

sioned. Unable to deter NATO, evidence suggests Milosevic switched tacks and tried to compel the alliance to stop bombing by forcing on it a dose of what it purportedly "feared most," namely, a massive refugee crisis. Although evidence is circumstantial, it appears Milosevic calculated that once the bombing started his best chance of success was to push forward with great alacrity to his primary objective of crushing the KLA—recognizing that doing so would generate a non-trivial number of refugees—and then to sue for peace and bargain from a position of relative strength.[97] (As the analysis that follows indicates, the patterns and timing of the population outflows are consistent with such a strategy.)

Evidence suggests Milosevic was gambling on the prospect that by that time discord and conflict within NATO[98]—and in the court of public opinion—would entice the alliance to deal, due to the heterogeneity of opinion among the alliance partners on two distinct fronts: bombing and refugee flows.[99] The U.S. Department of Defense even conceded as much in late 1999 in its *Kosovo After Action Report*, in which it noted that, "unable to challenge superior allied military capabilities directly," one of the "indirect means" of influence Milosevic employed was the intentional "creation of enormous refugee flows to create a humanitarian crisis."[100] Milosevic's offer to withdraw some troops from Kosovo on April 3,[101] followed by his decision to declare a unilateral ceasefire on April 6—coupled with his announcement that he had by that point achieved his objectives vis-à-vis the KLA—further suggests this was his intention.

Whatever his intentions, Milosevic's task became even more difficult once NATO bombing commenced because the stakes and the costs of backing down had changed for both sides. Exacting the desired response through compellence is, as a rule, more difficult than through deterrence because the costs of complying with the demands of the other side rise significantly. In contrast to deterrent threats, compellent actions more directly engage the prestige and passions of the put-upon states; in compellence, a state has "publicly committed its prestige and resources to a given line of conduct" that it is now asked to abandon.[102] Milosevic failed to appreciate

---

[97] "BETA Examines Milosevic's Kosovo Options," BETA News Service, March 4, 1999, offers a prescient echo of this theory, although it also predicts Milosevic would attempt to partition northern Kosovo, which did not happen.

[98] President Clinton himself acknowledged the conflicting domestic pressures and prerogatives facing NATO members in an early April press conference. "Crisis in The Balkans: President's Strategy: 'Our Plan Is to Persist Until We Prevail,'" *New York Times*, April 5, 1999.

[99] Lamberto Dini's postconflict acknowledgement that his government had been approached with a bilateral offer by Milosevic in April 1999 further supports this proposition.

[100] DOD, "Joint Statement on the Kosovo After Action Review."

[101] See, for instance, "Kosovo, the Untold Story."

[102] Robert Art, "The Functions of Force," *International Politics*, ed. Robert Art and Robert Jervis (New York: Harper-Collins, 1996), 159.

the magnitude of the task he set before himself because he did not or could not fathom the new and complex interplay that would be born of compellence. Although NATO shortsightedness may have led to a failure of deterrence, Milosevic's mistaken gamesmanship led to a conflict of greater ferocity than either side foresaw at the outset.

Timing and Pattern of Outflows

When Did the Expulsions Begin?

The assertion that Milosevic's campaign shifted to one in which he unleashed "demographic bombs" against NATO staging areas in Macedonia and Albania only *after* bombing commenced is borne out by several facts.[103] First, on March 22—two days *before* the alliance launched its airstrikes—in tacit acknowledgment that cleansing had *not* begun in earnest, NATO officials asked the KLA "to desist from terrorist attacks against Serbs in Kosovo so as to not give Belgrade a pretext to engage in ethnic cleansing."[104] Second, the first reports of mass expulsions began to emerge only *after* bombing had been under way for several days.[105] Third, significant numbers of refugees did not appear on the borders of Albania and Macedonia until several days after bombing began.[106] Indeed, two days after the bombing started, the UNHCR representative in Tirana gave a briefing to diplomats, local UN staff, and the director of the Albanian government Office for Refugees. They discussed the few recent arrivals (of which there had been none that day) and the state of preparedness of the organization. No one present expressed concerns or indicated they believed an impending crisis was brewing.[107] Fourth, the pattern and timing of outflows indicate that the expulsions were dictated (at least at the

---

[103] Although this was unequivocally not so when I first wrote about this case in 2000, this assertion is now relatively uncontroversial. For a more complete analysis of the timing and pattern of the outflows and killings, see Kelly M. Greenhill, "The Use of Refugees as Political and Military Weapons in the Kosovo Conflict," in *Yugoslavia Unraveled: Sovereignty, Self-Determination, and Intervention*, ed. Raju G. C. Thomas, 205–42 (Lanham: Rowman and Littlefield, 2003).

[104] Quoted in Christopher Layne, "Collateral Damage in Kosovo," *NATO's Empty Victory* (Washington, D.C.: CATO Institute, 2000), 52–53. See also Steven Erlanger, "US Issues Appeal to Serbs to Halt Attacks in Kosovo," *New York Times*, March 23, 1999.

[105] See, for instance, Layne, "Collateral Damage in Kosovo"; Paul Watson, "Airstrikes May Be Triggering New Massacres," *Los Angeles Times*, March 27, 1999; Jane Perlez, "US Stealth Fighter Is Down in Yugoslavia as NATO Orders Attacks on Serb Army Units: 'Ethnic Cleansing,'" *New York Times*, March 28, 1999.

[106] The OSCE cites UNHCR figures indicating that there were only 69,500 refugees throughout the region before March 24 but a total of 247,000 a week later and 450,000 four days after that. *Kosovo/Kosova*, 1:99.

[107] Judah, *Kosovo*, 239–40.

beginning of the war) by strategic and tactical requirements, as the following analysis indicates.

Patterns of Refugee Outflows

Statistical analyses of outflow patterns demonstrate that they occurred in three distinct pulses separated by periods of relatively light activity: Phase One, March 24–April 6, when most refugees came from western and southwestern Kosovo; Phase Two, April 7–April 23, when most refugees fled from the northern and central municipalities; and Phase Three, April 24–May 11, when most refugees hailed from western and southern municipalities.[108]

PHASE ONE   The first refugee pulse (which started on March 24, when the bombing started, and continued until April 6, when Milosevic declared his Orthodox Easter ceasefire) included the heaviest flow of the conflict, with migration concentrated in the Pec-Prizren corridor.[109] The nature of Phase One flows offers strong circumstantial evidence that Milosevic's initial campaign was directed at the KLA, first and foremost. NATO perhaps inadvertently acknowledged as much at the end of this phase when it accused Milosevic of continuing to "conduct counterinsurgency sweeps" in spite of his unilaterally declared ceasefire.[110] Outflows were particularly heavy in municipalities that were areas of strategic significance (along the Albanian border);[111] many were also known KLA strongholds, and they were all heavily targeted.

In addition, sending refugees across the borders to potential NATO staging areas also appears to have been a tactical objective during this initial pulse of expulsions.[112] FRY forces effectively emptied two cities (Pec

[108] See Patrick Ball, "Policy or Panic? The Flight of Ethnic Albanians from Kosovo, March–May 1999," http://hrdata.aaas.org/kosovo/policyorpanic/. This quantitative analysis is roughly consistent with my own qualitative assessment, derived from an examination of a variety of U.S. and European news sources; State Department, UNHCR, and OSCE documents; and reports from human rights organizations.

[109] Ibid. Other areas were also targeted—in particular, Kosovo Mitrovica and Pristina—although less intensively.

[110] See Thomas W. Lippman, "NATO Expands Fleet of Aircraft; Refugees Reappear at Kosovo Borders; NATO to Expand Fleet of Warplanes," *Washington Post*, April 11, 1999.

[111] Pec, Djakovica, and Prizren all sit on the border with Albania, and the main road through southwest Kosovo flows through Suva Reka. Djakovica, Orohovac, Suva Reka, and Pec were also known to have strong KLA presences. Prizren did not, although its strategic significance—straddling both the Albanian and Macedonian borders—made control of this municipality critical. Moreover, it is possible that a number of Prizren residents may have fled the KLA rather than the Serbs because the OSCE recorded numerous KLA attacks against perceived Serb loyalists; *Kosovo/Kosova*, chap. 5 (The Municipalities).

[112] In fact, we could make an argument that this was really the only intent of the expulsions. The expulsions, however, were for the most part not random; rather, they targeted

and Prizren) and more than 500 square miles of territory. This greatly surprised and unnerved NATO and the neighboring states of the FRY, including Macedonia, which shut its border until the alliance promised to airlift out of the region almost 100,000 refugees and to provide it with significant financial and logistical assistance.[113]

PHASE TWO   By the middle of Phase Two (roughly from April 7 to April 23), it is harder to interpret exactly what was happening, but what evidence exists suggests that Milosevic was probably still manipulating outflows in a tactically, if not strategically, significant way.[114] Migration was concentrated most heavily in the northern and central municipalities, although significant movements of people continued in areas previously targeted in the southwest.[115] Many of the municipalities targeted in Phase Two also hosted a significant KLA presence, particularly Srbica in the central Drenica region, which according to the OSCE, had been "a heartland" of KLA activity since its inception.[116] Outflows were also episodically stopped and restarted, as well as directed toward and away from particular border crossings.[117]

PHASE THREE   By the beginning of Phase Three (from roughly April 24, which coincided with the fiftieth NATO anniversary summit and the expansion of the NATO target set to include Milosevic personally, to May 11, when Milosevic lost his most important ally, Russia), Milosevic probably realized that the refugee gambit was going to fail—particularly after the NATO summit provided persuasive evidence that the alliance was not going to crumble, at least not imminently. During this phase, refugees came primarily from areas in the south and southwest, and included particularly heavy flows from Prizren. Flows were more modest than they had been previously, probably in large part because so many people had already fled.[118]

KLA strongholds and supposed sympathizers. Moreover, they appeared to be in large part orchestrated movements—they ebbed and flowed, shifted trajectories, and concentrations—and not simply an uncontrolled flood across the border.

[113] See the appendix; Michael Barutciski and Astri Suhrke, "Lessons from the Kosovo Refugee Crisis: Innovations in Protection and Burden-Sharing," *Journal of Refugee Studies* 14 (2001): 95–115; "Macedonia Fears It Could Become KLA Staging Ground," CNN, April 16, 1999.

[114] During this phase, flows were greatest from Kosovska Mitrovica and its southern neighbors, Vucitrn and Srbica, as well as from Kosovo Polje, Lipljan, and Istok, slightly further south and west.

[115] Ball, *Policy or Panic?* pt. 2.

[116] *Kosovo/Kosova*, chap. 5 (The Municipalities), Srbica.

[117] See, for instance, "Abrupt Stop in Refugee Flows Raises Fear," UN Wire, April 20, 1999.

[118] It is difficult to analyze the pattern of expulsions in Phase Three because almost 50 percent of those who crossed the border during this period had left their homes before April 24. See Ball, *Policy or Panic?* pt. 2.

Timing of Outflows

The timing of the observed population movements in Kosovo provide evidence that the FRY controlled the migrations to a large extent, starting and stopping them when necessary in an attempt to compel NATO to halt the bombing.[119] For instance, Phase One began with the start of the NATO bombing campaign and ended with Milosevic's self-declared Orthodox Easter ceasefire, at which time the ebbing flow of refugees was stanched by the surprise closure of the border. As suggested earlier, Milosevic may have hoped that NATO would accept a compromise at this point because it had been unable to stop FRY forces or to save the Kosovar Albanians from large-scale expulsions. As one observer noted when evaluating the state of play during this period:

> With help from Russian Prime Minister [Yevgeny] Primakov, Milosevic has begun a diplomatic counteroffensive aimed at making himself appear reasonable, even moderate. It is a measure that can hardly fail to sap NATO's already uncertain resolve. And for good measure, he has made a new friend in Iraqi President Sadaam Hussein [sic]—a leader well schooled in the art of turning military defeat into political triumph.[120]

Following the unequivocal rebuff by NATO of his ceasefire overture, Milosevic reopened the border on April 10,[121] at which time he reinforced the perception that he controlled targeted "demographic bombs" in the form of groups of refugees occasionally released for the final trek to a border crossing.[122] Observers on the ground sensed that there was "clear management of the flow of refugees."[123] FRY forces marched them around Kosovo in seemingly random patterns. As part of this herding, it is likely that refugees were used as human shields to protect FRY forces and materiel and to keep communication routes open.[124] They also were likely used to send signals to NATO that Milosevic, not the alliance, controlled the situation on the ground.

Finally, it is worth noting that no noteworthy flows occurred after early May, which for numerous reasons was probably when it became clear to Milosevic that it was time to make a deal.[125] First, the G-8 talks during the

---

[119] See, for instance, Thomas W. Lippman and Bradley Graham, "NATO Takes New Look at Options for Invasion," *Washington Post*, April 22, 1999.

[120] See Carnes Lord, "What Milosevic Really Wants."

[121] See Ball, *Policy or Panic?* pt. 2; John Gaps, "Allies Add Air Power; 600 Jets Deployed; More Refugees Flee," *Chicago Sun-Times*, April 11, 1999.

[122] Ball, *Policy or Panic?* pt. 2.

[123] Ibid., 110.

[124] See, for instance, *Kosovo/Kosova*, pt. 1, esp. 104–11.

[125] On May 10, Milosevic announced an end to attacks on the KLA, claiming that some units of the army and police were being withdrawn. NATO, however, disputed this claim.

first week in May had generated the broad outlines of a settlement that both Russia and the West were willing to consider.[126] (And after four days of secret meetings with Peter Castenfelt, Swedish financier, Milosevic could have been in little doubt of the Russians' intentions.[127]) Second, even the humiliating bombing of the Chinese Embassy on May 7 failed to crack NATO unity and resolve. Third, on May 13 President Boris Yeltsin replaced Prime Minister Primakov (a staunch supporter of the Serbs), which sent a clear signal to Milosevic that he had lost his most important international ally. Fourth, on the same day, even though a heated battle took place inside the Bundestag, Germany stood fast as a NATO partner, as did Italy when domestic turmoil arose within its government several days later. Fifth, and perhaps most telling, the second week in May saw a rush of new offers from European governments to accept Kosovars, which made it clear that the refugee gambit had decisively failed.[128] In short, by early May it would have been evident to Milosevic that, despite his attempts to shatter the alliance, NATO unity would not falter and neither refugees nor domestic dissent was going to lead the Europeans to defect. Accordingly, after mid-May outflows remained low until the end of the conflict in June.[129]

Why Did Milosevic's Gambit Fail?

Successful coercion requires making the cost of noncompliance sufficiently high that the target will be willing to accept the lower cost of backing down. Milosevic's attempted coercion via the use of refugees was doomed to fail because, in this case, the costs of concession actually rose over time. The (real and perceived) costs for NATO of backing down far exceeded those

[126] "Bombs over Belgrade, Diplomatic as Well as Military," *Economist,* May 8, 1999. This plan bore more than a passing resemblance to the plan that the Germans had started to float in mid-April. This proposal, which involved suspending the NATO bombing for at least twenty-four hours to allow Yugoslav forces to withdraw from Kosovo, also called for KLA disarmament and recommended a peacekeeping force that would perhaps operate under a UN mandate and include troops from Russia. It would be modeled loosely on the international stabilization force that was under UN mandate but NATO control in Bosnia. See, for instance, Judith Matloff, "Talk Still Drowned Out by Combat's Roar," *Christian Science Monitor,* April 16, 1999.

[127] Allan Little notes that Castenfelt "delivered a message that ended the Serbian leader's dreams of a Russian intervention. The Russian government was about to agree a peace plan with NATO and the Russian security forces had accepted it." *Moral Combat.*

[128] The offers included one from normally refugee-allergic Britain, which said it would take 1,000 a week, and from Italy, which said it would take 10,000 more and would ferry more aid to the camps in Macedonia. "Guns or Refugees—An Unequal Alliance?" *Economist,* May 8, 1999. Several weeks earlier, the United States had also reversed its policy and offered to take 20,000 refugees, and Canada agreed to take 5,000. Lippman and Graham, "NATO Takes a New Look."

[129] Ball, *Policy or Panic?* pt. 1.

of continuing the campaign for two completely contrary reasons. First, the alliance had ratcheted up its own costs of concession by leveraging much of its prestige on the success of its efforts. The prestige of NATO was further engaged by the efforts of a variety of groups—domestic and international NGOs, the KLA and its supporters, and humanitarian hawks—all of which were eager to raise the alliance's hypocrisy costs of inaction. Second, and conversely, NATO was able to mitigate the pain inflicted by Milosevic's demographic bombs—thereby effectively lowering the costs of noncompliance—by keeping these costs largely hidden from Western audiences and by forcing some of them back on Milosevic through the employment of a massive and extremely effective public relations and media campaign.

In some sense, it matters less how NATO responded to Milosevic's threat to unleash a flood of refugees than the fact that Milosevic appears to have tried to deter the alliance from attacking via such a threat. This is because, even if threats are well constructed and perfectly understood—which they were not in this case—they remain but one part of a target's calculus. As Lawrence Freedman has put it, "the threat itself will be one variable among many and not necessarily the most important: the interests at stake, the underlying political trends, the attitude of allies and so on must also be considered."[130]

The Importance of Preserving NATO

For much of the 1990s, NATO sought to redefine itself as the core of an enlarged security community and a tool for managing conflict within Europe and around its periphery.[131] It emphasized its ability—even its obligation—to maintain stability and safeguard human rights and democracy as key reasons for its continued existence. Perhaps Jamie Shea summed it up best when he stated, "NATO feels that Kosovo is a defining moment for the future of the alliance in showing NATO's determination to uphold values in the wider Europe."[132] Thus, it was widely believed that if NATO failed in Kosovo, against a foe no better than a "schoolyard bully" commanding an army of "thugs," its new *raison d'être* would be undermined, its credibility destroyed, and a dangerous precedent set.[133] As Tony Blair asserted dur-

---

[130] Lawrence Freedman, "Strategic Coercion," in *Strategic Coercion: Concepts and Cases,* ed. Lawrence Freedman (Oxford: Oxford University Press, 1998), 25.

[131] See, for instance, Joseph Lepgold, "NATO's Post-Cold War Collective Action Problem," *International Security* 23 (1998): 78–106.

[132] Quoted in Lippman, "NATO Expands Fleet of Aircraft."

[133] In fact, it was arguably this very same fear that had finally compelled the United States to take more aggressive action in Bosnia four years before. Only when it became clear that it was going to have to put its own troops into the region—if only to extract the troops of

ing the NATO summit, "many of our problems have been caused by two dangerous and ruthless men—Hussein and Slobodan Milosevic. . . . [Thus] one of the reasons why it is so important to win the conflict is to ensure that others do not make the same mistake in the future."[134] Even before the bombing started, General Clark reportedly told Madeline Albright that they would have to go ahead, even though they knew the consequences could be dire for Kosovar Albanians, because they had "put NATO's credibility on the line. [They had] to follow through and make it work. There [was] no real alternative."[135]

Even Henry Kissinger, although initially opposed to the NATO operation, wrote two weeks after it had begun, "NATO cannot survive if it now abandons the campaign without achieving its objective of ending the massacres."[136] And a month later Kissinger further opined,

> From the start, there has been a vast gap between the rhetoric and the means with which to back it up. Allied pronouncements have ritually compared Milosevic to Hitler. But the transparent reluctance to accept casualties signaled that the Alliance would not make the commitment necessary to overthrow the accused tyrant. Now, if the outcome is to be some kind of compromise, Milosevic will inevitably be legitimized and emerge as a valid interlocutor. By justifying the war in terms requiring total victory while conducting a strategy impelling compromise, NATO has maneuvered itself into a trap.[137]

In the end, NATO could not accept failure because it had so entwined its whole reason for being with the success of its mission in Kosovo. In essence, it made the costs of backing down impossibly large. As one U.S. Air Force officer put it, "There wasn't really any choice. I mean, really, Milosevic was a two-bit jerk, a real piece of sh-t. Do you think, even for a minute, we [i.e., NATO] could just roll over and play dead?"[138] And as

---

its European allies and humiliatingly declare the peacekeeping mission a failure—did the United States embrace more aggressive action. For a discussion of this conundrum and the anticipated humiliation associated with it, see Charles Boyd, "Making Bosnia Work," *Foreign Affairs* 77 (1998): 42–67; Andrew Neil, "Arkansas Kid Guns Down NATO," *Sunday Times,* July 23, 1995.

[134] Tony Blair, "Doctrine of the International Community." President Clinton also publicly put NATO on the hook, so to speak. See William Jefferson Clinton, "A Just and Necessary War," *New York Times,* May 23, 1999.

[135] Clark, *Waging Modern War,* 171. Albright reportedly responded, "Yes, I think so, too." Similar sentiments were echoed by U.S. military officers who served in Kosovo and by civilian defense planners in interviews I conducted at the Pentagon between July and September 2000.

[136] Henry A. Kissinger, "Doing Injury to History," *Newsweek,* April 5, 1999, 38–39.

[137] Henry A. Kissinger, "New World Disorder," *Newsweek,* May 31, 1999.

[138] Interview, August 2000.

Lieutenant General Short put it, "If we allowed this butcher, murderer and dictator to defeat the most powerful alliance on the face of the earth because we didn't have the stomach for collateral damage and we didn't have the stomach for unintended loss of civilian life, then we were going to cease to exist as an alliance."[139]

Thus, although many of European members of NATO resented their military reliance on the United States and frequently grumbled about its heavy-handed dominance of the alliance, its members were clearly unprepared to let NATO collapse.[140] Even Jacques Chirac, a frequent and vocal critic of NATO, proclaimed at the anniversary summit, "Unity and determination, total and unanimous."[141] The possibility that a real or perceived NATO failure in Kosovo could spell the death knell for the alliance led its European members to stifle (at least publicly) their criticism of the conduct of the war and to forgo all opportunities to defect from the stated NATO strategy.[142] Whatever the costs of sticking with an U.S.-driven alliance, at the time the Europeans obviously viewed them as lower than shouldering future costs alone.[143]

The Force Multiplier of Hypocrisy Cost Boosters

The costs of backing down were further elevated by a variety of domestic and international actors, many of which were members of what Michael

---

[139] Quoted in *Moral Combat.*

[140] William Drozdiak, "European Allies Balk at Expanded Role to NATO," *Washington Post,* February 22, 1998. As Philip Gordon pointedly asked, "If the (first) Yugoslav crisis on Europe's periphery—combined with a US policy that was erratic, uncertain, and domineering at the same time—was not enough to motivate...(adoption of) common security policies and military integration, what will?" "Europe's Uncommon Foreign Policy," *International Security* 22 (1997–1998), 76.

[141] Quoted in Doyle McManus, "Nineteen Countries Speak with One Voice," *Los Angeles Times,* April 24, 1999.

[142] Off the record, however, many diplomats were willing to be more critical of the United States, including several who "privately [said] they believe Albright [was] being far too hawkish." Matloff, "Talk Still Drowned Out." And as Kissinger put it the following month, "In Europe, the situation is more complex. The allies share our motives but are beginning to question our judgment. And they find themselves under increasing domestic pressure as the damage from the bombing of Serbia compounds the devastation of Kosovo." Kissinger, "New World Disorder."

[143] Although it has become popular in some circles to argue that the unity of the alliance was never in question, interviews with some of the principals, their diary entries, and their testimony before their respective legislatures suggests that such concerns were widespread—as was the belief that in some cases crises were only narrowly avoided. As Karl Kaiser, German government advisor, put it, "Some of the European allies believed they could not carry public opinion with them much longer. It was not easy for Germany. This country was particularly interested in getting the war ended. There was a possibility that the crisis could evolve in a way that could end up in a tragedy." Quoted in *Moral Combat.* See also House of Commons Select Committee on Foreign Affairs, "Fourth Report."

Ignatieff has called "the Something Must Be Done Brigade."[144] These actors—which included some human rights organizations, members of the media, and the KLA and its supporters—worked throughout the conflict to make NATO de-escalation impossible by publicly highlighting both the potential consequences of NATO inaction and the visible consequences of inadequate NATO action. For instance, in early April, Holly Burkhalter, then of Physicians for Human Rights, read an essay on National Public Radio, in which she urged the deployment of ground troops to stop what she believed was a genocide in the making. She proclaimed, "if President Clinton avoids taking the painful action necessary to expel Serb forces from Kosovo, he will be remembered as the President on whose watch three genocides unfolded."[145] Burkhalter later admitted that on the issue of genocide in Kosovo she "was wrong...but [maintained that] if you wait until it is proved to you six ways to Sunday, you haven't prevented it, have you?"[146]

Leadership Cost Escalation

Furthermore, leaders in some NATO capitals hoisted themselves higher on the hook of potential hypocrisy by trying to signal the resolve of NATO, both before and during the crisis. As Dennis McNamara, UNHCR special envoy for the Balkans, noted, "When you declare a war—NATO's first in Europe—to be primarily a humanitarian war with the main objective the return of refugees—you raise the political temperature enormously."[147] In 1998, even before the crisis turned into a war, Madeleine Albright had pledged, "We are not going to stand by and watch the Serbian authorities do in Kosovo what they can no longer get away with doing in Bosnia." Not long thereafter, however, she was forced to acknowledge the potential consequences of failing to live up to this pledge. As Albright put it, "Not only was it a *deja-vu* about the subject generally, but we were in the same room that we had been in during Bosnian discussions. I thought it behooved me to say to my colleagues that *we could not repeat the kinds of mistakes that had happened over Bosnia, where there was a lot of talk and no action and that history would judge us very, very severely.*"[148] Likewise, once

---

[144] Quoted in "An Undemocratic War," *Irish Times*, March 1, 2000.

[145] Holly Burkhalter, "Statement on Genocide in Kosovo," *All Things Considered*, National Public Radio, April 9, 1999.

[146] Pearl and Block, "Body Count."

[147] Quoted in Toby Porter, "The Partiality of Humanitarian Assistance: Kosovo in Comparative Perspective," *Journal of Humanitarian Assistance* (June 2000), www.reliefweb.int/rw/rwb.nsf/db900sid/OCHA-64CK3V?OpenDocument.

[148] Quoted in *Moral Combat*.

the bombing campaign had begun and outflow numbers were mounting, President Clinton declared:

> We have a lot of tough questions to answer about this operation, and I am quite sure that we cannot answer every one to everyone's satisfaction. But I would far rather be standing here answering these questions, with these people, talking about this endeavor, than I would to be standing here having you ask me why we are permitting a wholesale ethnic slaughter and ethnic cleansing and the creation of hundreds of thousands of refugees, and not lifting a finger to do anything about it.[149]

British Prime Minister Tony Blair too felt the pressure of adhering having to adhere to his own rhetoric.[150] As he put it shortly after the conflict ended:

> People used to say to me occasionally well for goodness sake Tony just don't talk about it at all, I'd say look it's quite difficult; I mean you're out there and people ask you; and as I say we don't have Milosevic's media and jolly good thing that we don't. But the fact is my guy's asking me, and your guys ask you, and you know you're expected to have some sort of answer to this.... The bottom line was we couldn't lose. If we lost, it's not just that we would have failed in our strategic objective; failed in terms of the moral purpose—we would have dealt a devastating blow to the credibility of NATO and the world would have been less safe as a result of that.[151]

The Media

Members of the media further helped raise the costs to NATO by publishing interviews (sometimes later discredited) with refugees, many of whom took NATO to task for failing to do more. For instance, one grandmother from Pec, whose two eldest sons were killed in earlier attacks, was quoted as claiming she was "sending [her] youngest son to join the KLA (Kosovo Liberation Army) [because]...I feel guilty that I stopped them all from joining earlier, because I put my faith in NATO."[152] Another refugee was quoted as asking, "If they didn't want to finish this war, why did they start it and leave us to take the punishment? How much more do we

---

[149] "Crisis in The Balkans: President's Strategy: 'Our Plan Is to Persist until We Prevail,'" *New York Times*, April 5, 1999. Clinton was clearly eager to avoid a repetition of that very criticism, which had been intense and stinging after the massacres at Srebrenica. Power, *Problem from Hell*, 430–31.

[150] See Garton Ash, "War We Almost Lost."

[151] Quoted in *Moral Combat*.

[152] Olivia Ward, "Refugees Lose Patience with NATO Strategy," *Toronto Star*, May 20, 1999.

have to pay?"[153] Some KLA supporters—including the infamous 16-year-old Rajmonda Rreci, who claimed she was joining the KLA to avenge the death of her sister—were later forced to acknowledge that their stories were untrue, but they remained unrepentant.[154] Besides, the effects could not be undone.[155] As Paddy Ashdown put it in the midst of the conflict, "This is the first war in history that is being fought for refugees. And we have set ourselves an unforgiving measure for judging its success. If they don't go back, we have lost."[156]

In short, even though their significance may pale beside the paramount issue of the survival of NATO, the material role of hypocrisy cost boosters should not be underestimated, nor in fact can their role really be disaggregated from the issue of preserving NATO. Consider that Ignatieff, for one, believes that the imposition of hypocrisy costs was decisive both in bringing about the intervention and in ensuring that NATO could not back down. "The war in Kosovo came about not through any democratic process, he says, but through pressure from media pundits just like him.... 'We have replaced institutional democracy through our representatives with a kind of media-ocracy.'... And the war lasted 78 days rather than two largely, Ignatieff claims, because politicians both in the United Kingdom and the United States knew they *had no democratic consent*."[157]

The Critical Role of the Kosovo Liberation Army—Active *Agents Provocateurs*

Further, it ought not be forgotten that it took time and a concerted effort by the KLA, its supporters, and international advocacy groups to turn what the *New York Times* called a "noticed but not dramatized" background problem into a major crisis that demanded an international response.[158]

---

[153] Ibid.

[154] Rreci, who later admitted she had actually been a member of the KLA and had known all along that her sister was alive, rationalized her lie by stressing that "other Kosovar girls had lost their sisters, and why shouldn't she do it for them?" Ultimately, however, Rreci admitted that what she had said was just KLA propaganda. Tom Regan, "Conned in Kosovo: A CBC Reporter's Dilemma," *Christian Science Monitor*, September 13, 1999.

[155] The Canadian Broadcasting Corporation (CBC) reporter who originally aired Rreci's story did produce a follow-up report, "The Truth about Rajmonda: A KLA Soldier Lies for the Cause," which examined not only her story but what it said about how news is reported from war zones. Ibid.

[156] Quoted in "Kosovo, the Untold Story."

[157] "An Undemocratic War."

[158] For instance, the need to take aggressive media-generating action was acknowledged by Veton Surroi, Kosovo Albanian political leader, who said, "As soon as we got the photographs we put them on the internet because that was the most horrendous thing we had seen until then. Kids, shot dead, were images of a war that people needed to see. We were shocked and we thought that other people needed to see this because this was getting out of control." Quoted in *Moral Combat*.

Although the 1998 Serb offensive was at least as brutal as anything that happened in the period leading up to the start of the bombing campaign a year later, during the first period, in the words of as Mary Robinson, Office of the UN High Commissioner for Human Rights, "No one was listening." An official in the office of then Italian Prime Minister Massimo D'Alema confirms this: "there were immense delays in facing up to the problem, particularly on the part of NATO and its European members."[159] U.S. officials later conceded: "At times it seemed that the administration was only paying 'sporadic' attention. And what attention the United States and the rest of the international community did pay to Kosovo was full of contradictions that would paradoxically increase the risk of NATO joining the conflict."[160] Indeed, it was only the active intervention of the KLA, aided by the international media, that shifted the stakes and forced NATO's hand. As Veton Surroi, the Kosovo Albanian political leader, noted: "There [was] a message...being sent to the Kosovars—if you want to draw international attention you have to fight for it. That is exactly it. You need to use violence to achieve your goals."[161] And so they did.

Consistent with the predictions of my theory, when the KLA *agents provocateurs* launched their armed challenge they also fully expected it to provoke massive Serbian retaliation in the form of a military offensive against the province. As Zymer Lubovci, KLA fighter, acknowledged, "We saw them [the Serbs] coming, so we prepared and opened fire....[I]t was guaranteed that every time we took action they would take revenge on civilians."[162] Furthermore, Hashim Thaçi, KLA leader and later prime minister of the province, subsequently admitted, "we knew full well that any armed action we undertook would trigger a ruthless retaliation by Serbs against our people....We knew we were endangering civilian lives, too, a great number of lives."[163]

Indeed, despite the costs, provoking such retaliation was a stated goal, in the service of mobilizing support for their campaign for independence, both within Kosovo and internationally.[164] As Alan Little observed, "The war in neighboring Bosnia taught them the value of a resort to the gun....From the remote wooded hillsides of rural Kosovo, they embarked on a strategy to draw the world's most powerful military alliance into their

[159] Ibid.
[160] "Kosovo, the Untold Story."
[161] Quoted in *Moral Combat*.
[162] Ibid.
[163] Ibid.
[164] Frelick, *Refugees as Weapons of War*; Lelyveld, "Defendant"; Alan J. Kuperman, "The Moral Hazard of Humanitarian Intervention: Lessons from the Balkans," *International Studies Quarterly* 52 (2008): 49–80.

struggle."[165] And as Dugi Gorani, Albanian negotiator, conceded, "Every single Albanian realized that the more civilians die, intervention comes nearer.... The more civilians were killed, the chances of international intervention became bigger, and the KLA of course realized that."[166] Alush Gashi, an advisor to Ibrahim Rugova, likewise acknowledged that prospect of NATO intervention "depends on how we look on CNN. People need to see victims in their living room."[167]

Arguably the Kosovars' expectation—that by instigating a violent Serbian response they would succeed in galvanizing international support—was largely an inadvertent consequence of a misreading of signals designed principally to deter Milosevic rather than encourage the KLA.[168] For instance, in January 1999, a U.S. official was quoted as saying that the KLA rebels "think we support their goals. But that's only because they're not listening to us. They hear the music, but they don't pay attention to the words."[169] Still, in line with Kosovar Albanian hopes and expectations, just two months later, NATO did intervene on their behalf. As Timothy Garton Ash concludes:

> There is no reason to doubt that Western leaders were concerned about this real human suffering. However, as politicians they were undoubtedly more concerned about the human suffering of the Kosovar Albanians than they were about that of the Congolese, Angolans, Sierra Leoneans, Rwandans, or Colombians, because television and the press covered Kosovo more intensely and graphically, with energetic commentaries from what one British minister sarcastically called the "something-must-be-done brigade." So [once the crisis made it to the international radar screen] this was also a war for which the mass media were implicitly and explicitly making a case.[170]

In the end, the vast majority of Kosovar civilians had to endure great suffering in support of their militant leadership's goals. Yet, by successfully portraying themselves as victims of Serb depredations—and by convincing the international media to cover (and then to exaggerate) this suffering—the KLA succeeded in their goal of ending Serb oppression of Kosovo, while further dooming Milosevic's simultaneous attempt to coerce the NATO alliance via the use of coercive engineered migration.

---

[165] Quoted in Moral Combat.

[166] Ibid.

[167] Quoted in interview in Bandow, "Hypocritical Humanitarianism," in *NATO's Empty Victory: A Postmortem on the Balkan War*, ed. Ted Galen Carpenter (Washington, D.C.: CATO Institute, 2000), 39.

[168] See, for instance, Crawford, *Hard Bargains, Fragile Peace*.

[169] Quoted in Michael Ignatieff, "The Dream of Albanians," *New Yorker*, January 11, 1999.

[170] Timothy Garton Ash, "Kosovo and Beyond," *New York Review of Books*, June 24, 1999.

As Richard Holbrooke admitted: "I don't believe that any of the liberation forces, or guerrilla forces of our lifetime moved more rapidly, or more successfully, from total obscurity to international standing and recognition than the Kosovo Liberation Army."[171]

Alleviating the Pain of Coercion

THE VALUE OF TROOPS IN ALBANIA AND MACEDONIA   When Milosevic launched demographic bombs against Albania and Macedonia, he probably hoped that, in addition to impeding KLA and NATO military operations, the refugees would overwhelm the local infrastructure and possibly destabilize the region.[172] Given how few preparations the West had made to accommodate the massive flows that emerged, this was a reasonable gamble. And for a time, it appeared that it might work. When the refugee crisis along the Macedonian border crossing near Blace "increased the potential costs of collaboration, key figures in the government threatened to publicly criticize the air strikes and ask NATO forces to leave the country."[173] This led the U.S. Embassy to intensify its efforts to solve the refugee crisis at Blace and placate the Macedonian government, which benefited handsomely as opportunists in this crisis.[174] (See the appendix for further details.)

In the end, however, here too Milosevic's gambit failed. Over 90,000 refugees were temporarily evacuated from the region, thus reducing pressures at the Macedonian border.[175] In addition, after promises of significant financial aid and logistical support were forthcoming, Macedonia did reopen its border (although it closed it again the following month when the promised aid was deemed insufficient and too slow in coming; see the appendix, case 53). And tens of thousands of NATO troops, in conjunction with UNHCR and the NGO community, provided relief to the refugees that remained, thereby further mitigating the pain Milosevic hoped to inflict on NATO and neighboring countries. Thus, although a week

---

[171] Ibid.

[172] Certainly some of the threats issued from Belgrade implied as much. For instance, Kathleen Newland, refugee expert, contends, "Milosevic very consciously directed refugee flows from Kosovo toward Macedonia rather than toward Albania because Macedonia had a much more complicated ethnic mix, was politically more fragile, and had its own problems with its own ethnic Albanian population." See *Refugees as Weapons of War.*

[173] Barutciski and Suhrke, "Lessons from the Kosovo Refugee Crisis," 101.

[174] Ibid.; Rey Koslowski, "The Mobility Money Can Buy," in *The Migration Reader: Exploring Politics and Policies,* ed. Anthony Messina and Gallya Lahav (London: Lynne Rienner, 2006), 578.

[175] Barutciski and Suhrke, "Lessons from the Kosovo Refugee Crisis," 101. See Richard Caplan, "Kosovo: The Implications for Humanitarian Intervention," *Forced Migration Review* no. 5 (1999), 7, for a breakdown of the locations to which the 91,000 Kosovars were transported during the Humanitarian Evacuation Program (HEP).

into the crisis it was claimed that "without international relief assistance, starvation [was] expected within 10 days to two weeks,"[176] catastrophe never struck. Ironically, therefore, even though ground troops were never sent into battle against Milosevic, effectively they degraded his refugees-as-weapons capabilities.

LOCALIZING THE PAIN   The containment of the vast majority of refugees in the Balkans and the relatively small number of NATO casualties also helped dampen the domestic costs of continuing the conflict. Consider just one of many examples of the palliative effects of refugee-related triage. In early April, Greece had pledged to offer 5,000 Kosovars temporary protection. But these 5,000 were not evacuated to Greece. Instead, like many other EU states, Greece opted to keep the Kosovars close to home, in their "first country of asylum "(Albania or Macedonia), in what Joanne van Selm has called "the buffer zone" between Greece and the source of the displacements.[177]

An examination of survey data is further illustrative. For example, although in mid-April 1999 87 percent of the British people polled still widely favored NATO action to protect Kosovar Albanians, only 15 percent of them were willing to accept any Kosovar refugees into Britain. Moreover, 56 percent of those polled said they would not sacrifice the life of a single British soldier to save the lives of the Kosovar Albanians.[178] Similarly, a poll in *Der Spiegel* in late March indicated that, although 64 percent of those in the western part of Germany supported air attacks on the FRY, only 33 percent supported the addition of ground troops to the operation. (The numbers for the eastern part of Germany were even lower.)[179] These data reflect the disparity in the sentiments and attitudes expressed by German and Italian political parties as well. Both incumbent governments

[176] Holger Jensen, "New Dangers Now Arise in Kosovo Crisis," *Denver Rocky Mountain News,* April 1, 1999. "The bilaterals, as the NATO armies came to be known, were hugely important in the relief effort, not only providing the logistical support traditionally associated with the role of the military, but also setting up and managing refugee camps on behalf of the governments that they represented." Toby Porter, "Coordination in the Midst of Chaos: The Refugee Crisis in Albania," *Forced Migration Review* no. 5 (1999).

[177] Joanne van Selm, ed., *Kosovo's Refugees in the European Union* (London: Continuum Publishing, 2000), 218.

[178] Gallup Poll, www.gallup.hu/gallup/self/polls/Kosovo/bombings.htm. To be fair, not all poll results are equally grim. Some European states supported hosting refugees, albeit only for a limited period.

[179] "Alle Hatten Skrupel," *Der Spiegel,* March 29, 1999. See also "Infratest Survey of April 3–5," quoted in Caroline King, "The New German Government and the Kosovo Conflict: A Painful Awakening," *Politik* (Summer 1999): 4–5. This level of support was replicated in many NATO countries, including Britain, France, and the Netherlands, where throughout the early part of the war support for the bombing—but not for the introduction of ground troops—was strong. See, for instance, Richard Boudreaux, "Europeans Hardened by Reports of Serb Atrocities," *Los Angeles Times,* April 1, 1999.

worried at different times that their coalition governments might fall, and episodically (particularly from left-wing elements in both countries) the pressure was intense.[180]

But both the sitting Italian and German governments were also concerned with the potential costs associated with appearing to be unreliable allies.[181] Thus, the evidence suggests, as long as the costs of NATO action appeared to be largely negligible to domestic audiences, support would hold.[182] As Ignatieff notes in *Virtual War*, Kosovo was a "virtual conflict," in which, while people suffered and died on the ground, the foreigners who become involved were able to view the war as if watching a sporting event on television; they were able to root for their team—the good guys—and then change channels. And even though the game was in deadly earnest, the deaths were mostly hidden, and above all, they were someone else's.[183] If, however, either Kosovar refugees with suitcases or NATO soldiers in body bags had started appearing at home, support likely would have plummeted.[184]

DOMESTIC CONTAINMENT POLICIES   An efficient and dexterous NATO public relations campaign cum media machine further aided the effort to make the costs of the campaign appear negligible to Western audiences. As Prime Minister Blair put it, "We had to take grip on the whole way the thing was run and organised because it was big—it wasn't just a military campaign it was also a propaganda campaign and we had to take our public opinions with us."[185] For several months, NATO members neutralized domestic opposition to the bombing campaign and sidestepped questions about whether it had inflamed the crisis, through the work of spokespeople who likened Kosovo to Cambodia under Pol Pot and likened FRY activities to "the Great Terror."[186] Tearful accounts by refugees, accompanied by pictures of clogged border crossings, filled Western television screens. At one point, Kenneth Bacon, Pentagon spokesman, went so far as to claim that "it would be much easier to attack Serbian military

[180] See Rathbun, *Partisan Interventions*, chap. 4; Croci, "Forced Ally?" esp. 44–45.

[181] See Rathbun, *Partisan Interventions*, chap. 4; Croci, "Forced Ally?" esp. 44–45.

[182] Reportedly, on the eve of the NATO summit, Clinton urged Blair to stop talking about the possibility of introducing ground troops into the campaign because "it caused domestic problems for allies." Dana Priest, "A Decisive Battle That Never Was," *Washington Post*, September 19, 1999.

[183] Michael Ignatieff, *Virtual War* (New York: Metropolitan Books, 2000), intro.

[184] As Secretary of Defense William Cohen had said during his time in the Senate, "And the hearts that beat so loudly and enthusiastically to do something, to intervene in areas where there is not an immediate threat to our vital interests . . . when those hearts that had beaten so loudly see the coffins, then they switch, and they say, 'What are we doing there?'" Quoted in Samantha Power, *Problem from Hell*, 455.

[185] Quoted in *Moral Combat*.

[186] Jensen, "New Dangers Now Arise."

targets on the ground in Kosovo following the 'temporary departure' of ethnic Albanians from Kosovo."[187]

In Germany, where the ruling Social Democratic Party (SPD) "was under enormous pressure to maintain the coalition or risk its collapse," the government "used references to genocide and comparisons to the Holocaust to maintain not only public backing, but also internal party support." As Brian Rathbun explains, in all of his Bundestag speeches, Defense Minister Rudolf Scharping, "recited a litany of abuses by the Milosevic government," and "Defense Ministry briefing sheets featured drawings by children in refugee camps of the tragedies they had experienced." But, "most controversially, Scharping made frequent mention of Operation Horseshoe, . . . whose authenticity was always shrouded in doubt."[188] Rathbun further notes that, "although many SPD members later privately said they were uncomfortable with how Scharping justified the war, they did not doubt the short-term effectiveness of the strategy. . . . He wanted to bring the parliamentary party behind him. It worked."[189]

Meanwhile, in Kosovo itself, journalists on the ground had access to on-site scanners and satellite communications, which enabled them to file stories with an ease and speed unprecedented in refugee camps.[190] This proved to be a double-edged sword when good information was hard to come by. "'We were all hamstrung,' a NATO official says. As the war dragged on, he says, 'NATO saw a fatigued press corps drifting towards the contrarian story: civilians killed by NATO's bombs. NATO bombs. [In response], NATO stepped up its claims about Serb 'killing fields.'"[191] For instance, on the same day the story broke about the accidental NATO bombing of a refugee convoy, NATO estimates of the number of people being killed by the Serbs also jumped, with General Sir Charles Guthrie, British chief of staff, declaring: "There are reports that thousands of young men have been murdered. I hesitate to quote a more precise estimate."[192] In the same vein, refugee reports that Serb soldiers used rape to drive expulsions "went from an assertion to an assumption of a systematic pattern in the span of a day."[193] And when D'Alema visited a refugee camp in

[187] Quoted in Michael Cameron, "NATO Raids Could Go On Indefinitely," *Hobart Mercury,* April 7, 1999.

[188] Rathbun, *Partisan Interventions,* 113.

[189] Ibid., 114.

[190] Peter Morris, "Humanitarian Interventions in Macedonia: An NGO Perspective," *Forced Migration Review* no. 5 (1999).

[191] Pearl and Block, "Body Count."

[192] Quoted in "Macedonia Fears."

[193] Frank Bruni, "Dueling Perspectives: Two Views of Reality Vying on the Airwaves," *New York Times,* April 18, 1999; Katherine Butler, "Briefings' NATO Spokesman Accused of Exaggerations by the French," *Independent,* April 10, 1999.

Albania at Easter, he and the press that covered the visit "engaged in tear-jerking descriptions of supposed Serbian atrocities in Kosovo."[194]

It is clear, at least in retrospect, that much of the coverage generated by the NATO media machine was exaggerated, misleading, or just wrong. For instance, a report released and widely disseminated by the U.S. State Department claimed that 100,000 Albanian men had been herded into a Pristina soccer stadium and held against their will. When one French journalist went to see for himself, however, he found the stadium empty.[195] Nevertheless, the propaganda campaign was extremely effective. It was instrumental in convincing the world that Milosevic alone was responsible for the tragedy that had unfolded and effectively neutralizing any benefit he had hoped to derive from the export of refugees.[196] (It is worth noting that Milosevic's brutal behavior during the earlier Bosnian war helped make the propaganda offered up during the Kosovo campaign more credible than it might otherwise have been.)

Moreover, ironically, in the end NATO was actually able to use the refugees to sustain support for its intervention. It fixed on them and succeeded in portraying their existence as the key reason for the intervention, even though that had become the defining goal of the mission only well after the bombing began.[197] As one close observer of the conflict has suggested, "Western public opinion would have turned against the bombardment, had it not been for the wrenching scenes of refugees pouring over the borders. The question would have been asked, 'How can we bomb a small country—whatever we think of its government—because it refuses to sign an agreement about the future of part of its territory?'"[198] In short, whatever its causes, the graphic images and media coverage of the heinous consequences of Milosevic's campaign reduced public antipathy to Kosovars, who were—at least during the critical period of the bombing campaign—viewed more as victims than as threats.[199]

Thus, in several states the level of commitment of the anti-migrant/refugee camp to keeping Kosovars out actually fell over time, thereby

[194] Croci, "Forced Ally?," 46.

[195] Pearl and Block, "Body Count"; Butler, "War in the Balkans."

[196] One illuminating example is offered by Jamie Shea's response to criticism of NATO after the bombing of the refugee convoy near Djakovica. Shea turned the argument on its head and asserted that the blame for the refugees' deaths lay with Milosevic, not with the pilots who make mistakes "in the heat of bombings." After all, "why was a refugee convoy escorted by Serb military vehicles on the Prizren-Djakovica road at 3:00 yesterday afternoon in the first place?" In Thomas Lippman, "Allies Confirm Civilian Attack," *Washington Post,* April 16, 1999."

[197] Thomas Lippman, "NATO Commits Troops, Aircraft to Help Feed, Shelter Refugees; Allies Discuss a Force to Ensure Safe Return," *Washington Post,* April 4, 1999.

[198] Judah, *Kosovo,* 251.

[199] See Matthew Gibney, "Kosovo and Beyond: Popular and Unpopular Refugees," *Forced Migration Review* no. 5 (1999): 28–30.

markedly reducing the vulnerability of the alliance to coercion. As Rey Koslowski has summed it up, first, the "refugee crisis quickly melted resistance among EU member states to extend temporary protection." Second, "the European media image of smuggled Kosovar Albanians changed. Smuggled 'illegal refugees' associated with criminal organizations suddenly were depicted as genuine refugees fleeing ethnic cleansing compared to the Holocaust. The KLA became viewed as 'freedom fighters' who were legitimate representatives of the Kosovars."[200] This sentiment was echoed by Marcello Foa, when speaking about the response in Italy: "When they see these horrible images on TV, they think that this is a new Holocaust, and they are really emotional. They are really—they really want to help them [the Kosovars]."[201] Table 3.1 illustrates this softening stance toward NATO bombing, reflecting a growing feeling in wavering states that bombing to protect Kosovars (even if it generated refugees) was justified and a general softening of attitudes toward Kosovar Albanians generally.[202]

And a Dash of Luck for Good Measure

In spite of the success of the NATO media campaign, after several months of bombing, rationalizations had grown threadbare in some circles. For instance, in Germany, pressure from within the SPD coalition began to mount by late April, and a special Green Party conference was held in early May. Two competing resolutions were forwarded, each of which demanded some measure of NATO de-escalation "because the air strikes had proven ineffective, inflaming rather than resolving the situation." The more radical of the two called for an outright end to the air campaign.[203] Support had also begun to flag again in Italy, where, after the bombing of the Chinese Embassy and a number of other NATO errors, support for the war effort dropped again.[204] Even in the United States—where support for bombing campaign had been consistently strong—by late May human rights and peace groups began to mobilize against it, insisting that the bombing campaign had failed to protect civilians targeted by the Serbs. These groups admitted that concerns about alleged Yugoslav atrocities

[200] Koslowski, "Mobility Money Can Buy," 578.
[201] "Views from Abroad."
[202] Although one must be cautious about assigning too much weight to public opinion data in isolation, they are useful for taking the temperature of a population and, more critically, for measuring shifts in that temperature. And, despite the lack of question continuity across space and time, these data further bolster the other evidence presented and clearly illustrate the hypothesized shifts in opinion over time.
[203] Rathbun, *Partisan Interventions*, 114–15.
[204] Croci, "Forced Ally?," 45.

TABLE 3.1
Shifts in Public Opinion in Wavering NATO Member States, Spring 1999

NATO Member State	Question	Date and Response	Date and Response	Date and Response
Italy	Are NATO airstrikes justified?	March 25: 27% yes	March 31: 40% yes	April 20: 62% yes
	Prime Minister D'Alema has said that after the first bombing the moment has come to return to diplomacy, while Mr. Clinton and Mr. Blair want to continue the bombing until Serbia signs the peace agreement. Which position do you support?	March 26: 77% return to diplomacy; 22% continue the bombing; 6% don't know	April 7: 60% return to diplomacy; 34% continue the bombing; 6% don't know	May 10: 62% return to diplomacy; 34% continue the bombing; 4% don't know
	Now, as you may know, President Milosevic heads the government of Yugoslavia, which NATO accuses of starting the war in Kosovo. In your view, should a settlement in Kosovo require that President Milosevic be removed from office?	April 22–24: 78% yes		
Germany	Are NATO airstrikes justified?	March 28: 56% yes	April 12: 60% yes	April 16: 68% yes
	Now, as you may know, President Milosevic heads the government of Yugoslavia, which NATO accuses of starting the war in Kosovo. In your view, should a settlement in Kosovo require that President Milosevic be removed from office?			April 22–24: 86% yes
Greece	Do you agree with your government's decision to support NATO airstrikes?	March 25: Greece condemned the bombing outright		April 20: 76% no
	Should Greece remain in NATO?			April 20: 53% yes; 26% no

(TABLE 3.1—cont.)

NATO Member State	Question	Date and Response	Date and Response	Date and Response
	Do Milosevic and his government support Kosovar human rights?		April 16: 53% no; 22% yes; 25% don't know	
	Would you volunteer to help the refugees?			April 20: 66% yes; of these, 98% said they would collect food and supplies, 86% said they would donate money, and 53% said they would work in a refugee camp

Sources: For Italy, Istituto per gli Studi sulla Pubblica Opinione/Cra-Neilsen; SWG-Trieste; Angus Reid Group for CNN. For Germany, *Bild Zeitung; Sueddeutsche Zeitung*; DIMAP; Angus Reid Group for CNN. For Greece, Institute V-PRC; ALKO.
Note: NATO, North Atlantic Treaty Organization.

had "made some of us think twice about what to do," but by mid-May it was time to agitate for a new approach.[205] Demonstrations were planned throughout the country, which were to culminate in a rally in the capital on June 5. Luckily for the administration and for the alliance as a whole, Milosevic agreed to the G-8 deal on June 3.

Case Evaluation

This case largely supports the propositions posed in chapter 1. A plethora of direct and indirect evidence suggests that refugee flows (and the threat thereof) were indeed employed strategically and coercively—and with fundamentally incompatible objectives—by a generator, *agents provocateurs*, and an opportunist. The outcome of this case also suggests the possibility

[205] Norman Kempster, "Peace Organizations Set to Take On Clinton," *Los Angeles Times,* May 21, 1999.

that in cases in which pariah generators and victimized *agents provocateurs* are simultaneously engaged in coercive engineered migration, the generators are likely to fare relatively poorly. This is true for a variety of reasons, all of which tend to redound to the benefit of the *agents provocateurs* and to the detriment of the generator(s). First, even if generators are provoked into responding in ways that create outflows, those actors will still be viewed as the true villains. Intentional targeting of civilians is generally viewed as internationally illegitimate behavior, and generators will tend to suffer for engaging in it.[206] This is especially true, as it appears to have been in this case, if the outflows that result are larger than anticipated or desired.[207] Second, objectively speaking, it is difficult to blame the victims of such attacks, particularly because they make the most sympathetic objects of media coverage.[208] Third, the kind of hit-and-run attacks in which *agents provocateurs* engage are more easily blamed on isolated rogue actors than is usually true for government-level responses. Interestingly, this is true even when the planning for guerrilla-type attacks is highly centralized and organized, and the responses are undertaken by isolated rogue military, paramilitary, and/ or police units.[209] In short, although further research is necessary to confirm this finding, this case suggests that, when competing groups engage in coercive engineered migration, *agents provocateurs* can be expected to fare better than generators.

There is also abundant evidence to suggest that Milosevic and the Yugoslav government apparatus, more broadly, did explicitly attempt to aggravate and exploit discord and disagreement within the alliance. As the nature, diversity, and delivery mechanisms of the threats issued indicate, this two-level coercion targeted both the leadership of individual member states and the domestic audiences within them (i.e., the internally divided populations who could, and in some cases did, pressure their governments). This was true both vis-à-vis concerns about the possibility of a mass migration crisis and intra-alliance disagreements about how to engage the Yugoslav government politically and militarily. Given the ample (and potentially costly) degree of heterogeneity of attitudes and

---

[206] See Gil Merom, *How Democracies Lose Small Wars* (Cambridge, UK: Cambridge University Press, 2003), chap. 1; Alexander Downes, *Targeting Civilians in War* (Ithaca, N.Y.: Cornell University Press, 2008).

[207] As previously noted, French Foreign Minister Vedrine admitted, "What most experts underestimated was that the collective memory of massacres in the Balkans was such as to unleash mass migrations." Quoted in "Kosovo, the Untold Story." In other words—consistent with Human Rights Watch's findings—many more chose to leave their homes than were directly or even indirectly impelled to leave; HRW, *Under Orders*.

[208] See Rory Braumann, "When Suffering Makes a Good Story," in *Life, Death and Aid: The Medecins Sans Frontieres Report on World Crisis Intervention*, ed. Medecins Sans Frontieres, 135–48 (London: Routledge, 1993).

[209] See *Kosovo/Kosova; Moral Combat.*

expectations within the key frontline states, it is not exactly remarkable that Milosevic believed for a time that he might succeed at fracturing the alliance, or at least causing one or more members to defect.[210] Moreover, it appears that coercion by swamping was attempted in neighboring states, in that Milosevic also sought to overwhelm the capacity of NATO to manage the humanitarian disasters that erupted along the Albanian and Macedonian borders, and to persuade the Macedonian leadership to end its cooperation with the alliance or face potential destabilization. (NATO itself has acknowledged as much.)

On the other hand, I found no evidence of a "smoking gun" in support of the proposition that Milosevic directly attempted to impose hypocrisy costs on NATO members. Instead, it appears he relied on the existence of discordant and highly mobilized interests to, first, deter the alliance from attacking and, then, cause it to fracture. At the same time, Milosevic understood well the normative and political constraints under which his (mostly) liberal democratic targets labored and recognized that these constraints limited their freedom of action in ways that could redound to his benefit. For instance, we now know that he spoke openly about the ability of his regime to "step over bodies and keep going," a freedom his liberal targets did not have.[211] It is likewise true that, while the campaign was underway, Milosevic attempted to cut bilateral deals with individual member states that were designed to not only make him look like a reasonable and humane man but also to undermine NATO unity.[212]

In contrast, the KLA *agents provocateurs* clearly tried to influence their targets through the use of the media and the imposition of hypocrisy costs. As the NATO intervention and its political consequences make clear, they were also obviously successful. As the following excerpt suggests, it was finally the obvious disconnect between the rhetorical commitments of the

[210] As previously noted, it has become popular in some circles to claim that NATO was never at risk. This is probably a safe assertion in terms of the fundamental survival of the alliance. But claims that defection by individual members from the mission or more broadly was never a realistic threat are belied by written evidence and by my interviews with European officials. See also Judah, *Kosovo;* Daalder and O'Hanlon, *Winning Ugly;* and "Kosovo, the Untold Story," on the stresses the conflict placed on the alliance and how—if Milosevic had not capitulated in early June—the center may not have held.

[211] Quoted in Borchgrave, "We Are neither Angels nor Devils."

[212] For instance, Lamberto Dini reports that he received a call from Milosevic, in which he proposed a deal to hand over Albanian activist Ibrahim Rugova. According to Dini, Milosevic said, "'I don't want to talk about the war now....I just want to arrange for Rugova's return. He would like to go to Macedonia,' he says, explaining that he cannot grant him that concession because his life would be in danger there. 'If you are agreeable, I shall have him fetched from Pristina with his family tomorrow. The aircraft can only arrive in the afternoon. I want them to travel by day.'" Quoted in "Kosovo, the Untold Story."

most powerful member of the alliance and its measurable lack of actual follow-through that forced NATO's hand:

> In Washington the first news of the Racak massacre presented a grotesque headache. The ghastly images put the administration of President Bill Clinton under pressure "to do something." But for a President still mired in the embarrassment and political paralysis of his impeachment for the Monica Lewinsky affair there was a wider concern.
>
> Typically for this administration, the issue that gripped Clinton's officials in the days after Racak was not a humanitarian one, but one of presentation: the thought that a looming crisis in Kosovo might overshadow the summit in Washington on 22 April to celebrate NATO's fiftieth anniversary.
>
> But Racak was also an embarrassment to Clinton and his advisers for another reason: it was the culmination of a period of fumbled foreign policy decisions by an administration that had seemed to sleepwalk through the previous 12 months of the Kosovo crisis. Racak cast that period in a sharp light.[213]

Whether there would have been political costs to be paid for further inaction is a counterfactual question that cannot be answered decisively. What can be said with certainty is that the administration obviously *believed* it needed to act to make the gap between rhetoric and (in)action disappear.[214] As General Clark put it, "Clearly, after Racak, extraordinary measures had to be taken."[215]

As Schelling has said, "a certain death may stun (a man), but it leaves him no choice."[216] When NATO presented Milosevic with the terms of the Rambouillet Accords, it dictated what probably seemed like certain death, and thus its attempt at coercion failed. But NATO was saved from failure because its shortsightedness was matched by Milosevic's substantial miscalculation of Western resolve, resilience, and resourcefulness and, most critically, the magnitude of the credibility stakes NATO had gambled on the success of this mission. Milosevic had hoped to use the threat of refugees to undermine NATO cohesion, and in this, he failed.

As figure 3.1 illustrates, despite initial wobbling—and fears within NATO about alliance stability—the coalition held, as did support for the operation. What relieved the pressure and sustained cooperation? For one thing, for some of the wavering members the FRY went from being seen

---

[213] Ibid.

[214] As one former NSC official put it, "So we made some mistakes. Maybe we were poorly prepared for what actually happened. But tell me how were we going to justify not doing anything when we were hearing things like 'a village a day keeps NATO away'?" Personal conversation, Lexington, Ky., November 2002.

[215] Quoted in *Moral Combat*.

[216] Schelling, *Arms and Influence*, 4.

H

Somewhat
vulnerable

DC, CB

Quadrant 1

Most
vulnerable

CC, CB

Quadrant 4

Intensity of
pro-camp
mobilization

Least
vulnerable

DC, DB

Quadrant 2

Somewhat
vulnerable

CC, DB

Quadrant 3

L

L   H

Intensity of anticamp mobilization

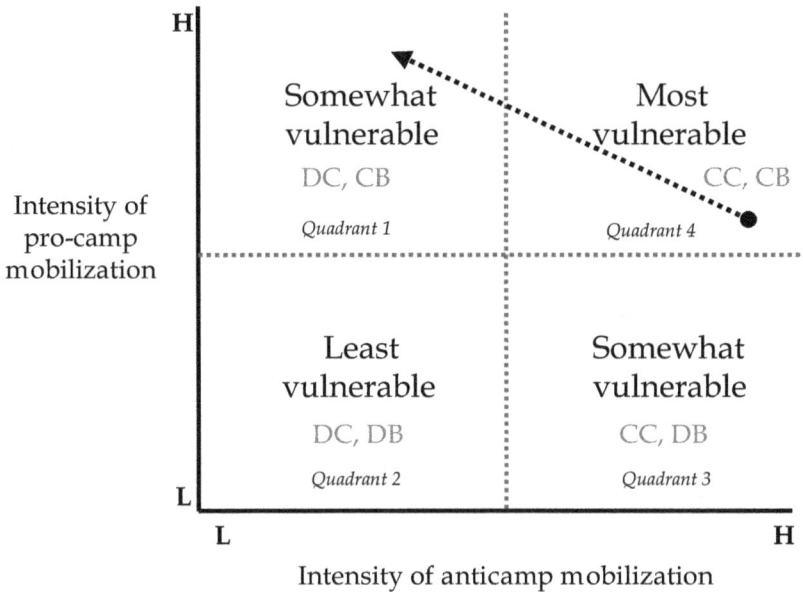

Figure 3.1. Why Milosevic failed. CB, concentrated benefits; CC, concentrated costs; DB, diffuse benefits; DC, diffuse costs; H, high; L, low.

as a victim of NATO belligerency to an aggressor. For instance, despite significant skepticism and hostility in some German political parties (particularly the Greens) toward the bombing campaign, even those in the left wing of the party concluded, as Brian Rathbun observed, that "simply ending a military campaign was not a viable option.... The Greens argued that the bombing would have to continue if Yugoslavia made no overtures." Experience with Milosevic had demonstrated "that he only negotiated under pressure."[217]

In addition, as already suggested, attitudes toward Kosovar Albanian refugees themselves softened. This process was aided by the Yugoslavs' own egregious behavior, as well as a deft NATO propaganda campaign, in which Milosevic was compared to Hitler and the fleeing Kosovars were compared to those fleeing a Nazi onslaught. By likening the mass outmigration to the Holocaust and casting Serb behavior as genocide, the Kosovar Albanians were (at least temporarily) transformed from threats into victims. Consequently, the concentration of support for the displaced in the pro-refugee/migrant camp skyrocketed while the level of opposition

---

[217] Rathbun, *Partisan Interventions*, 116. This position was part of the resolution passed at the May 1999 Green Party conference.

to them declined, thereby radically reducing NATO vulnerability to coercion over the course of the crisis. Indeed, somewhat ironically, this telegenically sympathetic group was critical in helping NATO preserve cohesion and diminish domestic criticism within its member states. (Although, according to Margarita Kondopoulou, the Greek media was something of an exception. Although the Kosovar Albanians were increasingly portrayed as sympathetic victims, NATO was portrayed as the real aggressor, with the Kosovar Albanians fleeing in response to NATO bombing raids.[218])

Criticism was also attenuated because the scenario that certain member states greatly feared, of being overrun with refugees, never materialized. Instead, the effects of the conflict were largely contained within the region, which kept the human (and, hence, the domestic) costs of the conflict low and broadly diffuse. In short, Milosevic also failed because NATO—with the assistance of the international media and the aggressive coverage-generating efforts of the KLA—succeeded in turning his refugee weapon back on him.

A Few Additional Conclusions and Parting Thoughts

Nevertheless, before we declare Milosevic's use of the refugee gambit a total failure, it is worth remembering that in the end the terms of the G-8 deal to which Milosevic agreed were preferable to those on offer at Rambouillet. Moreover, although he was ousted from power eighteen months later, it was not because of NATO bombs but because his own political and economic cronies and the Yugoslav people themselves had finally decided that the costs of international isolation and internal corruption had grown too great to bear. Thus, it was only after a September 2000 election, in which Vojislav Kostunica, Serbian economics professor, ran against him, that Milosevic was finally and truly defeated.

In the end, a close examination of the course of events demonstrates that even though Milosevic ultimately fell short, at least for a time, he came close to succeeding. This fact alone ought to give readers pause because, along with all of the purported lessons that keen observers and future adversaries may glean about the limits of coercion and the power of propaganda, they may also learn a thing or two about the potential firepower of demographic bombs. Moreover, cases in which one country faces a crisis largely alone (e.g., Italy in 1997 with Operation Alba) are likely to be more common than those in which a multilateral coalition such as NATO is the opposition/target.

---

[218] Kondopoulou, "Greek Media."

Finally, NATO intervention in Kosovo—driven as it was, at least in part, by the actions of the KLA and the support it garnered via intelligent use of the global media apparatus—may encourage other groups to manipulate international opinion via their own propaganda campaigns. By provoking attacks on themselves by their own governments, these groups may seek assistance with their bids for self-determination or for the overthrow of undemocratic governments, as the KLA now readily admits it did.[219] If former Prime Minister Blair's notion of when the principle of interference in the internal affairs of others states is acceptable (i.e., whenever oppression produces massive flows of refugees that unsettle neighboring countries) is embraced, it could provide a "virtual blank check" for future interventions.[220] Such a proactive stance may present a powerful incentive for those struggling for independence—and not one that we can afford to dismiss lightly. It can also serve as a handy fig leaf for actors who wish to support self-determination movements for their own self-serving political reasons, as the Russians amply demonstrated in the conflict over the breakaway Georgian province of South Ossetia in summer 2008.[221]

[219] See, for instance, *Moral Combat*.

[220] Granting of course that the appetite of many states for intervention has (at least temporarily) diminished in the aftermath of the troubled 2003 U.S.-led invasion of Iraq. See Ted Galen Carpenter, "Perils of the New NATO," in *NATO's Empty Victory: A Postmortem on the Balkan War*, ed. Ted Galen Carpenter (Washington, D.C.: CATO Institute, 2000), 178; Blair, "Doctrine of the International Community." (Blair's notion also conspicuously comports with the tenets of the UN Responsibility to Protect initiative.)

[221] See, for instance, "Russia Recognizes Georgian Rebels," BBC News, August 26, 2008.

4

An Invasion to Stop
the Invasion

The United States and the
Haitian Boatpeople Crises

I've seen this movie before, and I don't like it.
U.S. State Department official on the Haitian refugee crisis

Even before being sworn in for his first term as U.S. president—and leader of the world's sole remaining superpower—William Jefferson Clinton made the first foreign policy decision of his administration. Remarkably, perhaps, Clinton's initial foreign policy decision was not about the future of Russian nuclear weapons, the Iraqi no-fly zone, or even the future of the NATO alliance. Instead, it was a decision about how to deal with would-be asylum seekers from the tiny island nation of Haiti.[1]

Responding to the George H. W. Bush administration's treatment of those fleeing the repressive rule of the junta that had come to power in a coup in September 1991, candidate Clinton ran on a platform that included a promise to repeal what he had called the incumbent's "callous," "cruel," and "immoral" policy of repatriating all Haitians interdicted at

---

Epigraph: Ann Devroy and Barton Gellman, "Exodus From Haiti Strains U.S. Policy; Military Intervention Considered," *Washington Post,* July 2, 1994.

[1] Research materials for this chapter have been drawn from archival materials from JECL; contemporary U.S. and Florida state government documents; and a variety of secondary scholarly, popular, and journalistic sources. For additional perspective, I conducted interviews with former Carter and Clinton administration officials; U.S. diplomats formerly stationed in Port-au-Prince; U.S. military officers who participated in Haiti-related operations between 1991 and 1994; U.S. military officers responsible for Caribbean immigration enforcement at both SOUTHCOM and U.S. Coast Guard, Miami; a representative from the Haitian Refugee Center; officials from the administration of former Florida Governor Lawton Chiles; employees of the Miami District Office of the INS; and former Haitian boatpeople residing in Florida.

sea. Unfortunately for Clinton, however, many Haitians took him at his word.[2] His November 1992 victory stimulated such an "orgy of boat building" in impoverished Haitian coastal towns that by early January 1993 it began to appear that his inauguration bash might be overshadowed by a massive influx of between 50,000 and 200,000 boatpeople.[3] Acutely aware of the political damage such an influx might inflict on his fledgling administration, days before taking office the president-elect suddenly changed tack, declaring that the existing policy was not so "morally-reprehensible" after all and would remain in effect after his inauguration.[4] Although widely condemned by human rights activists, Clinton's move was effective at staving off both the anticipated political and migration crises, albeit only temporarily. The consequences of his policy flip-flop and rhetorical "tumble from the moral high ground" continued to haunt his administration for the next twenty-one months, eventually generating overwhelming pressure to respond militarily to resolve the ongoing political crisis and put an end to the Haitian exodus.[5] The crisis only came to a definitive end after Clinton launched the domestically unpopular Operation Restore Democracy—wherein more than 20,000 U.S. soldiers were dispatched to restore exiled Haitian president Jean-Bertrand Aristide to power—and only after somewhere between 60,000 and 100,000 Haitians had taken to the sea in a desperate attempt to reach the United States.[6]

[2] As one commentator put it at the time, "If politicians need evidence that people actually believe campaign promises, they need only look to the speeches of Bill Clinton and the reaction of the impoverished and politically oppressed people of Haiti. When candidate Clinton promised that he would change President Bush's policy of systematically turning back all Haitian refugees, Haitians did two things: They hailed Clinton as their savior, and they started building boats, many by ripping siding and roof beams from their houses to use as construction materials. A week ago, those planning their escape from Haiti spoke of President-elect Bill Clinton with reverence. His statements in favor of Haitian refugees had earned him a common saying, 'After God comes Bill Clinton.'" Howard W. French, "Haitians Express Sense of Betrayal," New York Times, January 17, 1993.

[3] Pamela Constable, "World Crises Won't Wait for a Transition in US," Boston Globe, November 30, 1992. Clinton's transition team reportedly feared that the inaugural would "be spoiled by television film of thousands of destitute Haitians being arrested on the high seas or, worse still, perishing during a vain bid to reach the US." Simon Tisdall, "US Ships Sail For Haiti to Halt Exodus," Guardian, January 16, 1993.

[4] Matthew Vita, "Clinton to Haitians: Stay Home; Influx Peril Sinks Campaign Pledge," Atlanta Journal and Constitution, January 15, 1993.

[5] Ibid.; David Malone, "Haiti and the International Community: A Case Study," Survival 39 (1997): 135.

[6] In addition, although the figures are imprecise, during the reign of the junta as many as 4,000 people were killed, around 300,000 became internally displaced, and thousands more fled across the border to the Dominican Republic; Robert Maguire, Edwige Balutansky, Jacques Fomerand, Larry Minear, William G. O'Neill, Thomas G. Weiss, and Sarah Zaidi, Haiti Held Hostage: International Responses to the Quest for Nationhood, 1986–1996, Occasional Paper no. 23 (Providence, R.I.: Watson Institute for International Studies, 1996). See also Kate Doyle, "Hollow Diplomacy in Haiti," World Policy Journal 11 (1994): 50–58; Ian Martin, "Haiti: Mangled Multilateralism," Foreign Policy 95 (1995): 72–89.

This chapter presents a longitudinal case study that explores why the Clinton administration decided to launch an invasion of the island nation, despite only tepid public support for, and significant congressional opposition to, military intervention. In the context of this examination, the chapter also tests my proposed explanation—that the decision to invade was a consequence of a successful exercise of migration-driven coercion—against the prevailing alternative explanation that it was simply a response to outflows that arose as an unintended externality of the junta's oppressive rule. The chapter likewise compares and contrasts the course and outcome of the 1991–1994 case with a successful precursor in the early 1980s and a demonstrable failure in the mid-2000s.

Interestingly, however, the 1991–1994 Haiti case did not commence as a case of migration-driven coercion. After raising his own potential hypocrisy costs to dizzying heights by promising to abandon the Bush repatriation strategy, in January 1993 the Clinton administration successfully fended off an imminent migration crisis and political fiasco by explicitly promising to reinstall exiled Haitian President Jean-Bertrand Aristide. But when a year into the first Clinton administration Aristide was no closer to being restored to power, the exiled Haitian leader went on the offensive, employing a strategy of coercive engineered migration. Largely as a consequence of his own rhetoric, Clinton became trapped in a kind of pincer movement between Aristide's two lines of attack: (1) his supporters within the United States (e.g., the Congressional Black Caucus and the Trans-Africa Lobby), who threatened to raise the domestic political costs of inaction to unacceptable levels, and (2) Aristide's demographic bombs from farther afield, who threatened to impose profound economic and political costs on the United States and on Clinton, if and when they arrived on U.S. shores. In the end, only by launching a military operation whose express mission was the restoration of democracy in Haiti could Clinton defang his critics at home *and* staunch the outflow from abroad. It was Aristide's coercive gambit that finally forced Clinton's hand and brought the crisis to a close.[7]

This case is noteworthy for several reasons. First, it demonstrates that this kind of coercion can be successfully conducted even from afar, seeing as Aristide was living in exile in the United States when he undertook actions designed to stimulate outflows from Haiti. Second, it provides a model

---

[7] This is not an interpretation that everyone shares. See, for instance, Monica Hirst, "Strategic Coercion in Latin America," in *Strategic Coercion: Concepts and Cases*, ed. Lawrence Freedman, 153–62 (Oxford: Oxford University Press, 1998). According to Hirst, the United States was actively trying to restore Aristide to power long before spring 1994. But the chronology of events and the apparent relative passivity of the United States, in September 1991 to early 1994 seem inconsistent with this claim.

illustration of the very real dangers of engaging in rhetorical grandstanding. The policies pursued under the Bush administration were no more injurious to the principles of refugee protection than those Clinton relied on. Yet candidate Clinton's decision to resort to normatively exalted rhetoric would lay bare these inherent contradictions and force him to take actions as president that his predecessor had successfully avoided. Third, Clinton's decision to intervene militarily in Haiti to restore its democratically elected leader to power, although he did so reluctantly, appeared to have marked a turning point vis-à-vis then emerging norms of justified intervention, a position that was advanced still further in the 1999 Kosovo campaign (see chap. 3) and in the period since.[8]

I begin this chapter by providing a short history of postwar U.S.-Haitian relations, including a brief examination of a 1979–1981 bilateral migration crisis, the consequences of which bore directly on the crisis in the 1990s. Then, to set the stage for what follows, I outline the background to the 1991–1994 crisis. Next, I explain how and why the strategies and tactics of the key actors shifted over the course of the crisis and analyze the consequences of these shifts in light of the responses they generated within the principal target state—the United States. At the same time, I evaluate whether these evolving strategies (and their accompanying tactical actions) comport with the predictions of my theory, in part by undertaking a constructive comparison with U.S. responses to the partially concomitant 1994 Rwandan genocide. Next, I evaluate the major propositions of this book in light of the evidence presented in this chapter and offer a few additional thoughts and possible implications of these cases. I conclude with a comparative examination of a follow-up proto-crisis that took place in February 2004, during which it appears that Aristide attempted unsuccessfully to reprise his 1994 success, and explore how and why the outcomes in 1994 and 2004 diverged so significantly.

Historical Precedents

Operation Restore Democracy was not the first military intervention that the United States undertook in the Caribbean or even the first on the island of Hispaniola. Between 1915 and 1934—in accordance with the Roosevelt Corollary to the Monroe Doctrine[9]—U.S. Marines had occupied Haiti and

---

[8] Moreover, the various constituencies in the United States calling for and opposing intervention ironically represented a total role reversal of their earlier attitudes toward U.S. military intervention; Malone, "Haiti and the International Community," 135.

[9] Thomas Weiss, "Haiti, 1991–1996: Why Wait So Long?" in *Military-Civilian Interactions: Intervening in Humanitarian Crises* (New York: Rowman & Littlefield, 1999), 170.

the neighboring Dominican Republic.[10] For a variety of reasons, it was not an occupation that served the island nation particularly well. First, although some infrastructure improvements were undertaken during the U.S. occupation, when the marines left in 1934 the country was little better off than it had been before they arrived. Although Haiti had once been the richest colony in the French colonial empire, when the United States withdrew it was still the poorest country in the Western hemisphere, a fact that remains true today. Second, the significant racial and social cleavages that existed between Haiti's majority impoverished black population and its mulatto-dominated elites were not improved during the U.S. tenure; in fact, they were reinforced.[11] Finally—and most problematically—the most lasting artifact of the occupation was the U.S.-created Garde d'Haiti, a well-organized and well-equipped military force that was subsequently (and repeatedly) used by the elites to oppress the majority.[12]

Nor was the period following Aristide's ouster the first time Haitian and U.S. immigration policies became inexorably intertwined with their foreign policies.[13] Such connections had existed since François "Papa Doc" Duvalier's accession to power in 1957 and continued through the reign of his son Jean-Claude "Baby Doc" Duvalier, who came to power on his father's death in 1971. Although both Duvaliers were widely recognized to be tyrannical and repressive leaders, the United States stalwartly supported them as bulwarks against communism in the Caribbean, particularly after Cuba fell to Fidel Castro in 1959.[14] The repressive rule of the Duvaliers drove tens of thousands of middle-class professionals from Haiti to the United States, so that as early as 1968 there were more Haitian physicians

[10] For a history of the occupation, see, for instance, Max Boot, *The Savage Wars of Peace: Small Wars and the Rise of American Power* (New York: Basic Books, 2002); Alex Dupuy, *Haiti in the World Economy: Class, Race, and Underdevelopment since 1700* (Boulder: Westview Press, 1989). Some have argued that it was the fact of the earlier occupation—and that the Americans left behind a powerful, albeit corrupt, paramilitary apparatus—that obligated the United States to intervene to restore democracy in the 1990s.

[11] See Dupuy, *Haiti in the World Economy;* Amy Wilentz, *The Rainy Season: Haiti since Duvalier* (New York: Simon and Schuster, 1989).

[12] See, for instance, Domingo Avecedo, "The Haitian Crisis and the OAS Response," in *Enforcing Restraint: Collective Intervention in International Conflicts*, ed. Lori Fisler Damrosh (New York: Council on Foreign Relations Press, 1993), 124. See also Weiss, "Haiti, 1991–1996"; Ernest H. Preeg, *The Haitian Dilemma: A Case Study in Demographic, Development, and US Foreign Policy* (Washington, D.C.: Center for Strategic and International Studies, 1996).

[13] See, for instance, Alex Stepick, "Unintended Consequences: Rejecting Haitian Boat People and Destabilizing Duvalier," in *Western Hemisphere Immigration and United States Foreign Policy*, ed. Christopher Mitchell, 125–55 (University Park: Pennsylvania State University Press, 1992).

[14] According to Naomi and Norman Zucker, successive U.S. administrations believed that "if the Duvalier stranglehold were loosened, the political disorder that followed would have led to a communist takeover." Naomi Flink Zucker and Norman L. Zucker, "US Admission Policies towards Cuban and Haitian Migrants," in *The Cambridge Survey of World Migration*, ed. Robin Cohen (Cambridge, UK: Cambridge University Press, 1995), 447.

overseas than inside the country.[15] Even so, migration from Haiti to the United States did not become politically problematic until the mid- to late 1970s, when the size and nature of the migratory stream shifted upward numerically and downward socioeconomically.[16] This quantitative up-surge culminated in an outflow that by 1980 was deemed to be of "crisis proportions." So politically problematic had the crisis become that then U.S. presidential candidate Ronald Reagan cited it—in conjunction with the notorious Mariel boatlift—as proof of the incumbent Jimmy Carter's ineffectual leadership.[17] Indeed, just as Clinton did fourteen years later vis-à-vis the post-1991 Haitian outflow, Reagan made effective political hay out of condemning Carter's efforts to shut off the boatlift, declaring "I can't agree with that. . . . As long as thousands are trying to get here, I can't understand the lack of humanitarianism in that."[18] As Lincoln Bloomfield, former NSC official in the Carter administration, admitted, "We got stuck in the middle, where there was no right answer. Taking them in got us in trouble. Trying to send them home got us in trouble. Locking them up *really* got us into trouble."[19]

Nor was the population outflow that followed Aristide's ouster the first one Haitian leaders successfully exploited for their own ends. According to regional experts, on various occasions both Papa Doc and Baby Doc Du-valier extracted financial and political concessions from the United States in exchange for keeping illegal immigration from Haiti under control.[20] For example, having successfully argued during the 1980 U.S. presidential election campaign that Carter's handling of the Cuban and Haitian crises demonstrated his incompetence, once elected, Ronald Reagan was keen

[15] Robert Rotberg, *Haiti: The Politics of Squalor* (Boston: Houghton Mifflin, 1971), 249. One study estimated that between 60 and 75 percent of highly skilled Haitians fled the island between 1957 and 1975; Aaron Segal, "Haiti," in *Population Policies in the Caribbean*, ed. Aaron Segal (Lexington, Mass.: D.C. Heath, 1975), 200. The flight of the highly skilled was viewed as relatively unproblematic because no numerical restrictions on immigration from the Western Hemisphere existed in this period and this group "easily met the 'qualitative' requirements." Aristide Zolberg, "From Invitation to Interdiction: U.S. Foreign Policy and Immigration since 1945," in *Threatened People, Threatened Borders: World Migration and US Policy*, ed. Michael Teitelbaum and Myron Weiner (New York: Norton, 1995), 145.

[16] See, for instance, Christopher Mitchell, "US Policy toward Haitian Boat People, 1972–93," *Annals of the American Academy of Political and Social Science* 534 (1994), 69.

[17] See, for instance, Antonio de la Cova, "US-Cuba Relations during the Reagan Admin-istration," in *President Reagan and the World*, ed. Eric J. Schmertz, Natalie Datlof, and Alexej Ugrinsky (London: Greenwood Press, 1997), 381–92.

[18] Quoted in Michael Getler, "Reagan Attacks Carter Policy on Refugees," *Washington Post*, May 17, 1980. Acknowledging concerns within the United States about unemployment, Rea-gan further noted, "if the building is burning, and there is still a chance to get people out of the upper-floor windows, you don't worry about jobs." Quoted in ibid.

[19] Interview, April 2001, Cohasset, Mass.

[20] Alan Dowty, *Closed Borders: The Contemporary Assault on the Freedom of Movement* (New Haven: Yale University Press, 1987), chap. 5.

to avoid finding himself subject to the same accusation. The threat of this eventuality coming to pass became more acute between Reagan's election and his inauguration, after members of the Republican party and the congressional delegation from Florida publicly called "for strong measures to curb the flow of Haitian boat people."[21] As Christopher Mitchell puts it, "Since the major public relations costs of appearing to have lost control of US borders were incurred in the politically strategic state of Florida, it was far preferable to deflect migration at sea rather than round them up and detain them within range of newspapers and TV stations in Miami."[22]

Thus, soon after assuming office, the pragmatic new president declared that the movement of undocumented Haitians to the United States had indeed become "a serious national problem" and formed a task force dedicated to tackling the issue.[23] Shortly thereafter, in one of the few documented examples of preemptive concession to coercive engineered migration, Reagan and Baby Doc concluded the 1981 U.S.-Haiti Interdiction Agreement. Under the agreement, the United States obtained the right to summarily return all Haitian boatpeople intercepted at sea, after preliminary screening for potential asylum claimants.[24] For its part, Haiti agreed to keep outflows to a minimum.[25]

[21]Stepick, "Unintended Consequences," 142. See also Vernon M. Briggs Jr., *Mass Immigration and the National Interest* (New York: M. E. Sharpe, 1996), 130. See also the memo to President Reagan from the task force established by him on March 6, 1981 in Task Force on Immigration and Refugee Policy, "Subject: What Policy Should the United States Adopt with Regard to Foreign Persons Who Enter South Florida without Visas?" Issue Paper no. 3, Washington, D.C., June 26, 1981.

[22]Christopher Mitchell, "The Political Costs of State Power: US Border Control in South Florida," in *The Wall around the West: State Borders and Immigration Control in North America and Europe*, ed. Peter Andreas and Timothy Snyder (Lanham: Rowman and Littlefield, 2000), 87.

[23]Reagan did so despite the fact that, at that time, Haitians made up less than 2 percent of the undocumented U.S. population. See "Testimony (before the US House of Representatives) of David Hiller, Special Assistant to the Attorney General, Coast Guard Oversight—Part 2," Hearings on Military Readiness of International Programs, Subcommittee on the Coast Guard and Navigation, Committee on Merchant Marine and Fisheries, 97th Congress, 1st session (1981); Presidential Proclamation 4865 of September 29, 1981, FR 28829, 46 *Federal Register* 48, 107, reprinted in 8 USC 1182 a at 820 (Su V. 1981), http://www.archives.gov/federal-register/.

[24]It is worth noting that between 1981 and the coup in 1991, 22,716 Haitians were returned to Haiti and only 28 were allowed to enter the United States to pursue asylum claims. U.S. Committee for Refugees, *World Refugee Survey 1995* (Washington, D.C.: USCR, 1996), 180.

[25]See, for instance, Lawyers Committee for Human Rights, *Refugee Refoulement: The Forced Return of Haitians under the US-Haitian Interdiction Agreement* (New York: Lawyers Committee for Human Rights, 1990). A U.S. State Department study team that traveled to Haiti in the late 1970s found that, as a rule, most Haitians encountered little resistance to their departure. Although departure without travel documents and exit authorization was a punishable offense under Haitian law, such offences were rarely prosecuted. Moreover, the only enforcement that usually occurred was when local authorities felt that they were "not adequately paid to ignore the activity." JECL, "Department of State Memorandum, June 19, 1979, Subject: State Department Study Team on Haitian Returnees," CR&J—White Box 23, Cubans and Haitians [8].

Officially, the United States offered nothing in return for Haitian co-operation, beyond some assistance in implementing the bilateral accord and a promise to provide Haitian citizens with more nonimmigrant visas. But off the record, U.S. officials admitted that they had promised to "de-emphasize human rights" and "look the other way on graft and corruption" inside Haiti.[26] Duvalier's government was also promised significant economic and security-related financial support.[27] And the Haitian Navy reportedly obtained free fuel from the U.S. Coast Guard, which it was then able to sell on the open market.[28] As Jorge Dominguez bluntly characterized it, "The Haitian government had been bought."[29]

As table 4.1 indicates, until the unseating of Baby Doc in 1986 this bilateral arrangement worked fairly well.[30] Haiti greatly reduced the size of its population outflows, and—until congressional pressure grew too great—the Reagan administration provided political and financial succor to Baby Doc's regime.[31]

But the end was not long in coming. In February 1986, just before he was due to be deposed, Baby Doc left the country and retired to the south of France.[32] It then took nearly five more years, four more presidents, two more coups, and two failed election attempts before Haiti held its first fully

[26] Stepick, "Unintended Consequences," 147. These claims appear to be confirmed by the fact that, in the three years that followed, the Reagan administration continued to maintain that "Haiti was making satisfactory progress in implementing political reforms," despite the fact that the U.S. Congress had come to very different conclusions and was working steadily to cut financial aid to the island nation. U.S. Congress PL98–151, "Continuing Resolution," 824; Stepick, "Unintended Consequences," 149. See also Christopher Mitchell, "Reviewing the Case Studies: Implications for Understanding Policy Choice," in *Western Hemisphere Immigration and United States Foreign Policy,* ed. Christopher Mitchell, 285–300 (University Park: Pennsylvania State University Press, 1992).

[27] Thomas Enders, then assistant secretary of state, testified before Congress that Haiti could not manage to control the departure of its citizens alone and that, in addition to assistance with the interdiction program, "the economic and security assistance requests for fiscal year 1982 will be essential to enable the Haitian government to deal with a severely strained economy." Quoted in Jorge Dominguez, "US-Latin American Relations," in *Immigration and US Foreign Policy,* ed. Robert W. Tucker, Charles B. Keely, and Linda Wrigley (Boulder: Westview Press, 1990), 158.

[28] Ibid. See also Stepick, "Unintended Consequences"; Zolberg, "From Invitation to Interdiction."

[29] Dominguez, "US-Latin American Relations," 158–59. See also Howard W. French, "Between Haiti and the US Lies a Quandary," *New York Times,* November 24, 1991, Week in Review; Zolberg, "From Invitation to Interdiction."

[30] The costs of this program were modest but not trivial, approximately $30 million per year for the full-time use of one Coast Guard cutter.

[31] For a discussion of how and why things began to deteriorate around 1984, leading to Duvalier's ouster two years later, see Stepick, "Unintended Consequences," 147–52.

[32] Reagan had concluded that it was more sensible to guarantee Baby Doc's safety and financial security than to await a bloodbath. For a fuller discussion of the period between Duvalier and Aristide, see Robert Rotberg, "Haiti in Turmoil: Politics and Policy under Aristide and Clinton," World Peace Foundation Reports no. 32, Cambridge, Mass., 2003; Alex Dupuy, *Haiti in the New World Order* (Boulder: Westview Press, 1997), 104; ibid.

TABLE 4.1
Apprehensions of Undocumented Haitian Migrants
to the United States (via Florida)

Year	Apprehensions
1980	24,530
1981	8,069
1982	134
1983	333
1984	836
1985	539
1986	3,595

Source: Adapted from Alex Stepick, "Unintended Consequences: Rejecting Haitian Boat People and Destabilizing Duvalier," in *Western Hemisphere Immigration and United States Foreign Policy*, ed. Christopher Mitchell (University Park: Pennsylvania University Press), 135.

"free and fair" democratic elections, in which populist priest Jean-Bertrand Aristide was swept into power with an impressive 67 percent of the vote.[33]

The 1991 Coup and the Advent of the Migration Crisis

A New Day in Haiti

Although the new Haitian leader was wildly popular with the impoverished black Haitian majority, he was despised by the country's small but powerful, mulatto-dominated, socioeconomic elite and by its military. Their hostility was not surprising, as both groups felt threatened by the wide-ranging economic and political reforms candidate Aristide had promised to implement.[34] Aristide further alienated the ruling class by his manner of governance.[35] He neglected to forge much-needed political alliances, eschewed involvement of the Haitian legislature in governance, engaged in widespread nepotism and patronage, and, critically, failed to condemn his supporters' behavior when they resorted to violence against

[33] The election of François (Papa Doc) Duvalier in 1957 was ostensibly democratic, but it had been widely condemned as corrupt. The 1990 election was held in response to an Organization of American States (OAS) offer and overseen by the organization.

[34] Avecedo, "Haitian Crisis," 131. See also Robert C. DiPrizio, *Armed Humanitarians: US Interventions from Northern Iraq to Kosovo* (Baltimore: Johns Hopkins University Press, 2002), 89.

[35] As Alex Dupuy puts it, "Aristide represented the worst fears of the prebendary state and the propertied bourgeoisie because he was not preaching a democracy that would protect the interests of all sectors of Haitian society equally. Rather, he advocated a democracy that would rectify past injustices and promote the interests of impoverished and excluded majority more than it would those of the privileged classes." *Haiti in the New World Order*, 104.

his political opponents.[36] Thus, few were surprised when—less than eight months after he assumed the presidency—Aristide was overthrown in an elite-supported military coup d'etat led by Lieutenant General Raoul Cedras,[37] Brigadier General Philippe Biamby (army chief-of-staff), and Lieutenant Colonel Joseph Michel François (police chief).

Back to the Future

After the coup, the junta engaged in widespread political repression. The armed forces and the police attacked, arrested, tortured, and occasionally murdered Aristide's supporters. At the same time, the junta stopped policing Haitian borders.[38] After a three-week interval—and days before an initial round of post-coup international trade sanctions imposed by the UN and the Organization of American States (OAS) was to come into effect—the first Haitians began to arrive on U.S. shores. Evidence suggests that the new military rulers were not actively encouraging people to leave; nevertheless, only rarely did they attempt to stop them. Instead, evidence suggests the Cedras-led junta attempted to use the tacit threat of a massive outflow as part of its strategy to accomplish two things: (1) dissuade the international community from imposing sanctions, a tactic that was mostly unsuccessful,[39] and (2) discourage the United States and Latin American states from taking active measures to unseat them, which was for a time successful.[40] As Cedras put it, he was "the pin in Haiti's hand grenade; if pulled, an explosion will follow."[41] In other words, although Aristide was the pivotal actor in the 1991–1994 Haitian migration drama,

[36] For instance, Aristide failed to condemn the practice of "necklacing," whereby his supporters placed burning gasoline-filled tires around their victims' necks. See Weiss, "Haiti, 1991–1996."

[37] Aristide had named him commander-in-chief of the military a few months earlier.

[38] Soldiers sometimes turned up to extort a payoff from rafters but rarely to stop departures. Greg Chamberlain, "US Offers Haiti Army $50m to Restore Democracy; Military agrees to observers' force as coast guard ships stand off shore," *Guardian*, January 18, 1993.

[39] Douglas Farah, "Coast Guard Patrols, Clinton's Switch on Repatriation Delay Haitian Exodus," *Washington Post*, January 21, 1993.

[40] Of course, this was an overdetermined outcome because few states were interested in taking military action in Haiti. The troika believed—for a long time, correctly—that the United States lacked the will to take actions strong enough to lead to its ouster. Reluctance within the Pentagon to consider an invasion, combined with the Bush administration belief that "the security of our country or the safety of our citizens was not at risk," meant "no serious consideration was given to the use of force to restore Aristide to power in Haiti." Interviews, July 2000, Washington, D.C., and April 2001, Cambridge, Mass. See also, for the first goal, Robert A. Pastor, "Haiti, 1994," in *The United States and Coercive Diplomacy*, ed. Robert J. Art and Patrick Cronin (Washington, D.C.: United States Institute for Peace, 2003), 122; and, for the second goal, James A. Baker III, *The Politics of Diplomacy* (New York: G. Putnam's Sons, 1995), 601–2.

[41] "Gathering Storm Clouds," *Maclean's*, July 25, 1994.

the leaders of the junta also played supporting roles. As will be discussed later in this chapter, critical roles were also played by other parties in the region, most particularly by the country of Panama.

The Bush Administration Response

Although the 1981 agreement was technically still in force after the coup, beginning in November 1991 a series of U.S. courts issued temporary restraining orders that prevented the Bush administration from forcibly repatriating Haitians interdicted at sea.[42] The administration thus found itself caught on the horns of a dilemma. Having condemned the coup and supported (albeit in a half-hearted way) the imposition of sanctions, the Bush administration was hard-pressed to claim that those fleeing were only economic migrants. Thus, beginning in November 1991, instead of being returned to the island after a cursory shipboard screening, those picked up at sea were transferred to the U.S. naval base at Guantanamo for screening as part of an "off-shore safe haven" program. Those found to have a credible basis for claiming asylum were then transferred to the United States to pursue their claims.

As UN and OAS sanctions—admittedly leaky because the border with the neighboring Dominican Republic was never effectively closed— continued to bite into the Haitian economy and the junta continued its repression, the tide of boatpeople began to swell significantly. By May 1992, the camp at Guantanamo was overflowing, 13,000 Haitians were still awaiting asylum screenings, new would-be refugees were being intercepted at rates of as high as 1,300 per day, and rumors abounded that more were on their way.[43] Within the Bush administration, mounting concern over the potential electoral consequences of a major Haitian boatlift in the summer before the presidential election produced a major policy shift. On May 24, 1992, Bush issued the Kennebunkport Order, a directive that effectively meant that the Interdiction Agreement was back in force.

Given the configuration of forces in support of and opposed to the admission of Haitians, Bush made a calculated political decision that he should be more worried about the probable political backlash associated with accepting the fleeing Haitians than the backlash of the Haitian community, their advocates, and refugee supporters, more generally.[44] "Mariel definitely left a shadow. Washington [was] nervous all year about the

---

[42] For instance, because of the prevailing conditions on the ground in Haiti, a lawsuit brought by the Haitian Refugee Center in November 1991 resulted in the temporary suspension of the policy of automatic repatriation.

[43] "Haitian Exodus Predictions Doubted," *St. Louis Post-Dispatch,* January 17, 1993.

[44] See Mitchell, "Political Costs of State Power," for a brief discussion of the political weakness of Haitians in the early 1990s.

Haitian influx," according to Father Richard Ryscavage, head of the U.S. Catholic Conference Office of Migration and Refugee Services, which provided social and legal services to some Haitian refugees.[45] Thenceforth, all Haitians interdicted on the high seas would be returned directly to Haiti, without prior screening.

Although little had changed on the ground in Haiti—if anything, conditions had deteriorated—the official line from Washington became that the boatpeople were fleeing economic deprivation, not political repression.[46] Off the record, however, some officials conceded the "problematic" nature of their position. One of Bush's "foreign policy aides" noted, "if you ask who faces the greatest danger of being killed or arrested as a result of political turmoil, a Cuban or a Haitian, I'd have to pick the Haitian."[47] Nevertheless, Haitians were again to be repatriated, whereas Cubans were not. Thus, from May 1992 until Clinton was forced to abandon the policy two years later, in-country processing became the only option for Haitians trying to legally enter the United States.[48]

The apparently "hypocritical" and "pandering" nature of Bush's position was not lost on those who believed that the United States had a responsibility to do better, as this *New York Times* op-ed by Leslie Gelb suggests:

> With little political incentive to please American blacks, Mr. Bush ignored refugees and starvation in Haiti and Somalia. In so doing, he forfeited America's moral leadership. For the first time since 1945, America has no moral basis for urging humanitarianism on others, and cannot credibly importune Europeans to care for refugees from Yugoslavia and Romania....All Presidents play politics with foreign policy in election years. But to keep his office Mr. Bush has, to an unprecedented degree, stroked the lesser instincts of Americans— and squandered America's credibility, moral leadership and power.[49]

Another lamented:

> It's so hypocritical, so mean. What's happened to America?...Bush must know these people will be persecuted, even shot at, when they return home.

---

[45] Quoted in "Send 'Em Back!" *Time*, June 8, 1992. And Ira Kurzban, an attorney for the Miami Haitian Refugee Center, lamented, "the Haiti policy played to the basest part of the Republican Party, the anti-alien group, the racists, to keep them from crossing over to Ross Perot." In ibid.

[46] Maguire et al., *Haiti Held Hostage*. During this same period, partisans of the coup started donning T-shirts and selling bumper stickers that proclaimed, "Haiti, love it or leave it."

[47] "Send 'Em Back."

[48] See, for instance, Americas Watch, National Coalition for Haitian Refugees, and Jesuit Refugee Service/USA, "No Port in a Storm: The Misguided Use of In-Country Refugee Processing in Haiti," no. 5, Washington, D.C., September 1993.

[49] Leslie H. Gelb, "Foreign Affairs; Mr. Bush, Statesman," *New York Times*, September 24, 1992.

Has he no heart?…It's not a question Bush likes to hear. Last week, in another classroom in a predominantly white and Republican suburb of Atlanta, a black father stood and asked if America no longer opened its arms to all refugees fleeing oppression. The President reddened and replied in a tone of bottled heat. "It's a very good question," Bush said, "and the answer is this: Yes, the Statue of Liberty still stands, and we still open our arms, under our law, to people that are politically oppressed. I will not open the doors to economic refugees all over the world."[50]

And still more trenchantly:

President Bush's treatment of Haitians fleeing their nation highlights glaring inconsistencies in US refugee policy. It also sets a woeful precedent that could prompt other countries to curtail assistance to refugees.…In turning away boatloads of Haitians without screening them, the US is violating the spirit, if not the letter, of a 1951 United Nations convention against such a practice, experts say. The State Department claims that the US technically is in compliance because it is turning the Haitians away before they reach US territory.…But the US never made that narrow distinction when, for a decade, it urged other nations to rescue Vietnamese boatpeople fleeing communism.[51]

The most significant criticism, however, came from Bush's rival for the presidency. As candidate Reagan had done in 1980, candidate Clinton was quick to use Bush's policy shift on Haiti as a political cudgel against him, denouncing it as "a blow to America's moral authority in defending the rights of refugees."[52] As previously noted, Clinton continued to wield this rhetorical weapon until the potential political consequences of doing so came back to haunt him in early January 1993. Elizabeth Drew, Clinton biographer, puts it plainly: the campaign strategy of having Clinton "appear [to be] more the activist in some areas…led him to say some things that he would later regret."[53]

With the assistance of the outgoing Bush administration—and fearing a massive outflow of as many as 150,000–250,000 Haitians[54]—the incoming president instituted what his advisors called, oddly enough, a

[50] "Send 'Em Back!"
[51] Robert S. Greenberger, "Washington Insight: Bush's Handling of Haitians Highlights Contradictions in U.S. Refugee Policy," *Wall Street Journal*, June 1, 1992.
[52] Quoted in J. F. O. McAllister, "Lives on Hold," *Time*, February 1, 1993.
[53] Elizabeth Drew, *On the Edge: The Clinton Presidency* (New York: Simon and Schuster, 1994), 138.
[54] See, for instance, "US Sends 22 Ships to Keep Haitians in Haiti," *St. Petersburg Times*, January 16, 1993; Steven A. Holmes, "US Sends Flotilla to Prevent Exodus From Haiti by Sea," *New York Times*, January 16, 1993; "Haitian Exodus Predictions Doubted."

"humanitarian" naval blockade.[55] The cordon, called Operation Able Manner, entailed the establishment of a naval barricade outside the 12-mile Haitian territorial limit to block an exodus; any intercepted boats were to be returned to the island. The U.S. Coast Guard, Navy, and Marines launched an operation to dispatch up to twenty-two warships, cutters, and patrol boats. Ironically, this meant there was a substantially larger naval presence in the area under the "humanitarian" Clinton than under the "racist" Bush, who had sent only two to three cutters to patrol the 600-mile route from Haiti to southern Florida since the September 1991 coup.[56] In any event, the "humanitarian" blockade was unnecessary because the feared exodus never materialized. Instead, a personal intervention by exiled President Aristide saved the incoming Clinton administration from its own preinaugural Mariel.

The Crisis That Was Not and the Critical Role of Jean-Bertrand Aristide

Like many *agents provocateurs*, Jean-Bertrand Aristide (following his ouster) was a weak nonstate actor, with few policy instruments at his disposal.[57] Even before Clinton took office, Aristide had recognized that "the threat of an exodus was one way to focus the attention of the international community, and especially the Clinton administration, on the political stalemate in Haiti."[58] Aristide had also recognized that he could use this threat to help achieve his primary goal—a return to power in Haiti. As Alex Dupuy has put it, "he hoped to convince Washington that, without his return, the crisis in Haiti and its consequences for the United States, especially the refugee dilemma, would not be resolved."[59] Aristide had failed in his attempts to persuade the Bush administration to reinstall him—after brief consideration, Bush had dismissed the idea of military intervention out of hand, declaring the return of Aristide "not worth the life of a single American soldier."[60] Aristide believed, however, that he would have more success with the incoming president. Hence, when President-elect Clinton

[55] The idea was that the military would interdict boats to prevent people from drowning. "We're looking at the general path they usually take coming out," said Jack O'Dell, Coast Guard spokesman. "We want to be in a situation where we can prevent any possible loss of life should the sea get rough." Quoted in Holmes, "US Sends Flotilla."

[56] "US Sends 22 Ships."

[57] See Dupuy, *Haiti in the New World Order*, chap. 7, for a description of Aristide's limited maneuvering room after the coup.

[58] Farah, "Coast Guard Patrols." This assessment accords with my interviews.

[59] Dupuy, *Haiti in the New World Order*, 142.

[60] Quoted in Martin Walker, "Immigration Fears Put US in Quandary over Haiti," *Guardian*, July 9, 1994.

approached him in early January 1993, Aristide was ready and willing to make a deal.[61]

It was agreed that in exchange for the U.S. government's adopting a more aggressive stance against the junta and working for his restoration to power, Aristide would help stop the impending migration crisis.[62] As Aristide put it:

> A "deal," as Americans like to call it, could be made between the two of us [President Clinton and me]. I would discourage the boat people and he would favor the return to democracy. The Haitian refugees would stay in the country and, in concert with the UN, the American president would put all his weight into the balance in order to get rid of the *de facto* power. This was a collaboration from which each side had something to gain.[63]

In justifying his decision to trust Clinton, Aristide avowed, "our first contacts had given me the impression of a change, even if his first decision contradicted his commitment to break with the junta....I had the sense that he understood the stakes and that his choice was for democracy. In short, he could play an essential role."[64]

Thus, while Clinton would concentrate his attentions on working with the UN to resolve the crisis, Aristide would work on convincing Haitians to stay at home. Aristide took a variety of public and private steps to make this happen. First, on January 16, 1993, Aristide announced in an interview that he had received private assurances from Clinton that the new administration would support his restoration as the leader of Haiti. "There is no doubt [Clinton] is supporting me," as he put it.[65] In their own pronouncements, transition team officials acknowledged Clinton's commitment to Aristide's return, but they were noncommittal as to the timing and strategy for implementation.[66] Nevertheless, Aristide was prepared to believe that Clinton would move quickly to see him restored to power. "I go with him, because that way we can have that democracy back

---

[61] See Dupuy, *Haiti in the New World Order*, 141; Doyle, "Hollow Diplomacy in Haiti"; Council on Hemispheric Affairs, "Clinton Missing the Boat on Haiti," Press Release no. 93.2, January 8, 1993; Vita, "Clinton to Haitians."

[62] Doyle, "Hollow Diplomacy in Haiti"; interviews, May 1999, Warrenton, Va., and April 2005, Cambridge, Mass.

[63] Jean-Bertrand Aristide (with Christopher Wargny), *Dignite'* (Paris: Editions du Sevil, 1994), 110. Robert Pastor confirms that such a deal was struck (he was in the room with Aristide when Clinton called); "Haiti, 1994," 124n. 14. Other U.S. officials concurred in interviews in May 1999, Warrenton, Va., and April 2005, Cambridge, Mass.

[64] Aristide, *Dignite'*, 110–11.

[65] Holmes, "US Sends Flotilla."

[66] Ibid.

in Haiti as soon as possible."[67] Second—sometimes with Clinton at his side and sometimes alone—Aristide broadcast numerous radio messages to Haiti urging his countrymen not to flee but, rather to stay home and fight.[68] Third, he made television appearances, including one on CNN, in which he told his interviewer, "You cannot imagine how happy I am when last night I was talking with President Clinton and seeing, now, together, it's so beautiful to work for democracy."[69] In the same interview, he also hinted strongly that he would soon return to Haiti as president. Fourth, in a letter and in a subsequent Voice of America broadcast, Aristide announced that "once international observers were in place, he would name a new prime minister, form a consensus government, and grant amnesty to the army."[70] Fifth, Aristide and his supporters in Washington and in south Florida made personal phone calls to Aristide's network of personal and political supporters on the ground in Haiti and told them to counsel those were considering taking to the sea to stay home.[71]

Aristide's personal entreaties and public media appearances proved extremely effective. The threatened exodus was averted. As one youth in Sunshine City, the largest and most wretched slum in Port-au-Prince, declared, "Aristide says wait for him. Okay, we'll wait, but if he doesn't come back, we'll go."[72] Another Haitian, a commercial pilot who "lived in the area for 35 years and flew over the region frequently" reported "the word is out not to go. They are going to wait it out....Right now there is no movement at all."[73] And as Reverend Antoine Adrien, Aristide's chief representative in Haiti, put it in a telephone interview at the time, "To be frank, I am more hopeful now, because before Mr. Clinton was promising the moon. Now he is promising something more real, to try to bring back democracy....Everyone knows that if there is real political will in Washington, the army cannot resist."[74] In short, Haitians declared that their primary reason for staying put was Aristide and his personal appeals, not the naval blockade.

Of course, one must be careful about assigning too much credit to Aristide in single-handedly forestalling the outflow. Undoubtedly a number of Haitians decided to remain simply because Clinton's policy shift made the prospect of asylum less likely. Nevertheless, in the days before

---

[67] Vita, "Clinton to Haitians."

[68] Pamela Constable, "In Departure from Pledge, Clinton Says He Will Send Haitians Back," *Boston Globe*, January 15, 1993.

[69] Quoted in Constable, "In Departure from Pledge."

[70] Dupuy, *Haiti in the New World Order*, 141.

[71] Interviews, February 2000, Miami, Fla., and July 2000, Washington, D.C.; Dupuy, *Haiti in the New World Order*, 141.

[72] Quoted in Chamberlain, "US Offers Haiti Army $50m."

[73] Quoted in Farah, "Coast Guard Patrols."

[74] Quoted in Constable, "In Departure from Pledge."

Aristide took to the airwaves, journalists on the ground had reported that, in the wake of Clinton's announcement, there was "little immediate indication that those planning to leave had changed their minds."[75] Moreover, Aristide was indirectly assisted in his efforts to convince Haitians that he would soon return by Jesse Jackson, who paid a visit to the island just after Clinton's inauguration. At a sermon in the Haitian capital, Jackson spoke before pro-Aristide parishioners and announced that "there [was] a new US policy for Titid [Aristide's nickname] to return." During his visit, Mr. Jackson also affirmed that Clinton had indeed made an agreement with Aristide that committed the United States to the exiled Haitian leader's return and said that he had heard this directly from White House officials.[76] He even went so far as to declare, "This could be Clinton's first foreign-policy victory. There is no reason it cannot happen in the first 100 days. Victory in Haiti would be far easier than in Bosnia or the Middle East."[77]

With the benefit of hindsight, it may seem peculiar to some that Aristide and others were so easily led to believe that Clinton would act in earnest, particularly as he had just reneged on one of his major campaign promises. Nevertheless, at the time many took Clinton seriously when he said he still believed "the policy should be changed.... I just don't think we can do it on a dime on January 20."[78] Although their impression of his credibility and commitment would soon shift, at the start of his first term, both opinion-makers and the U.S. public had very high expectations for William Jefferson Clinton.[79] A *USA Today*/CNN/Gallup Poll found that a majority of respondents believed Clinton would "create a new spirit of idealism," and an ABC/*Washington Post* poll found that 64 percent surveyed believed Clinton would try to keep his major campaign promises.[80] In short, it appears that many interested parties—Aristide included— simply believed Clinton needed a bit more time to follow through on his promises. For instance, one congressional staffer "active in Haiti policy"

---

[75] Douglas Farah, "Haitians Preparing Boats Denounce Policy Shift by Clinton," *Washington Post*, January 15, 1993.

[76] David Beard, "Jackson: New Administration Will Pressure Haitian Army to Reinstate Aristide," Associated Press, January 24, 1993; "Jesse Jackson Visits Haiti to Push for End of Military Rule," *Gazette*, January 23, 1993.

[77] Howard W. French, "Jackson, in Haiti, Cautions Military," *New York Times*, January 24, 1993.

[78] Quoted in Vita, "Clinton to Haitians."

[79] See, for instance, Andrew Kohut and Robert Toth, "Arms and the People," *Foreign Affairs* 73, no. 6 (1994): 47–61; Richard A. Melanson, *American Foreign Policy since the Vietnam War: The Search for Consensus from Nixon to Clinton* (Armonk: M. E. Sharpe, 2000); Richard Sobel, *The Impact of Public Opinion on US Foreign Policy since Vietnam: Constraining the Colossus* (Oxford: Oxford University Press, 2001).

[80] John Dillin, "Campaign Promises Dog Clinton's First Days," *Christian Science Monitor*, January 21, 1993, 1. The polls were taken January 14–17, 1993.

reported that Aristide and his backers believed Clinton's commitments were sincere, and they would give him time to fulfill them.[81] Likewise, Representative Charles B. Rangel (D-N.Y.), a long-time Haitian supporter, publicly argued in favor of giving Clinton's approach time to work.[82] This marked a sharp reversal for Rangel, who had been long critical of U.S. policy toward Haitians, declaring that summary repatriations "would not have happened if the refugees were Europeans."[83] (Rangel claimed to be impressed by Clinton's behind-the-scenes efforts to prod the OAS and the UN to take action on Haiti and was willing to give him a chance to succeed.[84])

Moreover, it must be remembered that, although there were myriad Haitian and human rights activists within the United States who were committed to the restoration of democracy in Haiti, many of them would have preferred to see someone other than Aristide assume the leadership role when that time came. Many potential supporters did not trust him.[85] His apparent embrace of the practice of "necklacing" did not help matters. A non-trivial number of other key actors simply did not like him. As one close observer diplomatically put it, Aristide was "unaccustomed to the need of compromise in politics and the tactics required of a parliamentary president."[86] Finally, there were still others who just thought he was unhinged. As Walter Slocombe, deputy under secretary for policy, later said, his own agency was staunchly opposed to risking soldiers' lives to put "that psychopath" back in power.[87] An unidentified State Department official who had worked closely with Aristide was somewhat more sanguine about Aristide's sanity, if not exactly a fan: "He can drive you crazy, but that doesn't mean he is crazy."[88] In short, Aristide's relatively low prestige and popularity within the United States at the outset of the first Clinton administration stymied the mobilization of those who favored action in support of Haitian migrants and tempered criticism of Clinton's

---

[81] Jon Sawyer, "Clinton's Reversal over Haiti Spawns New Diplomatic Ripples," *St. Louis Post-Dispatch*, January 16, 1993. The same congressional source also praised the work of Secretary of State Lawrence Eagleburger, who, after succeeding James Baker in August 1992, took a much more active role and pressed for UN intervention.

[82] Christopher Marquis, "Criticism in Capital Subdued," *Miami Herald*, January 16, 1993.

[83] Briggs, *Mass Immigration and the National Interest*, 150.

[84] Sawyer, "Clinton's Reversal."

[85] Patrick Brogan, "Why Clinton Will Gamble and Send in the Marines," *Herald*, July 9, 1994.

[86] Lester H. Brune, *United States and Post-Cold War Interventions: Bush and Clinton in Somalia, Haiti and Bosnia, 1992–1998* (Claremont, Calif.: Regina Books, 1999), 45.

[87] Quoted in Elaine Sciolino, "Haitian Impasse—A Special Report; Failure on Haiti: How US Hopes Faded," *New York Times*, April 29, 1994.

[88] *Congressional Record* 140, no. 62 (May 18, 1994), http://www.gpo.gov/fdsys/pkg/CREC-1994-05-18/html/CREC-1994-05-18-pt1-PgH53.htm.

own policy failings on the Haiti front, thus allowing the president to defer action for some time.[89] Simply put, the pro-camp just stayed home.

The Crisis That Was and the Critical Role of Aristide

Eighteen months later—in the wake of a second set of Haiti-related policy flip-flops that culminated in abandonment of the Kennebunkport repatriation policy—a new spate of boat building commenced, and Clinton again found himself boxed in. This time, however, there was no dodging the bullet. Aristide again played a pivotal role, but in stark contrast to the assistance he had provided in January 1993, the second time around the exiled Haitian president actually took actions that encouraged *more* Haitians to take to the sea. It was the sudden and precipitous increase engendered by these actions—from approximately 130 boatpeople per week before the crisis to 2,000–3,500 per day during early July 1994—that led, first, to the largest operation in U.S. Coast Guard history since World War II and, then, by the second week in September to a military operation designed to restore Aristide to power.

Token Efforts, Little Movement

After the January 1993 crisis had been averted and the immediate threat of a massive outflow was past, there was little acute pressure placed on Clinton to fix Haiti. The crisis became figuratively relegated to the back burner of the many policy issues occupying the new administration. Over the months that followed, the Clinton administration did play a role (if a limited one) in a number of multilateral (mostly UN-led) efforts designed to bring the crisis to a peaceful end.[90] However, despite his pre-inaugural promises to the contrary, Clinton more or less followed Bush's basic

[89] For instance, as late as October 1993—when the United States was theoretically moving toward the implementation of the Governor's Island Accords—Brian Latell, an intelligence officer for Latin America, prepared a psychological profile on Aristide that concluded he was mentally unstable. Such studies provided ammunition for anti-Aristide legislators and other influential figures such as Brent Scowcroft, former Bush NSC adviser, who described Aristide as "erratic" and concurred with then Senator Jesse Helms (R-N.C.) that Aristide was "probably a certifiable psychopath." Mark Danner, "The Fall of the Prophet," *New York Review of Books*, December 2, 1993.

[90] But, as Weiss notes, actions taken by the Security Council were "neither as rapid nor as vigorous" as they might have been, "due to the widespread unease among many developing countries that such action would set a precedent concerning intervention in the name of democracy and human rights." "Haiti, 1991–1996," 175. Moreover, the U.S. government reticence regarding Aristide further stymied progress. See Dupuy, *Haiti in the New World Order*, chaps. 6–7, esp. 167–68n. 6; Malone, "Haiti and the International Community."

policies of lax enforcement of OAS sanctions and of deferring to the OAS and the UN on negotiation of Aristide's return.

In effect, Clinton pursued a Janus-faced strategy.[91] On one hand, he condemned the coup and refused to recognize any of the governments installed by the military leaders; on the other hand, he began to pressure Aristide to make greater concessions to the junta leaders. It was reportedly believed that such measures would stall the return of Aristide until after his term expired in 1996. To achieve this goal, it was "necessary to appear to be encouraging a negotiated settlement of the crisis while allowing the Haitian military junta... to reject any deals that involved Aristide's return."[92] This position was justified on the grounds that Aristide had a poor human rights record and thus his restoration might lead to further strife on the island, particularly if he should reembrace his revolutionary agenda.[93] Clinton officials recognized that this was a risky strategy. But many within the administration believed that Aristide's lack of popularity within the United States, as well as among the Haitian elite, would protect the administration from the need to act more decisively.[94]

Then, in July 1993, the best chance for a resolution in quite some time seemed to be at hand. After a difficult period of negotiation—and under considerable pressure from Dante Caputo, UN special envoy, and Lawrence Pezzullo, Clinton administration envoy—Aristide and Cedras signed the so-called Governor's Island Agreement (GIA). The GIA provided for the return of Aristide (on October 30, 1993), political amnesty for the perpetrators of the September 1991 coup, and installation of a UN peacekeeping force.[95] Before the ink was dry on the accords, however, reports of escalating violence in Haiti began to emerge. Those opposed to the GIA—aided by the Front for the Advancement and Progress of Haiti (FRAPH) and former Tontons Macoutes—began threatening that they would prevent its implementation as well as begin assassinating Aristide supporters.[96]

---

[91] Malone, "Haiti and the International Community."

[92] Dupuy, *Haiti in the New World Order*, 139.

[93] Ibid., 140–41; Doyle, "Hollow Diplomacy in Haiti," 52.

[94] See, for instance, Pastor, "Haiti, 1994"; DiPrizio, *Armed Humanitarians*; Kim Ives, "The Unmaking of a President," in *The Haiti Files: Decoding the Crisis* (Washington, D.C.: Essential Books, 1994).

[95] United Nations, *Les Nations Unies et Haiti, 1900–1996*, UN Blue Book (New York: UN Department of Information, 1996), 28–48. Also, under the accord, Cedras was to retire on Aristide's—now officially supported—return, although, for his part, Aristide would name a new prime minister before he returned; wide-ranging political and legal reforms would be implemented; and military engineers from the United States and Canada to help rebuild the Haitian infrastructure. See United Nations, *Les Nations Unies et Haiti* (l'Accord Governor's Island, Document 74), 314–16.

[96] Militants also disrupted a meeting between the UN and the Haitian finance minister, holding the delegates hostage and threatening to kill ministry staff who favored Aristide's return.

Despite the rising violence and demonstrations, the UN and the administration moved to fulfill the July agreement. On September 23, the Security Council approved the deployment of 1,200 peacekeepers. In early October, the junta reneged on its promises to implement the accords, reaffirmed its opposition to Aristide's return, and dealt a telling blow to the GIA, which started the ball rolling toward a military confrontation. When the USS *Harlan County*, with two hundred lightly armed U.S. soldiers and twenty-five Canadian military trainers aboard, arrived within sight of Port-au-Prince on October 11, a hostile reception awaited it. While Haitian soldiers stood by, FRAPH-organized thugs blocked the docks and armed militants harassed waiting diplomats and journalists, shouting, "Kill the whites!" and "Somalia! Somalia!"[97] Following two days of deliberation, and with images of the U.S. soldier who had been dragged through the streets of Mogadishu just days before still fresh in the minds of those in Washington, Clinton ordered the *Harlan County* home.[98]

A Turning Point: Aristide Goes on the Offensive

After that littoral embarrassment, it appeared clear to the junta leaders in Port-au-Prince[99] and to Aristide and his supporters in Washington that the administration lacked both the desire to see the Haitian president returned to power and the will to push the junta out.[100] As Jocelyn McCalla, Haitian rights activist, put it, "Aristide basically decided that Clinton ha[d] abandoned him."[101] As Aristide himself puts it, "I was rewarded with the knowledge that Haitian policies in the United States are not decided by the White House. A politician makes decisions in accordance with his interests and not with his personal convictions. He may choose the speed of light or the snail's pace."[102] Having concluded that Clinton had in fact

---

[97] DiPrizio, *Armed Humanitarians*, 91.

[98] See, for instance, Mark Bowden, *Blackhawk Down: A Story of Modern War* (New York: Atlantic Monthly Press, 1999), 335.

[99] Those on the ground in Haiti appeared to come to the same conclusion. As Emmanuel Constant, leader of the dockside demonstration, put it, "My people kept wanting to run away. But I took the game and urged them to stay. Then the Americans pulled out! We were astonished. That was the day the FRAPH was [really] born. Before, everyone said we were crazy, suicidal, that we would all be burned if Aristide returned. But now we know he is never going to return." Quoted in Martin, "Haiti," 72–73.

[100] Many reports suggest that the junta felt secure in backing away from the GIA because there was so much disagreement within the United States—and the OAS and UN, for that matter—on which tack to take. It has even been suggested that U.S. officials indirectly thwarted the *Harlan County* landing by suggesting the UN would be easily deterred. DiPrizio, *Armed Humanitarians*, 205n. 27.

[101] Jocelyn McCalla, of the National Coalition for Haitian Refugees, quoted in Phil Gunson, "Aristide Attacks Refugee Policy," *Guardian*, April 8, 1994.

[102] See Aristide, *Dignite'*, 110–11.

chosen a sluggish tempo,[103] Aristide decided to go on the offensive, and his weapon of choice was migration-driven coercion.

AVENUE A: TURN UP THE POLITICAL THERMOSTAT   As noted previously, Aristide had long been "seen in the US as a marginal figure without clout in Washington, [and thus] not well-placed to press his suit with the Administration."[104] But by late 1993 the tide had turned. Despite outstanding apprehensions about Aristide, those concerned with the plight of Haiti and its people had run out of patience with Clinton. In the absence of plausible alternatives, this frustration redounded to Aristide's benefit, and he began to be viewed as the best hope of seeing democracy restored to Haiti in the foreseeable future. Acting "on expert advice" and "seizing on a vacuum in Washington's Haiti policy in early 1994," Aristide confronted the administration head-on.[105] Having concluded that domestic politics was the real "governing factor in Clinton's lurching Haiti-related policy shifts,"[106] Aristide decided that the most expedient way to attack the administration was to escalate the domestic political pressure on two fronts: by upping the hypocrisy costs associated with the U.S. Haitian refugee/migration policy and by increasing the prospective political and economic costs associated with an unending flow of Haitian boatpeople. Aristide was assisted on the domestic political front by the legitimacy that the OAS and the UN had already invested in his claims, as well as by a wide variety of supporters, including members of the Congressional Black Caucus, the Trans-Africa Lobby, a variety of newly motivated civic and religious groups, and the liberal wing of the Democratic Party.[107] Aristide was likewise aided on the migration-threat front by the respect and esteem in which the impoverished majority in Haiti held him. To give teeth to his threats, Aristide publicly declared Clinton's Haiti policy "racist" and a "cruel joke" and announced that in six months he would rescind the 1981 U.S.-Haitian Interdiction Agreement—which had permitted Washington to intercept Haitians at sea and repatriate them.[108] As one observer put it at the time, the repudiation of the agreement "forces the White House out of its foxhole."[109]

---

[103] At the same time, it has been argued that Aristide would never have been willing to return without a contingent of U.S. troops to shield him from assassination. So, even if Clinton had moved faster, Aristide might still have pushed for a military-backed reinstallation. Interviews, February 2000, Miami, Fort Lauderdale, and Wilton Manors, Fla., and April 2005, Cambridge, Mass.

[104] Malone, "Haiti and the International Community," 135.

[105] Ibid.

[106] Carl Mollins and Luke Fisher, "Troubled Waters," *Maclean's*, July 18, 1994.

[107] Malone, "Haiti and the International Community," 135.

[108] Ibid., 157. See also Steven Greenhouse, "Aristide to End Accord That Allows US to Seize Refugee Boats," *New York Times*, April 8, 1994.

[109] Jocelyn McCalla, of the National Coalition for Haitian Refugees, quoted in Gunson, "Aristide Attacks Refugee Policy."

WITH A LITTLE HELP FROM SOME NEW AND OLD FRIENDS   The help offered by Aristide's allies took a variety of forms. First, in response to growing repression and an increase in the number of killings on the ground in Haiti, the more liberal members of Congress—on whose support Clinton was dependent to pass his broad social agenda—began to mobilize and exert pressure in favor of a shift in the administration's position toward the junta and Haitian boatpeople.[110] Representative Major R. Owens (D-N.Y.), whose district included a large Haitian community, for instance, argued for military action "because it signals to Haiti's military leaders that the days of blessings and mixed signals are over.... Maybe the president will have the guts to stand up to bring the illegal terrorist government [of Haiti] down."[111]

Second, Randall Robinson, executive director of the Trans-Africa Lobby, wrote a scathing letter to the *New York Times*—which ran in a full-page ad format—in which he accused Clinton of willful ignorance and gross ineptitude in dealing with Haiti.[112] The letter was signed by more than one hundred prominent Americans, including civil rights, religious, and labor leaders; a variety of Hollywood celebrities; and members of Congress, who—in the letter—also accused the Clinton administration of pursuing a racist policy toward the Haitian refugees and demanding the return of Aristide to power.[113]

Third, Robinson also announced that he would go on a hunger strike until the administration fired Lawrence Pezzullo (the U.S. envoy to Haiti) and changed its policies toward both the junta and the refugees.[114] (Pezzullo was widely viewed as openly hostile to Aristide.) What ultimately became a twenty-seven-day ordeal was covered on a daily basis by a *Washington Post* reporter, who shared with readers the graphic details of Robinson's weight loss and physical deterioration. Robinson had long been advocating amplified efforts to oust the junta, but the objective of his highly publicized hunger strike was much narrower—the end of the summary repatriation policy. "All we need to do is undertake a hearing to separate the economic refugees from the political refugees.... I end this fast when we give the people a hearing."[115]

---

[110] Dupuy, *Haiti in the New World Order,* 156.

[111] Ann Devroy and Bradley Graham, "US to Bar Haitians Picked Up at Sea," *Washington Post,* July 6, 1994.

[112] Randall Robinson, "Haiti's Agony, Clinton's Shame," *New York Times,* April 17, 1994.

[113] Dupuy, *Haiti in the New World Order,* 156.

[114] Kevin Merida, "TransAfrica Leader to Fast in Protest," *Washington Post,* April 12, 1994; Steven Greenhouse, "Aristide Condemns Clinton's Haiti Policy as Racist," *New York Times,* April 22, 1994.

[115] "Treat Haitians Fairly," *New York Times,* April 22, 1994.

Fourth, the Congressional Black Caucus introduced legislation reiterating Robinson's demand that Pezzullo be replaced and calling for tougher sanctions against the junta.[116] Although by mid-July 1994 the measure had not yet come up for a vote, it hardly mattered; the White House had adopted virtually all the provisions of the bill as U.S. policy toward Haiti. As one congressional staffer who closely followed the issue noted, the bill "was a blueprint for what was done in the coming months. [It] was what they rallied around and pushed for. And they got almost everything." As another State Department official put it, "The basic components of the [B]lack [C]aucus approach—the military is the problem, Aristide is the solution; we shouldn't move away from him even two inches; we should do nothing that smacks of any kind of alternative to Aristide, like work with a prime minister"—all that was adopted.[117]

Finally, domestic dissent from one of the president's core bases of support—African Americans—further highlighted the significance of the mobilization (and counter-mobilization) of concentrated interests in determining the efficacy of coercion. Although quiescent and passive from late 1991 to early 1994, this avowedly pro-migrant group mobilized in force in early 1994. At the same time, the concentration of interests opposed to the admittance of Haitians was high from the outset and grew still higher over time. See table 4.2 for a sample of public opinion data from summer 1994, during which the crisis heated up again in earnest. As the data make clear, the public was highly divided—and markedly polarized—over how to respond to the crisis.

The highly mobilized dissent also led to significantly elevated levels of network news coverage of the Haitian crisis and the events surrounding it, particularly following Robinson's hunger strike and a nearly concomitant rise in protests in favor of admitting the fleeing Haitians. (The crisis had previously dropped in prominence as a lead story soon after the widely anticipated 1993 inaugural refugee crisis failed to materialize.[118]) In late April–early May 1994, nearly 66 percent of the network stories on Haiti featured criticism of Clinton's policies by Randall Robinson, members of the Congressional Black Caucus (some of whom were arrested during

---

[116] The fact that the number of caucus members had grown from twenty-six to forty after the 1992 election meant that by mid-1994 it was playing an instrumental role in administration decision making. (This was particularly true because some within Congress and within the administration counted on the caucus to provide critical support for Clinton's initiatives on health care and welfare reform, as well as on the crime bill. Steven A. Holmes, "With Persuasion and Muscle, Black Caucus Reshapes Haiti Policy," *New York Times*, July 14, 1994; interviews with former Clinton administration officials, July 2000 and May 2001, Washington, D.C.

[117] Quoted in Holmes, "With Persuasion and Muscle." This statement accords with my own interviews.

[118] Warren P. Strobel, *Late-Breaking Foreign Policy: The News Media's Influence on Peace Operations* (Washington, D.C.: USIP, 1997), 186.

TABLE 4.2
Shifts in U.S. Public Opinion During the Second Phase of the Haitian Boatpeople Crisis, May–September 1994

Question	Date and Response	Date and Response	Date and Response
Do you favor the use of military force to restore democracy in Haiti?	~ May 7–10: 25–36% yes Sources: [2, 6]	July 13–17: 39% yes Source: [1]	September 15: 40% yes Source: [6] September 16: 56% yes Source: [4] September 19: 34% yes Source: [5]
Do you support the use of military force to stop the refugees?		July 13–17: 56% yes Source: [1]	
The elected president of Haiti, Jean-Bertrand Aristide, was overthrown by the Haitian military in 1991. In order to remove the military and restore President Aristide to his position, do you favor or oppose the United States sending in ground troops?			September 19: 40% yes (Democrats, 49%; Republicans, 29%; Independents, 44%) Source: [3]
Haitian immigrants (are now):		July 13–17: 6% a good thing for the U.S.; 45% a bad thing for the U.S.; 42% have no effect Source: [1]	
Should the U.S. summarily turn back boats loaded with Haitians seeking asylum in this country?	April 7: 52% yes (Democrats, 42%; Republicans, 65%; Independents, 53%) Source: [2]	June 18: 62% yes Source: [6]	
Why do Haitians try to come to this country: "to seek a better life" or "to escape persecution"?	May 7: 66% "to seek a better life" Source: [2]		

Sources: 1: ABC News; 2: Boston Globe; 3: CBS/New York Times; 4: CNN/Gallup Poll; 5: Knight-Ridder; 6: Washington Post–ABC News Poll.

protests outside the White House), and others.[119] In short, the bulk of the media coverage during this period focused on the policy struggle that pitted Haiti policy critics against the administration, which found itself forced to publicly acknowledge the shortcomings of its policies.

Moreover, charges of U.S. culpability for the state of affairs in Haiti were also increasingly publicly and frequently articulated, as the following editorial illustrates: "Of all the intractable foreign policy knots frustrating the Clinton administration, Haiti seems the toughest to cut. The crisis there is so acute—*and so very much induced by past US actions*—that passivity is no longer possible."[120] The head of the American Bar Association Coordinating Committee on Immigration Law similarly argued that, although charges of racism were being used to "blur the debate," it was undeniably true that the U.S. government's repatriation policy was "a knee-jerk insensitive reaction to a human tragedy of which our foreign policy played a substantial part."[121]

In short, Clinton was soon forced to admit the efficacy of the activists', and particularly Robinson's, tactics. "I understand and respect what he's doing.... We ought to change our policy. It hasn't worked."[122] Within a week of making this candid admission, Clinton reversed course on three major policy positions, exactly in line with activists' and Congressional Black Caucus demands. First, he replaced the unpopular Pezzullo with William Gray III, former member of the House and president of the United Negro College Fund. Second, he announced a shift in U.S. refugee policy, whereby thenceforth all Haitians interdicted at sea would be granted proper asylum hearings aboard U.S. ships or in third countries. Third, he proclaimed U.S. willingness to support tougher economic sanctions against the junta.[123] Although the administration claimed these shifts had been in the works for a long while, and were not the result of domestic political pressure, one aide acknowledged, "Of course, the pressure does matter. We live in a cocoon here."[124]

These policy reversals led Robinson to end his hunger strike, eased caucus pressure, and quieted Clinton's domestic critics for a short period. They did not, however, make the crisis evaporate. In fact, inadvertently—and

[119] Ibid., 185.
[120] "Haitian Futility," *Nation* 258 (1994), 819.
[121] Robert Juceam, quoted in Henry J. Reske, "Courts Wrangle over Haitians," *ABA Journal* 78 (1992), 30.
[122] Clinton, quoted in ibid. See also "Haitian Impasse—A Special Report."
[123] President Clinton's statement at a White House press conference, May 8, 1994, in *Public Papers of the Presidents of the United States, William J. Clinton, 1994, Book I*, (Washington, D.C.: Office of the Federal Register), 859–63. And at the urging of the United States, shortly thereafter the UN Security Council adopted extensive new sanctions against Haiti and demanded that the leaders of the junta step down.
[124] Quoted in "Pressure Drop," *Nation* 258 (1994), 737.

in very short order—these policy shifts made the problem much worse. By repudiating the summary repatriation policy, the Clinton administration spawned a new spate of boat building in Haiti and helped provoke a new outflow, thereby also providing further ammunition for Aristide in his attempt to convince the administration that, unless he was returned to power, the crisis in Haiti would continue indefinitely, as would the ongoing boatpeople problem.[125]

AVENUE B: RAISE THE REFUGEE THREAT   Just as the White House was hoping that the junta was starting to feel the heat of the new sanctions (and would soon step down), mass outmigration from Haiti resumed in earnest and shifted the most acute pressure back on to the United States. The renewed surge began only days after a U.S. naval ship started screening and processing Haitians in Jamaican waters on June 15, as part of the new policy under which all Haitians were to be treated like potential refugees.[126] Within three weeks, nearly 18,000 Haitians had been intercepted—each of whom had to be individually screened. Intelligence reports suggested more were on their way.[127] (These reports were given particular credence because, just two days before, the U.S. Coast Guard had intercepted 3,458 in a single day, the highest one-day total ever.) And while Guantanamo had been reopened only the previous week, the facility was already close to reaching its 12,500-person capacity.

The upsurge not only threatened to overwhelm the facilities at Guantanamo but also reignited anxieties in Florida of a large influx of Haitians.[128] This, in turn, ignited the political fears among state leaders, since both the governorship and a Republican-held U.S. Senate seat were up for grabs in the November elections. Even before the new influx commenced, Governor Lawton Chiles had filed a lawsuit against the federal government for the $739 million he claimed the state paid out in education, welfare, and other services for illegal immigrants the previous year. And Senator Bob Graham (D-Fla.) quickly became one of the strongest voices in Congress calling for an invasion to restore Aristide. As one report put it at the time, "Although [Graham's] public reasons are high-minded, his mailbag and calls from constituents stress that Florida has too many immigrants already."[129] As one such constituent put it:

> I prefer, even if we have to go in with our armed forces to Haiti and stay there
> for 10 years, that we put a stop to this illegal immigration.... That would be

---

[125] Dupuy, *Haiti in the New World Order,* 142.

[126] "Taking to the Boats," *US News & World Report,* July 11, 1994.

[127] James Adams, "Clinton Considers Covert Operations against Haiti," *Sunday Times,* July 3, 1994.

[128] "Which Haiti Policy?" *New York Times,* July 7, 1994.

[129] Walker, "Immigration Fears."

still cheaper than having to let all these people into the country on welfare and Medicaid....We ought to go in there and return their president make those military officers get out. Otherwise, it's going to be our problem in Florida for a longer time than 10 years.[130]

The administration was finding it increasingly difficult to put a positive spin on what was quickly turning into a major policy crisis—the trajectory of which increasingly seemed pointed toward a military response. Clinton officials found themselves compelled to acknowledge that the crisis disrupted their preferred strategy—a gradual tightening of sanctions designed to bring about a return to democracy without military intervention. "We're seized by the refugee surge, and this has accelerated the discussion of other options," conceded one senior administration official.[131] Another, a senior State Department official, admitted, "We cannot absorb this magnitude of outflow indefinitely, [which] raises the urgency of finding a resolution to the problem."[132] Still another official conceded, "We'll be good through the middle of next week. But is this a sustainable policy? No."[133] "Undoubtedly the numbers have been much higher than what we had expected," said another. "Now, we'll just have to wait and see and pray that this time we have a policy that will get them down to a manageable level."[134]

In evaluating just how vulnerable the Haitian crisis had made the Clinton administration by summer 1994, it is worth noting that the president found himself unable to talk about much else. For instance, any policy success he might have hoped to garner from the July 1994 G-7 summit in Naples was undermined by the Haitian problem. For one thing, on his arrival in Italy, Clinton remained on Air Force One for half an hour to be briefed on the Haitian situation by Vice-President Al Gore, a fact widely reported by the international press corps.[135] For another, although Clinton did not mention Haiti in the opening statement at his news conference on the Naples waterfront, "questions about the troubled island dominated his meeting with reporters," and he "took pains to defend the [most] recent switch in policy."[136]

---

[130] Lewis Wussler, Florida voter, quoted in Bill Cotterell, "Immigration: Newcomers Cost Floridians Higher Taxes," *St. Petersburg Times*, May 22, 1994.

[131] Quoted in ibid.

[132] "Taking to the Boats."

[133] Quoted in Elaine Sciolino, "Allies Wax Unenthusiastic about Peace Force for Haiti," *New York Times*, July 9, 1994.

[134] Quoted in Roberto Suro, "Clinton's Gamble with Haiti Hinges on Refugee Response," *New York Times*, July 11, 1994.

[135] See, for instance, Martin Walker and Jonathan Freedland, "Panama Shuts Off Haiti Safety-Valve for US," *Guardian*, July 8, 1994.

[136] Craig Hines, "Panama Decision Frustrates Clinton; Hunt On for Haitian Refugee Havens," *Houston Chronicle*, July 9, 1994.

AN UNHELPFUL ARISTIDE   It is apparent that administration officials mistakenly believed Aristide would again come to their aid to staunch the swelling outflow. Officials set up an airborne radio service—which could override all Haitian radio frequencies—to enable Aristide to speak to the Haitian people.[137] But whereas during the first crisis Aristide had been instrumental in stopping the flow, this time around Aristide steadfastly refused to cooperate.[138] Indeed, he instead began to speak out *against* Clinton's appeals to Haitians not to flee the country. "It would be immoral to ask people whose very lives are at risk to stay in Haiti," Aristide said, "a Haiti I am compelled to describe as a house on fire."[139] He also declared—in marked contrast to his January 1993 entreaties—that "It's better to die on the high seas than to live kneeling at the feet of the putschists. Take the risk rather than experience deprivation and repression...in spite of the American reception."[140] And—in a clear demonstration that Aristide both recognized the power of the refugee weapon and was actively wielding it against the Clinton administration—he declared that "stopping the flow of boat people constitutes an essential motive for the American government in its attempts to get out of crisis. [But] there is no solution without a return to democracy."[141]

THE ROLE OF THE REFUGEES   Aristide's messages gave encouragement to Haitians, who responded by taking to the sea. Boats were prepared in nearly every village along the southern coast of Haiti, with the explicit goal of putting more pressure on the United States to hasten Aristide's return. As mentioned in chapter 1, one villager put it plainly, declaring, "We cannot get arms to fight.... The only way to fight is to get the Americans to keep their promises. The only way to do that is to do what they fear most [come to the United States]."[142] Like their exiled leader, Haitians understood well the political significance of their flight, both for Aristide and for the U.S. president. "If Clinton wants to stop the refugee situation, he has to bring Aristide back.... The refugee issue is a trump card that Aristide is holding and right now he's going to play it to his advantage."[143]

---

[137] Martin Walker, "Refugee Tide Swamps US Haitian Policy," *Guardian*, June 29, 1994.
[138] Jack R. Payton, "Haiti's Isolation Deepens as Flights to US Cut Off," *St. Petersburg Times*, June 25, 1994; Pilita Clark, "Haiti Risks Invasion after Expulsions," *Sydney Morning Herald*, July 13, 1994; Elaine Sciolino "Haiti Invasion Imminent, Envoy Says," *New York Times*, July 4, 1994.
[139] "Incident at Baie du Mesle," *Time*, July 11, 1994.
[140] Aristide, *Dignite*, 78–79.
[141] Ibid., 80.
[142] "Incident at Baie du Mesle."
[143] Garry Pierre-Pierre, "Haitians Are Undeterred by New Clinton Policy," *New York Times*, July 7, 1994.

Indeed, many Haitians interviewed said that only Aristide's personal plea asking them to stay in Haiti would prevent them from leaving. "Right now only the little priest can make me stay."[144] "We won't believe in anyone again—only Aristide. Send Aristide back, and there will be no more boat people."[145] "We know that if we take to the boats it will help Aristide. No one told us this, we just know it is true. We are not afraid to die in the sea if it helps to return Aristide."[146] "If Clinton picks us up today, then we will try again tomorrow. . . . we will be on the next boat. That is what Mr. Clinton must understand. Unless we have our president back, we would rather die at sea than die here."[147]

Further encouragement to take to the sea came from the fact that shipboard asylum petitions were being approved at a relatively generous rate of 30 percent, compared to the average rate of 6.6 percent that had prevailed since the processing centers in Haiti were opened in February 1992.[148] The proportion of Haitian applicants granted refugee status reached as high as 40 percent at one point, due at least in part to increased work by private human rights organizations that helped Haitians apply for refugee status.[149] This placed still further pressure on the Administration to find a more permanent solution.

Moreover, it appears that the second time around many Haitians did not even try to reach Florida. Rather, they aimed only to get beyond (if only, just beyond) Haiti's 12-mile territorial limit, to use what Haitians called "a shark visa."[150] In addition to interview data, two other sources of evidence support this proposition. First, the type of boats used to flee had

[144] Ibid.

[145] Marilyn Greene, "Fewer Fleeing Haitian Shores," USA Today, July 29, 1994.

[146] "Incident at Baie du Mesle."

[147] Witzer Joseph, quoted in Farah, "Haitians Preparing Boats." At the same time, some of those who fled did not return after Aristide had been returned to power. Thus, it is possible they would have come whatever Aristide had advised. Several Haitians that I interviewed said they simply took advantage of the shift in U.S. policy; that is, July 1994 seemed an auspicious time to seek asylum. One put it plainly, "I had no job, no work. My brother told me it was a good time." Others said they planned to return to Haiti once they had made more money, moved their families, and/or had become citizens. Interviews, February–March 1999 (Miami, Fort Lauderdale, and Wilton Manors, Fla.).

[148] Of the first 1,111 Haitians processed, 338 received asylum. By contrast, between February 1992 and June 1994, only 3,875 out of 58,793 applications were approved. According to U.S. officials, this was largely due to two factors. First, by July 1994, Haitians received a significantly more sympathetic hearing from the examiners deciding refugee status than they had previously, in part because of the consequences of the tightened economic sanctions. Second, UNHCR officials were observing the process and explaining to the Haitians their rights, in effect preparing them better for the U.S. interviews. Devroy and Gellman, "Exodus from Haiti."

[149] Ann Devroy and Daniel Williams, "Stay Home, Clinton Tells Haitians; Surge in Boat People Spurs Talk of Invasion That Aristide Opposes," Gazette, June 29, 1994.

[150] Gary Pierre-Pierre, "Taking a 'Shark Visa' Proves Perilous to Fleeing Haitians," Houston Chronicle, July 6, 1994; interview, April 2005, Cambridge, Mass.

shifted from larger craft, carrying hundreds, to dozens of smaller boats, each of which could accommodate fewer than twenty-five people. These were boats that were ill-suited for a voyage to Florida; indeed, many were little more than rafts that had been constructed from materials taken from—and off—Haitians' own homes.[151] According to a Haitian dock-worker, "They are using boats that can't reach Miami. They go out so they can get picked up."[152] Second, Haitians started leaving from all over the island, not just from areas where the currents were favorable. As one U.S. Coast Guard official put it, "so many people were taking to the high seas from points where they could not possibly get to the United States that it was clear that the refugees' only intention was to be rescued at sea."[153] "It feels as if they have got all these boats and we don't have enough ships," said another U.S. naval officer.[154]

"But like a gambler who feels too far behind to quit," Clinton put more chips on the table and announced yet another major policy shift.[155] The administration proclaimed that henceforth it would send all Haitians to temporary camps around the Caribbean, in the expectation that they would be deterred from fleeing once they realized they would end up in an offshore camp rather than in Miami. But this policy too soon fell apart.

The administration's new plan was thrown into a tailspin when, suddenly and without warning, Panamanian President Guillermo Endara abruptly reneged on his (reluctantly concluded) agreement to temporarily house 10,000 Haitians for up to six months.[156] As one reporter put it at the time, "the Panama fiasco added to the impression of an Administration daily lurching this way and that over Haiti."[157] Not only was the administration suddenly short 10,000 slots for would-be refugees, but also it suffered the humiliation of being rebuked by the leader of a country that

[151] Payton, "Haiti's Isolation Deepens."

[152] Carmelo Loiseau, a dockworker, quoted in "Taking to the Boats."

[153] Dave Todd, "Clinton Policy a Failure," *Ottawa Citizen*, July 2, 1994.

[154] Commander Bob Reininger, U.S. Navy, quoted in Jason Vest, "Risky Exodus of Refugees Swells Anew," *Chicago Sun-Times*, June 28, 1994.

[155] Roberto Suro, "Clinton's Gamble with Haiti Hinges on Refugee Response," *New York Times*, July 11, 1994.

[156] Endara claimed that U.S. officials had browbeaten him into saying he would accept the refugees. "I felt mocked and intimidated.... They treated me as if this were a banana republic." Quoted in Walker, "Immigration Fears," 14. (Endara may also have decided to reconsider, once it became evident that he was likely to face some domestic political backlash of his own if the Haitians were admitted; they were no more welcome in Panama than they were in Florida.)

[157] As Larry Birns, director of the Council on Hemispheric Affairs, put it at the time, the Panamanian defection was "a devastating blow to the Clinton policy, and exposes its utter bankruptcy. There is an overwhelming hostility to the US policy throughout the Caribbean islands, where governments and opinion-makers say that to let themselves become dumping grounds for Haitian refugees simply abets Washington's racism." Walker and Freedland, "Panama Shuts Off Haiti Safety-Valve."

owed its freedom to a U.S. military intervention only five years before. As a *New York Times* editorial put it at the time:

> And when the Administration is publicly humiliated by a Latin leader as indebted to Washington as Panama's President, Guillermo Endara....it is a sign that US credibility in the region has sunk to an alarming new low. If even Mr. Endara has no compunctions about thumbing his nose at the US and walking away from diplomatic understandings, what is to be expected of Gen. Raoul Cedras and his sneering cronies in Haiti's junta?[158]

The situation became sufficiently tense that in the middle of the Naples Summit, an "unnamed Senior Administration official" gave a previously unscheduled "Background Briefing" to journalists on assignment at the summit to discuss the fallout associated with the Panamanian defection.[159] In the days and weeks that followed, the administration tried hard to re-place the 10,000 slots with commitments from other countries, some as far afield as West Africa.[160] But these efforts were largely unsuccessful, height-ening pressure to bring the crisis to a close.[161]

In the end, without the assistance of Aristide to stop the flow, the assis-tance of Caribbean nations to contain the flow, or the tolerance of the state of Florida to bear the flow, the administration was forced to move toward a military solution. Columnist William Raspberry summed it up:

> There was no trouble-free path for American diplomacy. Haiti's military leaders seemed determined to remain in power unless and until they were forced out, and Americans had demonstrated that they had no taste for doing what was necessary to force them out. Clinton tried to split the difference: threatening military action he didn't want to undertake in the hope that Ce-dras and the others would take him seriously and leave voluntarily. As a result, the American president found himself on the brink of an invasion for which, despite his earnest explanations, there was virtually no political sup-port at home.[162]

---

[158] "Needed: Steady Hands on Haiti," *New York Times,* July 9, 1994.

[159] Office of the [White House] Press Secretary (Naples, Italy), "Background Briefing by Senior American Official," July 8, 1994, Briefing Room, 7:50 p.m.

[160] Ibid.

[161] A few states—specifically, Dominica, Antigua, Barbuda, and Grenada—did express a willingness to help but only for cash, only for a finite period, and only if the numbers were small. Robert Greenberger, "US Sends Marines to Waters off Haiti, Steps up Efforts to Divert Boat People," *Wall Street Journal,* July 6, 1994.

[162] William Raspberry, "Brilliant or Stupid? Robinson, Fauntroy Are Irreconcilable on Haiti," *Pittsburgh Post-Gazette,* September 22, 1994.

There was in fact some support, but unfortunately for Clinton that support was highly "polarized, with the general tendency toward disapproval."[163] Although the quantity and intensity of support for intervention did grow over time, from about 27 percent (8% strongly and 19% somewhat strongly) in favor of using U.S. troops to restore Aristide in December 1993, to 47 percent (15% strongly and 32% somewhat strongly) in favor in July 1994, the quantity and intensity of disapproval also grew during this period—from 57 percent (34% strongly and 23% somewhat strongly) opposed to approximately 67 percent (33% strongly and 34% somewhat strongly) opposed the following July.[164] However, these numbers essentially flip-flopped if the mission was to evacuate Americans to stop the flow of Haitian refugees to U.S. shores![165]

Operation Restore (Uphold) Democracy

Hence, despite significant remaining congressional objections and a highly polarized public, on September 15, 1994, Clinton gave a nationwide address, announcing that the United States would intervene to "protect our interests, to stop the brutal atrocities that threaten tens of thousands of Haitians, to secure our borders, to preserve stability and promote democracy in our hemisphere, and [in a nod to his promise to Aristide, perhaps?] to uphold the reliability of the commitments we make and the commitments others make to us."[166] Just two days before, the State Department had released its third interim report on human rights in Haiti, which compared the current situation to the worst excesses of the Duvalier days.[167] In an attempt to garner support for the mission, Clinton drew explicitly on this report in his speech, recounting a litany of politically motivated killings, torture, and rape and declaring, "General Cedras and his accomplices alone are responsible for this suffering and terrible human tragedy."[168]

Given more time before the November congressional elections and a better set of options, Clinton might have chosen not to invade. In electoral terms, there was little to be gained by getting the approach right on Haiti, but there was much to lose by putting another foot badly wrong. Polling data made clear that Americans disapproved of Clinton's handling

[163] Eric V. Larson and Bogdan Savych, *American Public Support for U.S. Military Operations from Mogadishu to Baghdad* (Santa Monica, Calif.: RAND, 2005), 44.

[164] Ibid., 45.

[165] ABC News poll, July 17, 1994, in "Americans Favor Haiti Invasion to Stop Refugees," Reuters, July 26, 1994.

[166] "Text of President Clinton's Address on Haiti," *Washington Post*, September 16, 1994.

[167] "Haitian Regime as Bad as Duvalier, US Says," USIA Wireless File, September 15, 1994.

[168] "The Crisis in Haiti," reprinted in U.S. Department of State Dispatch, September 19, 1994, 605.

of foreign policy generally and strongly opposed his sending troops into Haiti to restore Aristide.[169] it had begun to appear, however, that intervention was the only way to bring the escalating crisis to an end in the foreseeable future.[170] Neither promises nor threats had swayed the junta leaders. The outflows showed no sign of abating, and Aristide's deadline for abrogating the 1981 agreement was fast approaching. At the same time, domestic pressure from the pro-camp and from advocates of military action remained steady or was growing[171] while opposition to Haitians (whether referred to as migrants or refugees) was also steadily mounting.[172] At the same time, many of those opposed to an invasion were simultaneously criticizing Clinton for failing to protect the U.S. borders.[173] In short, it became clear that the political costs of failing to act were guaranteed but that, if handled deftly, the political payoff of a success might boost Clinton's popularity and (at a minimum) clear Haiti off the public's radar screen before the November elections.

In short, the level of anti-migrant mobilization remained high while the level of pro-Haitian mobilization rose, leaving Clinton increasingly vulnerable to coercion. Moreover, the opinion shared by (some) former Clinton officials and Aristide advisors was that the deposed leader would never have returned without U.S. troops at his back. As one official bluntly put it, "He would have found a way to undermine any peace deal that did not involve US military protection, just as he had several times before. He was frankly very afraid, afraid he would be taken out and shot."[174]

Luckily for the administration, the need for an unpopular forced-entry operation evaporated following a last-minute agreement between a U.S. delegation—led by former President Jimmy Carter, former Chairman of the Joint Chiefs-of-Staff General Colin Powell, and former U.S. Senator Sam Nunn—and the leaders of the junta, which was concluded only after it was clear that an invasion was afoot.[175] The junta agreed to step down in exchange for amnesty for its members and the Haitian military as well as "golden parachute" packages. How generous these packages ultimately

---

[169] Larson and Savych, *American Public Support for U.S. Military Operations*, 44–47.

[170] As Secretary of State Christopher put it at the time, "The timing of this is really dictated by what's going on in Haiti. We seem to be running out of other options." Quoted in Robin Wright, "Christopher Calls for Unity on Haiti; GOP Leaders Reject Consensus Appeal," *Los Angeles Times*, September 12, 1994; interview with Clinton administration NSC official, May 2000, Washington, D.C.

[171] Linda Feldmann, "Haiti Invasion 'Option' Splits US Lawmakers," *Christian Science Monitor*, July 15, 1994.

[172] Malone, "Haiti and the International Community," 133.

[173] Ibid.; John Dillin, "Zbigniew Brzezinski Prediction: US Will Intervene in Haiti Mess," *Christian Science Monitor*, May 6, 1994.

[174] Interview with former administration official and U.S. diplomat, April 2005, Cambridge, Mass.

[175] Malone, "Haiti and the International Community," 133; Weiss, "Haiti, 1991–1996," 183.

were remains in dispute. Some sources report that they were quite size-able and included the unfreezing of the junta members' assets (e.g., Ce-dras reportedly got to keep "the $100 million fortune" he had allegedly compiled while in power) and the leasing of junta-owned property (e.g., the United States reportedly agreed to pay Cedras $5,000 per month to "rent" his house).[176] Others claim, however, that the payouts made to junta members were rather more modest.[177]

A Constructive Comparison

Is it easy to argue that the relative concentration of interests mattered in the cases in which action was eventually taken and policies changed. But what about those cases in which action remained untaken and policies, unchanged? As a measure of whether the strength of concentration of in-terests matters, it is instructive to compare the U.S. responses to Haiti in spring 1994 to its response to the Rwandan genocide, which was occur-ring contemporaneously. In the period April 1–May 30, 1994, the *New York Times* ran eight articles that focused on the U.S. response to the situation in Rwanda, which represents slightly less than 10 percent of the total num-ber of articles (namely, ninety-one) on Rwanda published in the *New York Times* during this period. These included less than a handful of editorials, one of which condemned the UN failure to help Rwandan refugees—while noting at the same time that "Somalia provides ample warning against plunging open-endedly [*sic*] into a 'humanitarian' mission"[178]—and an-other that praised the U.S. decision not to intervene:

> The Clinton Administration has rightly resisted a clamor for instantly ex-panding a minuscule United Nations peacekeeping force to halt the human carnage in Rwanda. An ill-planned military debacle might only deepen the conflict there and jeopardize peacekeeping missions elsewhere....[T]o enter this conflict without a defined mission or a plausible military plan risks a repetition of the debacle in Somalia.[179]

As one reporter put it at the time:

> there is no political will, either in Washington or other capitals, to inter-vene....Washington's thinking is rooted in a decision last year, following the

[176] Dupuy, *Haiti in the New World Order*, 160.
[177] See, for instance, Pastor, "Haiti, 1994."
[178] "Cold Choices in Rwanda," *New York Times*, April 23, 1994.
[179] "Look before Plunging into Rwanda," *New York Times*, May 18, 1994.

death of 18 American soldiers in Somalia, to oppose a peacekeeping operation for Burundi, arguing that tribal warfare was so intense that the number of forces needed to stop it would be too high for public opinion to accept. There will be no political cost at home for such an approach.[180]

The assertion that inaction would be cost-free was demonstrably correct. In testimony before the U.S. Congress on May 18—by which time it was evident to many that a genocide was underway in Rwanda—Madeleine Albright, then U.S. representative to the UN, declared that it would be "folly" for a UN force to venture quickly into the "maelstrom" in central Africa.[181] Not a single member of Congress disagreed or suggested that the United States had a moral obligation to respond.[182] The Republican humanitarian hawks, who favored air strikes in Bosnia, had little appetite for intervening in Rwanda.[183] Even the Congressional Black Caucus, busy lobbying for a shift in Haiti policy, said little. A few exceptions to this stance could be found in letters to the editor by Jeri Laber, the head of Human Rights Watch–Helsinki, on April 20, and by Alain Dextexhe of Medecins Sans Frontieres. As noted in chapter 1, the Clinton administration assiduously eschewed use of the word *genocide*, at least in part because of the "enormous amount of responsibility" they perceived they would incur should they use the term.[184] In short, the Rwandan genocide—although clearly publicly salient by April 25, 1994—failed to catalyze a mobilized, highly concentrated, and thus potentially politically damaging response on the part of those who favored taking action. At the same time, on the other side of the debate—those opposed to intervention—the bulk of the contemporaneous media coverage suggested neither that intervention was appropriate nor that the U.S. president was responsible.

The situation was little different in Europe, even though its territory was geographically closer to Rwanda and its people had more binding

[180] Elaine Sciolino, "For West, Rwanda Is Not Worth the Political Candle," *New York Times,* April 15, 1994.

[181] Douglas Jehl, "US Is Showing a New Caution on UN Peacekeeping Missions," *New York Times,* May 18, 1994. One senior administration official acknowledged, "this is a blood frenzy." In ibid.

[182] Sciolino, "For West."

[183] For instance, in an appearance on *Face the Nation* in mid-May, Senator Bob Dole (R-Kans.) made clear he did not think the United States had "any national interest [in Rwanda]....I hope we don't get involved there. I don't think we will. The Americans are out." Quoted in ibid.

[184] Douglas Jehl, "Officials Told to Avoid Calling Rwanda Killings 'Genocide,'" *New York Times,* June 10, 1994. Those publicly defending the administration position argued that "the first obligation before joining in so unequivocal a castigation" is to be absolutely sure of the facts. As a responsible Government, you don't just go around hollering 'genocide,'" said David Rawson, the U.S. ambassador to Rwanda. "You say that acts of genocide may have occurred and they need to be investigated." In ibid.

historical ties. As one reporter put it, "in this conflict between humanitarian impulses and cold calculation of national interest, realpolitik is winning. European governments deplore the slaughter in Rwanda but are not willing to take the risks inherent in trying to stop it."[185] In fact, although France eventually launched its own limited intervention, Operation Turquoise, by late May, Italy was the only European country that expressed a willingness to even consider joining a UN mission to Rwanda. In terms of media coverage, television coverage was extensive, but few newspapers gave the genocide regular front-page attention, and the bulk of the reporting focused on the difficulties facing those who wanted to help. One London newspaper columnist offered an explanation for foreign reluctance to react forcefully to the killings in Rwanda: "Rwandans are thousands of miles away.... Nobody you know has ever been on holiday to Rwanda. And Rwandans don't look like us. They have even less clout than Bosnian Muslims."[186] Few disputed this characterization. Another disheartened (Canadian) commentator concurred, noting, "The trouble is that Rwanda is too far away and not quite important enough.... Only the electronic shrinking of the world into a global media village has put the horror of such a conflict uncomfortably under our noses. In a world with less efficient communications, the West would care even less."[187]

By way of comparison, in the same April 3–May 30 time frame, the *New York Times* ran approximately ninety articles on Haiti, sixty-three of which focused on Clinton's role. It also published seven editorials and op-eds, one of which praised Clinton's decision to finally institute sanctions that might "bite." The others—which carried titles such as "In America, Abandoning Democracy," "Treat Haitians Fairly," and "Words, Words, Words"—all criticized Clinton administration policy as hypocritical, scandalous, ineffective, and grossly in need of reform. For example, consider the following op-ed piece by columnist Bob Herbert, in which he notes that:

> The Supreme Court, in its ruling last June, acknowledged that the forced repatriation of refugees at sea "may even violate the spirit" of the United Nations [Refugee] treaty. The Court went as far as to suggest that the drafters of the treaty had not specifically protected refugees at sea because they "may not have contemplated that any nation would gather fleeing refugees and return them to the one country they had desperately sought to escape.... Randall

---

[185] Stephen Kinzer, "European Leaders Reluctant to Send Troops to Rwanda," *New York Times*, May 25, 1994.

[186] Quoted in ibid.

[187] Peter Millar, "Live and Let Die: We Should Fight in Rwanda, but We Won't," *Gazette*, May 28, 1994.

Robinson has lost a dozen pounds or so, and if the Administration doesn't change its policy regarding Haitian refugees he will lose a dozen more. He doesn't want to die but he believes the moral issue here is big enough to risk dying for. The United States, he believes, cannot become a barrier to liberty, a nation that sends the seekers of democracy back into the inferno.[188]

Four days after this column ran—in an explicit acknowledgement of the political pressure he was suffering—Clinton announced the policy shift that ended repatriation without screening.

Thus although the total number of *New York Times* articles published was virtually identical for Haiti and Rwanda, Haiti had the potential to cause real political harm, whereas Rwanda did not, and this made all the difference. Consider that in late April—at the height of the massacres in Rwanda—Aristide publicly declared Clinton's policy of forcibly returning refugees to Haiti "genocidal" and "racist," and he compared their treatment to that of Jews before the Holocaust. In response, then National Security Adviser Anthony Lake reportedly invited Aristide to hold talks to review U.S. policy.[189] In contrast, when a human rights representative "quietly came to lobby [Lake] for United States action [in Rwanda]," Lake reportedly told him he "would be unsuccessful in pressing for an intervention unless a great deal of popular protest began to occur."[190] It is worth noting that during the period in question not a single Haitian died trying to reach the United States—or if one did, his or her death was not reported in the U.S. press[191]—whereas up to 800,000 were slaughtered in Rwanda.

Case Evaluation

The findings of this case largely support the key propositions of this book, with one notable qualification. First, the nature and the motivations of the challengers were consistent with the predictions of the theory. The (incidental, if you will) generators were, indeed, weak illegitimate leaders of the poorest country in the Western Hemisphere. On one hand, evidence suggests Cedras and his cadre made a horrible miscalculation in not doing more to restrain the departure of boats and rafts.[192] (It was only in July

---

[188] Bob Herbert, "In America; Fasting for Haiti," *New York Times*, May 4, 1994.

[189] "Aristide: 'Its A Genocide,'" *Miami Herald*, April 22, 1994.

[190] Quoted in William F. Schulz, *In Our Own Best Interest: How Defending Human Rights Benefits Us All* (Boston: Beacon Press, 2002), 10. See also David Rieff, "The Precarious Triumph of Human Rights," *New York Times Magazine*, August 8, 1999.

[191] But between twelve and twenty people did die in Haiti due to political-related violence.

[192] See, for instance, Mitchell, "Political Costs of State Power."

1994 that the first evidence emerged of attempts to stop outflows from Haiti, when after "calling the mass exodus a political action," Haitian soldiers began searching for and destroying boats that were being readied to depart for the United States.[193]) On the other hand, however, although the junta was removed from power, its members reportedly departed with very attractive retirement packages. Moreover, under the terms of the settlement they were—to use Jimmy Carter's own term—turned into "honorable men."[194] Cedras, Biamby, and Francois were permitted to stay in power up to a month before Aristide's return, granted amnesty for all human rights abuses committed by themselves and their underlings since the 1991 coup, and (reportedly) left in possession of millions of dollars that they made breaking the oil embargo.[195] So, as exits go, the junta could have fared far worse.

The predictions regarding the nature and behavior of the principal *agent provocateur*, Aristide, were also borne out. As a deposed and exiled political figure, Aristide was forced to rely on the support of advocates and the international community; their assistance in heightening the hypocrisy costs for the target state was invaluable in Aristide's quest for reinstatement. He was also helped immeasurably by the actions of Haitians themselves, who stayed in Haiti when asked and took to the sea when needed. In short, the timing, shifting size, and changing nature of outflows over time were correlated much more tightly with Aristide's entreaties to Haitians to either stay put or to leave than with shifts in either general levels of violence or state-imposed repression on the ground. That hundreds were to die by following Aristide's orders, and in the service of his restoration, was a risk of which both Aristide and his supporters publicly expressed a willingness to take.

Aristide was also clearly successful in his exercise of coercive engineered migration. Although the post-1991 case did not begin as attempted coercion, only Aristide's instrumental escalation of the crisis finally brought it to a close—largely on his desired terms. Despite a long-standing reluctance to intervene and a desire to avoid reinstalling Aristide, the Clinton administration was forced to do both to reduce the growing hypocrisy, political, and monetary costs associated with failing to act. Moreover, this case represents the first known instance in which the United States not only intervened in the hemisphere to restore a popularly elected president

---

[193] "Incident at Baie du Mesle."

[194] "Agreement Sets Conditions for Haitian Leaders to Retire," USIA Wireless File, September 19, 1994.

[195] See Douglas Farah, "US Assists Dictators' Luxury Exile," *Washington Post*, October 14, 1994; Dupuy, *Haiti in the New World Order*, 160. On this last point, there is some disagreement. Most suggest the junta did well financially, but Robert Pastor is skeptical; see Pastor, "Haiti, 1994."

to power, but also found itself cajoled into restoring a man "who had been branded by the US as a radical firebrand" and who was intensely disliked and distrusted by many in the U.S. government.[196] To add insult to injury, the United States still had to offer side-payments to the coup leaders to entice them to leave without the use of force, and thus without the risk of incurring casualties.

It bears noting, however, that if Panama had not defected from its commitment to house Haitians in summer 1994, it is possible that intervention might have been avoided, and thus Aristide's gambit could have turned out very differently. If Panama had followed through on its promise, the administration might have had an easier time convincing other states to help share the burden. Nevertheless, historical precedent does not suggest we should invest too much faith in this counterfactual. For instance, when former President Carter approached a variety of countries for help with the Mariel crisis, he had little success. Although more a significant amount of financial aid was promised, pledges to actually receive exiles numbered no more than the original 10,800 Cubans who surged into the Peruvian Embassy in April 1980—there were no offers to take any of the 125,000 who arrived in the United States as part of the boatlift. And the pledges of accommodation that were made were often hedged in some way. For instance, Brazil said it would take those specifically asking to go there. France said it would "take French-speakers with ties in that country," and Canada said it would take three hundred but then back-pedaled, claiming that "so far we haven't found any Cubans who said they wanted to go to Canada."[197] Moreover, most Latin American countries adopted the diplomatically convenient position that the Mariel crisis was a bilateral issue between the United States and Cuba, and since the refugees' country of first asylum was the United States, these states bore no legal obligation to accept them.[198]

Second, evidence suggests that the existence of domestic discord and a high level of polarization (heterogeneity) within the target state was critical to coercive success. Even before the intervention, close observers and analysts of Haiti noted, "political criticism of the interception policy has helped induce the US government to act in favor of a democratic regime in Haiti. Such a political trend would undercut the argument that Haitian boat people are fleeing political persecution and would bolster the policy of repatriation."[199] Likewise, there is an abundance of evidence to suggest

[196] Farah, "US Assists Dictators' Luxury Exile."

[197] Christopher Dickey, "22 Nations Offer Limited Aid for Cuban Exodus," *Washington Post*, May 9, 1980.

[198] By September 1980, only eighty-eight Cubans had been resettled outside the United States. Charles Babcock, "Civiletti Says US Can't Block Fla. Refugee Influx," *Washington Post*, September 20, 1980.

[199] Mitchell, "US Policy," 69.

that the challengers in this case did not stumble into the exploitation of this heterogeneity by accident. For instance, numerous reports have confirmed that the junta leaders felt secure in resisting Washington's demands because there was so much disagreement about which tack to take, both within the United States—between the executive and Congress, among different agencies, and within the public—and among the international bodies dealing with the crisis (e.g., the OAS and UN).[200]

Similarly, both Aristide and his supporters (as well as average Haitians) made numerous references to the critical role that U.S. domestic politics played in their thinking and their actions. In short, there was a nearly ubiquitous recognition of the power of domestic conflict to drive international outcomes.

Third, it would be hard to argue that hypocrisy did not matter because it was only after Randall Robinson and the Congressional Black Caucus took up their respective causes that Washington policies began to bend.[201] Despite this fact—and this is the major qualification—I argue that, in this case, hypocrisy costs served more of a supporting role than an instrumental one. Op-ed columnists from both the left and the right (e.g., Bob Herbert and William Safire in the *New York Times*) condemned both Bush and Clinton—at least episodically—throughout the post-coup period, yet there was little significant change in policy until 1994. In other words, because critical columns appeared throughout the crisis, it seems evident that they alone were insufficient to cause a policy shift. It was only in conjunction with the expectation of escalating political and economic costs that hypocrisy costs really mattered. Nevertheless, it was clear that the Clinton administration had to find a solution to the Haitian crisis because a hypocritical policy that allowed for continued interdiction was not sustainable. As Bob Pastor puts it:

> By tragic accidents, by Haitian sabotage or snipers, or by the difficulty of installing democracy in a country that had never really had it. Any of these problems would jeopardize his ability to lead both at home and abroad. He [Clinton] was therefore not ready to cross that Rubicon and invade Haiti until he realized that his prestige and power were at risk *for failing to deliver on his repeated pledge* to restore Aristide to power. The Congressional Black Caucus and other liberal groups exerted important influence. *Clinton knew that they would constantly remind him of his promise, and they were among his most reliable supporters.*[202]

---

[200] Whether this is true is unclear. In some sense, however, it is irrelevant because the message was crystal clear. Within the United States, there was profound disagreement about how to proceed, and thus U.S. credibility was critically compromised.

[201] "Which Haiti Policy?" A18.

[202] Pastor, "Haiti, 1994," 138.

Moreover, Clinton fared far worse than Bush—even though Bush arguably pursued the more consistently harmful policies from the perspective of actual hypocrisy—because Clinton found himself hoist on his own rhetorical petard. As columnist Clarence Page observed, "I find Clinton on the subject of race to be uplifting, yet perplexing. He knows human nature well enough to sing the right words and music. Yet when his feet hit the floor on thorny issues like Haiti, they seem to dance out of step."[203] In short, as suggested in chapter 1, condemnation—and its consequences— will be more acute for those actors who employ lofty rhetoric and then try to avoid living up to that rhetoric than for those actors who simply and consistently behave in a politically expedient manner. Moreover, Clinton's critics on the Haiti issue were members of his natural constituency—not so for Bush—thus, the hypocrisy costs to be borne were still higher.

As illustrated in figure 4.1, at the outset of the crisis, only those opposed to the admittance of Haitians were highly mobilized; this allowed the Clinton administration to continue to repatriate Haitians despite its earlier promises not to do so. Then, once this consistently high concentration of opposition was coupled with newly concentrated, hypocrisy costinfused pressure from the previously quiescent African American activists and their supporters, Clinton found himself unable to satisfy both of these irreconcilable constituencies and thus highly vulnerable to coercion. Faced with a seemingly insoluble dilemma, the administration felt it had little choice but to do as Aristide demanded, in order to stop the outflow at its source and make the problem disappear.

Still, concession occurred late in the game. Evidence suggests this was true in part because of all of the usual dysfunctions that tend to characterize decision making in powerful liberal democracies—including hubris, credibility problems, bureaucratic inattention, and information asymmetries. But it also appears that there was one special circumstance that made the intelligence-failure part of the problem more forgivable/understandable in the case of Haiti. Specifically, one reason U.S. officials failed to predict the scope of the second migration crisis in summer 1994 was that, in their search for new boat building, U.S. military helicopters and airplanes flying over Haitian beaches did not include in their assessments the tiny boats used by those just trying to get past the 12-mile barrier, a stratagem that had not been anticipated. This made a tremendous difference in their calculations regarding the size of a potential outflow because it can take a year to build a boat large enough to reach Florida but it takes less than two weeks to build one that can reach beyond the 12-mile limit.[204]

[203] Quoted in Ronald I. Perusse, *Haitian Democracy Restored, 1991–1995* (Lanham, Md.: University Press of America, 1995), 74.

[204] Tom Squitieri, "Haitian 'Numbers' A Surprise; US Admits Refugee Tide Not Expected," *USA Today*, July 6, 1994.

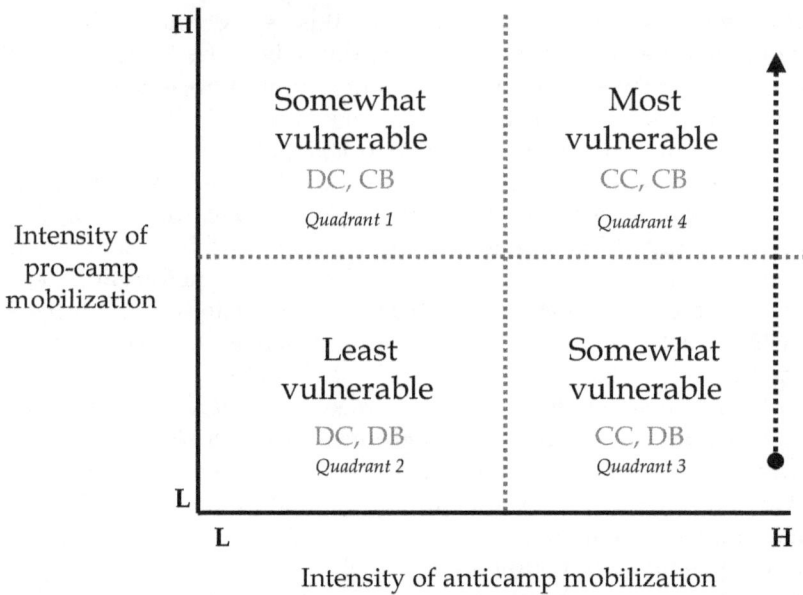

Figure 4.1. Why Aristide succeeded. CB, concentrated benefits; CC, concentrated costs; DB, diffuse benefits; DC, diffuse costs; H, high; L, low.

Refugee Threat Redux—Aristide under Siege, 2004

A decade after Aristide's striking coercive success and return to power, a new political crisis was looming. The man the United States had reinstalled and who had once been regarded as "the nation's hope for democracy" was increasingly viewed by Haitians as a corrupt and untrustworthy autocrat. Frustrations mounted as national elections were delayed and the parliament ceased to function. Although opposition had been building for months, full-scale violence finally broke out in early February 2004. Protesters took to the streets complaining of human rights abuses by the government, and armed gangs seized control of police stations in several cities and demanded Aristide's resignation.[205]

The French—the former colonial rulers of Haiti—entered the fray and added their voices to those calling for Aristide to step down. For its part, the United States adopted a more supportive, albeit ambiguous, stance. On February 12, then Secretary of State Colin Powell told the Senate Foreign Relations Committee, "the policy of the administration is not regime

[205] Carol J. Williams, "Doubts Linger on Aristide's Exit," *Los Angeles Times*, March 1, 2005.

change, President Aristide is the elected president of Haiti, [although we are] 'disappointed' in Aristide's failure to build 'a functioning, stable democracy.'"[206] Five days later, on February 17, Powell announced that, although Aristide must share some blame for the violence, the United States "cannot buy into a proposition that says the elected president must be forced out of office by thugs and those who do not respect law and are bringing terrible violence to the Haitian people."[207] At the same time, the United States publicly embraced the CARICOM Plan, a power-sharing agreement that would have allowed Aristide to serve out his term with substantially reduced powers; however, it refused to commit U.S. troops to protect him.

This relatively supportive U.S. stance shifted abruptly little more than a week later, however, fast on the heels of a public declaration by Aristide that, absent the insertion of previously requested, armed international assistance, another Haitian migration crisis was likely to follow. At a press conference in English, Creole, French, and Spanish, Aristide proclaimed:

> Should those killers come to Port-au-Prince, you may have thousands of people who may be killed. We need the presence of the international community as soon as possible. We may have more Haitians leaving Haiti by boat for Florida.... Unfortunately many brothers and sisters in Port-de-Paix will not come down to Port-au-Prince; they will take to the sea, they will become boat people. How many will die before reaching Florida? I don't know.[208]

Whether or not Aristide's comments were intended to serve as a new coercive threat, they were manifestly viewed as such by the administration of George W. Bush. As James Foley, U.S. Ambassador to Haiti, put it, "He was trying to trigger an international intervention to save his presidency."[209] The move was a rapid and demonstrable failure.

Less than twenty-four hours later, President Bush warned Haitians against trying to escape the violence and turmoil on the island by sailing to the United States, saying that any Haitians caught doing so would be turned back.[210] Boats were deployed in a kind of cordon in the Caribbean Sea, designed to act as both a deterrent and as a net for anyone who

---

[206] Quoted in Christopher Marquis, "US Officials Hint at Support for Haitian Leader's Ouster," *New York Times*, February 12, 2004.

[207] "France Ponders Haiti Peace Force," BBC News, February 18, 2004.

[208] Quoted in Marika Lynch, Susannah A. Nesmith, and Martin Merzer, "Aristide to World: Help Stop Bloodshed," *Miami Herald*, February 25, 2004; and in Carol J. Williams, "Aristide Appeals to World for Aid: Haitian Leader Warns of a Tide of Refugees," *Los Angeles Times*, February 25, 2004.

[209] Quoted in Williams, "Aristide Appeals to World for Aid."

[210] "Boat People Fleeing Haitian Crisis," CNN, February 26, 2004.

decided to attempt the crossing.[211] At the same time, U.S. officials, including Secretary Powell, suddenly announced that—despite previous U.S. statements to the contrary—Aristide's resignation was an "increasing possibility" and "more a feature of the [ongoing] discussions than it was before."[212] On February 28, the White House went further, newly asserting that "the long-simmering crisis is largely of Mr. Aristide's doing" and that "his own actions have called into question his fitness to remain in office."[213]

The very next day, the United States sent an aircraft to Port-au-Prince to "help" Aristide decamp for renewed exile, this time far from the United States, in the Central African Republic. And although in the days leading up to Aristide's flight from Haiti the UN Security Council had denied his request for military intervention to quell the uprising, it authorized an international military force just hours after he left the country.[214]

This incident was over almost as soon as it began, with few political costs incurred by the Bush administration. Although suspicions regarding Aristide's departure were raised in diplomatic circles and in the press, the pro-camp mobilized only haltingly. In the period leading up to Aristide's ouster, thirty members of the Congressional Black Caucus urged the president in a published statement to do "everything in his power to protect the people and the government of Haiti" and stressed "the urgent need for the United States to actively insert itself in the crisis and for the president to personally become engaged in what may become a human catastrophe in our own hemisphere."[215] Yet, after Aristide's summary departure, none offered sustained criticism of the administration's actions.[216] Public protests were likewise lackluster and short-lived.[217]

---

[211] Although the Pentagon denied it (ibid.), some reports emerged that the United States also had a plan to temporarily house Haitians at Guantanamo if the flow got too large to allow summary repatriation. As Michael Ratner, president of the Center for Constitutional Rights, who for decades dealt extensively with the Haitian boatpeople issue, described it, "what they have been able to develop is a system of boats that surround Haiti[,] of US ships that can stop, they think, every single Haitian. In addition, we have seen reports...that they set up in Guantanamo as many as 50,000 beds for possible refugees." Precisely where and for how long they would have housed them there if a crisis erupted—given the concomitant presence of detainees from the "war on terror" is unclear. Quoted in "Aristide Warns of Possible Refugee Crisis in Haiti," *Democracy Now*, February 25, 2004, www.democracynow.org/2004/2/25/aristide_warns_of_possible_refugee_crisis.

[212] "Boat People Fleeing Haitian Crisis."

[213] Williams, "Doubts Linger on Aristide's Exit."

[214] Ibid.

[215] "Boat People Fleeing Haitian Crisis."

[216] Subsequent calls for a UN investigation into the sudden departure of Aristide were rebuffed. "US, France Block UN Probe into Aristide Ouster," Inter Press Service, April 13, 2004; Williams, "Doubts Linger on Aristide's Exit."

[217] For instance, on February 28, Aristide supporters numbered close to 2,000 in a protest along Eastern Parkway in Brooklyn, N.Y. (home to the second-largest Haitian diaspora

The lackadaisical response of the pro-camp was due in no small part to the fact that the shine had once again gone off Aristide. In the decade following the U.S. intervention—during which approximately $900 million in U.S. development aid had been poured into the country—Haiti had made little progress. Moreover, elections held in 2000, one of which brought Aristide back into power, were widely viewed as fraudulent.[218] In fact, by February 2004, Aristide had grown so unpopular that fully 56 percent of Haitian Americans polled asserted that the economic and political situation in Haiti had been better under the [profoundly corrupt and nepotistic] Duvaliers, whereas only 14 percent thought times were better under Aristide. Forty-six percent of those surveyed rated Aristide's job performance as poor or mediocre versus the 23 percent that gave him a good or excellent rating.[219] As Robert Maguire, long-time Aristide supporter and director of international affairs at Trinity College, put it at the time, "Aristide has felt that his power was strong enough that he feels he doesn't have to play the traditional Haitian political game. He has alienated many, many people."[220]

Conversely, mobilization by members of the anti-migrant/refugee camp was high. Not only had the general popularity of Haitian boatpeople not—to put it mildly—grown since 1994, but 2004 was also an election year.[221] The congressional contingent from Florida cautioned the president on the dangers of another Haitian migration crisis for them, for him, and for the country. Then Senator Bob Graham (D-Fla.), one-time presidential candidate, specifically warned of a brewing "humanitarian catastrophe" and said the region "was on the edge of the volcano of crisis in Haiti yet again."[222] Moreover, the attention of the U.S. public was focused elsewhere—on the rapidly worsening situation in Iraq, among other things. Thus, the crisis generated relatively limited (and short-lived) media attention. In short, low pro-camp mobilization coupled with high anti-camp

---

population). At a protest the following week—*after* Aristide's removal—the number of supporters had dwindled to five hundred, before the protests ceased altogether. Jeremy Smerd, "After Aristide: On Streets and Airwaves, the Haitian Diaspora Confronts Chaos at Home," http://smerd.wordpress.com/2004/03/09/after-aristide-on-streets-and-airwaves-the-haitian-diaspora-confronts-chaos-at-home/.

[218] "US Distances Itself from Haiti's Election Process," CNN, November 25, 2000. As John Conyers Jr., Congressional Black Caucus member, put it on CNN, "Unfortunately, there were irregularities that occurred in the election and there is a post-election problem of the vote count that is threatening to undo the democratic work of the citizens of Haiti."

[219] "Haitians in US Nostalgic for Duvalier Era," Reuters On-line, February 20, 2004, www.haiti-info.com/spip.php?article1367.

[220] Quoted in Marquis, "US Officials Hint at Support for Haitian Leader's Ouster."

[221] Ibid.; "Aristide Warns of Possible Refugee Crisis in Haiti." Recall also that the incumbent president's brother, Jeb, was then governor of the Sunshine State.

[222] "Aristide to World."

mobilization and limited public attention to the issue meant that a successful coercion redux was never a realistic option for Aristide.

That said, despite Aristide's declining popularity, the administration had originally been prepared to leave him in place until the end of his term, particularly since there was little enthusiasm for taking renewed military action in the Caribbean in 2004. But when—just after Haitian rebels made clear they would resist the U.S.-backed power-sharing agreement—Aristide made the mistake of intimating an uncontrolled outflow might be forthcoming, he essentially signed his own political death warrant. As Richard Boucher, U.S. State Department spokesman, candidly put it, "We can't be called upon, expected or required to intervene every time there is violence against a failed leader. We can't spend our time running around the world and the hemisphere saving people who botched their chance at leadership."[223]

[223] State Department noon briefing, March 4, 2004, www.globalsecurity.org/military/library/news/2004/03/mil-040304-usia04.htm.

5

North Korean Migrants, Nongovernmental Organizations, and Nuclear Weapons

It's clear that the Chinese have enormous leverage over North Korea in many respects. But can they exercise that leverage without destabilizing the regime? Probably not.
DANIEL SNEIDER, Associate Director for Research, Asia-Pacific Research Center, Stanford University

The 1990s were a tough decade for the North Koreans. In 1991, they lost their superpower patron with the fall of the Soviet Union, and in 1994, they lost their patron saint with the death of the Great Leader Kim Il Sung, who had ruled North Korea since its founding shortly after World War II. For not wholly unrelated reasons, the 1990s were also marked by a series of devastating famines, which resulted in the deaths of between several hundred thousand and several million North Koreans[1] and the flight of several hundred thousand more across the Tumen River and into the Yanbian Prefecture of northern China.[2]

Epigraph: Quoted in "The China-North Korea Relationship," *A Council on Foreign Relations Backgrounder* (July 2009), http://www.cfr.org/publication/11097/.

[1] To compensate for the loss of foreign aid that accompanied the demise of the USSR and to boost its supply of arable land, North Korea pursued a policy of massive deforestation during this period. This policy resulted in devastating floods and massive erosion, which in turn reduced rice and maize production by more than 60 percent over a fifteen-year period. The famines were, then, worsened and deepened as a consequence of internal North Korean politics. Andrew S. Natsios, *The Great North Korean Famine: Famine, Politics and Foreign Policy* (Washington, D.C.: United States Institute of Peace, 2001). Refugee reports place the number of dead at between 1 and 3.5 million; however, based on its body counts, the World Food Program believes the real death toll was far lower. See John Gittings, "Life on a Diet of Roots, Grass and Seaweed; While the Capital Gets a Facelift, North Korea Has Run Out of Food," *Guardian*, April 29, 1999, 16.

[2] Most fled northward toward Yanbian—where the North Korean, Chinese, and Russian borders meet—because crossing the Tumen River was viewed as easier than penetrating the

Paradoxically, however, the country also benefited somewhat from its weakness and instability during this troublesome decade. For one thing, after the disintegration of the USSR, China became the main trading partner of North Korea. After briefly trying to make Pyongyang pay like a "normal nation," Beijing changed tack and began offering large quantities of aid (both overt and covert), for fear that otherwise famine might precipitate a collapse of the country—creating millions of refugees and perhaps bringing U.S. troops in a unified Korea to its border.[3] More or less concomitantly—with the country now under the control of Kim Il Sung's eccentric and rather less popular son, Kim Jong Il—North Korea also successfully leveraged its structural weaknesses into a lucrative agreement to freeze its nascent nuclear program in return for U.S. aid and assistance in building civilian nuclear reactors.[4] In short, U.S. fears of a nuclear North Korea coupled with Chinese (as well as South Korean and even Russian) fears of a massive North Korean outmigration granted this relatively weak actor noteworthy bargaining strength against its significantly more powerful international counterparts.[5]

From one perspective, a decade later little had changed. Although the movement of North Koreans across the border had slowed markedly by 2002, the issue continued to complicate—some would even say, "plague"—relations between states in the region and with the United States farther afield. And, just as they had in the mid-1990s, migration-related fears continued to redound to the benefit of North Korea on the nuclear front. The United States wanted North Korean neighbors to pressure it to relinquish its recidivistic nuclear ambitions—which had been reinvigorated

---

heavily mined demilitarized zone (DMZ) that divides North and South Korea. Moreover, not only is the Tumen River little more than a creek at the border crossing, but in Yanbian, Korean is widely spoken and many of its inhabitants are themselves ethnically Korean. Scott Snyder, "Transit, Traffic Control, and Telecoms: Crossing the 'T's' in Sino-Korean Exchange," *Comparative Connections*, 4 (2002), http://csis.org/files/media/csis/pubs/0201qchina_korea.pdf.

[3] Interview with Dr. John Park, Korea scholar, April 2003; Marcus Noland, "Why North Korea Will Muddle Through," *Foreign Affairs* 76 (July–August 1997): 105–18.

[4] See, for instance, Scott Snyder, *Negotiating on the Edge: North Korean Negotiating Behavior* (Washington, D.C.: United States Institute of Peace, 1999), esp. chap. 3; Mark Habeeb, *Power and Tactics in International Negotiations: How Weak Nations Negotiate with Strong Nations* (Baltimore: Johns Hopkins University Press, 1988); Hans Binnendijk, *How Nations Negotiate* (Washington, D.C.: National Defense University, 1987); T. V. Paul, *Asymmetric Conflicts: War Initiation by Weaker Powers* (Cambridge, UK: Cambridge University Press, 1994).

[5] Research materials for this chapter were drawn from a variety of primary and secondary sources, including an array of international newspaper, journal, magazine articles and articles that appeared in the Foreign Broadcast Information Service (hereafter FBIS). For additional perspective, I conducted interviews with UNHCR officials, regional scholars, a staff member from former U.S. Senator Edward Kennedy's (D-Mass.) office, and several U.S.-based academics who have engaged in track-two diplomatic efforts with the North Koreans. I also had conversations with a former Chinese government official and two South Korean policymakers, both of whom agreed to speak "on background."

by, among other things, President George H. W. Bush's inclusion of North Korea in the odious "axis of evil." But the concerns of its neighbors about potential regime collapse meant Washington's wishes went unheeded.[6] Of course, for its part, North Korea had little interest in precipitating a massive outflow, only in demonstrating it *could* generate one, if pushed.

From another perspective, however, a great deal had changed. Beginning in 2002, a loose coalition of international activists and NGOs—a network of sorts—tried to catalyze precisely the kind of outflow that the North Korean government eagerly sought to avoid and its neighbors so vehemently feared. This chapter offers a case study of the multifaceted attempts at coercive engineered migration that were undertaken on the Korean peninsula during this period—attempts in which North Koreans were used as coercive instruments against China, against South Korea, and both by and against the North Korean regime itself. Intriguingly, one of these attempts was explicitly aimed at bringing down the North Korean regime, whereas another was expressly (albeit tacitly) aimed at propping it up.

This case offers a useful test of the propositions advanced in this book for several reasons. First, the case boasts a range of challengers, not only an active (yet relatively reluctant) generator but also aggressive *agents provocateurs* and opportunists, whose goals and aims in stark opposition to one another. It also offers significant variation in regime type and in the degree of vulnerability across targets; in short, it is a rich case. Second, although North Korea was a distinctly unwilling generator of migrants, its bargaining position on the nuclear front nevertheless benefited immeasurably from its neighbors' fear of outflows. Indeed, as implied, these fears significantly undermined attempts by Washington to persuade North Korea's neighbors to pressure Pyongyang into backing down. This also makes this an important case, one that demonstrates with clarity how fears of potentially destabilizing population movements can circumscribe the range of maneuvering of even a superpower.

In this chapter, I first outline the aims and strategies of the actors in this case while simultaneously examining whether these strategies (and their accompanying tactical actions) are consistent with the predictions of my theory. Then, I explore the reactions of the targets to the maneuvers of the challengers and ask whether these maneuvers had their intended effects. Next, I revisit the major propositions advanced in chapter 1 and evaluate them in light of the evidence presented in this chapter. Finally,

---

[6] In fact, North Korea reportedly fears such an event as much as its neighbors, particularly a Romanian-style revolution, during which the incumbent leadership was summarily executed. David Wall, "When North Korea Collapses," *Guardian*, December 1, 2002.

I offer a few additional thoughts about and possible implications of this particular case.

The Challengers, Their Goals, and Their Targets

North Korea: A Reluctant Generator

Soon after North Korea embarked anew on its mission to obtain nuclear weapons, a debate arose among Korea experts about Kim's motives in this latest round of brinksmanship.[7] Some argued the aim was normalization of relations with the West, and thus Kim sought aid to help implement further liberalization without precipitating a total collapse of the economy.[8] In support of this proposition, they pointed to the fact that after the crisis in the mid-1990s Kim undertook significant economic reforms and made overtures designed to foster better relations with the West.[9] Others were less sanguine, asserting Kim was merely engaged in short-term blackmail, motivated by his need to acquire enough foreign aid to weather the latest domestic economic crisis.[10]

Desperate or not, tactical or strategic, both sides agreed the new nuclear crisis was simply another in a long line of self-created crises designed to "turn up the pressure on the US, but [which] has impacts in the region."[11] As one close observer put it, the North Korean pattern of "drama and catastrophe" was a tried and true strategy for them—a kind of atomic "trick or treat," if you will.[12] Robert Gallucci, who negotiated the 1994 U.S.-North Korean nuclear agreement, echoed this sentiment, suggesting that the North Koreans "don't have much in the way of a negotiating position....All they have is the threat of doing harm. This is their major asset."[13] As Kim himself conceded, "[Our] missiles cannot reach the

[7] Western diplomats who have dealt with him (e.g., former U.S. Secretary of State Madeline Albright) say Kim Jong-Il is no fool but a well-briefed politician who knows exactly what he is doing. Moreover, through satellite TV, his own sources, and hours of Web surfing, he also knows significantly more about the West than the West knows about him. Chris Cobb, "North Korea's High Roller," *Ottawa Citizen*, January 11, 2003.

[8] David Kang, in ibid.

[9] For instance, he unilaterally cleared land mines from the DMZ and admitted kidnapping Japanese in the late 1970s and early 1980s to teach North Korean spies Japanese; Marcus Noland, "Economy's Ills Shape DPRK Crisis," *BBC News*, April 23, 2002.

[10] See Cobb, "North Korea's High Roller"; Natsios, *Great North Korean Famine.*

[11] Robert Einhorn, quoted in Sean Gordon, "North Korea Turns Up Heat on Opponents," *Ottawa Citizen*, December 31, 2002.

[12] Snyder, *Negotiating on the Edge*, 43. See also William M. Drennan, "Nuclear Weapons and North Korea: Who's Coercing Whom?" in *The United States and Coercive Diplomacy*, ed. Robert Art and Patrick Cronin (Washington, D.C.: United States Institute of Peace, 2003), 157–224.

[13] Quoted in Michael Dobbs, "North Korea Policy Confounds US; after Breakdown in Recent Talks, Some See Need for Bolder Strategy," *Washington Post*, May 20, 1997.

United States, and if I launch them, the US would fire back thousands of missiles and we would not survive. I know that very well. But I have to let them know I have missiles. I am making them because only then will the United States talk to me."[14]

North Korea felt it could safely raise the nuclear stakes with the United States due to the shield afforded it by its neighbors' concerns about its potential collapse; as such, they were simply unwilling to risk the kind of escalation Washington favored.[15] "It [was] essential to give [the Koreans] a way to back down," as one Korea watcher put it, "because the United States was unable to muster enough international pressure to cow [them]."[16] Xia Yishan, a political scientist at the Chinese Institute for International Studies in Beijing, summed up regional attitudes in stressing the belief that "pressure alone [on Pyongyang was] not enough. We also need patience."[17] Even then-outgoing South Korean President Kim Dae-jung—who was rarely critical of the United States—concurred, arguing, "pressure and isolation have never been successful with communist countries."[18] And, as James Laney and Jason Shaplen presciently observed in a March 2003 *Foreign Affairs* piece, "those who think they can outwait Pyongyang by isolating it or pressuring it economically ... are likely to be proven wrong. ... Pyongyang enjoys an inherent advantage in any waiting game: Beijing." To guard against collapse of North Korea, China will continue to allow "food and fuel (sanctioned or unsanctioned) to move across its border with the North," as indeed they continue to do five years later.[19]

The reasons why North Korea's neighbors were more concerned about the short-term consequences of destabilization and an influx of refugees than the long-term prospect of a nuclear (and possibly proliferating) North Korea remain somewhat opaque. But, whatever the rationale(s) behind that calculation, the fears that a potential mass migration engendered within

[14] Choe Hak Rae, former publisher of *Hankyoreh Shinmun* (recalling a conversation he had with Kim Jong-Il in the summer of 2000), quoted in Peter Maas, "The Last Emperor," *New York Times Magazine,* October 19, 2003.

[15] See, for instance, Avery Goldstein, "The North Korean Nuclear Challenge and American Interests: Getting the Priorities Right," November 6, 2003, www.nautilus.org/fora/security/0344_Goldstein.html.

[16] Einhorn, quoted in Gordon, "North Korea Turns Up Heat," A7. See also Joseph Kahn, "To China, North Korea Looks Radioactive," *New York Times,* February 2, 2003; Bill Nichols, "US Allies Afraid of Pushing North Korea Over the Edge," *USA Today,* December 30, 2002; Sonni Efron and Ching-Ching Ni, "Showdown with Iraq: China Is Wary of Toeing the US Line," *Los Angeles Times,* February 24, 2003; *Economist,* October 14, 2006.

[17] Quoted in Efron and Ching-Ching, "Showdown with Iraq."

[18] Quoted in ibid. For his part, Russia's foreign minister suggested that a policy of isolation would backfire and could "only lead to a new escalation in tension." In ibid.

[19] James T. Laney and Jason T. Shaplen, "How to Deal with North Korea," *Foreign Affairs* 82 (2003): 27.

probable recipient states offered North Korea powerful bargaining lever-age it would otherwise have lacked. Concerns were so great that in Janu-ary 2002 Chinese, Russian, and South Korean military officials gathered in Seoul for a week of simulated computer scenarios based on a hypothetical flood of 100,000 refugees into the South.[20] Another such exercise followed two years later, and in 2003 Chinese state media reported a seven-day exercise close to the mountainous North Korean border without giving its exact location or purpose. Some analysts speculated that the (unusual) reporting of this exercise was actually a signal by the People's Liberation Army (PLA) that it was prepared for any eventuality. But most analysts thought it more likely that the Chinese were simply training troops to pro-tect the border in the event of a North Korean collapse.[21] And, in 2006, China took the further step of building a fence along part of its border with North Korea.[22]

Such efforts were not lost on Pyongyang, for whom the fear of cross-border population movements served as an effective general deterrent and, as of this writing, continues to do so. As stated at the outset, although North Korea did not want to generate a major outflow, it needed to main-tain a credible threat of being willing and able to do so and, thereby, also maintain its relative bargaining strength despite its aggregate weakness. It was—and continues to be—a successful strategy.[23] The same cannot be said, however, of the tack pursued by the *agents provocateurs,* who sought to use mass migration to end the reign of the "Hermit Kingdom."

Aggressive *Agents Provocateurs:* A Coalition of Activists and Nongovernmental Organizations

In 1989, Hungary opened its barbed-wire border with Austria and al-lowed thousands of East Germans vacationing in Hungary to escape com-munism. This tide turned into a flood, hastening not only the collapse of East Germany but also the fall of the Iron Curtain. From early 2002 until (at least) well into 2005, a loose organization of activists and at least seven international human rights NGOs—with funding from one to two dozen more—sought to replicate the eastern European experience in northeast

---

[20] James Brooke, "Bush Urged to Press China on Providing Relief for Refugees Secretly Fleeing North Korea," *New York Times,* February 11, 2002.

[21] Oliver August, "China and US Flex Muscles," *Times,* January 24, 2003.

[22] Norimitsu Onishi, "Tension, Desperation: The China-North Korean Border," *New York Times,* October 22, 2006. Although the collective attempt to stimulate a mass outflow had subsided by that point, Chinese fears had not.

[23] Although the Chinese adopted a somewhat harder stance toward North Korea in 2007 and 2008, they remained committed to propping up the regime up through monetary and political assistance.

Asia.[24] As one UNHCR official put it, "These guys are serious. Regime change by refugee flow; this could be 'the next big thing.'"[25]

This loose network of activists and NGOs—a number of which were religious organizations—had both immediate and more long-range goals. They targeted China and South Korea, and explicitly attempted to impose hypocrisy costs on both states with the very visible use of would-be North Korean asylum seekers. Primarily, the network sought to focus international attention on the plight of the North Koreans and to force the Chinese government to recognize them as refugees with a right of asylum—rather than as economic migrants—and to set up transit camps in the border region to help facilitate further flight.

Concomitantly, they pressured the South Korean government to take in more North Koreans. As one of the leaders of the movement put it, we are "simply bringing attention to a human tragedy that is inconvenient for politicians...[and] working for the overthrow of the North Korean regime."[26] "The theory [is] that if UN refugee camps are established on the China-North Korea border, they will incite a flood of North Korean refugees who want to escape political oppression in North Korea, leading to the same type of regime collapse in North Korea that occurred in East Germany," just without the Berlin Wall.[27]

The activists also sought to bring information about the outside world to North Koreans by sending small radios into the country by balloon and by staging very visible protests at the Panmunjom border crossing. The group viewed these steps as critical because, absent real information about life outside, there would be "no uprisings like those in former East European countries and no defections on a mass scale."[28]

Although there were many "ground troops" who played instrumental roles in this coalition, a few key figures appear to have masterminded the scheme. The most widely known is Norbert Vollertsen, German physician and activist, a controversial figure who served as an aid worker in North Korean hospitals until he was expelled in 2000. According to Vollertsen, his immediate goal was to persuade China to offer protection to North Koreans seeking refuge instead of repatriating them. He shamelessly sought to exploit the Chinese desire to be viewed as a real "world player," asserting

[24] James Brooke, "China Called Likely to Oust 78 North Koreans," New York Times, January 22, 2003; John Burton, "Protests against China's Stance on N. Koreans," Financial Times, July 2, 2001.
[25] UNHCR official, personal communication, December 2002.
[26] Robert Marquand, "One Man's Quirky Fight for Suffering North Koreans," Christian Science Monitor, December 2, 2002, 1.
[27] Brad Glosserman and Scott Snyder, "Borders and Boundaries: The North Korean Refugee Crisis," PacNet Newsletter 21 (2002), www.csis.org/pacfor/pac0221.htm.
[28] Burton, "Protests against China's Stance."

that "during the six party talks, China [could] prove that it *really deserves to be a member of the international community* by opening its border to North Korean refugees and in this way become the 'Hungary of the Far East.'"[29] "As a German who witnessed the fall of the Wall," Vollertsen declared, "I understand the destabilizing impact an exodus of refugees can have on totalitarian regimes."[30] He further went on to note:

> As a German, I also know about Neville Chamberlain's appeasement policy towards Nazi Germany, how badly it failed, and how disastrous were its consequences. The only way to truly help the North Korean people and to end Pyongyang's nuclear blackmail is to hasten the collapse of Kim Jong Il's murderous regime.[31]

Taking aggressive steps—even though they were widely derided by some of his NGO colleagues—was necessary, according to Vollertsen, because in the early 2000s "the North Koreans [were] laughing at the international community. But if you apply pressure, they will respond. Now is the chance."[32]

Another key figure in the network was Kim Sang Hun, South Korean human rights activist. In the 1970s, Kim worked for Amnesty International, and in the decades that followed he worked for other international organizations, including the UN Development Programme and the World Food Program (WFP). Upon retirement, Kim decided to devote himself to publicizing human rights violations in North Korea, to helping North Korean defectors escape, and to bringing down the regime.[33] Kim firmly believed, "If China would grant refugee status to North Koreans, so many would immediately flee that the regime would disintegrate. 'You don't need to bring an expensive aircraft carrier to solve the North Korea problem.'"[34]

Several religious leaders also played key roles. One was Reverend Tim Peters, an evangelical pastor and head of the Seoul-based charity Helping Hands Korea. Peters became a devoted activist soon after moving to Seoul in 1975 as a lay missionary, following "a highly transforming conversion

[29] Nobert Vollertsen, "South Korea's Spoilers," *Wall Street Journal*, August 22, 2003.

[30] Nobert Vollertsen, "Prison Nation: Why North Koreans Cheered Bush's 'Axis of Evil' Designation," *Wall Street Journal*, February 5, 2003.

[31] Ibid.

[32] Vollertsen, quoted in interview with Donald MacIntyre, "Diary of a Mad Place," *TIME Asia*, January 22, 2001. In fact, even before the engineered outmigration project started in earnest, Vollertsen's own aid agency distanced itself from his statements and proposed schemes.

[33] "Human Rights Activist Honored by TIME," *Chosun Ilbo*, April 24, 2003; Kim Sang Hun, in an interview with Donald MacIntyre, "One Man against Kim Jong Il," *TIME Asia*, April 28, 2003.

[34] Quoted in MacIntyre, "One Man against Kim Jong Il."

to Christ."[35] Because Peters was less of a lightning rod than Vollertsen, more than any other Westerner Peters reportedly "became the public face" of the network. Peters self-consciously described his role as one of the founders, and managers, of a Korean Underground Railroad, whose cause was "as urgent" as its predecessor, which transported African American slaves from the U.S. South to freedom in the north.[36]

Also significant was the Reverend Douglas Shin of the Los Angeles–based Korean Peninsula Peace Project, who claimed he was "fighting everyone who is preventing us from helping the North Koreans. What are our motivations? Sometimes we just want to help people. Sometimes we feel hatred for the dictatorship. Sometimes we see a war and North Korea's pending collapse. Sometimes maybe we are fighting the Chinese dictatorship as well."[37] Shin claimed that he and his compatriots were prepared take whatever steps were necessary in the service of their cause. "Some people will perish, but the majority will get out. . . . There will be a continuous flow until the end" (i.e., the fall of Kim Jong Il's government).[38] The activists and sympathetic NGOs, such as Life Funds for North Korean Refugees and Helping Hands, also targeted the South Korean "sunshine policy," which was viewed as far too conciliatory toward the North. As Vollertsen put it, "If all you have is sunshine, well that's a desert. In nature, you need both sun and rain; I am a rainmaker. We work together."[39]

That these men and their followers sought to affect regime change via the employment of coercive engineered migration was self-evident. Whether they could succeed, however, was another matter.

The Strategy

In support of their coercive attempts, the activists engaged in a two-pronged attack. The first prong centered around the staging of dramatic escapes and bids for asylum, ideally captured on film and subsequently distributed to major news outlets to maximize the international impact of these events. The second prong was directed at raising public consciousness of the issue and mobilizing pressure on targets in several distinct ways: first, by exhorting the United States and other Western governments to demand that the Chinese and South Korean governments do more to live up to their moral obligations to those fleeing the North Korean regime;

---

[35] Donald MacIntyre, "Running out of the Darkness," *TIME Asia,* April 24, 2006.
[36] Ibid.
[37] Quoted in Elisabeth Rosenthal, "More Koreans Give China the Slip," *New York Times.*
[38] Quoted in ibid.
[39] Robert Marquand, "One Man's Quirky Fight for Suffering North Koreans," *Christian Science Monitor,* December 3, 2002.

second, by appealing directly to public opinion in East Asia in the hope that the targeted populations would pressure their governments to accept more North Koreans and embrace them as refugees; and third, by trying to shame UNHCR and the WFP into pressuring the Chinese government into changing its policies on North Koreans, lest these organizations be viewed as hypocritical themselves.

The selections excerpted next are illustrative of this strategy in action. As the theory predicts, the activists and their supporters attempted to influence target behavior by highlighting the disparity between rhetoric of the target governments about North Koreans and their actions (i.e., by imposing damaging hypocrisy costs). An op-ed, published in the *Washington Post* in July 2001, articulates clearly what would become the explicit network agenda approximately six months later:

> The first obstacle is the Chinese government, which has signed an international convention on protection of refugees but refuses to respect its terms....it will not allow the UNHCR to operate in the area or screen the arrivals, instead ludicrously insisting that all are mere economic migrants not suffering from persecution by the world's strictest totalitarian government. Earlier this year an extraordinary total of 11.8 million South Koreans signed a petition to the United Nations asking for better treatment for the refugees. But it's not clear their own government is entirely on board. South Korean officials have not pressed China to grant the refugees access to the UNHCR or freedom to travel to the South, instead preferring what they call "quiet diplomacy."...
>
> But it may also be that some in South Korea and in the West fear success....though South Korea hopes for unification with the North some day, it fears a precipitous collapse of the Pyongyang regime that would swamp it with refugees. Thanks to such concerns, North Korea's refugees have been hemmed into a miserable no-man's land, both diplomatically and literally. The bravery of the Jung Tae-jun family last week at last put their suffering on the international agenda. The United Nations and the Bush administration should act to keep it there—by beginning a serious campaign to give the UNHCR access to the thousands of families left behind.[40]

Another asserted:

> Neither the United Nations nor Western governments have pressed Beijing hard enough on this matter; the assumption seems to be that China can't be expected to take action that might embarrass its fellow Communist regime. But if China can commit to the rules of the World Trade Organization, it should no longer be allowed to flout the refugee convention with impunity.

[40] "Escape from a Prison-State," *Washington Post*, July 3, 2001.

Japan, the United States and other Western governments must make clear to Beijing that the way to avoid further incidents around consulates and embassies is to use the UNHCR, rather than its security thugs, to manage a problem that will not go away.[41]

Still others sought to outrage the public through the use of graphic imagery, disturbing historical analogies, and colorful hyperbole. One called on the international community to pressure China to behave like "other civilized nations" and recognize North Koreans as refugees because "in the 20th century the world stood by as the Nazis killed millions of Jews, the Khmer Rouge slaughtered a third of Cambodia's population, and millions of people were murdered in Rwanda. This should not be repeated. The world must not turn its back on the horrors taking place in North Korea."[42] Still another opined that:

Just when I was feeling sentimental about leaving China, they issued wooden clubs to the police guarding the diplomatic compound where I live. It wasn't hard to guess what they were for. The heavy, yard-long truncheons were for hitting North Korean refugees, in case any more tried to burst into diplomatic buildings and defect. [The Chinese would be enforcing] its treaty with North Korea promising to return Korean runaways. It is one of many traces of Maoist poison still hidden in the system behind the glittering facades of Beijing and Shanghai, the Starbucks cafés and Porsche showrooms.... China sticks to the letter, but not the spirit, of its international promises. It has signed up to a United Nations treaty on protecting refugees. As so often, Beijing has found a loophole to avoid its obligations, insisting that the North Koreans are illegal migrants, not refugees.[43]

And in yet another—after detailing a brutal death of a North Korean, beaten with an iron pipe for the crime of "'crossing the border'...by the officials of one country while officials from another country simply watched"—the author implored the United States to "use economic leverage to make China comply with the international [refugee] treaties it has signed." Barring that, she advocated a worldwide boycott of Chinese goods and called on the International Olympic Committee to find a new location for the 2008 Games.[44]

[41] "Asylum in China," *Washington Post*, May 12, 2002.
[42] "China Refuses to Assist North Korean Refugees," *San Antonio Express-News*, Editorial, August 6, 2002.
[43] David Rennie, "Mao's China Still Lives—and It Carries a Big Stick," *Daily Telegraph*, March 22, 2002.
[44] Suzanne Scholte, "Border Brutality; China Must Not Be Allowed to Aid and Abet North Korea's Murderous Regime," *Washington Post*, October 26, 2002.

Established voices in the human rights community also weighed in, but in less evocative and inflammatory language and probably not in the service of the cause of the *agents provocateurs*. Nevertheless, their intention to impose hypocrisy costs is clear. The U.S. Committee on Refugees (USCR) proclaimed China "in violation of its international obligations as a signatory to the *UN Refugee Convention*.... There is little doubt that North Koreans fleeing to China are refugees."[45] Furthermore, following the November 2002 publication of the Human Rights Watch report, *The Invisible Exodus: North Koreans in the People's Republic of China*, its Washington director for Asia acknowledged that "North Korea bears the main responsibility for this exodus of refugees.... But [asserted that] the Chinese government has important responsibilities, too. Forcibly returning asylum seekers is a blatant violation of international law."[46]

Curiously, some groups traditionally viewed as "good guys" (i.e., pro-refugee/migrant protection) themselves came under attack. For instance, UNHCR was singled out for criticism for its "complicity" in Chinese attempts to deny the North Koreans refugee status. In December 2002, several human rights activists announced that UNHCR would "be the target of our actions in the future" because "the one agency with the authority to force a solution has chosen to sit on its hands. It's not just collusion, it's culpable negligence to the point of complicity."[47] Soon thereafter, the *Wall Street Journal* published a scathing criticism of UNHCR inaction on the North Korean front. Claudia Rosett, writer and journalist, implored:

> So what can the UNHCR do? Plenty, if the UN bothered to insist on upholding its own mandate and promises. Not only is the Chinese government a signatory to the UN's 1951 convention and additional protocols guaranteeing protection for refugees; Beijing actually holds a seat on the UNHCR's executive committee. Beyond that, and even more germane, China and the UNHCR signed a bilateral treaty in 1995 that guarantees each side the right to call for swift and binding arbitration in the event of a dispute over refugee policy. All the UNHCR has to do is invoke it. But don't hold your breath. The scandal here is that neither UN Secretary General Kofi Annan nor UNHCR head Ruud Lubbers seems to care enough to even make an audible peep, let alone enforce their own conventions and treaties to help the famished, fleeing North Koreans.... [According to U.S. Senator Sam Brownback, who

---

[45] Jana Mason, USCR policy analyst, quoted in "USCR Condemns China's Forced Return of North Korean Refugees," USCR Press Release, January 22, 2003.

[46] "China: Protect Rights of North Korean Asylum-Seekers," Human Rights Watch Press Release, November 19, 2002, http://staging.hrw.org/press/2002/11/nkreport.htm.

[47] Willy Fautre of Human Rights Without Frontiers and Tarik M. Radwan of Jubilee Campaign USA, both human rights advocates, quoted in James Brooke, "China Facing Protests Over the Plight of North Korean Refugees," *New York Times*, November 30, 2002.

recently visited North Korea, there is] "not much interest in pressing the Chinese."

Not only is this UN behavior craven and cruel, it is dumb. Were the UN to insist on providing safe haven, or merely safe passage, for refugees flowing out of North Korea through China, the result could be not only the saving of thousands of lives, but quite possibly an exodus that could end the menace emanating from Pyongyang by bringing down the regime. China might not like the idea, but under genuine international pressure, Beijing might be persuaded to cooperate.[48]

Such criticism was strenuously rejected by UNHCR, whose spokesperson responded, "Picketing our offices does not solve the problem. We don't run China.... [Moreover], we have a long-standing request with the Chinese to get access to the border. Where we are hosted by a government, we have to operate with a government's consent."[49] As another UNHCR official put it, "the pressure is real. Misguided, but real. Fortunately, in a weird way, UNHCR is protected because it is even now widely viewed as a European refugee agency."[50]

DRAMATIC ESCAPES, SCINTILLATING REALITY TV   Whatever the impact of the print media campaign, the activists did not stop there. Rather, they sought to take advantage of 24/7 global media by staging a series of media-grabbing dramatic escapes and bids for asylum, spectacles which would ideally be captured on film to maximize their international impact. This prong of the campaign had two phases: (1) embassy crashings, in which would-be asylum seekers attempted to breech the security of an embassy compound and claim asylum within that country, and (2) boatlifts, in which would-be asylum seekers took to the sea with the expectation that they would be rescued by passing ships and delivered to a country where they could claim asylum. The first phase of embassy crashings heated up in spring 2002, but, although the first boatlift of North Koreans in five years landed in South Korea that same August, the boatlift project did not begin in earnest until the following January.[51]

According to Kim, the idea of storming embassies was hatched at a Kentucky Fried Chicken restaurant in downtown Seoul during a

[48] Claudia Rosett, "The U.N.'s Twisted Refugee Policies," *Wall Street Journal Europe*, January 2003.

[49] Kris Janowski, UNHCR spokesman, quoted in Brooke, "China Facing Protests."

[50] UNHCR official, interview, January 2003 (via telephone, from Cambridge, Mass., to Geneva, Switzerland).

[51] Jonathan Watts, "North Koreans Flee by Boat," *Guardian*, August 20, 2002.

brainstorming session with Vollertsen.[52] As Vollertsen described it: "We agreed that helping North Korean defectors to enter a foreign embassy in Beijing would be an effective way to bring the issue to international attention.... Our plan was to conduct as many operations as possible, to keep the issue in the news and ratchet up the international pressure on Beijing."[53]

In preparation for their scheme, Kim interviewed Koreans in China while Vollertsen scoped out vulnerable embassies. And over the following year, the network staged a number of successful, albeit small-scale, embassy crashings before the Chinese implemented sufficient new security measures (detailed later) to ensure that future attempts would fail. Thus, for a short time, the crashing strategy was a tactical triumph. With few exceptions, those who managed to breech the compounds were granted asylum abroad, and the activist network garnered a great deal of press coverage.

Why were they successful? The targeted embassies were carefully chosen and then reconnoitered to help improve the chances for success.[54] The events themselves were carefully stage-managed. As Shin put it in fall 2002, early on "we had someone on the spot. It was like teaching a baby how to walk. We took them [the would-be refugees] by the hand and led them in."[55] Which embassies were targeted was no coincidence, either. The March 2002 crashing of the Spanish embassy, for instance, was driven by the fact that at the time Spain held the rotating presidency of the European Union and a major EU summit was to be held in Barcelona just days after the incident.[56] News of the Spanish crashing was also leaked to CNN ahead of time, so that footage of the defectors rushing into the embassy could be captured on tape and then distributed across the globe.

In fact, most crashings were leaked to news organizations ahead of time. Sometimes this led to their failure—as in an attempted September 2002 escape at the Ecuadoran Embassy, of which the Chinese government had also been forewarned. But it also resulted in some powerful TV images; what became a highly publicized and embarrassing scuffle outside the Japanese Embassy in Shenyang in early May 2002 would probably not have attracted much attention but for the fact that the tipped-off South

[52] MacIntyre, "One Man Against Kim Jong Il." Another version of events suggests that the original planning and coordination occurred in connection with the Third International Conference on North Korean Human Rights and Refugees, held in Japan, February 9–10, 2002. Those assembled publicly criticized the human rights record of China and demanded that China not only grant North Koreans refugee status but also permit foreign NGOs and religious groups to help them resettle in third countries.

[53] Vollertsen, "Prison Nation."

[54] For more on a successful attempt in which would-be refugees managed to locate two small openings in the wall of an otherwise impenetrable compound, see ibid.

[55] Rosenthal, "More Koreans Give China the Slip."

[56] David Hsieh, "N. Korean Defections in China Staged by Activists," Straits Times, March 16, 2002.

Korean Yonhap News Agency captured the whole thing from a window across the street. The resulting footage showed a group of five North Koreans making a dash for the embassy gate. Two men got inside (but were later removed), but three others—two women and a small child— were dragged back across the street, kicking and screaming, by Chinese guards.[57] The film, shown repeatedly on Japanese television, was effective at mobilizing public opinion. This already embarrassing situation was then exacerbated by comments by the Japanese ambassador to Beijing that suggested the Foreign Ministry was more concerned about damage control than about the events that had transpired.[58]

Similarly, there was widespread outrage in Seoul when footage was shown of a June 2002 incident at the Korean compound in Beijing. Chinese public security officials forcibly entered the compound and dragged away a North Korean who was seeking asylum, despite protests, scuffles, and blows to South Korean diplomatic personnel and employees who tried to prevent the removal of the man, whose son remained inside the compound. The footage evoked a strong negative reaction from the South Korean public, mitigated only by its preoccupation with the ongoing World Cup events. Here, again, the timing and choice of embassies was not accidental. At the time, Vollertsen declared that "the World Cup is the best opportunity to get our message across [as] there will be hundreds of international journalists and television crews in the country."[59] And as Shin put it, when speaking about the would-be refugees who stormed the South Korean compound, "The Chinese will let them go while their team is in South Korea. How can they not let them go? It's a save-face standoff. In the end, the Chinese will close their eyes and say, O.K."[60] (And they did.) It is worth noting in passing that in this same period (during the World Cup) ABC *Nightline* ran a provocative segment about the underground and North Koreans fleeing to China.

IF AT FIRST YOU DON'T SUCCEED, ADOPT A NEW ANALOGY   After a time—and subsequent to the implementation of enhanced security

[57] John Gittings, "Scuffle Highlights the Plight of North Korean Refugees," *Guardian*, May 14, 2002. Following all the bad publicity, the two sides engaged in a round of mutual recriminations and rationalization. The Japanese accused the Chinese of violating the Vienna Convention on Diplomatic Relations—although on the film three Japanese consular officials are shown "walking calmly across the compound. One of them pick[ed] up the Chinese guards' caps, which had been knocked off in the struggle, and hand[ed] them back to their owners." Not exactly much of a protest. For their part, Chinese Information Office Minister Zhao Qizheng asserted their guards had "blocked the intruders in a very short time, even at the risk of sacrificing their own lives." In ibid.

[58] Glosserman and Snyder, "Borders and Boundaries."

[59] Quoted in Andrew Ward, "Activist Plans More Defections by N. Koreans," *Financial Times*, March 21, 2002.

[60] Quoted in Don Kirk, "World Cup Factor Could Help Refugees," *International Herald Tribune*, May 31, 2002.

measures by the Chinese—it became evident that embassy crashings needed to be replaced by something more effective, as well as something that could increase the number of escapees from a handful to a boatload. (In spite of its visible successes, only a few hundred North Koreans successfully "escaped" via embassy crashings.) The East German–Hungary model was thus abandoned in favor of another historical analogy. If the embassy crashings were reminiscent of the first phase of the Mariel boatlift in Havana and the beginning of the end of Communism in eastern Europe, the new strategy of helping North Koreans escape China by sea was "in deliberate imitation of the 'boat people' of Vietnam."[61] Supporters of the so-called boat people project planned to smuggle thousands of refugees through Chinese ports and into international waters, from where they would seek asylum in South Korea and Japan. As Vollertsen explains, "We made extensive plans for vessels to carry refugees across the Yellow Sea from China to South Korea."[62]

The project—concocted in summer 2002 by Vollertsen and Shin—got off to a disastrous start in January 2003 when Chinese authorities arrested dozens of asylum seekers as they prepared to board a pair of fishing boats.[63] The thwarted plan had been for two separate groups to sail from Yantai to Chuja, an island off the South Korean southern coast, and to Sasebo, a port city on the southernmost main island of Japan, Kyushu. The boat escape was to have been the activists' largest, and most aggressive, operation yet.[64] As Shin put it at the time, "we are prepared to die doing this. We will try again soon, maybe a month from now, or maybe a few days."[65] Vollertsen, for his part, declared, "This failure will spur us to be more effective next time."[66]

The network was not so naïve as to believe it would succeed at bringing down the North Korean regime simply by publishing a bunch of op-eds in national newspapers and creating some must-see TV. Nevertheless, its members believed that if they were able to exert sufficient pressure on the Chinese to get them to acquiesce to the establishment of border camps (i.e., if their creation catalyzed a massive outflow), then things might get interesting. Still, the network could not do this alone. It required assistance from a powerful backer such as the United States. Hence, the fact that the vast majority of op-eds calling for action were published in U.S. papers was probably not a coincidence, nor was the fact

---

[61] Richard Lloyd Parry, "North Korean Refugees to Be 'Boat People,'" *Times*, January 28, 2003.
[62] Vollertsen, "Prison Nation."
[63] Brooke, "Bush Urged to Press China."
[64] Barbara Demick, "58 N. Korean Defectors Held," *Los Angeles Times*, January 20, 2003.
[65] Quoted in ibid.
[66] Quoted in Philippe Pons, "Forcibly Returned Refugees Face Punishment in N. Korea," *Guardian*, January 30, 2003.

that Vollertsen and others repeatedly testified before the U.S. Congress during their ill-fated attempt at migration-driven coercion.

Increasingly Less Passive Opportunists: A U.S.-Based Coalition

Protected from the direct effects of a massive exodus, a disparate coalition within the United States—comprising Bush administration officials, policy experts, legislators from both sides of the aisle, and members of the Christian Coalition—supported the activist strategy.[67] This group of opportunists tried hard, albeit unsuccessfully, to persuade China not to repatriate North Korean migrants, believing, like the network they supported, that the establishment of camps in northern China could "set off a chain reaction" similar to what had happened in eastern Europe.[68] As one senior administration official put it, "When Hungary and Czechoslovakia opened their borders to East Germans, it helped speed the collapse of the Berlin Wall. Supporting refugees from North Korea could stress their system, too."[69] As Victor Cha, Korea scholar, put it, "If this regime were actually to collapse, it won't be through an elite coup. Real regime change will come from the bottom, from people who can't oppose the regime but who can vote with their feet."[70]

Support for this migration-driven, bottom-up destabilization strategy grew steadily in certain circles after North Korea announced the resumption of its nuclear program in October 2002—particularly since some supporters believed this was the only way short of an invasion to affect regime change in North Korea.[71] Then U.S. Secretary of Defense Donald Rums-

[67] See, for instance, Marian Wilkinson, "US Prepares to Open Door to Flood of North Korean Refugees," *Sydney Morning Herald,* July 30, 2003.

[68] James Dao, "US Is Urged to Promote Flow of Refugees from North Korea," *New York Times,* December 11, 2002.

[69] To further shield itself against the consequences of a possible outflow from North Korea, after the September 11 terrorist attacks, in June 2002 the United States announced that anyone thinking of targeting U.S. compounds should note that "no diplomatic compound will tolerate unidentified persons breaking through security for any reason.... [Moreover], US diplomatic personnel are not authorized to grant asylum to asylum seekers entering a US compound." Testimony given by U.S. Assistant Secretary of State Arthur Dewey, to a Senate Judiciary Subcommittee, June 21, 2002, http://usinfo.state.gov/regional/ea/easec/dewey.htm.

[70] Quoted in Dao, "US Is Urged to Promote Flow."

[71] This represented a noteworthy switch from the stance taken by the previous administration, which in early 2000 had provided tacit support for the incumbent regime by remaining silent in the wake of the illegal repatriation by Russia of seven North Koreans whom UNHCR had deemed legitimate refugees deserving of asylum. "Total silence was how one UN official described the Western response to the forced repatriation. This was a direct and clear violation of international law. In most parts of the world, the Americans would be outraged. Aid officials said the silence fits a pattern that started last year when North Korea indicated it was suspending its development of weapons of mass destruction. Foreign governments grateful for the easing of tension over North Korea's weapons programs have been

feld was a particularly avid proponent, and in April 2003 his advisors reportedly circulated a classified memo proposing that the United States
team up with the PRC to press for the ouster of the North Korean leadership.[72] Then Chairman of the U.S. Senate Foreign Relations Committee
Richard Lugar concurred, arguing publicly that resettling North Korean
refugees in the United States and urging other countries to do the same
could "spark a greater flow of North Koreans from their gulag-like country" and perhaps "hasten the fall of the Pyongyang regime."[73]

Others, both within the administration and elsewhere in Washington,
were less enthusiastic and found even discussion of this strategy counterproductive at best.[74] Skeptics argued that the North Koreans would simply crack down harder on border crossers. "This is not the East German
regime. It's much more brutal," according to one dubious Bush administration official.[75] Another opined, "North Korea has been isolated for years.
Its main domestic policy is isolationism, or self-reliance. If hundreds of
thousands die of starvation, it will not bring down Kim Jong Il."[76]

Moreover, critics argued, it was simply "ludicrous" to think that the
PRC—acting as intermediary between the Democratic People's Republic
of Korea (DPRK; North Korea) and the United States—"would join in
any American-led effort to bring about the fall of the DPRK government.
The last thing the Chinese wanted was a collapse of North Korea that
would create a flood of refugees into China and put Western allies on
the Chinese border."[77] "The Chinese might turn up the heat on the North
Koreans—as we witnessed with the temporary shut down of petroleum
supplies—but they [would not] do anything that might endanger the
North Korean regime; they are too worried about the domestic political
consequences."[78]

---

less energetic about opposing Pyongyang on refugees or pressuring North Korea's leaders
to distribute foreign food aid equitably to its famished population, aid officials say." John
Pomfret, "N. Korean Refugees Insecure in China," *Washington Post*, February 19, 2000.

[72] David E. Sanger, "Administration Divided over North Korea," *New York Times*, April 21,
2003.

[73] Bruce Klingner, "The Tortuous North Korean Refugee Triangle," *Asia Times On-line*, September 22, 2004, www.atimes.com/atimes/Korea/FI22Dg01.html.

[74] Distribution of the Rumsfeld memo apparently created anger within the State Department because its argument was so clearly at odds with the State Department approach
of trying to convince Kim, in the words of one senior administration official, "that we're not
trying to take him out." Ibid. See also Joo Yong-joon, "Powell Downplays Regime Change
Talks," *Chosun Ilbo*, April 24, 2003.

[75] Quoted in Dao, "US Is Urged to Promote Flow."

[76] Quoted in James Kynge, "New Korean War Is Beijing Nightmare as Tensions Rise," *Financial Times*, December 30, 2002.

[77] Senior Bush administration official, quoted in Sanger, "Administration Divided over
North Korea."

[78] Interview with John Park, April 2003 (Cambridge, Mass.).

This general assessment was echoed in the Laney and Shaplen *Foreign Affairs* article:

> North Koreans are a fiercely proud people and have endured hardships over the last decade that would have led most other countries to implode. It would therefore be a mistake to underestimate their loyalty to the state or to Kim Jong Il. When insulted, provoked, or threatened, North Koreans will not hesitate to engage in their equivalent of a holy war. Their ideology is not only political, it is [also] quasi-religious.[79]

Whether the United States or other states provided more assistance than simple financial support for the activists or their network remains a matter of speculation.[80] Nevertheless, whereas previous attempts by Congress to encourage refugees from North Korea had been blocked by successive U.S. governments concerned about Chinese and South Korean opposition, in late 2003 a sea change took place.[81] President George W. Bush explicitly and publicly endorsed a policy of assisting those fleeing North Korea. Having already proclaimed to the *Washington Post* that he "loathed Kim Jong Il," he declared that he disagreed with those who claimed, "We don't need to move too fast because of the financial costs. Either you believe in freedom and worry about the human condition, or you don't."[82]

Primary and Secondary Target Responses

Despite the explicit policy shift of the Bush administration, neither China nor South Korea was prepared to let North Korea collapse, nor was either willing to support a sustained indefinite policy of squeezing the North. Both states remained greatly concerned about the unquestionably costly—and potentially destabilizing—consequences of a massive influx,

---

[79] Laney and Shaplen, "How to Deal with North Korea."

[80] See, for instance, Hsieh, "N. Korean Defections" and the STRATFOR.com North Korea coverage, which suggested that the United States might support such a strategy. Others, such as Roberta Cohen of the Brookings Institution, argued that Washington would rather see the Pyongyang regime improve than collapse because its sudden disintegration could overwhelm the South and create political and economic turmoil. Roberta Cohen, "Aid Meant for the Hungry," *New York Times*, May 16, 2002.

[81] Marian Wilkinson, "US May Welcome Korean Refugees," *Age*, July 30, 2003.

[82] Dao, "US Is Urged to Promote Flow." For a similar argument from the other side of the aisle, which explicitly suggests both that (1) the Democrats' failure to demand improvements in North Korean human rights conditions as a minimum prerequisite to any substantial détente between the two countries makes them subject to accusations of hypocrisy and (2) this failure may push Korean Americans into the arms of the Republican Party (the clear party of the pro-camp on this issues), see Bruce B. Lee and Michael O'Hanlon, "Wrong on North Korea," *Baltimore Sun*, July 13, 2005.

and both gleaned less inspirational lessons from the fall of the Berlin Wall than did the international *agents provocateurs* and the opportunists in Washington.

China

In particular, China worried about the potential *political* consequences of an eastern European redux, namely the potentially destabilizing effect of waves of refugees in Chinese northeastern provinces, where a sizable Korean minority already lived.[83] Chinese think-tank experts "privy to high-level leadership deliberations" claimed the leadership was extremely wary of the U.S. desire to promote the collapse of Kim Jong Il's regime.[84] One unidentified Chinese source was quoted as saying, "This risks exploding out of control. Everyone knows about the Hungary example. We don't want that to happen here."[85] Another—an advisor to both the Chinese and North Korean governments—asserted, "If we gave them refugee status, millions would pour over our doorstep. That would cause a humanitarian crisis here and a collapse of the North. We can't afford either."[86] And as Li Bin, the Chinese ambassador to Seoul, put it, "Beijing is concerned that a flood of asylum bids by the thousands of North Korean defectors hidden in China could create instability in the region and strain its relations with the two Koreas and the international community. The issue could bring about difficulties for the improving relationship between South Korea and China."[87]

Moreover, and more fundamentally, the Chinese believed they had "no compelling reason to push for Korea's immediate political reintegration, even by peaceful means," insofar as they viewed North Korea as "a useful buffer zone that contributes to their national security."[88] A senior Chinese official added further historical perspective, declaring, "Humanitarian problems, no matter how urgent, must not be politicized. The Korean diaspora that resulted as our turbulent modern history took its course teaches this painful lesson."[89]

[83] See "Paris Report on US Hopes That China Will Influence North Korea," FBIS, January 10, 2003.

[84] Bonny S. Glaser, "Beijing Ponders How Hard to Press North Korea," *PacNet Newsletter* 54 (2002), www.csis.org/pacfor/pac0254.htm.

[85] Quoted in John Pomfret, "N. Korea Refugees Leave China; Beijing's About-Face Ends Embarrassing Month-Long Standoff," *Washington Post*, June 24, 2002.

[86] Quoted in John Pomfret, "China Cracks Down on N. Korean Refugees," *Washington Post*, January 22, 2003.

[87] Quoted in Ward, "Activist Plans More Defections by N. Koreans."

[88] Chae-Jin Lee, *China and Korea: Dynamic Relations* (Stanford: Hoover Institution, 1996), 171–72.

[89] Quoted in "Inopportune Refugee Policy," *Weekend Australian*, July 26, 2003.

In the end, China faced a diplomatic dilemma—trying to remain cozy with a stable North Korea while improving ties with Western countries critical of its human rights practices. As one Western diplomat put it, "Beijing [was] keen to maintain its relationship with and influence in Pyongyang and the refugee issue was becoming a real problem."[90] But, as a non-democracy, I would argue, China was relatively less susceptible— although not immune—to the imposition of hypocrisy costs. It was also better able to simply absorb these costs or deflect them without paying noteworthy domestic political penalties. Evidence bears out this proposition. The intent of the activists was the improvement of the plight of the North Koreans. But the international spotlight did not have the desired effect; in fact, it backfired. As Peter Hayes, executive director of the Nautilus Institute, a Berkeley-based nonprofit that focuses on Asian security issues, put it at the time, groups involved in smuggling out refugees "are taking what appears to be a shortcut but in fact is not a shortcut but a dead end."[91]

Although a signatory to the 1951 Refugee Convention, China consistently argued that the North Koreans were not refugees but economic migrants who had crossed the border primarily for financial reasons and often stayed for only a short time before returning to North Korea with goods and money for their families.[92] Thus, the Chinese maintained, they were perfectly within their rights to repatriate those North Koreans who crossed into China.

At the same time, however, before the network launched its attempt at coercion, the Chinese were inclined to "let sleeping dogs lie" and take no action against the migrants or those helping them. With the exception of a brief period during summer 2001, in the midst of the nationwide Strike Hard campaign "against corruption and social ills,"[93] the tacit modus operandi that had been in place since the late 1990s was that the PRC would tolerate quiet activities by South Korean NGOs to assist North Koreans in China, and even to facilitate their asylum in South Korea via third countries, but that public attention to these activities would not be tolerated.[94]

[90] Oliver August, "Dreams of Freedom End in Nightmare of Deportation," *Times*, February 7, 2003.

[91] Quoted in Matthew Yi, "Californians Reach Out to Help Korean Refugees," *San Francisco Chronicle*, February 15, 2003.

[92] "China Snubs UN Plea over North Korean 'Refugees,'" FBIS, January 23, 2003. In fact, in August 2002 aid workers in the border region who interviewed hundreds of North Koreans estimated that only 5 percent of new arrivals technically qualified for refugee status under the 1951 Convention. Elisabeth Rosenthal, "North Koreans Widening Escape Route to China," *New York Times*, August 5, 2002.

[93] Snyder, "Transit, Traffic Control and Telecoms."

[94] Scott Snyder, "Clash, Crash, and Cash: Core Realities in the Sino-Korean Relationship," *Comparative Connections* 4 (2002), www.csis.org/pacfor/cc/0202Q.html.

Thus, although the Chinese government was unprepared to officially welcome large numbers of North Koreans, its pre-coercion behavior suggests that its leaders were nevertheless somewhat sympathetic to the migrants' plight and prepared allow some number of defectors to settle in, or at least to pass through, their country.

But after the activist network mounted its very public campaign, the blind eye that had previously been turned to those who managed to cross the border focused, and the high-profile escapes and accompanying publicity compelled China to shut down the de facto underground railroad.[95] "It [became] too sensitive," according to one South Korean who was active in the Yanbian Korean Christian community. "[In 2001], you could meet with [refugees] officially even. Now, that's impossible."[96] Wu Dawei, Chinese ambassador to Korea, concurred: "At a stage where the inter-Korean relations are improving, it is better not to deal with such sensitive matters if possible."[97]

In short, the activist gambit garnered media attention and facilitated the escape of several dozen North Koreans, but "the hubris accompanying their dramatic and unexpected success" set into motion a harsh and effective—and totally predictable—response from Beijing.[98] As one China scholar bluntly and acidly noted:

> In shortsighted pursuit of individual publicity and on a bet that the PRC government had no choice but to accept international humiliation, these NGO activists have needlessly put at risk hundreds of North Korean refugees who might have otherwise quietly followed an admittedly arduous but relatively effective route to South Korea. One need only examine the Falun Gong case to recognize that public demonstrations in Beijing and premised on surprising or embarrassing China's public security department and senior leadership are counterproductive and do not persuade the Chinese leadership to respond constructively to these issues.[99]

[95] Ibid.

[96] Gady A. Epstein, "Stemming Flow of N. Korea Refugees," *Baltimore Sun*, February 24, 2003.

[97] "Chinese Ambassador Reveals Position on NK Refugees," *Chosun Ilbo*, March 27, 2001.

[98] That this reaction was hardly unanticipated is clear from a February 2002 letter to the editor of *CanKor* (a weekly e-clipping service devoted to news and analyses of the DPRK). Tom McCarthy, the writer, notes that it might be useful for those recommending "putting pressure on China" to open refugee camps to promote change in North Korea to "reflect for at least a moment on the consequence of their actions. [Namely,] China will simply close its borders with North Korea, thereby solving everybody's 'refugee' problems. It's not hard to see who the losers will be." Tom McCarthy, "China and North Korean Refugees," letter to the editor of *CanKor*, February 13, 2002, www.vuw.ac.nz/~caplabtb/dprk/china_refugee.html.

[99] Snyder, "Clash, Crash, and Cash."

The expectation of the activists was that this means of escape would force the Chinese to cooperate and to build refugee camps along the border.[100] But, in fact, the Chinese appear to have felt more vulnerable to the consequences of a North Korean downfall than the hypocrisy costs imposed by the network and its supporters.[101] Thus, with the assistance of the North Koreans themselves, the Chinese government began to crack down on the migrants and on those who helped them, and to cleanse its border provinces of escapees. Chinese and North Korean police began actively rounding up and returning North Koreans with the help of Kim Jong Il's son, Kim Jong Nam.[102] In addition, undercover North Korean agents reportedly posed as would-be refugees to infiltrate the NGO network.[103]

According to some estimates, Beijing returned 80,000 of the 100,000–300,000 who had fled to escape the famines of the 1990s.[104] The Chinese also tightened border security (via the installation of infrared cameras and increased patrols), stepped up arrests and prosecutions, and denied entry visas to activists known to have attempted to publicize the North Koreans' plight.[105] Not surprisingly, the number of successful escapes nosedived.[106] The Chinese also increased security around diplomatic compounds in Beijing and Shenyang by sending notices requesting cooperation and by constructing or adding barbed-wire-fenced areas to keep North Koreans from going over the walls.[107]

Nevertheless, concerns over potential hypocrisy costs were not wholly absent. The consistently proactive, yet defensive, Chinese rhetoric on the issue of repatriation demonstrated a clear sensitivity to charges that they were flouting their international obligations. The Chinese Foreign Ministry steadfastly maintained, "these people entered China's territory illegally because of economic reasons and they are not refugees and they cannot be considered as refugees. [Moreover, we] believe the UN refugee commission also has a clear awareness of China's position. And in

[100] Kirk, "World Cup Factor Could Help Refugees."

[101] "US Civil Leader Urges China to Let UN Deal with NK Refugees," *Korea Times*, June 27, 2003.

[102] Brooke, "China Called Likely to Oust 78 North Koreans."

[103] In unconfirmed reports, advocates claimed spies came to churches and to the campus of a private university in the city of Yanji supported by Korean and U.S. Christian funds. Because Chinese and North Korean security forces did thwart a number of the attempted operations, it appears that some infiltration did occur. See Epstein, "Stemming Flow of N. Korea Refugees."

[104] Oliver August, "Dreams of Freedom End in Nightmare of Deportation," *Times*, February 7, 2003; "Influx of N. Korean Defectors Could Cause Problems," *Daily Yomiuri*, February 21, 2003.

[105] See, for instance, "South Korean Goes on Trial in China," Associated Press, May 15, 2003.

[106] MacIntyre, "Running out of the Darkness."

[107] Epstein, "Stemming Flow of N. Korea Refugees."

handling these cases, we adhere to the international laws, domestic laws and regulations on the basis of the humanitarian spirit."[108]

Moreover, in a separate statement, the Foreign Ministry spokesperson took direct aim at the activists and sought to justify Chinese actions on national security grounds, declaring,

> I want to point out that recently some international organizations or citizens used the North Korean illegal immigrants to steadily create trouble. These actions violate China's laws and harm social stability....So as to those who violate China's laws, plan and organize people to illegally enter China, the Chinese government will take measures to crack down on them based on Chinese law and protect Chinese social stability.[109]

In addition, some Chinese officials—and most particularly those in the Ministry of Foreign Affairs (MFA)—remained concerned about the "image projected by [their] strong-arm tactics," even if they felt they could rationalize them.[110] This same group also reportedly believed that, if managed correctly, the crisis could provide Beijing with an opportunity "to boost its image as a responsible major power willing to actively contribute to the maintenance of peace and stability in the Asia-Pacific region."[111] As one senior, Beijing-based PRC research fellow put it in October 2003, "China's in an interesting and unfamiliar situation whereby people [are] seek[ing] refugee status in China—usually it's the other way around."[112] Thus, in what was widely interpreted as an MFA victory (over the ministries of Public Security and State Security) in a "bureaucratic brawl" over the potentially embarrassing embassy crashings, the Chinese continued to facilitate the transfer of refugees to safe third countries.[113] Observers believe the MFA won the tussle because of the highly publicized and humiliating miscalculations regarding the pursuit of North Koreans (by Chi-

---

[108] Ibid. The Chinese reiterated this position in June 2003 in response to a claim by UNHCR Ruud Lubbers that China had relaxed its position on repatriation. Lui Jin Chao, Chinese Foreign Ministry spokesman, stated that China would handle the "illegal migrants" according "to international law and Chinese law." Jim Randle, "Chinese Deny Policy Change on North Korea," *Voice of AmericaNews.com*, June 17, 2003, www.globalsecurity.org/wmd/library/news/china/2003/china-030617-voa01.htm.

[109] "PRC FM Spokesman Says China Confirms DPRK Refugees Arrested, Warns Aid Groups," FBIS, January 21, 2003.

[110] David Hsieh, "Coming Next: New Human Wave; Experts Say the Number of North Korean Refugees Using China to Get to the South May Rise to More than 1,000 This Year," *Straits Times*, June 26, 2002.

[111] Bonny S. Glaser, "Beijing Ponders How Hard to Press North Korea," *PacNet Newsletter* 54 (2002), www.csis.org/pacfor/pac0254.htm.

[112] Comments shared with me by John Park from his communications with "a senior PRC research fellow," in October 2003 (in Cambridge, Mass.).

[113] Ibid.

nese officials from the Public Security Bureau) into the Japanese and South Korean diplomatic compounds in spring 2002.[114] In any case, this domestic turn of events suggests that hypocrisy played a role, albeit a limited one, even in China.

Even so, Chinese concerns about hypocrisy costs and/or their desire for an international prestige boost were clearly insufficient to catalyze the kind of policy shift that the network and its supporters in Washington sought. Still, some within the Washington Beltway believed it would be possible to get the Chinese on board by convincing them that South Korea and the United States would take in more escapees. (Of course, the South Koreans were not too fond of this idea.) "China doesn't want to have to feed tens of thousands of refugees. But if they thought these people would only stay a few weeks, it might change their mind," according to one senior Bush administration official.[115] To this end, in November 2002 U.S. Senator Sam Brownback (R-Kans.) and Senator Ted Kennedy (D-Mass.) proposed a bill that would earmark up to $80 million to "feed, clothe, and move to safety" those North Koreans seeking to flee.[116]

In the end, however, those who thought the Chinese could be persuaded to change their position, via either moral or financial suasion, were mistaken. As John Park put it, "Of course, the Chinese are concerned about their international image. But they are *really* concerned about the future of their own power."[117] Overall, the Chinese leadership perceived the risks associated with a potential North Korean collapse as being far more threatening than any costs that the activist network, alone or in conjunction with the United States, could inflict. Nor did they find the side-payments on offer attractive enough to warrant a policy reevaluation.[118]

---

[114] Ibid.

[115] Quoted in Dao, "US Is Urged to Promote Flow."

[116] Brooke, "China Facing Protests."

[117] Interview, April 2003, Boston, Mass.

[118] The claim that side-payments and promises to resettle North Koreans outside the region would soften Chinese attitudes toward an institutionalized underground railroad was raised again in a 2007 op-ed, in which the authors asserted, "The Chinese government's cost-benefit calculus regarding these refugees would change drastically if Washington weighed in as their advocate. If the United States (along with other governments) provided informal assurances that China is merely a way station for North Koreans—assuaging any official fears about a permanent foreign refugee population—it may well be possible to convince Beijing to cooperate in the relocation mission (or at least to look the other way as it takes place). Should it do so, many of the problems that Beijing seems to fear will vanish of themselves: if those refugees can be quickly processed by the United Nations refugee commission or similar offices, for example, Beijing need no longer worry about the risks imposed by a large, illegal population along its border with North Korea." Nicholas Eberstadt and Christopher Griffin, "Saving North Korean Refugees," *New York Times*, February 19, 2007. China's reaction to similar claims from 2002–2005, however, suggests that the Chinese would be far less amenable to such a scheme than the authors suggest.

South Korea

Whereas China was most concerned about the *political* consequences of a massive outflow, South Korea had long been acutely worried about the *economic* costs of a sudden collapse of the North, having witnessed the consequences of German reunification,[119] as well as having dealt with the after effects of the 1997 Asian financial crisis.[120] Analysts from the Korea Development Institute (KDI), the leading South Korean quasi-governmental economic think tank, argued that the German experience demonstrated that national unification involves enormous costs and that "convinced a large number of South Koreans that sudden economic integration in Korea...will result in disaster."[121] These concerns were not necessarily unwarranted. In 1997, analysts calculated that if South Korea were to absorb the North, the cost of unification—defined as the capital investment needed in North Korea to choke off the incentive for mass migration—would be on the order of US$1 trillion.[122] Indeed, two South Korean unification studies specialists, Kim Kyu-wan and Park Seong-jo, captured this fear when they named their book on the relevance of the German experience for Korea: *North and South: Dead if United*. It is noteworthy that this potentially inflammatory title "did not cause any protest among its numerous reviewers: its authors said what is accepted as increasingly obvious."[123] The articulation of such fears was (and remains) commonplace in South Korean television and print media.

The conflicting prerogatives at play in the minds of South Koreans—political allegiances, economic concerns, and security-related dangers associated with both weapons of mass destruction and general peninsula

---

[119] Raymond Whitaker, "The Dark Horses of 1994; North Korea: Kim's Weak Finger on a Big Trigger," *Independent*, January 1, 1994. During the 1994 crisis, a Western diplomat reported fears of political collapse as well: "There's a worry that they [the South Koreans] may be swamped. The first fear is that subversives could slip in pretending to be defectors, and they're also concerned about upsetting the social balance." Richard Lloyd Parry, "N. Koreans Flee 'in Hundreds,'" *Independent*, March 16, 1996.

[120] See "A Fig Leaf," *Asia Times*, June 15, 2001.

[121] Ha-Cheong Yeon, "Economic Consequences of German Unification and Its Policy Implications for Korea," KDI Working Paper no. 9303, Korean Development Institute, 1993, 23; Hong-Tack Chun, "A Gradual Approach toward North and South Korean Economic Integration," KDI Working Paper no. 9311, Korean Development Institute, 1993, 4, quoted in Nicholas Eberstadt, "Hastening Korean Reunification," *Foreign Affairs* 76 (1997): 77.

[122] Marcus Noland, Sherman Robinson, and Monica Scatasta, "Modeling North Korean Economic Reform," *Journal of Asian Economics* 8 (1997): 15–38. For a different perspective on the costs of reunification, see Eberstadt, "Hastening Korean Reunification." Nevertheless, even under optimistic scenarios, North Koreans would have powerful incentives to head South. As Noland points out, the potential for such migration is enormous—assuming a person carrying some belongings could travel 20 miles a day, 40 percent of the population of North Korea lives within a five-day walk of the DMZ.

[123] Andrei Lankov, "Bitter Taste of Paradise: North Korean Refugees in South Korea," *Journal of East Asian Studies* 6 (2006), 113.

(in)stability—engendered a kind of head-in-the-sand reaction vis-à-vis a potential mass influx. Indeed, the issue was viewed as so sensitive that it was not even discussed during high-level North-South talks in August 2002.[124] At heart, Seoul feared that accepting North Koreans unconditionally would undermine its ongoing sunshine policy of engagement.[125] "The sunshine policy and the refugee issue are at odds, [and] the biggest victims of [it] are the refugees," as one South Korean activist put it.[126] Similarly, Moon Chung-in, a professor of political studies at Yonsei University in Seoul, argued that the government feared sending "a mixed signal" by supporting the refugees and the activists assisting them:

> What they are doing is good from a humanitarian perspective. But from a diplomatic point of view it could create problems. Neither the South Korean government nor society is ready to accommodate the refugees. We have to make a distinction between idealism and realism. Right now, we have about 1,300 defectors and refugees living in South Korea, but we are failing to give good treatment to them. If we can't handle 1,300, how can we handle so many more?[127]

Yet the situation was not quite that straightforward, and just closing the door was not really an option. Specifically, the South Korean position was complicated by its codified constitutional commitments. Under Articles 2 and 3 of the Constitution of the Republic of Korea, as reaffirmed by its Supreme Court in 1996, *anyone* from the Korean peninsula is considered a South Korean citizen, and every North Korean refugee has the right to resettle in South Korea.[128] Thus, when Ban Ki-Moon, then South Korean foreign minister and now UN secretary-general, made the impolitic statement that South Korean would not allow any more North Koreans to defect to the South, he was forced to backtrack, claiming instead that Seoul could not assume "unlimited responsibility" for all North Korean refugee seekers.[129]

Nevertheless, by the mid-2000s, Seoul had reportedly accepted only approximately 6,500 North Korean refugees since the end of the Korean War more than half a century before.[130] Seoul has been historically reticent

---

[124] Robert Marquand, "A Refugee's Perilous Odyssey from North Korea," *Christian Science Monitor*, August 16, 2002.

[125] Han Park, in ibid.

[126] Julie Chao, "Neighbors Balk at North Korean Refugees," *Atlanta Journal-Constitution*, December 29, 2002.

[127] Ibid.

[128] Pomfret, "N. Korea Refugees Leave China."

[129] Klingner, "The Tortuous North Korean Refugee Triangle."

[130] Valerie Reitman, "Leading His Flock of Refugees to Asylum," *Los Angeles Times*, October 27, 2002; Lankov, "Bitter Taste of Paradise," 107.

to implement policies that would help large numbers of North Korean migrants reach freedom in the South, despite public entreaties about pan-Korean brotherhood and the clause in the constitution that makes all Koreans citizens of South Korea.[131] Although legally required to accept all North Korean defectors, in practice the government has traditionally turned away all but those with valuable intelligence information.[132] As Nicholas Eberstadt has noted, "the South Koreans have not been famously sympathetic."[133] For his part, Vollertsen was forced to concede,

> the South Korean government has largely turned a blind eye to the plight of their "brothers" to the north, and in many cases has actually hindered their escape....Read this again, for I wish to stress the shame of it: South Korean authorities worked actively to foil our attempts to bring North Korean refugees to freedom. But under South Korean law, North Korean refugees cannot be turned away. It's time for Seoul to live up to this promise.[134]

As Vollertsen's comments make plain, South Korea was by many measures a theoretically attractive target for the imposition of hypocrisy costs and coercive engineered migration, more generally. During the period in question (as well as since), however, South Korea was (and remains) largely shielded from normative entrapment by the unwillingness of China to cave to the activists' demands or to recognize the fleeing North Koreans as refugees. As a result, the outflow North to South remained small, and South Korea had relatively few North Koreans with which to deal. For his part, Vollertsen claims that South Korea even engaged in active interdiction. As he put it: "Our plans to cross the Yellow Sea were foiled in part by South Korean authorities who used surveillance, interception and minders to disrupt our plans."[135] Whatever the case, there was still a fiftyfold increase in the number of North Koreans defecting to South Korea between 1995 and 2004—from 41 to 1,894.[136]

[131] Klingner, "The Tortuous North Korean Refugee Triangle."

[132] Michael Baker, "N. Korean Refugees Gain a Crusader, but So Far No Help," *Christian Science Monitor*, May 16, 2001. According to Lankov, until the early 1990s, the overall number of defectors was nominal—five to ten per year. Most were North Korean elites because only members of privileged groups had exit options. Among the early defectors were pilots who flew their fighter jets to the South, diplomats who defected while stationed overseas, soldiers of elite units who knew how the DMZ was protected and could outsmart the guards, and fishermen who managed to deceive their supervisors and sail their boats south. Lankov, "Bitter Taste of Paradise," 109.

[133] Quoted in Dao, "US Is Urged to Promote Flow."

[134] Vollertsen, "Prison Nation."

[135] Ibid.

[136] Lankov, "Bitter Taste of Paradise," 111. Still, to put these figures into perspective, the number of East Germans who defected to the West in 1962–1988 was 562,261—approximately 21,000 per year.

At the same time, from the mid-1990s, defectors began to come from less privileged groups, such that the defector community began to resemble much more closely the North Korean society as a whole. If anything, as Andrei Lankov, a Korean area specialist, argues, geographically or socially disadvantaged groups became overrepresented among North Korean refugees. And, in 2002 alone, "defectors committed 89 crimes, or 28.4 crimes per 1,000 defectors. Since the average crime level in Korea was 16.7 per 1,000, this indicates that the crime rate among the defectors was 1.7 times higher than the South Korean average."[137] With this in mind, it is perhaps not surprising that public opinion data suggest that, if attempts by the activists to mobilize South Koreans had any effect at all, it mobilized them in a direction that ran counter to what the network wanted (see table 5.1). In other words, as the number and socioeconomic complexity of the would-be refugees rose—and the lessons of the German experience became ever more apparent—South Korean attitudes toward fleeing North Koreans actually hardened rather than softened.

For instance, one possible interpretation of the data is that, between 1998 and 2004, the number of people who thought South Korea should admit those fleeing from the north shifted from as much as 72 percent *in favor* to 62 percent *opposed*. At the same time, during the very period when the network was trying to stimulate the opposite effect, South Korean attitudes toward the North Korean leadership softened rather than hardened, while their attitudes toward the United States—and particularly the Bush administration—hardened rather than softened. This may well have been a consequence of the efforts of the sitting South Korean government. After all, Roh Tae Woo's 2002 electoral triumph was achieved largely on a platform of anti-Americanism and continued support for the sunshine policy.

Whatever the cause, the obvious consequence was that migration-driven coercion by the activist network, designed to replicate the East German (or the Indochinese) experience on the Korean peninsula, was not destined to succeed. As Roe himself said, during a visit to Germany in April 2005, Germany should be seen as a negative example to be avoided by Korea. As a *Korea Times* piece on North Korean migrants reiterates, South Korean public and elite behavior as well as public opinion data all point in the same direction with respect to the attempted coercion—failure.[138]

[137] Ibid., 111, 123.
[138] Untitled document, *Korea Times*, April 14, 2005.

TABLE 5.1
Shifts in South Korean Public Opinion vis-à-vis the North Koreans, December 1998–December 2004

Question	Date and Response	Date and Response	Date and Response	Date and Response
Should North Korean defectors be admitted to South Korea?	December 1998: 43% unconditionally; 29% selectively; 22% under no condition *Source:* [3]			
Should North Koreans who escape be allowed to come to South Korea?		2000: 41.9% no *Source:* [4]		
Should civic groups arrange North Korean defections to the South?				
Do you approve of the South Korean government's North Korea policies?			February 2004: 4.6% approve; 57.2% disapprove *Source:* [5]	December 2004: 50% approve; 42.6% disapprove *Source:* [5]
Do you think North Korea is changing (for the better)/reforming?			February 2004: 45.8% yes *Source:* [5]	December 2004: 60.4% yes *Source:* [5]
Who/which represents a greater threat to South Korea's security?		September 2003: 42% Kim Jong-Il; 38% George W. Bush *Source:* [2]	January 5, 2004: 39% United States; 33% North Korea *Source:* [1]	December 22–23, 2004: 62% no; 32% yes *Source:* [5]
What is your biggest interest in the North-South inter-cooperation projects?				December 22–23, 2004: 40% linkage of roads and railways; 31.5% construction of a permanent meeting place for separated family members *Source:* [5]

Sources: 1: *Chosun Ilbo;* 2: Gallup Poll; 3: *Joong Ang Ilbo* and Citizens Coalition for National Reconciliation; 4: Survey conducted by Yun In Jim, Korea University; 5: Unnamed "research firm" in Seoul, announced by South Korean Unification Ministry.

That said, South Korea was also protected by Chinese intransigence. In a bilateral case of coercion, as Lankov's following observation suggests, the outcome might well have been different:

> The South Korean government to a large extent remains a prisoner of earlier nationalist rhetoric and political ambitions of bygone regimes. It has to maintain the fiction of "one Korea," since any open challenge to this assumption is bound to produce an outcry from all quarters, including even the North Korean government and its Seoul sympathizers. At the same time, the actual interests of the South Koreans, the sole constituency of the democratically elected Seoul administration, seem to be in collision with the unification rhetoric. The public and elite opinion in Korea perceives unification as a potential disaster that should be prevented or at least postponed to some uncertain future when some painless solution might become miraculously available.[139]

Unfortunately for South Korea, such a painless solution appears chimerical at best, at least for the foreseeable future. Meanwhile, as of this writing, some actors continue to actively lobby in favor of actions that would place South Koreans in just the bind they are so eager to eschew. In defending their plan to re-create the Chinese underground railroad that was shut down after the activists' failed attempt at coercion, Nicholas Eberstadt and Christopher Griffin argue, "Some will worry loudly about international resettlement for tens (never mind hundreds) of thousands of North Korean refugees, but the logistical issues are basically solved in advance: as a matter of national law, South Korea is obliged to welcome them all."[140]

Case Evaluation

This case bears out, in the main, the key propositions forwarded in chapter 1. North Korea, the reluctant generator, was a weak semi-legitimate actor with limited recourse to alternative avenues of influence. Although its government was reluctant to precipitate an actual outflow, the potential consequences of such an outflow provided North Korea with significant leverage, at least with its neighbors, if not with the United States. Likewise, the *agents provocateurs* were also relatively weak actors who perceived themselves as engaging in a kind of altruistic Machiavellianism, in which the deaths of some fleeing North Koreans was an acceptable

[139] Ibid., 129.
[140] Eberstadt and Griffin, "Saving North Korea's Refugees."

price to pay in the service of the larger goal of the overthrow of the North Korean regime. As Vollertsen put it, "Despite arrests and beatings [and, obviously, deaths], my friends and I will continue our efforts to create a steady flow of refugees through Western embassies in China, by boat across the Yellow Sea, and at the Russian-North Korean border."[141] And as (ever less passive) opportunists, the nature and role of the coalition within the United States was also consistent with the predictions of my theory; despite its relative strength and superpower status, militarily changing the North Korean political landscape was not a viable option, making coercive engineered migration appear an attractive alternative.

In addition, there is ample evidence to suggest that the *agents provocateurs* and the opportunists in this case tried to influence their targets by threatening to generate political crises within the target states of China and South Korea and by shaming them internationally. Evidence also suggests they attempted to do so, at least in part, through the use of the media and the imposition of hypocrisy costs. This was the explicit—and well-documented—strategy of the activist *agents provocateurs*. The opportunists within the United States dabbled with the strategy as well.[142] However, this coalition of Bush administration officials and sympathetic members of Congress seemed more committed to effecting change by attempting to convince the Chinese to change their position (while simultaneously offering rhetorical support for the UNHCR attempts to do the same) and by directly supporting the activities of the activist network.

Attempts to influence South Korean behavior similarly failed. In fact, the attempts to mobilize support for mass North Korean defections actually appeared to contribute to a further slide in support among the general South Korean public, which had commenced with the 1997 Asian financial crisis. To be clear, this decline was not a steady one, although it became pronounced following the upsurge in outflows stimulated by the network in 2002. In late 2004 and early 2005, for instance, the South Korean government tightened its policies vis-à-vis would-be defectors and cracked down on brokers who purportedly arranged mass defections.[143]

---

[141] Vollertsen, "Prison Nation."

[142] But given the problematic U.S. stance toward those North Koreans who sought asylum at U.S. embassies, such attempts led, instead, to the successful imposition of hypocrisy costs on the United States by the South Koreans and a softened stance. See Donald G. Gross, "After the Breakthrough, Now What?" *PacNet Newsletter* 27 (2002), www.cis.org/pacfor/cc/0202Qus_skorea.html. Gross notes that South Korean Foreign Ministry officials "criticized the US for showing no concern over the fate of refugees," and "perhaps stung by this criticism, the administration offered strong support to the ROK in a new dispute with China over refugees…and indicated it would raise the issue of refugees with North Korea when its bilateral talks resumed."

[143] Park Song-wu, "Poverty Forces Over 50% of NK Defections," *Korea Times*, December 5, 2004.

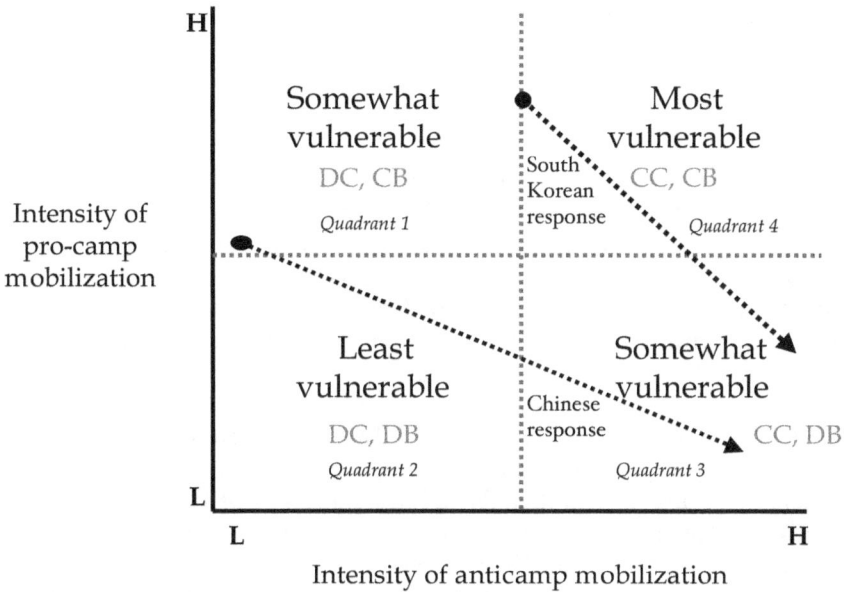

Figure 5.1. Why the NGOs and activists failed. CB, concentrated benefits; CC, concentrated costs; DB, diffuse benefits; DC, diffuse costs; H, high; L, low.

Both moves were supported by a majority of South Koreans, and neither generated noteworthy dissent or pro-camp mobilization. This may have been, at least in part, due to the fact that by this time most South Koreans viewed North Koreans as economic migrants rather than political refugees. Interestingly—although its results might be treated with some skepticism—by 2004 over 55 percent of North Korean defectors surveyed by the South Korean Unification Ministry said they had fled for economic reasons, "to avoid destitution and starvation," whereas only 9 percent cited "political dissatisfaction" as a reason they had left.[144] In sum, as illustrated in figure 5.1, the activists' coercive gambit failed in South Korea because the concentration of interests in favor of "keeping North Koreans at home" increased over the course of the crisis and the concentration of interests in favor of admitting them markedly declined.

Although the evidence is far from conclusive, the mixed Chinese reaction to the imposition of hypocrisy costs further supports the idea that liberal democracies are particularly susceptible to them. As a liberalizing—but

[144] Those interviewed were defectors who fled in January 2000–June 2004; cited and quoted in ibid.

still authoritarian—state, China has relatively wide latitude in its policy responses to coercive engineered migration. It took full advantage of that freedom by resisting calls for the creation of refugee camps, tightening its border controls, and repatriating many North Koreans living in China. At the same time, some of the Chinese reactions—the installation of barbed wire around embassies and the transfer to safe-asylum countries of individuals who managed to find a (highly publicized) way to claim asylum— suggest that the government was acutely aware of—and somewhat sensitive to—the imposition of hypocrisy costs. Moreover, the staunch Chinese adherence to the idea that all North Koreans were (and continue to be) economic migrants demonstrates a recognition that acknowledging that some might be legitimate asylum seekers would impose serious constraints on its behavior. As it is, when and where China felt exposed, it took (and continues to take) steps to reduce its potential vulnerability to charges of hypocrisy. The tragic consequence of this is, although this strategy left China less exposed, it also left the hapless North Korean migrants in an even sorrier state than before this coercive exercise commenced. Their underground railroad was closed down, and many of their connections within China dried up. In short, the strategy of the network failed utterly. Conversely, of course, the success of the tacit strategy pursued by North Korea is equally clear.

This case also highlights the possibility that successful coercive engineered migration becomes vastly more difficult when one of the targets is also a generator. In other words, imposing unacceptably high hypocrisy costs on the illiberal Chinese regime would have been challenging in any event. The fact that the activists wanted the Chinese to do something that could catalyze the very catastrophe that concession usually allows targets to avoid may well have made the activist endeavor impossibly hard.

Further Implications of This Case

It seems at least possible that the activist strategy of trying to impose hypocrisy costs on China would have been more effective had September 11 never happened. After the terrorist attacks, not only did it become significantly more difficult to get an issue such as the plight of the North Koreans on to the public radar screen for a sustainable period of time, but during the time frame in which this attempted coercion took place, the United States was far less likely to directly attack the Chinese with hypocrisy costs than it would have been. Even a cursory examination of the Bush administration reaction to the pre-9/11 E-P3 incident in April 2001 provides ample, if only circumstantial, evidence in support of this proposition.

In addition, it is a bit odd (and thus noteworthy) that the most powerful state in the world, which also happened to have 100,000 troops stationed in the region, on land or afloat, began to explicitly embrace the idea that coercive engineered migration might be the most expedient and desirable way to bring down North Korea. Nevertheless, it is completely understandable. As long as a collapse in northeastern Asia replicated what had happened in eastern Europe—which administration officials decided was plausible, if not probable—virtually all the costs would have been borne by those in the region; little wonder that President Bush was not deterred by the financial costs argument. Obviously, the situation would be different if such a collapse had resulted not in a flood of civilians north but the march of a million soldiers south.

Similarly, although the answer to the question of why the long-term consequences of a nuclear (possibly proliferating) North Korea are more palatable to its neighbors than the potential short-term fallout from the collapse of the regime remains opaque, the recognized tendency of states to discount the shadow of the future is a strong contender.[145] It may also be the case that North Korean neighbors believed it aimed to acquire (and then employ) its nuclear weapons principally as means—bargaining, financial, or deterrent—to nonoffensive ends.

Finally, this case should put the nail in the coffin of assertions that migrants and refugees do not represent a "real" security issue. The inexorable connection between the North Korean nuclear crisis and the migrant/refugee problem cannot be denied. If the fact that the ability of the sole world superpower to cow one of the weakest countries in the world was actively impeded by the threat of a mass migration does not represent a real security issue, it is unclear what does.

[145] See Kenneth A. Oye, "Explaining Cooperation under Anarchy: Hypotheses and Strategies," World Politics 38 (1985): 12–18.

6

Conclusions and
Policy Implications

You might think, from a perusal of the British papers this week, that
thousands of illegal 'scrounging gypsies'...had just swept across
the European plains to stage a full-frontal assault on the White Cliffs
of Dover.
**ALAN TRAVIS (UK Home Affairs Editor) and IAN TRAYNOR (European
Editor), the *Guardian***

After the 1999 Kosovo conflict, it was widely argued that a new and different armament—the refugee as weapon—had entered the arsenals of the
world. One scholar even went so far as to declare, "the nature of war [it-
self] has changed; now the refugees *are* the war."[1] As I have demonstrated,
however, the instrumental exploitation of engineered cross-border migrations is neither a new nor a particularly unusual phenomenon. Rather,
such exploitation has a long and influential history that includes both war
and peacetime use. Indeed, in this book I have identified at least fifty-
six attempted cases of migration-driven coercion (or coercive engineered
migration) between 1951 and 2006 alone—nearly three-quarters of which
were at least partially successful in achieving their stated goals. I also have
proposed a theory to explain how, why, and under what conditions this
tactic is likely succeed and fail.

In particular, I have argued that there are two distinct, but overlapping, pathways by which this kind of unconventional coercion can be effected. One is predicated on overwhelming the capacity of the target state
to absorb or manage migration crises; the second is predicated on a kind

---

Epigraph: Alan Travis and Ian Traynor, "Britain's Little Refugee Problem," *Guardian,* October 22, 1997.

[1] Comments of Professor Martha Minow, Harvard Law School, at a conference on the Kosovo conflict at Brandeis University, December 11, 2000.

of political blackmail aimed at exploiting competing political interests within the target state. Although both function as two-level coercion by punishment strategies, swamping focuses on manipulating the *ability* of targets to accept/accommodate/assimilate a given group of migrants or refugees, while agitating focuses on manipulating the *willingness* of targets to do so. Through large-N analysis, I have demonstrated that, although exceptions exist, the majority of coercive attempts in the developing world rely primarily (but not exclusively) on swamping, whereas most attempts in the developed world focus more directly on agitating.

The data have further revealed that, although the objective dangers posed to targets tend to be greater in the case of swamping, the probability of coercive success tends to be greater in the case of agitating. Indeed, the data have shown that coercive engineered migration tends to be most often attempted (and most often successful) against generally more powerful, liberal, democratic targets. As noted at the outset, this is not to suggest that coercive engineered migration is some kind of superweapon. Nevertheless, for highly resolved challengers with few other options at their disposal, discriminate targeting of particularly vulnerable targets can result in favorable outcomes, at least relative to the available alternatives.

So, why does this method of nonmilitary persuasion ever work? Arguably, it most often succeeds because it is a strategy that merges the international and domestic concerns of a state into one and transforms its domestic normative and political virtues into international bargaining vices. This perverse transmutation is possible for two reasons. First, although liberal democracies are likely to have made normative and juridical commitments to protect to those fleeing persecution (and sometimes privation), some segment of the societies within liberal states is usually unwilling to bear the real or perceived costs of upholding these commitments. As one journalist and commentator put it, "When you put their cruelties to the political class, you are often treated to a bluff lecture on pragmatism. We agree with much of what you say, you're told, but live in the real world, son. There's only so much immigration society can take. We're civilised people, but you should see our swinish voters."[2]

Second, liberal democratic targets are also most likely to be (quite transparently) constrained in international bargaining arenas by domestic political checks and balances. Thus, their attempts to credibly commit to policy actions that are likely to engender negative and concentrated costs domestically are less likely to be taken seriously internationally. Such targets are further constrained by the potential imposition of hypocrisy costs, a special class of reputational costs that can be imposed when targets claim

---

[2] Nick Cohen, "Comment: Lies for Lives: Forget about Principles, Asylum Seekers Are Only Welcome If They Guarantee Our Future Prosperity," *Guardian*, February 11, 2001.

to espouse migration-related human rights norms, but (attempt to) engage in behavior that abrogates those norms.

In the case-study portion of the book, I examined and illustrated the proposed casual mechanism(s) in fine-grained detail. I tested the proposed theory in a variety of longitudinal case studies, chosen from three continents, that spanned the time period from the mid-1960s (the height of the Cold War) through the mid-2000s (the post–Cold War era). In chapter 2, I examined three cases of migration-driven coercion by a single coercer—Cuba under President Fidel Castro—against three different U.S. administrations, in 1965, in 1994, and, most notoriously, in 1980, in the guise of the Mariel boatlift. In chapter 3, I explored three distinct attempts at coercion against a multilateral target (the NATO alliance) in the lead-up to and during the 1999 Kosovo conflict—one by a generator, one by an *agent provocateur*, and one by an opportunist. In chapter 4, I examined another three temporally distinct migration-driven coercive attempts, this time involving Haitian boatpeople, the first of which started in the late 1970s and the last of which concluded in the mid-2000s. Because two of the three Haitian cases occurred contemporaneously with two of the three Cuban cases (and the targets were the same), constructive comparisons were drawn between what were otherwise rather distinct outflows. In chapter 5, I examined another multifaceted case of coercion, this time on the Korean peninsula, by multiple state and nonstate actors—by a generator and an *agent provocateur*—against one democratic and one nondemocratic target. Because these attempts occurred in the context of the Korean nuclear crisis of the early 2000s, the case also illustrated how fundamentally national and international concerns merge in this kind of coercion and also how migration-related fears can prove even stronger and more influential than concerns about the proliferation of weapons of mass destruction.

Some of the coercive attempts in chapters 2–5 focused on stakes as relatively low and straightforward as financial aid; others focused on stakes as high and complicated as military intervention and regime change. Although the cases examined in this book included both successes and failures, it is worth reiterating that the observed outcomes were not simply and directly correlated with the nature and gravity of the demands made. (For further evidence in support of this observation, see the appendix.) Still more interesting, despite the broad geographic and temporal diversity of these cases, what they share in common not only largely comports with the predictions of my theory but also significantly exceeds what distinguishes them.

The broad theoretical implications of this book were outlined in the introduction and explored at some length in chapter 1. In this chapter, I therefore focus exclusively on cross-case patterns and their practical implications. I also tackle the question of what current trends appear to portend for the future, offer policy recommendations for targets facing the (potential) threat of coercive engineered migration, and briefly explore the generalizability of my theory beyond the realm of migration.

Crosscutting Patterns and Their Implications

The findings in this book join the body of research that suggests that liberal democratic targets can be hobbled by their very nature in international crisis bargaining. Specifically, the case evidence suggests that challengers exploit three distinct democratic strengths/virtues: (1) their moral and ethical constraints and impulses, (2) their level of societal transparency, and (3) the nature and consequences of their domestic political divisions. In each of the cases examined, there was direct and/or indirect evidence that at least some of the challengers understood well the moral, ethical, and legal constraints under which their targets operated. In some of the cases, the available evidence is only circumstantial, and thus the conclusions cannot be considered definitive. For instance, as of this writing, I have not uncovered evidence that Kim Jong Il's regime specifically sought to manipulate the constraints imposed by the status of China as a signatory of the UN Refugee Convention. On the other hand, the Chinese decision to studiously avoid calling fleeing North Koreans *refugees* cannot have been lost on their neighbor, nor can the fact that the Chinese have been pouring large sums of financial, energy, and food aid into North Korea since the initial rumors of the possible destabilization of that country first arose in the mid-1990s.

Moreover, a good deal of evidence has emerged that supports the proposition that challengers willfully and intentionally manipulated and took advantage of "the 'psychological' weaknesses of Western societies...to good effect."[3] In short, challengers unleashed flows that they knew targets would be unable to simply stop (i.e., by closing their borders) or instigated flows that they knew targets would be compelled to intervene to stop. In both eventualities, targets were more often than not compelled to concede to at least some of the demands posed by their challengers to bring the crises to a close. This was as true at the height of the Cold War as it was in the decades that followed. Although outcomes did not always accord with what challengers desired, it was a rare case indeed in which targets could simply ignore the threats of challengers and dismiss their escalatory

[3] James Gow and James Tilsley, "The Strategic Imperative for Media Management," in *Bosnia by Television*, ed. James Gow, Richard Paterson, and Alison Preston (London: British Film Institute, 1996), 103. See also Marjan Malesic, ed., *The Role of the Mass Media in the Serbian-Croatian Conflict* (Stockholm: SPF, 1993), 11.

responses out of hand. Even the 2004 Haitian case, which culminated in Aristide's summary removal from power, precipitated a response from the chosen target, then the world's sole superpower.

Similarly, although the level of transparency within liberal democracies—coupled with the fact that democratic leaders remain accountable to their constituents should they fail to uphold their claims—is viewed by many as making democracies more credible, the findings of this book indicate (at a minimum) that the conditions under which this holds are more limited than is often acknowledged. In the cases examined, both challengers and the displaced themselves behaved in ways that indicated that they often found threats and promises made by targets regarding their (un) willingness to absorb refugees and migrants *incredible*; this was true in the Balkans, on the Korean peninsula, and in the Caribbean. Challengers also appeared to find many threats made by targets to use force to stop outflows equally incredible—hence, the need for a seventy-eight-day bombing campaign against Milosevic in Kosovo in 1999 and the need to commence a forced-entry operation into Haiti before the junta would step down in 1994. The very visible existence of domestic (and/or intra-alliance) divisions over how crises should be handled convinced challengers that target threats were not to be taken seriously. That said, in some cases coercive gambits unequivocally failed. Nevertheless, it is clear that the existence of domestic and/or intra-alliance political turmoil offered enough reasonable doubt to materially and adversely affect the abilities of targets to influence the behavior of challengers.

Moreover, the very public nature of democratic decision making not only undermined (or at least impeded) the ability of targets to make credible claims ex ante, it also heightened the probability that concession would eventually result. As Bob Pastor has put it, "In the post-Cold War era when the sole superpower is needed to catalyze the international community on behalf of humanitarian goals, the president's inability to threaten pariah regimes may mean, paradoxically, that force is needed more often and with more intensity than if his threats were taken seriously."[4] In short, credibility is a major problem for weak actors trying to convince more powerful ones to comply with their demands, but it can also be significant problem for powerful states that happen to be democracies.[5]

As suggested at the outset, however, variation exists across liberal democracies—particularly in the degree to which their executives possess

---

[4] Robert Pastor, "The Delicate Balance between Coercion and Diplomacy: The Case of Haiti, 1994," in *The United States and Coercive Diplomacy*, ed. Robert Art and Patrick Cronin (Washington, D.C.: USIP, 2003), 138–39.

[5] Ronald Rogowski, "Institutions as Constraints," in *Strategic Choice and International Relations*, ed. David A. Lake and Robert Powell (Princeton: Princeton University Press, 1999), 125–26.

or lack policy autonomy. It is thus hardly surprising that the (highly decentralized and normatively exposed) United States appears to have been
the single most popular target of this kind of coercion in the last half century. Nevertheless, because immigration and asylum policy have become
so profoundly politicized, the influence of legislators and the public has
increased, even in societies where lawmakers and public opinion have
traditionally held less sway. So although strong (centralized) and weak
(decentralized) liberal democracies are differentially vulnerable, this difference may be less acute today than it has been historically.[6]

In addition, as the North Korean case suggests, even non-democracies
appear to recognize the power of hypocrisy costs to inflict political harm,
even though such states are less susceptible than their more democratic
counterparts. Despite the fact that hypocrisy costs are only a theoretical
construct, the cases illustrate that their consequences are viewed as real
by both challengers and targets. For instance, in the 1980 U.S.-Cuba case,
officials on both sides explicitly took note of the fact that the United States
would find itself trapped between its codified commitments and its competing political prerogatives (the Americans, ruefully; the Cubans, glee-
fully). And Castro tried to further heighten U.S. hypocrisy costs in the
midst of the crisis by helping Haitians stranded in the Caribbean make
it to the United States and then publicizing their subsequent detention in
Florida. Recognition of the political dangers of these inherent contradictions can be found in each of the cases, although to be clear this policy tool
was not always employed. For example, in the Kosovo case I found no direct evidence that Milosevic sought to impose hypocrisy costs on NATO,
although he demonstrably did attempt to exploit the disagreements and
conflicts of interest that existed among alliance members. On the other
hand, the KLA and its supporters admitted to attempting to impose hypocrisy costs, and at least some NATO members felt their effects.

Nevertheless, hypocrisy costs did not play an equally important role in
all cases. For instance, Haitian activists and some op-ed writers engaged
in low-level hypocrisy-cost imposition throughout the immediate post-
1991 coup period under George H. W. Bush's administration—but to no
avail. Although administration officials acknowledged their awareness of
these costs, they did not feel sufficiently pressured to shift their policies in
response. But once candidate Clinton entered the scene, the stage was set

[6] See, for instance, Ryan K. Beasley, Juliet Kaarbo, Jeffrey S. Lantis, and Michael T. Snarr,
Foreign Policy in Comparative Perspective: Domestic and International Influence on State Behavior
(Washington, D.C.: Congressional Quarterly Press, 2002); Christian Joppke, *Immigration and
the Nation-State: The United States, Germany, and Great Britain* (Oxford: Oxford University Press,
2000); Adrian Favell, "The Europeanization of Immigration Politics," European Integration
On-line Papers no. 2, 1998, http://eiop.or.at/eiop/texte/1998-010a.htm. See especially, Ian
Buruma, "Mind the Gap," *Financial Times Sunday Magazine*, January 10, 2003, 28–30.

for a different outcome. Clinton lowered his own hypocrisy-cost threshold during the presidential campaign by promising to overturn what he called the "callous" and "racist" Bush policy; this meant that, once Aristide and his supporters escalated their attacks in the spring of 1994, Clinton had little choice but to concede. (These actors were also, as already noted, aided by the fact that Aristide's supporters were natural Clinton constituents; thus, Clinton was more susceptible to the costs they threatened to impose than George H. W. Bush had been.)

In other words, holding the migrant group in question and the degrees of normative and political liberalization all constant, targets can still vary significantly in their levels of vulnerability. Articulating a pro-active norms-laden initial position leaves target leaders more susceptible to charges of hypocrisy and vulnerable to potential coercion than leaders who eschew such rhetoric. Hence, this book also illustrates the very real dangers associated with pursuing a rhetorically robust strategy for short-term political gain. Tough moralizing talk may be cheap in the short run—particularly if the "talker" is not in a position to do more than criticize (i.e., if he or she is a member of the opposition party and/or only a candidate running for office). But that same actor may soon find him- or herself suffering the consequences of deploying escalatory rhetoric if he or she comes into power before the issue or crisis in question has been resolved.

This is one of the great ironies of coercive engineered migration. In trying to garner prestige points while also signaling resolve to would-be coercers, targets actually increase their susceptibility to it. This is true for several reasons. First, high-minded rhetoric served in some cases to narrow targets' room for maneuver—in other words, it reduced the sized of their policy win sets—thereby making attempted coercion look more attractive to would-be challengers. Second, rhetorical grandstanding can be particularly dangerous due to the nature of leaders' influence on the public agenda. In making statements about their commitments to migrants or refugees—either generally, or with regard to a particular group—leaders inadvertently increase their own vulnerability to coercion, should they be called on to uphold such commitments in future.[7] Third, research suggests that although leaders do appear to possess some power to influence what appears on the public's radar screen, leaders have rather less power to influence the nature of the resulting media coverage once issues become salient.[8] Fourth, even if public opinion is not what David Price calls

<hr>

[7] See, for instance, Leon V. Sigal, "Who? Sources Make the News," in *Reading the News*, ed. Robert Karl Manoff and Michael Schudson, 9–37 (New York: Pantheon, 1986).

[8] On the power of the executive to influence the public agenda, see, for instance, Jeffrey E. Cohen, "Presidential Rhetoric and the Public Agenda," *American Journal of Political Science* 39 (1995): 87–101; George C. Edwards III and B. Dan Wood, "Who Influences Whom? The President, Congress, and the Media," *American Political Science Review* 93 (1999): 327–43.

"activated," research suggests that leaders feel compelled to deal with sa-lient issues—even if highly conflictual—for "the simple reason that they might be blamed for inaction" if they did nothing.[9]

The findings from the case studies also support the contention that co-ercive engineered migration is rarely a strategy of first resort for genera-tors. As suggested in chapter 1, this is probably due to the fact that flows tend to grow larger and less controllable than coercers generally desire. In some cases, there is direct evidence to support that generators hoped for smaller outflows (e.g., the testimony from Castro insiders), and in other cases, there is circumstantial evidence in support of this proposition (e.g., Milosevic's border closure and unilateral ceasefire declaration). In some of the cases examined, moreover, generators even publicly lamented the fact that any outflows were necessary. Nevertheless, the cases also dem-onstrate that, when potential generators are very dissatisfied with the *status quo* and/or anticipate an imminent worsening of the situation, they may willfully accept the risk that a massive outflow might become destabilizing—or precipitate a military response—and employ coercion by design, not by accident.[10]

Across the cases, moreover, if concession did result, it often came late in the game, leaving targets with larger migrant or refugee populations than anticipated or desired. This appears to be a consequence of the fact that, as is often the problem with coercive strategies that promise escalating punishment, "instead of being convinced that the perpetrator's resolve to inflict maximum damage if demands are not met, the opponent is more likely to be convinced that the coercer will never escalate far above current restrained levels."[11] In short, targets frequently fail to take seriously the threats of challengers until an outflow has been initiated.

Confident of their superior strength and position, powerful targets fail to recognize until late in the game that they might lose. The added tragedy is that not only does this lead to more migrant victims but it also leads to suboptimal outcomes for both sides. Because it is so easy for generators to lose control of outflows, and because the costs associated with absorbing large numbers of unwelcome migrants clearly exceed those of absorbing few or none, it seems self-evident that both sides should avoid such an outcome. Yet often they do not.

[9] Timothy E. Cook, *Governing with the News* (Chicago: University of Chicago Press, 1998), 127. See also David E. Price, "Policy Making in Congressional Committees: The Impact of 'Environmental' Factors," *American Political Science Review* 72 (1978): 548–74.

[10] See Meir Statman, "Lottery Players/Stock Traders," *Financial Analysts Journal* 58 (2002): 14–21; Daniel Kahneman and Amos Tversky, "Prospect Theory: An Analysis of Decision Making under Risk," *Econometrica* 47 (1979): 263–91.

[11] Robert A. Pape, *Bombing to Win: Air Power and Coercion in War* (Ithaca, N.Y.: Cornell University Press, 1996), 28.

In stark contrast, however, the cases also suggest that *agents provocateurs* tend to prefer larger (rather than smaller) outflows. This appears to be a consequence of two disparate factors. First, the greater the outflow, the more victimized the *agents provocateurs* appear in the eyes of international observers—this precise sentiment was expressed by the KLA in the Kosovo case. The more victimized and, hence, more worthy of sympathy a group is, the more likely it is that it will garner the outside support necessary to achieve its goals. Second, the larger and/or the more illimitable the outflow—or, more specifically, the more the size of the flow deviates from the size and speed of normal cross-border movements—the more threatening it appears to potential recipient states and, hence, the greater the likelihood that these states will intervene to staunch it. This was true in Kosovo as well as in Haiti, and it is this fear that animated North Korea's neighbors.

With the issue of flow size in mind, it is also worth noting the critical role that the displaced themselves can play. When refugees and migrants cooperate with challengers (as the majority of Kosvoar Albanians did with the KLA), the probability of coercive success increases significantly. In contrast, when the displaced pursue their own agendas (e.g., leave in greater numbers than is preferred, choose a different destination than is desired, or fail to do what is expected of them on arrival), they can undermine the strategy of coercers and doom their attempts to failure. (See, for instance, case 2 in the appendix, which details the failed U.S. attempt to use engineered migration against North Vietnam in the mid-1950s.)

In addition, migrants can upend stable equilibria between *potential* challengers and targets as well as torpedo active and tacit arrangements that may exist between them. For instance, it has been argued that had the Haitian junta done more to restrain those who took to the sea in response to Aristide's entreaties in summer 1994, the United States probably would not have intervened to remove the military rulers from power.[12]

Beyond what the preceding conclusions suggest, what does the evidence from the past tell us about what to expect in the future?

The Growing Strength of Norms and the Efficacy of Coercive Engineered Migration

As noted in the introduction, a quarter century ago Myron Weiner, political scientist and migration specialist, noted that the number of state-directed

---

[12] Christopher Mitchell, "The Political Costs of State Power: U.S. Border Control in South Florida," in *The Wall around the West: State Borders and Immigration Control in North America and Europe*, ed. Peter Andreas and Timothy Snyder (Lanham: Rowman and Littlefield, 2000), 81–98.

outmigrations began to rise significantly in the early 1970s. Eighty-seven percent of the cases of coercive engineered migration identified in this book likewise transpired after 1970. This is probably no coincidence. Perversely and tragically, it appears that the growth of humanitarian norms since the end of World War II—and particularly since the early 1970s when the number and influence of NGOs truly began to blossom—has actually inadvertently strengthened weak actors prepared to employ this kind of coercion, particularly (but not exclusively) against liberal democratic targets.[13] This is because, as the norms governing appropriate state behavior have grown in strength and in number, so has the leverage of those who seek to exploit these norms for good and for ill. As Louis Henkin, international law expert, observed in the late 1970s, "Human rights have assumed a high place in the rhetoric of international relations and most governments, moved to adhere to international covenants, cannot lightly disregard them."[14] One NGO activist put it more bluntly, "NGOs must influence the UN system to ensure that the real human rights picture emerges. *Whether we like it or not, the UN is a system that can be used.* We have to change the opinion of governments on human rights."[15]

The end of the Cold War allowed further expansion of the global agenda, as well as inclusion of issues and voices that had been excluded in the bipolar struggle that had dominated global affairs. But as the strength of norms promoters has grown, so has, concomitantly and inadvertently, the strength and visibility of those who would exploit these norms and the existence of hypocrisy costs for their own benefit. Moreover, the very nature of the Cold War itself probably further contributed to this phenomenon. It was after all portrayed as an epic battle between liberalism and communist authoritarianism, one which was fought largely in the public sphere, via massive propaganda campaigns touting the superiority of liberal precepts and values—many of which are synonymous with those promulgated under the human rights regime.

Taken together, these developments can only be viewed as a case of the law of unintended consequences in action, in which the growing strength of humanitarian norms since the end of World War II has invested power in the hands of a number of weak actors who would otherwise have little. This proposition is consistent with Thomas Risse and Stephen Ropp's

[13] See Margaret Keck and Kathryn Sikkink, *Activists beyond Borders: Advocacy Networks in International Politics* (Ithaca, N.Y.: Cornell University Press, 1998), chap. 4; Sanjeev Khagram, James V. Riker, and Kathryn Sikkink, eds., *Restructuring World Politics: Transnational Social Movements, Networks, and Norms*(Minneapolis: University of Minnesota Press, 2002).

[14] Louis Henkin, *How Nations Behave* (New York: Council on Foreign Relations, 1979), 236.

[15] Marwaan Macan-Markar, "Asian Activists Say Human Rights Principles being Eroded at UN," Inter Press Service, December 16, 2002, www.cyberdyaryo.com/features/f2002_1216_04.htm.

finding that the stronger the transnational advocacy network becomes and the more vulnerable the norm-violating government is to external pressure, the more likely it is that the violator will have to engage in tactical concessions to placate its critics.[16] As Stephen Krasner, political scientist and former director of policy planning in the U.S. State Department, has put it, "Compliance and enforcement mechanisms for [human rights accords]...have strengthened the positions of sympathetic national actors and changed domestic conceptions of appropriate policy."[17] The irony is that as pressure to adhere to these humanitarian norms has grown so has the leverage of those who seek to exploit them, as the ease with which potential targets can be entrapped has likewise grown.

Evidence suggests that the rise of humanitarian norms has made the instigation of refugee flows easier for *agents provocateurs* as well. As Fiona Terry has argued, the establishment of the international refugee regime has been especially significant because it has facilitated the creation of "humanitarian sanctuaries," which offer guerrillas legal protection, access to resources, and a mechanism by which guerrilla movements can control civilian populations and legitimize their leadership.[18] Whether these developments are sustainable, however, is an open question. In what may be a kind of blowback effect, evidence suggests that targets are actively tightening their immigration laws and asylum policies, and otherwise reducing their explicit normative commitments to the protection of the most vulnerable populations of the world. As former British Prime Minister Tony Blair put it, although the values of the 1951 Refugee Convention are indeed "timeless, we should stand back and consider its application in today's world."[19]

Policy Implications and Recommendations

Are potential target states compelled to respond as Blair suggests, to rethink their commitments, tighten their laws, and narrow the openings

---

[16] Thomas Risse and Stephen C. Ropp, "International Human Rights Norms and Domestic Change: Conclusions," in *The Power of Human Rights: International Norms and Domestic Change*, ed. Thomas Risse, Stephen C. Ropp, and Kathryn Sikkink (Cambridge, UK: Cambridge University Press, 1999), 234–78.

[17] Stephen Krasner, *Sovereignty: Organized Hypocrisy* (Princeton: Princeton University Press, 1999), 126.

[18] See Jean-Christophe Rufin, *Le Piege Humanitaire: Suivi de Humanitaire et Politique Depuis la Chute du Mur*, rev. ed. (Paris: Jean-Claude Lattes, 1993), in Fiona Terry, *Condemned to Repeat? The Paradox of Humanitarian Action* (Ithaca, N.Y.: Cornell University Press, 2002), 8–10.

[19] Marilyn Achiron, "A 'Timeless' Treaty under Attack," *Refugees Magazine* 123 (2001), www.unhcr.org/publ/PUBL/3cdfd3e19.html. "Britain to Push for Launch of Pilot Scheme in East Africa," *Guardian*, June 20, 2003.

at their borders? Not necessarily. Although imperfect, there are options available that can help protect potential target states and those they have previously committed themselves to protect. States faced with the threat of coercive engineered migration have at least three distinct policy options: (1) play this two-level bargaining game with greater acumen, (2) make the game less attractive to potential challengers, and (3) change the potential contestants so that the probability that anyone will choose to play declines. It is not clear that there is one right answer, and none of the three is a panacea. What *is* clear, however, is that potential target states can and should be better prepared for the significant possibility that their sheer material strength may offer insufficient protection against an unconventional attack.

Option One: Play the Game, but with a Better Grasp of the Rules

Because coercive engineered migration is relatively common, potential targets need not treat each crisis as if it were sui generis. There are lessons from past cases of migration-driven coercion, from negotiations in more traditional coercive environments, and from the bargaining literature on which policymakers can draw to deter or assuage challengers and to forestall recidivistic predation. For one thing, history shows that in some circumstances targets might be best served by negotiating with would-be challengers in the early stages of a potential crisis, despite strong predispositions against doing so. As noted in chapter 2, the United States could probably have avoided at least two of its three Cuban migration crises had it not ex ante flatly rejected Castro's calls for bilateral negotiations. Indeed, evidence suggests the United States did dodge another potential Cuban crisis in April 1995 in just this way. To be clear, choosing to concede to threats as soon as a challenger makes them can generate its own costs in terms of reputation and credibility. Early concession may, for instance, encourage challengers to threaten potential targets ever more frequently and with growing demands.[20] Nevertheless, more careful monitoring of the prevailing conditions on the ground in potential sending states, coupled with more aural acuity if and when potential challengers begin making threatening noises, could lead to earlier diplomatic intervention, which in turn could stave off domestic discord, unnecessary crises, and political embarrassments.

---

[20] See, for instance, Robert Jervis, *Perception and Misperception in International Politics* (Princeton: Princeton University Press, 1976), chap. 3, for a discussion of the potential dangers of appeasement.

Under certain conditions, targets may even decide to make preemptive concessions to potential challengers to forestall crises before they start, as, for instance, Reagan did with the side-payments associated with the 1981 U.S.-Haiti Interdiction Agreement. Here again, however, there are dangers associated with early concession to challenger demands—tacit or actual. For example, China began to pour significant resources into North Korea in a preemptive attempt to stave off a crisis in the mid-1990s, and it has been (almost) continuously been doing so ever since. Nevertheless, the price of these side-payments surely appear nominal to the Chinese, as least compared to the potential costs associated with a sudden collapse of the North Korean regime.

Option Two: Make the Game Not Worth Playing by Eroding the Power of the Migration Weapon

Through a careful combination of pro-active public policy, education, research, and generous side-payments, potential targets may be able to reduce their vulnerability by undermining, or at least diminishing, the ability of challengers to use migrants and refugees as coercive instruments. Specifically, if a target can prevent an outflow from being perceived or treated as a real crisis, it can significantly degrade the potency of this weapon. Facilitating degradation may not be easy, however, because both challengers and interested outsiders usually have powerful incentives to keep outflows as salient and contentious as possible. Nonetheless, there are several concrete steps that potential targets can take that may mitigate, if not eliminate, their vulnerability.

First, states can develop and be prepared to implement comprehensive and politically acceptable contingency plans, both to actively cope with specific emergencies and to help prevent local infrastructure(s) from being overburdened.[21] Specifically, to be better prepared for potential influxes, governments should not wait until active outflows arise to court communities that might be persuaded to take migrants—either for short- or long-term stays—in exchange for attractive economic and/or political compensation packages. Theoretically, this is what the U.S. federal government and the state of Florida did after the Cuban and Haitian crises in summer 1994. They should also not wait until crises arise to make communities that are likely ports of entry or landing zones aware that

---

[21] As Christian Holmes, director of the Cuban-Haitian Task Force, put it when discussing the failure of the United States to respond appropriately to the Mariel boatlift, "When you have a crisis situation…where there is not a clear legal history, legal precedent or clear law, it makes it very hard to respond to the event." Interview with Christian Holmes, quoted in David W. Engstrom, *Presidential Decision Making Adrift: The Carter Administration and the Mariel Boatlift* (Lanham: Rowman and Littlefield, 1998), 98n119.

practicable response plans exist. For instance, although the details remain classified, both state and federal officials claim that a mutually acceptable contingency plan is finally in place that should allow the United States to manage a massive outflow from Cuba or Haiti.[22] A failure to engage in this kind of contingency planning may place targets in binds in which they find themselves subject to subsidiary opportunistic coercion in the midst of an already ongoing crisis. The successful Macedonian coercion of NATO in the middle of the Kosovo crisis is just one example.

Alternatively, just as governments conduct exercises in which relevant actors respond to simulated terrorist attacks, pandemics, and natural disasters,[23] they might also conduct (more and more visible) exercises designed to combat migration-related unnatural disasters. Indeed—Although we can be little more than cautiously optimistic about their effects—such exercises could in principle fulfill a dual role within the two-level game environment in which this kind of coercion takes place. That is, exercises could simultaneously send a deterrent message to potential coercers and a pacifying message to domestic audiences while also leaving target governments and their citizens better physically and psychologically equipped to confront outflows and influxes, if and when they arise.[24]

Second, potential target governments may choose to launch preventive education campaigns designed to affect the attitudes of the citizens who are the proxy targets of these punishment-based coercive strategies. Such campaigns might be aimed at improving perceptions of particular migrant or refugee groups, or of migrants and refugees in general. History and research demonstrate that attitudes toward groups—for better and worse—can and do shift over time.[25] Japanese Americans, for instance, are now "valorized by the media and by policymakers alike as members of the 'model minority.'"[26] But they were initially described by detractors as "different in color; different in ideals; different in race; different in ambitions; different in their theory of political economy and government. They

[22] Interviews with state and federal officials, May 2000, Miami, Fla., Washington, D.C. At the same time, it is worth noting that similar claims were made *before* either of the 1994 crises commenced.

[23] See, for instance, "Project Argus—Protecting against a Terrorist Attack," 2007, www.gloucestershire.police.uk/counterterrorism/Project%20Argus/item3986.html; and "Bethesda Terror Attack Drill Tests Emergency Resources," November 13, 2008, http://www.simulationinformation.com/cms/index.php?option=com_content&task=view&id=1196.

[24] On the downside, they could also alarm target populations and catalyze greater opposition. But pretending this kind of coercion does not happen has not worked either.

[25] See, for instance, Daniel J. Tichenor, *Dividing Lines: The Politics of Immigration Control in America* (Princeton: Princeton University Press, 2002).

[26] Stephanie J. DiAlto, "From 'Problem Minority' to 'Model Minority': The Changing Social Construction of Japanese Americans," in *Deserving and Entitled: Social Constructions and Public Policy*, ed. Anne L. Schneider and Helen M. Ingram (Albany: State University of New York Press, 2005), 81.

speak a different language; they worship a different G_d. They had not in common with the Caucasian a single trait."[27] Attitudes toward specific groups can also be changed on much shorter time scales, if in relatively shallow ways, as the Kosovo case makes clear.[28]

Other campaigns might focus on educating publics about the true costs and benefits of inflows. The majority of studies have found that over time immigration generally either has no effect or represents a net gain for most industrialized countries.[29] But, because these effects tend to be unevenly distributed, concomitantly making provisions for those destined to bear the brunt of the costs is critical. Educational outreach may be particularly appropriate in states facing falling birthrates and aging populations, such as Germany, Japan, and Italy, where inflows could provide a much-needed boost to declining tax bases.

Direct beneficiaries of migrant and refugee labor may even be persuaded to take up the cause. For instance, in November 2003, John Forrest, the whip of the federal Nationals Party in Australia, began lobbying his government to take a more sympathetic attitude to refugees who want to remain in that country permanently, because they provide a valuable source of (undersupplied) labor for the table grape-, citrus-, and vegetable-growing industries in his district.[30] Such initiatives may be undertaken on the national level as well. In 2005, for instance, the Canadian government announced plans to encourage a quarter million new immigrants per year to settle there, citing the value of influxes as a "fundamental driver of the economy of tomorrow."[31]

To be clear, education is no magic bullet either. Truly committed members of specific pro- or anti-refugee/migrant camps are unlikely to be converted.[32] Education might, however, change the minds of those on the fence—or keep them firmly on it—and, depending on the prevailing

[27] Page Smith, *Democracy on Trial: The Japanese American Evacuation and Relocation in World War II* (New York: Simon and Schuster, 1995), 49.

[28] See, for instance, Benjamin I. Page and Robert Y. Shapiro, *The Rational Public: Fifty Years of Trends in Americans' Policy Preferences* (Chicago: University of Chicago Press, 1992).

[29] "Let the Huddled Masses In," *Economist*, March 29, 2001. See also Roger Lowenstein, "The Immigration Equation," *New York Times Sunday Magazine*, July 9, 2006, in which Lowenstein notes, "You can find economists to substantiate the position of either chamber, but the consensus of most is that, on balance, immigration is good for the country. Immigrants provide scarce labor, which lowers prices in much the same way global trade does. And overall, the newcomers modestly raise Americans' per capita income. But the impact is unevenly distributed; people with means pay less for taxi rides and household help while the less-affluent command lower wages and probably pay more for rent. The debate among economists is whether low-income workers are hurt a lot or just a little."

[30] Michelle Grattan, "Nats MP Goes In to Bat for Refugees," *Age*, November 9, 2003.

[31] Canadian Immigration Minister Joe Volpe, quoted in Joel Millman, "Canada's Open Door to Immigrants Is Seen as Crucial for Growth," *Wall Street Journal*, May 23, 2005.

[32] See, for instance, James Stimson, *Tides of Consent: How Public Opinion Shapes American Politics* (Cambridge, UK: Cambridge University Press, 2004).

strength and concentration of the committed pro- and anti-interests in a particular crisis, this could make all the difference. Moreover, a growing body of research suggests that personal exposure to members of other ethnic and racial groups significantly increases tolerance of, and greater affinity for, these groups writ large.[33] In the United States, for instance, those born after 1978 (the so-called "Millennials") are the most diverse generation in U.S. history, and their attitudes toward race are dramatically different from their predecessors. They evince almost universal acceptance (94 percent) "of interracial dating and marriage and less concern about the economic or cultural impact of immigration. For them, race is 'no big deal.'"[34] Over time, this shift could translate into a smaller pool of candidates for the anti-refugee/migrant camp and reduced state vulnerability to coercion.

Third, potential targets could more actively cultivate the support of other states that could share the burden in the event of outflows. This strategy was employed (with varying degrees of success) in Southeast Asia vis-à-vis Indochinese refugees during the 1970s and 1980s, in Europe throughout the Yugoslav wars of dissolution in the 1990s, and in the Caribbean during a variety of crises between Cuba and the United States and Haiti and the United States from the 1980s to the mid-2000s. A variation on this theme is the aforementioned practice of warehousing asylum seekers in their home region or in the states of first asylum, within areas that have euphemistically been called "safe havens." However, while warehousing tends to serve the needs of potential target states and keeps the contradictions inherent in their behavior somewhat hidden from domestic audiences, it can cause significant political problems within the states doing the warehousing. (Recall that fears of just such an outcome led Panama to rescind its promise to host 10,000 Haitians in summer 1994, thus helping force the U.S. government's hand vis-à-vis the long-delayed, forced-entry military option.)

Nevertheless, states seeking foreign aid or other forms of international support might be persuaded to oblige target states under the right conditions. Recall that, early in the Kosovo crisis, an escalating refugee crisis on the Macedonian border at Blace was solved in just this manner.[35] Likewise, Australia solved several of its own potential migration crises

[33] See, for instance, Lauren M. McLaren, "Anti-Immigrant Prejudice in Europe: Contact, Threat Perception and Preferences for the Exclusion of Migrants," *Social Forces* 81 (2003): 909–36.

[34] Ruy Teixeira, "New Progressive America: Twenty Years of Demographic, Geographic, and Attitudinal Changes across the Country Herald a New Progressive Majority," Center for American Progress, Washington, D.C., 2009, 32, www.americanprogress.org.

[35] Michael Barutciski and Astri Suhrke, "Lessons from the Kosovo Refugee Crisis: Innovations in Protection and Burden-Sharing," *Journal of Refugee Studies* 14 (2001), 101.

by furnishing substantial financial aid to the cash-strapped Pacific island nation of Nauru. (Still, it must also be noted that Nauru—recognizing and exploiting the strong disinclination of the Australian government to admit the displaced—then responded with its own successful opportunistic attempt at coercive engineered migration.[36])

Fourth, targets may simply choose to abrogate relevant humanitarian norms, either by underlining national security concerns or by refusing to recognize those fleeing as worthy of protection. Of course, targets that choose to (or simply appear to) abrogate said norms run the risk of incurring significant reputational and hypocrisy costs. Under certain conditions, however, leaders may deem this price preferable to the aggregate domestic political ramifications of accepting more migrants. This was clearly the position adopted by Australian Prime Minister John Howard in 2001, who found himself subject to widespread international recrimination after his administration refused refuge to 438 asylum seekers who were rescued from a sinking boat by the Norwegian cargo ship, *Tampa*.[37]

To try to circumvent charges of hypocrisy, targets may simply attempt to change existing domestic and/or international laws so that they can eschew claims that they are abrogating norms while still engaging in behavior that runs counter to accepted precedents. Since the September 11 terrorist attacks, for instance, many states have been able to evoke and employ national security rationales as grounds for challenging existing commitments with greater facility (and more widespread public receptivity) than was the case previously.[38] Indeed, according to James Hampshire, since 9/11, governments have sought to "disembed" liberalism from migration policymaking by attacking both its political and normative liberal underpinnings.[39] Although such responses might be tactically effective, they endanger and threaten to further undermine protections for those fleeing violence and persecution, the true victims of this kind of coercion. There is some evidence, however, to suggest that the pendulum may be swinging back as the 2001 attacks recede into the distance.[40]

[36] For a particularly informative discussion of Nauru's blackmail strategies, see the transcript of NPR *This American Life*, December 6, 2003, www.thislife.org.

[37] See, for instance, "Soldiers Frog-March Asylum Seekers off Ship," *Guardian*, October 2, 2002.

[38] For an international accounting of the migration-related legislation and other security measures enacted after 9/11, see International Organization for Migration, "International Terrorism and Migration," June 2003, app., www.belgium.iom.int/pan-europeandialogue/documents/terrorism%20migration.pdf.

[39] James Hampshire, "Disembedding Liberalism? Immigration Politics and Security in Britain since 9/11," in *Immigration Policy and Security: U.S., European and Commonwealth Perspectives*, ed. Terry E. Givens, Gary P. Freeman, and David L. Leal (London: Routledge, 2008), 118.

[40] For some specific examples of pro-refugee/migrant camp pushback, see Peter Nyers, *Rethinking Refugees: Beyond States of Emergency* (London: Routledge, 2006), 125–31. See also

Option 3: Change the Contestants to Decrease
the Probability of Play

Undertaking radical regime change or other actions designed to change
the conditions on the ground in potential sending states is a third option
available to target states. Although the impulse to go this route has been
tempered somewhat by the U.S. experience in Iraq, it is far from dead;
indeed, in some circles, it is even growing in strength.[41] The impulse has
also been making strange bedfellows of groups that normally would have
little to do with one another.[42] As one UNHCR official told me, "This could
be the next big thing. [We] field a lot of queries on this topic from the
evangelical "right" on the Hill. Interestingly, as long as we keep mum on
abortion and contraception, these fellows are some of the strongest refugee advocates in the US."[43] A similar sentiment was expressed by another
"human rights watcher," who mused, "I always thought there was more
in common between Human Rights Watch and the Bush administration
than either would be comfortable thinking, because they are both revolu-
tionaries—in my view, quite dangerous radicals. They believe that virtue
can be imposed by force of law and force of arms."[44]

At the same time, those who favor the regime change option need to remain cognizant that the overthrow of a sitting dictator and an increase in
economic development may actually increase emigration from that state
in the short run. This, for instance, is what many in the U.S. government
fear will happen when Fidel (or Raul) Castro dies. This tendency, known
as a "migration hump" reflects the fact that economic development tends
to disrupt traditional economic and political relationships and traditionally noncompetitive sectors and also provides prospective emigrants with
the economic means to emigrate.[45] Moreover, those formerly in power
and their supporters may also migrate or simply flee in large numbers
during the "hump" period.

A further complication is the fact that migration crises that trigger
humanitarian intervention may lead to the "rapid reclassification of unwanted 'illegal migrants' into bona fide refugees" with temporary protection

---

Agnes Hurwitz, *The Collective Responsibility of States to Protect Refugees* (Oxford: Oxford University Press, 2008).

[41] Ted Permutter has come to the same conclusion, drawing on the case of Operation Alba
in 1997. Permutter, "The Politics of Proximity: The Italian Response to the Albanian Crisis,"
International Migration Review 32 (1998): 203–22.

[42] See, for instance, "Australian Responsibility to Protect Fund," 2009, http://r2pasiapa
cific.org/index.php?option=com_content&task=view&id=91&Itemid=98.

[43] UNHCR official, personal communication, December 2002.

[44] David Rieff, quoted in George Packer, "The Liberal Quandary over Iraq," *New York Times
Sunday Magazine*, December 8, 2002.

[45] See, for instance, *International Migration and Trade* 28 (1994), www.worldbank.org.

status (TPS). The extension of TPS to displaced people who employ smugglers has the knock-on effect of reducing the number of services smugglers need to provide to facilitate their successful entry into destination
countries.[46] Hence, smugglers can take advantage of crises that catalyze
military responses to expand their operations at the expense of state efforts
to control clandestine migration.[47]

Still more troubling is the prospect that smugglers too could get into the
migration-driven coercion game; that is, the number of potential contestants could rise rather than fall over time. As John Salt and Jeremy Stein
have noted, as human trafficking expands, smugglers—rather than their
migrant and asylum seeking customers—are making more decisions about
their clients' ultimate destinations.[48] Because "part of the smugglers' success in getting migrants across borders is the smugglers' ability to change
routes and destinations in order to overcome obstacles that states put in
their way," they are particularly well placed to circumvent target state de-
fenses.[49]

It does not require a significant stretch of imagination to envision how
smugglers themselves might get into this two-level bargaining game, either on their own behalf or as intermediaries for states or other nonstate
actors. Indeed, human smugglers are already exploiting liberal target normative commitments. In one case, for instance, traffickers arranged for
children wearing lifejackets to be thrown overboard from a leaking boat
in the hope that the Australian Navy would rescue them, in what was described as "an outrageous attempt at moral blackmail."[50]

The capacity for heightened exploitation and manipulation of population movements exists; whether the incentives to do so will follow remains to be seen. Consider, however, that in the midst of the Kosovo crisis
aid workers estimated that, during the last week in April 1999 alone, 1,000
refugees per day were successfully transported across the Adriatic and
then helped to claim asylum or to disappear within Italy.[51] It has been estimated that Albanian smugglers made DM 10 million by smuggling Kosovar Albanians in the initial weeks of the war.[52] What would governments
have paid to discourage them from doing so? And at what political cost?

[46] See Rey Koslowski, "The Mobility Money Can Buy," in *The Migration Reader: Exploring Politics and Policies,* ed. Anthony Messina and Gallya Lahav (London: Lynne Rienner,
2006), 571–87.
[47] Ibid., 580.
[48] John Salt and Jeremy Stein, "Migration as a Business: The Case of Trafficking," *International Migration Review* 35 (1997): 467–94, in ibid., 581.
[49] Ibid.
[50] "Drama on the High Seas," *Mercury,* October 10, 2001.
[51] Frederika Randall, "Italy and Its Immigrants: Refugees from the Balkan Peninsula," *Nation,* May 31, 1999.
[52] Koslowski, "Mobility Money Can Buy," 578.

Final Thoughts and a Few Predictions

At the end of the day, the fact remains that cross-border population movements present a real ethical conundrum for Western liberal democratic regimes. As a rule, liberal democracies are reluctant to insist that governments restrain the exit of their citizens simply because they or others are disinclined to accept them. These regimes likewise believe in the right of emigration, but simultaneously embrace the principle that states retain the right to determine who and how many will be permitted to enter.[53] Most have accepted the principle of *non-refoulement* enshrined in the 1951 Convention and 1967 Protocol. Yet, at the same time, they have not adopted a universal right to asylum; instead, the granting of asylum remains at the discretion of the receiving state.[54]

When push comes to shove, liberal democracies wish to be in the position neither of having to force people to return home against their will nor of having to press governments to prevent their people from leaving. As John Coleman Bennett put it more than forty years ago, "No government would be justified in letting down all barriers, because the interests of its own country should be guarded....This is a hard problem with which we shall have to live, [that] prudence and generosity will be in conflict."[55] Rather, what states really want is for governments to stop repressing political dissidents and persecuting minorities, so they do not want to leave in the first place.[56] This situation becomes further complicated by the actions of oppressed groups themselves, which—acting as *agents provocateurs*—may see no better way to promote their own agendas than by provoking government attacks on themselves.

What does this portend for the future? It is not wholly clear. But the available evidence suggests that, as long as nascent and actual mass migrations pose a threat, intentional or otherwise, target states will be driven to take broader and more pro-active steps to decrease their vulnerability to outflows. Thus, the current Western trend toward ever-tighter immigration restrictions—despite declining birthrates in many places—is likely to continue. This will, thereby, further weaken the framework that undergirds the 1951 Convention and 1967 Protocol.

Nevertheless, this push and pull remains a dynamic process, and for every action, there is an equal (or greater) opposite reaction. While targets act to

---

[53] Myron Weiner and Michael Teitelbaum, *Political Demography, Demographic Engineering* (London: Berghahn Books, 2001), 120.

[54] Carl Kaysen, "Refugees: Concepts, Norms, Realities, and What the United States Can and Should Do," in *Threatened People, Threatened Borders: World Migration and US Policy*, ed. Michael Teitelbaum and Myron Weiner (New York: Norton, 1995), 246.

[55] John Coleman Bennett, *Foreign Policy in Christian Perspective* (New York: Scribner, 1966), 57.

[56] Weiner and Teitelbaum, *Political Demography, Demographic Engineering*, 120.

reduce their susceptibility to this brand of coercion, NGOs and other norm-promoting actors simultaneously continue to push for the expansion of the definitions of who is worthy of protection and what constitutes morally appropriate behavior.[57] To the extent these initiatives are successfully—and on several fronts, the jury is still out—they increase target vulnerability to coercion by altruistically minded actors as well as by more self-serving ones.

Consider, for instance, the burgeoning influence of the human security movement and its supporters, who contend that the international community has an imperative to provide protection to vulnerable people of the world. Similarly, in response to the Australian reaction to the *Tampa* incident, Norway proposed new international legislation that would pledge all coastal states to accept shipwrecked boatpeople, wherever they are found.[58] Such progressive developments serve to further expose (and even, in some cases, increase) the contradictions between the competing domestic political imperatives of states and their domestic and international normative commitments. In other words, hypocrisy costs are not new, and their sources appear to be growing. Moreover, norms-promoting groups have also grown measurably more aggressive in their attempts to impose hypocrisy costs on states that appear to be in violation of their international obligations.[59]

When push comes to shove, it may appear to some targets that the only way to combat these ever-increasing and more visible contradictions is to do more to keep would-be refugees and migrants in their countries of origin. As states have come to view migrant flows as potential security threats to international and regional security, the UN Chapter VII "threat to international peace" clause has been invoked to justify intervening in internal conflicts, particularly if they are generating substantial outflows.[60] Indeed, the new paradigm of the refugee regime, according to Bill Frelick of the USCR, is "to prevent refugee flows from occurring rather than assist refugees in exile."[61] This is because, as another observer has suggested:

> It is not just the pictures of horror on the television screen that determine foreign policy today. It is the fear of massive immigration of refugees.... Civil

---

[57] See, for instance, Yasemin N. Soysal, *The Limits of Citizenship: Migrants and Postnational Membership in Europe* (Chicago: Chicago University Press, 1994); David Jacobson, *Rights across Borders: Immigration and the Decline of Citizenship*, 2nd ed. (Baltimore: Johns Hopkins University Press, 1997).

[58] "Norge Anbefaler Nye Lover om Flyktninger," *Aftenposten*, April 27, 2003.

[59] For one particularly potent example, see "UNHCR Slams Australian Treatment of Boat People," 2003, www.unwire.org/UNWire/20031112/449_10350.asp.

[60] Gil Loescher, "Protection and Humanitarian Action," in *Global Migrants, Global Refugees*, ed. Aristide R. Zolberg and Peter M. Benda (New York: Berghahn, 2001), 172.

[61] Bill Frelick, "Preventing Refugee Flows: Protection or Peril?" *World Refugee Survey 1993* (Washington, D.C.: U.S. Committee for Refugees, 1993), 5.

wars are nasty things—but it is when they threaten to erupt with hundreds of thousands of the poor and dispossessed crossing borders and destabilising their neighbours that outside action becomes necessary. A Europe and an America that were created out of the mass movement of persecuted or defeated peoples are no longer willing to accept this as the inevitable outcome of an unstable era.[62]

In sum, as long as potential target states remain keen to avoid letting refugees and migrants in and equally keen to avoid being seen as trying to keep them out, the desire to keep things uneventful at home may well lead to more political and military activism abroad. Nevertheless, because foreign activism often generates significant material costs that offset the hypocrisy costs it circumvents, it remains an open question whether and for how long target state voters and taxpayers will be willing to pay them.

Further Applications of the Theory

As noted at the outset, the use of population movements as instruments of coercion represents but one of the ways in which weak actors exploit the adherence of targets to legal norms while flagrantly violating those norms themselves. Another that has gotten a good deal of press in recent years is the use of civilian noncombatants to undermine the ability of powerful democracies to successfully conduct military operations. This application of the theory relies on undermining the overwhelming advantages advanced liberal states tend to possess in terms of firepower, technology, and training, by exploiting their respect for—and usual adherence to—the norm against targeting noncombatants. For instance, Somali warlords regularly used women and children as human shields against coalition forces during Operation Provide Comfort. During the 1999 war in Kosovo, Serb forces routinely exploited refugees as protection for their convoys to discourage the NATO alliance from attacking them, and in Bosnia, they used UN peacekeepers and aid workers as shields against air attack.[63] In the first phase of the ongoing conflict in Afghanistan, Taliban fighters regularly placed military equipment in the vicinity of population centers as a deterrent to attack; and in the latter phase, the use of human shields as a deterrent to targeting of personnel has become a regular feature of the conflict. When states engage in behavior that (appears to) self-consciously violate the norms they profess to espouse, combatants can then use the

---

[62] Adrian Hamilton, "Holding Back the Human Tide," *Observer*, July 10, 1994.
[63] Daniel Byman and Matthew Waxman, *The Dynamics of Coercion* (Oxford: Oxford University Press, 2002), 145.

media and norms-promoting groups to impose hypocrisy costs on their adversaries.[64] These examples represent only one dramatic and timely application of a norms-driven coercive strategy; there are numerous others— including torture, sanctions, embargoes, and terrorism—all of which deserve close examination. Comparing and contrasting findings across these various applications could also yield some important theoretical and policy implications in arenas far removed from migration.

Furthermore, states and their leaderships are not the only targets of hypocrisy-based political pressure. As noted at the outset, the avowedly green energy company, BP, is a recurrent target of environmentalists whenever it attempts to undertake actions that run counter to its stated environmentally friendly ethos. As one journalist has described the situation:

> It may seem unfair that BP is the target of environmental and social-responsibility movements. [Some might ask whether] Greenpeace et al. [shouldn't be] going after Exxon Mobil, which still tries to sow public skepticism towards global warming theories and has reportedly worked behind the scenes to remove a prominent scientist from the United Nations climate change panel and still refuses to pay $5 billion in punitive damages ordered by an Alaskan court after the 1989 Valdez oil spill? *But BP has, by virtue of its slogans and its actions, tried to seize the moral high ground and so is judged by a different standard.*[65]

For better and for worse, BP is far from alone. Norms, just like human beings, can be wielded as coercive weapons, and they can be wielded in the service of beneficent and altruistic goals, as well as self-serving and immoral ones.

---

[64] See, for instance, Thom Shanker, "Gates Tries to Ease Tension in Afghan Civilian Deaths," *New York Times,* September 18, 2008; Kelly M. Greenhill and Michael J. Boyle, "Killing with Kindness? The Impact of NGOs and IOs on Civilian Casualties in Wartime," paper presented at the 2008 Annual Meeting of the Political Science Association, Boston, August 2008.

[65] Darcy Frey, "How Green Is BP?" *New York Times Sunday Magazine,* December 8, 2002; National Public Radio, "No Cash on the Barrel, *On the Media,* August 24, 2007, www.onthe media.org/transcripts/2007/08/24/07.

Appendix

Coding Cases of Coercive Engineered Migration

Below are brief synopses of all possible cases of coercive engineered migration between 1951 and 2006 that I have identified as of this writing. Of these sixty-four cases, fifty-six appear definitive and eight are suggestive. The heading for each mini-case contains the following information:

1. The identity of the coercer(s), followed (in parentheses) by the type of coercer: G, generator; AP, *agent provocateur;* or O, opportunist
2. The identity of the target(s)
3. The year(s) of the real or threatened crisis
4. The identity [in brackets] of the displaced group
5. The outcome of the coercive attempt: *Success, Partial Success, Failure,* or *Indeterminate.*

For capsule presentations of this information, see again tables 1.1 and 1.3. The summaries themselves contain key details, including the objectives sought by the coercer(s). As appropriate, these mini-cases also highlight noteworthy idiosyncracies as well as broader historical consequences and policy implications.

Federal Republic of Germany (O)—United States, 1953 [East Germans]; *Partial Success*

In the early 1950s, widespread public discontent with the draconian economic policies of the East German Communist Party culminated in what became known as the June Uprising of 1953. The unrest also provoked the movement of over 300,000 people across the border into West Germany (the Federal Republic of Germany [FRG]) during 1952 and the first half of 1953. At the time, West German Chancellor Konrad Adenauer decried what he believed to be a deliberate attempt by the East Germans and the Soviets to alter the FRG demographic make-up while also self-consciously exploiting the ongoing crisis himself, with the objective of extracting political and financial assistance from the United States.[1]

As refugee numbers mounted, Adenauer publicly warned that the influx had the potential to destabilize the FRG, absent aggressive action and the infusion of substantial assistance. He further asserted that the crisis ought to be treated as an international problem (read a U.S. problem) because, he maintained, it resulted from the political shortcomings of the Potsdam Agreement.[2] With these assertions as a backdrop, Herbert Blankenhorn, a key Adenauer foreign policy advisor, traveled to Washington on a secret mission in March 1953 and asked for US$100 million. The following month, Adenauer made his own trip to the U.S. capital, during which he raised the request to US$250 million, to be divided between the FRG and West Berlin.[3]

Eisenhower administration officials were skeptical of Adenauer's dire prognostications about the possible fate of the FRG, believing instead that he was manipulating the crisis to improve his odds of winning the upcoming elections.[4] Nevertheless, they were prepared to reward Adenauer for his pro-Western stance and keen to bring what could have become a costly migration crisis to a close. Thus, "to satisfy Adenauer's domestic needs, [the United States] gave the appearance, publicly, of complying with his requests."[5] Although the amount the United States ultimately delivered was less than Adenauer had hoped (approximately $115 million), the financial infusion provided him with a highly publicized economic boost. He also obtained sought-after political support, including a U.S. diplomatic communiqué acknowledging the possibility of continued and enhanced burden sharing and aid to come.[6] Adenauer was decisively reelected in the fall of 1953. (Case 1)

[1] Soviet archives have since demonstrated, however, that Adenauer was wrong. Neither the Soviets nor the East Germans had instigated, or even favored, a massive outflow. See Valur Ingimundarson, "Cold War Misperceptions: The Communist and Western Responses to the East German Refugee Crisis in 1953," *Journal of Contemporary History* 29 (1994): 463–81. The United States seems to have recognized as much at the time. See DDEL, Papers as President of the United States (hereafter PAPUS) (Ann Whitman file), Dulles-Herter Series (hereafter DHS), Box 2; Walter B. Smith, Acting Secretary, "(Top Secret) Memorandum for the President, Subject: Clarifications of Conclusions on Psychological Warfare at the Chiefs of Mission Meetings in September," November 6, 1953.
[2] The Potsdam Agreement was drafted and adopted by the major World War II victors—the USSR, the United States, and the United Kingdom—in July and early August 1945. Among other things, it outlined policy for the occupation and reconstruction of Germany.
[3] Ingimundarson, "Cold War Misperceptions." (Notably, in his memoirs Adenauer makes no mention of this request, although he discusses this trip to Washington.)
[4] DDEL, PAPUS (Ann Whitman File), DHS, Box 2; "(Top Secret) Memorandum for the Secretary of State from the President" (attached to memo above it), October 23, 1953.
[5] Ingimundarson, "Cold War Misperceptions," 471. Eisenhower had just come into office that January and was committed to upholding his campaign promise to slash government spending.
[6] Ibid.

South Vietnam/U.S. Central Intelligence Agency (CIA) (G)— North Vietnam, 1954 [North Vietnamese]; *Failure*

Following the 1954 partition of Vietnam at the 17th parallel, the government of South Vietnam—with the active assistance of the U.S. CIA—instigated a mass migration from north to south. Article 14(d) of the 1954 Geneva Accords stipulated that "any civilians residing in a district controlled by one party who wish to go and live in the zone assigned to the other party shall be permitted and helped to do so by the authorities of that district" within a three-hundred-day period. Although a noteworthy number of Vietnamese surely would have moved south in any case, nothing was left to chance.

Under the leadership of Colonel Edward Lansdale, the Saigon office of the CIA launched a propaganda campaign and conducted psychological operations aimed at maximizing the size of the outflow. It sought to create the perception that North Vietnam was plagued with civil unrest and disorder, whereas South Vietnam was stable, welcoming, and economically vibrant.[7] For those it induced to leave, the CIA provided free transportation by air and sea.[8] In the end, somewhere between 450,000 and 1 million northerners (mostly Catholics) fled south.[9]

This mass migration, dubbed Operation Passage to Freedom, was intended to boost the anticommunist population of the south and, by extension, to dissuade the North Vietnamese leader Ho Chi Minh from pressing forward with demands for reunification elections—which the accords stipulated were to be held in July 1956.[10] The prodigious size of the outflow was expected to produce the added benefit of embarrassing and delegitimizing the North in the lead-up to the scheduled vote.[11]

Although many within the Eisenhower administration were dubious of the plan, Lansdale vehemently believed Hanoi would be deterred from demanding national elections after such a clear demonstration of the "bankruptcy" of the North

---

[7] George C. Herring, *America's Longest War: The United States and Vietnam, 1950–1975* (Boston: McGraw Hill, 1986), 44. The CIA hired astrologers to predict hard times in the north and good times in the south, disseminated horror stories of Chinese communist regiments raping young Vietnamese women and even spread rumors that those who stayed behind might be subject to a U.S. atomic bomb attack. Catholics in particular were encouraged to flee with slogans such as "the Virgin Mary is going south." Stanley Karnow, *Vietnam: A History* (New York: Viking Press, 1983), 221–22; Kathryn C. Statler, *Replacing France: The Origins of American Intervention in Vietnam* (Lexington: Kentucky University Press, 2007), 150.

[8] Seth Jacobs, *Cold War Mandarin: Ngo Dinh Diem and the Origins of America's War in Vietnam, 1950–1963* (Lanham: Rowman and Littlefield, 2006).

[9] It has been suggested that between 750,000 and 2 million more would have left had the Viet Minh not intervened. Herring, *America's Longest War,* 56; John Prados, "The Numbers Game: How Many Vietnamese Fled South in 1954?" *VVA Veteran* (January–February 2005), www.vva.org/archive/TheVeteran/2005_01/feature_numbersGame.htm; Robert Turner, *Vietnamese Communism: Its Origin and Development,* Hoover Institution Publication 102 (Stanford: Hoover Institution Press, 1975). Resettlement costs, which were borne almost exclusively by the United States, amounted to $80 million in 1955 and 1956 alone. Statler, *Replacing France,* 152.

[10] Karnow, *Vietnam,* 222.

[11] Jacobs, *Cold War Mandarin,* 45; Brian Crozier, "The Diem Regime in Southern Vietnam," *Far Eastern Survey* 24 (1955), 56.

Vietnamese regime and the popularity of the alternative.[12] Contrary to Lansdale's expectations, however, Ho was undeterred. He rationally surmised he would win any nationwide election; having come to the same conclusion, South Vietnamese Prime Minister Ngo Dinh Diem simply refused to hold them. The Eisenhower administration backed Diem up, asserting that free elections were impossible given current conditions in Vietnam; the Soviet Union and China did nothing. Absent external support, Ho was powerless to force the election question. Consequently, Lansdale's key objective was met, although not for reasons he anticipated. Vietnam would not be reunified for another two decades,

The U.S./South Vietnamese–instigated mass migration ultimately proved intensely counterproductive. For one thing, "the massive flight of the Catholics actually made [Ho's] rule easier, since their fanatical anti-Communism [did] not nag him."[13] For another, the outflow ironically helped to undermine Diem's own regime. Few of the refugees from the north ever effectively integrated into South Vietnamese society. And Diem's favoritism toward his northern co-religionists caused tensions that gave rise to what became known as the Buddhist crisis of 1963, which culminated in Diem's downfall and assassination. Furthermore, possibly the most important (and tragic) consequence of Operation Passage to Freedom was its U.S. policy legacy. It cemented in the minds of a number of political and military officials the idea that, having encouraged the flight south, the United States had a moral, political, and economic obligation not only to the refugees but also to ensuring that the South did not fall to communism, thus limiting U.S. options in the years that followed.[14] (Case 2)

Algerian rebels (AP)—French allies, particularly the United States, esp. 1956–1960 [Algerians]; (somewhat serendipitous) Partial Success

As the French-Algerian War (1954–1962) escalated, Algerian Front de Libération Nationale (FLN)/Armée de Libération Nationale (ALN) rebels increasingly undertook actions they anticipated would provoke repressive, refugee-generating reprisals by the French military. Such actions were part and parcel of FLN/ALN attempts to internationalize their struggle—a strategy viewed by many as the only successful path to independence.[15] The adoption of this strategy, the brutality of

[12] According to Lansdale, the communists' "stock with the public in North Vietnam was so abysmally low that they wouldn't dare put it to a vote, let alone chance a contest against Diem, whose popularity was at a peak." While acknowledging "powerful motivations for the rice-deficit North to gain control of the rice-surplus South," Lansdale was sure its leaders knew "they couldn't win this goal via the ballot box." L. Edward Lansdale, *In the Midst of Wars: An American's Mission to Southeast Asia* (New York: Harper and Row, 1972), 346–47, 348.

[13] Karnow, *Vietnam*, 224.

[14] Frankum, *Operation Passage to Freedom*, 207; Statler, *Replacing France*, 152.

[15] Alistair Horne, *A Savage War of Peace: Algeria, 1954–62*, rev. ed. (New York: Penguin Books, 1987), esp. chaps. 6, 12. Some insurgents even believed the United States could single-handedly force France to grant Algeria independence; the insurgents simply had to find a

the French response to it, and the brutality of French counterinsurgency tactics, more generally, led to the displacement of over 2 million Algerians over the course of the war. A significant majority of them found themselves languishing in refugee camps in Morocco and, especially, Tunisia. Taking advantage of the impunity that Tunisian "neutrality" offered the insurgents and the protection it granted their refugees, the ALN/FLN in turn used the camps as staging areas from which to launch cross-border attacks and ambushes.[16] In late summer 1957, the rebels stepped up these attacks, with the explicit intention of provoking a French response so as to gain international sympathy and support and to influence the debate in the UN General Assembly that fall.[17] But, although French casualties mounted as a result of ALN attacks, due to the Cold War context of the conflict the success of the internationalization strategy was limited.[18] Some criticisms were publicly and privately leveled, but support for France among its allies remained relatively steadfast, and episodic calls to intervene on behalf of the Algerian "victims" were summarily dismissed.[19]

Attitudes shifted decisively, however, after the French launched a retaliatory strike against the ALN-controlled Tunisian border village and refugee camp at Sakiet-Sidi-Youssef in early February 1958.[20] The timing of the attack could not have been less auspicious.[21] First, it was a market day, which heightened the civilian death toll from the attack. Second, Red Cross delegates had visited the village that morning to set up an infirmary and a school as well as to distribute refugee assistance. This meant that not only were the pre- and post-attack disparities abundantly evident but also that there were more outside observers in the area

way to convince it to do so. Irving M. Wall, *France, the United States, and the Algerian War* (Berkeley: University of California Press, 2001), 24.

[16] Horne, *Savage War of Peace*, 267. By 1958, the FLN infrastructure in Tunisia was reportedly the largest and most important element of its military and civilian logistical support system. Charles R. Shrader, *The First Helicopter War: Logistics and Mobility in Algeria, 1954–62* (London: Greenwood Press, 1999), 175.

[17] Wall, *France*, 102.

[18] Robert Asprey, *War in the Shadows: The Guerrilla in History* (New York: Doubleday, 1975), 661.

[19] The FLN was bemused by the concomitant U.S. commitments to opposing colonialism and opposing communism—which produced a schizophrenic policy that privileged Cold War imperatives over liberal principles while seeking to alleviate the humanitarian consequences of doing so. As one rebel mused, the United States "helps us through the U.N. with wheat and food, and . . . furnishes her ally, France, with the finest military hardware . . . to kill us off. Which way do the Americans want us, dead or alive?" Quoted in Yahia H. Zoubir, "US and Soviet Policies towards France in North Africa," *Canadian Journal of History* 30(1995), 458.

[20] In the months leading up to the French strike, numerous attacks had been staged from the village/refugee camp. In January, for instance, a French patrol was ambushed just outside Sakiet and a plane was brought down by machine-gun fire. The French responded with angry warnings, but on the morning of February 8, another plane was hit from Sakiet and forced to make an emergency landing. Three hours later, a squadron of U.S.-made B26 bombers flattened the village, leaving eighty-six dead and many more seriously wounded. A. Aroua, *Reading Notes on French Colonial Massacres in Algeria*, trans. J. Hamani-Auf der Maur, 1102, www.hoggar.org/books/Massacres/42Colonial.pdf.

[21] The bombing would have been less significant had France not already generated significant discomfiture among its allies with its devastating regroupment policies, widespread use of torture, and indiscriminate reprisal violence. Horne, *Savage War of Peace*, 243–44.

than usual.[22] Thus, when "journalists, film makers, Tunisian, French, foreigners rushed to the scene," the village that had been "untroubled in the morning was three-quarters in ruins."[23]

Regardless of whether the mission was authorized by the French government—debate persists even today—it was a monumental error, one recognized by French military intelligence as having "incalculable" tactical, diplomatic, and moral consequences.[24] Not only did the incident generate widespread international opprobrium, but it also catalyzed a French ministerial crisis and precipitated a shift (long-desired by the FLN) in the stance of French allies regarding both how the war should end and the nature of the postwar settlement (i.e., Algerian independence). In the end, although the Algerians lost on the battlefield, they won the political war, in no small (if serendipitous) part because of the opportunistic exploitation of their own refugees and the camps that housed them. (Case 3)

Austria (O)—United States and Western Europe, 1956 [Hungarians]; *Success*

By dint of its geographical location, Austria was predestined to become one of the countries most directly affected by the Hungarian Revolution of October–November 1956. The outflow of refugees from Hungary was initially modest and largely composed of communists unseated during the uprising. But, following the Soviet crackdown in early November, the numbers pouring over the Austrian border rapidly swelled to well over 150,000. Not only did this human tidal wave boost the population of Austria by about 3 percent over the course of just a few days, it also led to fears that the Soviet Red Army would soon follow the refugees and reoccupy the country, whose postwar occupation had ended only a year before.[25]

The economic and security dangers this massive influx presented for Austria were indisputable; the open question was how they would be managed and by whom. From the outset, the United States—which was arguably somewhat abashed about inadvertently contributing to the Hungarian crisis through its Cold War "liberation rhetoric"—had made clear its willingness to provide some material assistance.[26] As the crisis mounted, however, it soon became clear that Austrian expectations about what an acceptable aid package would consist of vastly outstripped what was on offer, both from the United States and Austrian Western European neighbors.[27]

[22] Ibid.; see also Wall, *France*, 111.

[23] Aroua, *Reading Notes*, 1102. Moreover, Red Cross trucks had been hit, and the majority of the victims were women and children.

[24] Wall, *France* 111. As Horne puts it, nothing "could have done more to 'internationalize' the war than the French bombing of Sakiet." *Savage War of Peace*, 250.

[25] Johanna Granville, "Of Spies, Refugees and Hostile Propaganda: How Austria Dealt with the Hungarian Crisis of 1956," *History* 91, no. 301 (2006): 62–90.

[26] DDEL, PAPUS (Ann Whitman file), DHS, Box 8; "Phone Calls, 11/9/56-5."

[27] Austria had particularly high expectations for the United States because it viewed U.S. radio broadcasts as instrumental in stimulating the crisis in the first place. Miklox Szabo,

Austrian officials then upped the ante by publicly announcing that if sufficient assistance were not quickly provided, Austria would be unable to "retain the refugees." Moreover, if efforts to resettle Hungarians elsewhere in the world were not accelerated, Austria would be "forced to introduce immediate measures" that might entail border closure and repatriation.[28] Such sentiments were echoed in private settings as well.[29] (Interestingly, the dynamic interplay that accompanied Austrian threats and U.S. responses was studiously monitored by diplomats in the Soviet Foreign Ministry.[30])

In short order, Eisenhower announced that the U.S. attorney general would use his discretionary authority to immediately grant admission to 15,000 additional refugees and that, when these numbers had been exhausted, the situation would be reexamined. Other countries responded in kind. Of the 175,369 refugees that crossed the Austro-Hungarian border between October 23, 1956 and September 13, 1957, 83 percent were transferred to other countries. In the end, the United States absorbed about 38,000, after initial offers to resettle the majority had to be scrapped due to congressional opposition.[31] Most significantly, only 12,000 (less than 7 percent) remained in Austria. Austria fared well on the financial front as well. All crisis-related costs were borne by outsiders.[32] Apparently concerned about potential hypocrisy costs, the United States agreed to pay a significant share of these costs even though it strongly suspected Austria was padding the bills to obtain additional funds. (On Vice-President Nixon's return from Austria in December 1956, he and his team reported that very "possibly the Austrians were exploiting the situation to obtain longer term profits in the construction of new housing units and in construction of barracks, etc."[33])

All this said, however, the Hungarian crisis was not one that the Austrians had sought; in fact, they surely would have eschewed it, given the option. Still, skillful and effective crisis manipulation left Austria far better positioned both economically and politically than would otherwise have been the case. It reportedly even

---

Homeless in the World (Budapest: Pannonia Press, 1960), 38, in Cheryl Benard, "Politics and the Refugee Experience," *Political Science Quarterly* 101 (1986): 39–62.

[28] Granville, "Of Spies, Refugees and Hostile Propaganda," 73. For his part, Charles D. Jackson, psychological warfare expert and Eisenhower advisor, urged quick action, warning that "if the pressure on Austria becomes much greater, it's conceivable that the Austrian border guards will be instructed to turn back the refugees." In point of fact, Austria did shut its borders for a time, forcing 17,000 or so to flee to Yugoslavia instead. DDEL, PAPUS (Ann Whitman file), NSC Series, Box 8, "313th Meeting of the NSC, February 21, 1957"; Ferenc Cseresnyés, "The '56 Exodus to Austria," *Hungarian Quarterly* 40 (1999): 86–101.

[29] During Vice President Richard Nixon's December 1956 visit, for instance, Chancellor Raab stated point-blank, "the present refugee problem clearly exceeds Austria's resources." DDEL, PAPUS (Ann Whitman file), NSC Series, Box 8, "313th Meeting of the NSC, February 21, 1957"; DDEL, PAPUS (Ann Whitman file), DHS, Box 8; Department of State, "Memorandum of Conversation," December 26, 1956, Subject: Hungarian Refugees.

[30] Granville, "Of Spies, Refugees and Hostile Propaganda."

[31] See, for instance, Melvin J. Lasky, ed., *The Hungarian Revolution* (New York: Praeger, 1957).

[32] The largest donors were, in descending order: the Vatican, Spain, France, the FRG, Switzerland, and the United States. Szabo, *Homeless in the World*, 63.

[33] U.S. State Department, "Memorandum of Conversation," December 26, 1956.

paved the way for Austria to shift its foreign policy orientation from a regional to a global focus.[34] (Case 4)

United States (G)—Soviet Union, 1961
[East Germans]; *Indeterminate*

In summer 1961, in the midst of the last major Cold War Berlin crisis, the United States at least entertained—and possibly implemented—a plan to use the threat of stimulating a mass migration westward to pressure the Soviet Union to back down on Berlin. In a partially declassified memo to U.S. Secretary of State Dean Rusk from Deputy Commandant Allen Lightner, the senior U.S. diplomat in Berlin, Lightner asserted that:

> the prospect of intolerable loss of refugees and/or fears of incipient revolt might well lead [Nikita] Khrushchev to cease pressing toward Berlin decision....In short, it is possible we may have here one of the most important deterrents to Sov[iet] action on Berlin, in which case situation perhaps calls for something more than "our helping advertise facts to the world." [text still redacted]...In this connection consideration might also be given to reminding Sov[iet]s through informal diplomatic channels of our restraint with respect to the refugees; fact that neither West Germans nor allies have ever urged East Germans to flee to the West; on contrary policy has been one of discouragement, and even at present time policy is to refrain from anything that could be construed as urging anyone to come West. At appropriate time might be useful to drop hints that we could easily change this policy which could overnight drastically worsen internal GDR [German Democratic Republic] situation....Sov[iet]s should realize it is neither in their interest nor ours that situation in East Berlin be permitted to deteriorate to point of internal disorders that could lead to uprising similar to 1953 or to Hungarian Revolt of 1956.[35]

Whether the United States followed through with this proposed plan remains unclear, although the proposal did receive further consideration by the John F. Kennedy administration. It is also noteworthy that the Berlin Wall was erected early the following month—making large-scale flight from the East impossible—and, following a short-term, albeit dangerous, escalation over an incident at Checkpoint Charlie, the Soviets did back down in Berlin.[36] (Case 5)

---

[34] Michael Gehler, "From Non-alignment to Neutrality: Austria's Transformation during the First East-West Détente, 1953–1958," *Journal of Cold War Studies* 7 (2005): 104–36.

[35] U.S. Department of State, telegram, "From US Embassy Berlin (Deputy Commandant Allen Lightner) to US Secretary of State, Refugee Problem May Deter Soviets from Going Ahead with Treaty," July 24, 1961, No. 87, Control No. 15686; see also U.S. Department of State, telegram, "From US Embassy Berlin (Dowling) to US Secretary of State," July 31, 1961. Both are available through the DNAS.

[36] Raymond L. Garthoff, "Berlin 1961: The Record Corrected," *Foreign Policy* 84 (1991): 142–56.

Cuba (G)—United States, 1965 [Cubans]; *at least Partial Success*

On September 28, 1965, Cuban President Fidel Castro announced that, on October 10, the port of Camarioca would be opened so that any Cubans who wanted to leave for "the Yankee paradise" could do so. Likewise, anyone who wished to travel to Cuba to retrieve relatives would be permitted to do so. By unleashing this demographic bomb against the United States, Castro effectively demonstrated how easily he could disrupt U.S. immigration policy. Virtually overnight, and with little warning, the Cuban government presented the Lyndon Baines Johnson administration with a major migration crisis.

Having failed to anticipate this possibility, the administration was ill-prepared to respond. U.S. officials were simultaneously concerned with the potential political, logistical, and economic problems associated with a massive influx and disturbed by the prospect that the spectacle would "make the US look powerless." LBJ and his advisors nevertheless felt they had little choice but to respond with contempt and call what they assumed was Castro's bluff.[37] Thus, on October 3, Johnson publicly proclaimed that the United States would continue to welcome all those Cubans who sought refuge.

Within a week it became evident that hundreds, if not thousands, of Cuban Americans were planning to travel to Cuba to claim relatives. By October 9, the exiles had organized a flotilla of boats and set out for Cuba. Confronting a larger and more imminent influx than anticipated, the very next day LBJ blinked and began a series of secret negotiations with Castro to normalize the outflow. The result was a Memorandum of Understanding that established procedures and means for the movement of Cuban refugees to the United States.[38] On the same day the memorandum was signed, Castro closed the port of Camarioca, limiting the total number of Cubans who reached U.S. shores during the crisis to fewer than 3,000.[39] (See chap. 2.) (Case 6)

Biafran rebels (AP/O)—United States, 1967
[Biafrans]; *Partial Success*

Within months of the outbreak of the Nigerian Civil War (or Biafran War) in May 1967, the breakaway region was encircled by far more powerful Nigerian government forces. After a year of fighting, Biafra had lost half of its territory, as well as all its major towns, airports, and seaports, its refining capacity, and

[37] David W. Engstrom, *Presidential Decision Making Adrift: The Carter Administration and the Mariel Boatlift* (Lanham: Rowman and Littlefield, 1998), 20.
[38] From LBJL, National Security Files of McGeorge Bundy, CHRON FILE Oct 21–31, 1965 [2 of 2], "Memorandum for the President from McGeorge Bundy, Subject: Latin American Developments," October 21, 1965. This was followed, that December, by the establishment of an open-ended airlift, which continued until 1973.
[39] LBJL, National Security Files of McGeorge Bundy, CHRON FILE Nov 1–12, 1965 [2 of 2], "Memorandum for the President from McGeorge Bundy, Subject: Latin American Developments," November 3, 1965; U.S. Coast Guard, *The "Other" Boatlift: Camarioca, Cuba, 1965,* www.uscg.mil/history/uscghist/camarioca1965.asp.

even its oilfields. What territory remained was choked with displaced people, and the regime was short on food, ammunition, and funding. In short, Biafra appeared on the brink of collapse. But skillful manipulation of the suffering of the refugees in the region allowed the Biafran leader (Lieutenant) Colonel Chukwuemeka Odumegwu Ojukwu to stave off defeat for far longer than anyone anticipated.

Ojukwu and his subordinates self-consciously undertook actions (and forbid others) that ultimately increased the number of war-related refugees and IDPs.[40] The Biafrans did so with the express intent of exacerbating and expanding the crisis to provoke international sympathy and guilt, encourage external intervention, and catalyze the provision and distribution of aid. So successful were these efforts that the end of the war found more than 3 million refugees crowded into a 2,500-square-kilometer enclave. As one observer put it, "Because direct appeals for war materials met with negative responses, it became clear to [the Biafrans] that a hunger wracked skeleton of a Biafran child with long arms, swollen legs and the dry face of an old man with protruding stomachs was a more effective way of appealing for help and converting sympathy into political action."[41] To ensure that the message about this somewhat self-inflicted humanitarian tragedy got out, the Biafran government hired international public relations firms to promote its cause.[42]

The plight of the Biafran displaced produced waves of alarm and anxiety in both Europe and the United States.[43] In fact, the war reportedly became the most pronounced issue in European foreign affairs in 1968, and, in the United States, was second only to Vietnam.[44] It also galvanized the largest privately organized relief operation in history to that point. At its height, more than forty relief flights (most also carrying arms and ammunition) made the flight every night.[45] These flights not only were vital in providing food and medical supplies, but also served as an invaluable source of revenue for the insurgents. Concomitantly, Ojukwu refused to allow the creation of a protected land corridor for the delivery of supplies; this worsened his own people's situation, but also ensured that the dramatic and telegenic airlift remained necessary.[46] A number of external actors were cognizant of the ongoing manipulation, but did little or nothing to stop it. A 1969 CIA report

[40] Joseph Thompson, *American Policy and African Famine: The Nigeria-Biafran War, 1966–1970* (New York: Greenwood Press, 1990).

[41] Interview with Ojukwu, quoted in Ted Gogote Badom, *Foreign Intervention in Internal Wars: The Case of the Nigerian Civil War 1967–70* (Lund: Studentlitteratur, 1997), 251–52.

[42] Clifford Bob, *The Marketing of Rebellion: Insurgents, Media, and International Activism* (New York: Cambridge University Press, 2005), 25.

[43] As one author put it, "The spectacle of mass starvation among refugees packed into fetid camps as the federal noose slowly tightened galvanized Western opinion." Martin Meredith, *The Fate of Africa: From the Hopes of Freedom to the Heart of Despair* (New York: Public Affairs, 2005), 204.

[44] John J. Stremlau, *The International Politics of the Nigerian Civil War* (Princeton: Princeton University Press, 1977), xii.

[45] These flights were made possible in large part because the United States sold eight long-range aircraft to a Catholic relief organization "at a laughable price." Meredith, *Fate of Africa*, 204.

[46] Ibid., 204–5.

admitted, for instance, "In an effort to obtain sympathy for its cause, Biafran leaders encouraged numerous foreign observers to visit refugee areas where conditions were worst....It seems reasonable to assume that most Biafran farmers and their families were not starving."[47]

Ojukwu and his supporters' machinations helped stave off defeat for the better part of two years; they obtained diplomatic support, food aid, and direct and indirect military assistance. Full-scale intervention was not forthcoming, however, and the Biafrans eventually lost the war. In the end, the competing configuration of great power interests in Nigeria blunted the impact of the support the Biafrans received and prevented a more uniform and concerted multilateral response.[48] Ultimately, therefore, the Biafrans were only partially successful in their use of coercive engineered migration.[49] (Case 7)

Israel (G)—Jordan, 1967 [Palestinians]; *Indeterminate*

At the conclusion of the Six-Day War in June 1967, King Hussein of Jordan alleged in talks with U.S. diplomats that Israel was attempting to force him into direct peace talks by threatening to overwhelm his country with war refugees.[50] (Roughly 500,000 Palestinians were displaced by the fighting, and a million were under Israeli control in what became known as the Occupied Territories.) This case is difficult to code for several reasons. On the one hand, public talks between Jordan and Israel were not held and the two countries did not sign a peace treaty until 1994; thus, one could reasonably code the case a failure. On the other hand, it is now known that Jordan was engaged in private discussions with the Israelis for several years before the Six-Day War—a fact unknown by the United States until at least 1967. Moreover, shortly after the war ended, Jordan reportedly did approach Israel with a peace plan that was designed to solve the refugee problem,

---

[47] Quoted in Zaki Laïdi, *The Superpowers and Africa: The Constraints of a Rivalry, 1960–1990* (Chicago: University of Chicago Press, 1990), 47.

[48] Whereas France, China, and Portugal provided military aid and diplomatic support, the United States refused to do so. As was the case in Algeria, during the Cold War the United States was generally more committed to supporting its (in this case, British) allies—which were steadfastly behind the Nigerian government—than to defending the right to self-determination. (The Soviets too supported the government.) As Assistant Secretary of State for African Affairs Robert Moore put it, in defending the U.S. decision not to take the issue to the UN, "In the view of so many states, the humanitarian and political issues are so intertwined that relatively few believe that one could be considered without the other. In this circumstance, serious doubts are unavoidable as to whether the UN at this time could help." *New York Times*, July 5, 1968.

[49] Still, the insurgents might be viewed as personally successful, although their rebellion was defeated. Ojukwu went into peaceful exile in Cote d'Ivoire, and efforts to have him extradited failed. The rebels were reabsorbed into the Nigerian federal army, and civil servants returned to their posts. "Nigerian Civil War," Library of Congress Country Studies, www. workmall.com/wfb2001/nigeria/nigeria_history_civil_war.html.

[50] LBJL, "(Secret) Telegram from Ambassador to Jordan, Burns to the Secretary of State," (circa) July 31, 1967, National Security Files of the Special Committee of the National Security Council, Box 11,12,13, Refugees Folder.

among other things; consequently, one might code the case as a success.[51] Finally, although it is clear that the Israeli leadership was keen to see as many Palestinians as possible leave Israeli territory—and, in fact, some harbored hopes that they could be resettled in Iraq[52]—whether Israel actually intended to use the refugee weapon to force Jordan to the peace table remains unclear. (In fact, Golda Meir once expressed fears that if Jordan produced a peace plan, Israel would unfortunately have to sign it.[53]) (Case 8)

Jordan (O)—United States, 1967 [Palestinians];
Short-term Success; Long-term Failure

King Hussein of Jordan also used the 1967 crisis (and same Palestinian refugees) to persuade the United States to increase its pressure on Israel to make concessions and to compel it to allow refugees from the war to return home.[54] The United States believed that repatriation of "West Bankers" would free the Jordanian government "from the immediate pressure of a new large homeless group that [would] blame the Government for its lot" while also helping the Jordanians "reinforce their claims that the *status quo ante* on the West Bank must be reestablished and that unilateral Israeli moves changing the complexion of the population cannot be tolerated."[55]

On one level, Hussein's demand was not unwelcome. U.S. diplomats acknowledged at the time that the crisis offered LBJ "a remarkably opportune justification for condemning Israel on an issue, which will help to indicate to moderate Arabs that we are sensitive to the needs of the Arab people without costing us politically at home."[56] McGeorge Bundy advised LBJ to "Put us on record in favor of a real attack on the refugee problem....This is good LBJ doctrine and good Israeli doctrine."[57] Moreover, like much of the rest of the world, administration officials had been moved by dramatic televised images of the displaced. These "ugly images" led many governments to demand that Israel allow the refugees to

---

[51] Tom Segev, *1967* (New York: Metropolitan Books, 2005), 517–18.
[52] This would be a kind of quid pro quo for Israeli acceptance of Iraqi Jews; ibid., 527.
[53] Ibid., chap. 21.
[54] In response to the U.S. ambassador's assertion that the ball was in Hussein's court to move the process forward, the king retorted that he could use the refugees to "launch a very effective international propaganda campaign against the government of Israel" if he chose. LBJL, National Security Files of the Special Committee of the National Security Council, Box 11,12,13, Refugees Folder: "(Secret) Telegram from Ambassador to Jordan, Burns to the Secretary of State," (circa) July 31, 1967.
[55] LBJL, National Security Files of the Special Committee of the National Security Council, Box 11,12,13, Refugees Folder: US Department of State Director of Intelligence and Research (Thomas L. Hughes), "(Confidential) Intelligence Note to the Secretary: West Bank Refugee Return Off to a Modest Start," July 19, 1967.
[56] Ibid.; "(Secret) Informal Memorandum (to Walt[er] Rostow and Mac[George] Bundy) on 'Israel's Approach to the Refugees,'" June 26, 1967.
[57] Quoted in Michael B. Oren, *Six Days of War: June 1967 and the Making of the Modern Middle East* (New York: Ballatine Books, 2002), 254.

return.[58] In short, the Johnson administration was, at least at the outset, willing to comply with the Jordanian appeal. To that end, Israeli Foreign Minister Abba Eban was told "the President meant business when he called for 'justice for refugees.' We will measure Israel's good faith in seeking reasonable settlement in large measure on this issue.... Without serious Israeli movement, there can be no peace, and it will become less and less possible for the United States to support reasonable Israeli demands."[59] Israel eventually agreed to allow a larger number to return as part of the well-publicized Operation Rescue. Initially, 20,000 were to return, but only 14,000 managed to do so before the operation was concluded.[60]

LBJ kept up the pressure for some months, and evidence suggests the Israelis found his threats persuasive. The Israelis feared, for instance, that the United States might withhold the fifty F-4 Phantoms they were keen to acquire if the Israelis failed to produce a plan to settle the refugees.[61] They even appear to have been convinced that the United States might force them to withdraw from the newly acquired territories.[62] With the administration increasingly distracted by the situation in Vietnam and the approaching election season, however, by February—March 1968, U.S. pressure had more or less ceased. In the end, the United States stood by Israel, did not compel it to withdraw from the territories, and did not uphold its threats regarding the Palestinian refugee problem. (Case 9)

Pakistan (G)—India, 1971 [East Pakistanis]; *Failure*

An estimated 10 million refugees crossed the border from East Pakistan into India following the outbreak of a civil war between the geographically divided eastern and western provinces of Pakistan in December 1971. India accused the Pakistani leadership of deliberately instigating the outflow both to solve its own internal

[58] Israeli ambassadors overseas wrote home that "television broadcasts from the bridges and tent camps set up by the UN on the eastern side of the river were damning.... 'The most terrible impression is made by scenes of fathers with children in their arms, begging our guards to let them go back to their wives and children still on our side,'" wrote Israel's ambassador in Germany. He added, "We cannot stand up, here or in other countries, to the wave of protest, which we believe will also have political implications." Segev, *1967*, 540–41. Even Israeli Foreign Minister Abba Eban was "shocked by scenes he saw on television during a visit to New York" and hastily arranged for "a televised return of [a small number of] refugees" (541).

[59] LBJL, National Security Files of the Special Committee of the National Security Council, Box 11,12,13, Refugees Folder: "(Secret) Memo For the Secretary from the Acting Secretary," undated.

[60] Segev, *1967*, 542.

[61] Ibid., 571–74. It is worth noting that the Israelis had conducted an internal study, which concluded that they could successfully relocate 250,000 families to the West Bank without incurring any significant economic hardship. But it was kept "top secret because it demonstrated there was no economic barrier to settling the refugees in the West Bank—a conclusion that could result in international pressure" (528n. 18).

[62] During a January 1968 meeting with Israeli Prime Minister Levi Eshkol, Johnson reportedly quipped that "You claim you want peace. In fact you only want a piece of this and a piece of that." Ibid., 573. See also Oren, *Six Days of War*, 326–27.

political problems—by forcing the East Pakistani Hindu population into India—and to pressure India into ceasing its support for Bengali freedom fighters, the Mukti Bahini.[63] (The Indians were indeed providing arms and logistical assistance, as well as refuge and training within India, for the insurgents.)

Unfortunately for Pakistan, however, Indian officials responded by declaring the potentially destabilizing inflow a *casus belli* and sending in its armed forces. Indeed, the Indian ambassador to the UN claimed that its use of force was a justified response to the Pakistani "new crime of 'refugee aggression.'"[64] Following less than two weeks of hostilities, the Indian occupation of East Pakistan led to the partition of the country, and the new state of Bangladesh was born.[65] Within months, the vast majority of refugees were repatriated. (Case 10)

Uganda (G)—United Kingdom, 1972 [British Ugandans]; *Failure*

On August 5, 1972, President Idi Amin announced his intention to expel all Asians from Uganda within three months, in what has been widely regarded as an act of simple economic expropriation (i.e., a case of dispossessive engineered migration). Up to 80,000 of those due to be pushed out were British passport-holders. However, this expulsion threat was issued more or less concomitantly with Amin's entreaties to the British to reverse their recently taken decisions to reduce military assistance to his country and cancel the dispatch of a military training team. The British reportedly decided to retract their support in the wake of a rising number of atrocities perpetrated against Ugandan civilians and, perhaps more important, the conduct of joint Soviet-African military exercises. Amin provided a ninety-day notice so the British could rescind their decision regarding aid and assistance. They did not oblige him.

Interestingly, the British appear to have anticipated that Amin might resort to the use of coercive engineered migration against them. In May 1972, High Commissioner Richard Slater sent a dispatch to the British Foreign Secretary, in which he noted that, although they (the British) would be unable to influence Amin by withdrawing support, any move taken against him "would be fraught with consequences for our community [i.e., the thousands of British passport-holders in Uganda] for which we are at present ill-prepared." Simon Dawbarn, Foreign Office official, later concurred, noting "we must go on doing business with Amin" because "we have too many hostages in Uganda," referring again to British passport-holders.[66] (Case 11)

---

[63] Richard Sisson, *War and Secession: Pakistan, India, and the Creation of Bangladesh* (Berkeley: University of California Press, 1990).

[64] United Nations Security Council Resolution, 1606th Meeting, December 4, 1971, 17.

[65] Myron Weiner and Michael Teitelbaum, *Political Demography, Demographic Engineering* (London: Berghahn Books, 2001), 129–30.

[66] Marc Curtis, *Unpeople: Britain's Secret Human Rights Abuses* (London: Vintage Books, 2004), excerpt available at: http://markcurtis.wordpress.com/2007/02/13/the-rise-of-idi-amin-in-uganda-1971-72/.

Bangladesh (O)—Burma, 1978–early 1980s
[Burmese Muslims (Rohingyas)]; *Success*

Bangladesh (O)—Burma, 1989–1992
[Burmese Muslims (Rohingyas)]; *Success*

In the early 1980s, Bangladesh responded to an influx of Burmese Muslims—created largely as a consequence of the Burmese policy of settling non-Muslim Burmese in the Arakan region—by threatening to arm the Bengali-speaking Muslim refugees (Rohingyas) and help them return to Burma if settlement was not halted. The Bangladeshis' threat succeeded in significantly reducing, but not wholly stopping, the outflow for the better part of the decade.[67] (This case illustrates the seemingly unusual situation in which a counter-crisis is threatened in response to an inflow.)

At the end of the 1980s, another outflow materialized, this time driven by Burmese government confiscation of land in the Arakan for a military base and the concomitant forced conscription of Rohingyas as unpaid laborers. The outflow ended with a signed agreement in April 1992, which provided for the "safe and voluntary" return of the Rohingyan refugees. During the reprise, Bangladeshi leverage may have been greater because aid for the Muslim insurgents was reportedly flowing in from outside sources, including Islamist organizations based in Pakistan and Saudi Arabia.[68] (Cases 12 and 31)

Association of Southeast Asian Nations (ASEAN) and Hong Kong
(O)—Western states, especially the United States, 1978–1982
[Vietnamese boatpeople, other Indochinese]; *Success*

In the wake of the wars in Vietnam, Cambodia, and Laos, over 1.4 million Indochinese fled, or were expelled from, their home countries. The numbers leaving Vietnam by sea grew rapidly in the late 1970s, giving rise to the term "floating human time bomb." In the four months between March and June 1979 alone, about 150,000 boatpeople arrived in East and Southeast Asia—about twice the number of all those resettled since 1975.[69]

As the outflow escalated, ASEAN member states issued a joint communiqué, warning that they had "reached the limit of their endurance and [had] decided they would not accept new arrivals."[70] As for those "'illegal immigrants/displaced

---

[67] Weiner and Teitelbaum, *Political Demography, Demographic Engineering*, 129; Myron Weiner, *The Global Migration Crisis: Challenge to States and to Human Rights* (New York: Harper Collins, 1995), 23.

[68] Myron Weiner, "Rejected Peoples and Unwanted Migrants in South Asia," in *International Migration and Security*, ed. Myron Weiner (Boulder: Westview Press, 1993), 159.

[69] W. Courtland Robinson, *Terms of Refuge: The Indochinese Exodus and the International Response* (London: Zed Books, 1998), 50.

[70] Speaking for ASEAN, more generally, the Singaporean foreign minister warned, "the exodus from Vietnam was a dangerous weapon aimed at the region. Each junkload of men, women and children sent to our shores is a bomb to destabilize, disrupt and cause turmoil

persons/refugees' already being given temporary shelter," if they were not returned or resettled *outside* the region in a timely fashion, all this "scum, garbage and residue"—as they called the displaced—would be expelled.[71] The communiqué followed close on the heels of a public statement by then Deputy Prime Minister Mahatir Mohamad that "any Vietnamese caught on Malaysian soil would be shot on sight."[72] Because Malaysia, Thailand, Singapore, and Indonesia received the majority of the initial arrivals, they were the first to implement what became known as the push-back policy, whereby boats were towed back to sea and refused landing. Later, many landed in Hong Kong, prompting its governor to likewise warn, "if nothing effective [is] done internationally, patience in the recipient territories could snap, with disastrous results."[73]

In short order, it became clear that Western states, and especially the United States, could no longer simply refuse to call the Indochinese "refugees" and hope that the neighboring states would accept responsibility for them. Their growing refusal to accept responsibility—coupled with dramatic, globally televised consequences of this shift in policy—generated enormous Western media attention and public concern. By early 1979, "the media began to depict the boatpeople as victims of 'an Asian holocaust.'"[74] The United States in particular was singled out for "unique responsibility towards the refugees from Indochina."[75] Treating the crisis as a local, regional problem was simply no longer an option.

Despite the fact that it was widely understood that the outflow was being (at a minimum) encouraged by the Vietnamese, neither the United States nor its allies had much leverage over Vietnam nor did they have much immediate desire to offer Vietnam rewards for stemming the flow. Consequently, targets effectively had only three choices: accede to the push-back policy and pay the associated hypocrisy costs, attempt to exert counterpressure on ASEAN countries and Hong Kong to accept the refugees and assume the strategic risks associated with doing so, and concede to the challengers' demands and bear the costs of the crisis.[76] The targets chose concession. To institutionalize the arrangement, an international conference

---

and dissension in ASEAN states. This is a preliminary invasion to pave the way for the final invasion." Quoted in ibid., 53.

[71] Quoted in ibid., 50–51. The widely publicized Malaysian refusal to permit 2,500 Vietnamese to disembark from a chartered freighter in November 1978 underscored the gravity of their demands. Barry Wain, "A Proven Way to Help Refugees—Brutality," *Wall Street Journal*, October 1, 1982. But the Malays were hardly alone. The Thais, Indonesians, Singaporeans, and Filipinos all pushed boats back to sea or set up naval blockades that prevented them from reaching territorial waters in the first place. Although good data are scarce, estimates placed the resulting death toll at about 200,000–250,000.

[72] Robinson, *Terms of Refuge*, 51; Gil Loescher and John Scanlan, *Calculated Kindness: Refugees and America's Half-Open Door, 1945 to Present* (New York: Free Press, 1986), 140.

[73] Leonard Davis, *Hong Kong and the Asylum Seekers from Vietnam* (New York: St. Martin's Press, 1991), 7.

[74] Loescher and Scanlan, *Calculated Kindness,* 140. See also Robinson, *Terms of Refuge;* Astri Suhrke, "Indochinese Refugees: The Law and Politics of First Asylum," *Annals of the American Academy of Political and Social Science* 476 (1983): 102–15.

[75] Quoted in Loescher and Scanlan, *Calculated Kindness,* 137–38.

[76] Because only the Philippines was a signatory to the 1951 Refugee Convention, UNHCR lacked leverage to persuade these states to provide even temporary asylum.

was held in Geneva in July 1979. The conference resulted in promises to double the number of third-country resettlement slots to more than a quarter million, to pledge financial payments to cover the costs of the resettlement, and to increase the provision of financial incentives to $160 million (more than double what had been provided during the previous four years). It also resulted in a promise from the Vietnamese government to "make every effort" to forestall departures in the first place.[77]

In short, the opportunistic challengers fared well, particularly in light of the fact that they were quite capable of absorbing the Indochinese had they so chosen. In the words of Poul Hartling, UN High Commissioner for Refugees, "the numbers involved in Southeast Asia [were] not unmanageable." Indeed, China and Vietnam accepted far higher numbers "with far fewer complaints." But these states wanted little to do with Vietnamese refugees, still less if they were ethnic Chinese.[78] And through the vigorous employment of ruthless tactics and skillful exploitation of the crisis, they succeeded in fully transferring the financial, political, and economic onus of settling these people to the West and, in the process, benefited financially.[79] In doing so, "control over the outflow of people from Vietnam was restored by undercutting the right of peoples facing persecution to move out of danger and flee their country."[80] (Case 13)

Vietnam (G)—United Nations Security Council/United States, late 1979 [Vietnamese boatpeople]; *Indeterminate*

On May 30, 1979, UNHCR and Vietnam signed a Memorandum of Understanding, which served as the foundation for what became known as the Orderly Departure Program (ODP). The idea was that lists of would-be departees would be matched with lists from potential receiving countries. Those who appeared on both lists would be allowed to leave. Those who appeared on only one list would be subjects of discussion and negotiation.

It remains somewhat unclear whether the Vietnamese extracted a quid pro quo, although given shifts in their behavior prior and subsequent to this period it is at least possible that they did.[81] U.S. Senator Ted Kennedy had recommended that the United States offer various inducements to Vietnam "with a view

---

[77] Loescher and Scanlan, *Calculated Kindness*, 145; Office of the UN High Commissioner for Refugees (UNHCR), *State of the World's Refugees 2000* (Geneva: UNHCR, 2000), 84.

[78] Robinson, *Terms of Refuge*, 51–52.

[79] Gervase Coles, "Approaching the Refugee Problem Today," in *Refugees and International Relations*, ed. Gil Loescher and Laila Monahan (Oxford: Oxford University Press, 1989), 380; Robinson, *Terms of Refuge*, 51–52.

[80] Loescher and Scanlan, *Calculated Kindness*, 145–46.

[81] At the time, some observers questioned Vietnamese motives. Some asked whether the Vietnamese were attempting to extract concessions and improve their international standing (as they explicitly did a decade later). Others suggested they were simply attempting to impart some legitimacy to ongoing attempts to export "undesirable elements, like the ethnic Chinese." Robinson, *Terms of Refuge*, 57.

toward resolving outstanding bilateral issues including the refugee problem."[82] It is, however, also possible that Vietnam feared a cutoff in extant assistance from elsewhere in the world (e.g., the European Community) if it failed to cooperate.[83] (U.S. attempts to resume relations with Vietnam during 1977 and early 1978 had foundered on Vietnamese insistence that U.S. reconstruction aid precede the establishment of diplomatic relations.[84]) In any case, Vietnam explicitly promised UN Secretary General Kurt Waldheim that "for a reasonable period of time, it would make every effort to stop illegal departures." And virtually overnight, arrivals plummeted, from 56,941 in June 1979, to 17,839 in July, and 9,734 in August. In the final four months of the year, the number fell still further, to approximately 2,600 per month.[85] (Case 14)

Thailand (O)—United States and China, 1979–1980s
[Cambodians/exiled Khmer Rouge]; *Success*

The Vietnamese invasion of Cambodia in December 1978 stimulated a massive outflow of Cambodians to surrounding countries, including Thailand. At first, the numbers were relatively small, and the Thais wavered about how to respond. But, over time the numbers grew significantly, and in March 1979, the Thai Army commander-in-chief announced, "We think we have had enough trouble and need not increase the size of the burden.... When they have recovered, they will be pushed back across the border."[86] The Thais then episodically closed the border to further arrivals and undertook mass deportations and push-outs.[87] Both China and the United States responded rapidly.[88]

Although Thailand remained concerned about the burdens the Cambodians would impose, its leaders "determined rapidly to avail themselves of insistent Chinese offers of assistance for Thai security and for Khmer resistance to Vietnam's occupation of Cambodia."[89] In addition to bearing much of the financial burden for the Cambodian refugees, the Chinese government pledged to decrease support for insurgents operating in Thailand, to guarantee Thai security in the event of a Vietnamese attack, and to sell the Thai government oil at subsidized rates.[90] For its part, the United States agreed to support the Thai military, and

[82] Loescher and Scanlan, *Calculated Kindness*, 138.
[83] See ibid., 143.
[84] Ibid.
[85] Ibid., 145–46.
[86] Robinson, *Terms of Refuge*, 45.
[87] Ibid., chap. 4.
[88] We now know that the United States and China cooperated in this decision. Zbigniew Brezezinski, then U.S. national security advisor, has since averred, "I encouraged the Chinese to support Pol Pot. I encouraged the Thai to help the D.K. [Democratic Kâmpuchéa]." Quoted in Elizabeth Becker, *When the War Was Over* (New York, Touchstone, 1986), 440.
[89] Daniel Unger, "Humanitarian Assistance in Cambodia," in *Refugee Manipulation: War, Politics and the Abuse of Human Suffering,* ed. Stephen Stedman and Fred Tanner (Washington, D.C.: Brookings Institution, 2003), 27.
[90] William Shawcross, *The Quality of Mercy: Cambodia, Holocaust and Modern Conscience* (New York: Simon and Shuster, 1984), 126, in Fiona Terry, *Condemned to Repeat? The Paradox*

Bangkok became the principal residual U.S. ally on the Southeast Asian mainland throughout the decade that followed.[91] The United States also agreed, along with other donor states, to contribute to a kind of parallel fund-matching program designed to directly benefit Thais and the Thai government, called the "Thai affected villages" program.[92] Although the result was not coercion-related, Thailand further benefited from the refugees' presence because they provided a buffer between itself and the Vietnamese Army.[93] (Case 15)

Haiti (G)—United States, 1979–1981 [Haitians]; *Success*

In the years following the dictator Papa Doc Duvalier's accession to power in Haiti in 1957, tens of thousands of middle-class professionals fled from Haiti to the United States. This exodus continued after Duvalier's son, Baby Doc, assumed power in 1971. Migration flows from Haiti to the United States became politically problematic at the end of that decade, when the number of Haitian migrants began to skyrocket while their average socioeconomic status concomitantly began to plummet.[94] This numerical upsurge culminated in an outflow that was deemed to be one of crisis proportions, and that was cited in 1980 by then presidential candidate Ronald Reagan, in conjunction with the concomitant Mariel crisis, as proof of the incumbent President Carter's ineffectual leadership.[95]

Eager to avoid being similarly tarred, in January 1981, shortly after his inauguration, President Reagan formed a task force dedicated to tackling the issue of Haitian migration. Soon thereafter, in one of the few documented examples of a preemptive concession to coercive engineered migration, Reagan and Baby Doc concluded the U.S.-Haiti Interdiction Agreement. Under the agreement, the United States obtained the right to summarily return all Haitians intercepted at sea, after a preliminary screening for potential asylum claimants. For its part, Haiti agreed to keep outflows to a minimum. In return, officially, the United States offered only financial assistance in implementing the bilateral accord and a promise to provide Haitians with more nonimmigrant visas. Off the record, however, U.S. officials admitted they had also promised to "de-emphasize human rights" and "look the other way on graft and corruption" inside Haiti, as well as to provide "significant" economic and security-related financial support.

of Humanitarian Action (Ithaca, N.Y.: Cornell University Press, 2002), 121. See also Robinson, *Terms of Refuge*, 27–28.

[91] Gil Loescher, *Refugee Movements and International Security* (London: Brassey's for the International Institute for Strategic Studies, 1992), 35.

[92] Benard, "Politics and the Refugee Experience," 623.

[93] Myron Weiner, *Security, Stability and International Migration* (Cambridge, Mass.: Center for International Studies, 1991).

[94] Christopher Mitchell, "US Policy toward Haitian Boat People, 1972–93," *Annals of the American Academy of Political and Social Science* 534 (1994), 69.

[95] See, for instance, Antonio de la Cova, "U.S.-Cuba Relations during the Reagan Administration," in *President Reagan and the World* (London: Greenwood Press), 381–92.

The Haitian Navy also reportedly obtained free fuel from the U.S. Coast Guard, which it was then able to sell on the open market.[96] (See chap. 4.) (Case 16)

Haitian-focused NGOs (AP/O)—United States and Haiti, 1979–1981 [Haitians]; *Failure*

During the 1979–1981 migration crisis, a group of Haitian nongovernmental activists seeking to discredit and ultimately bring down Baby Doc Duvalier's regime not only encouraged Haitians to flee the island but also—once on U.S. soil—to declare themselves (truthfully or not) victims of direct persecution. Despite widespread abuses in Haiti, the scheme rarely worked; of the 30,000 or so Haitians who arrived in the United States between 1972 and 1980, fewer than 100 were granted refugee status.[97] Nevertheless, the advocates surmised that by fixing the attention of the U.S. media on Haitian migrants—via maximizing asylum claims, encouraging "hunger strikes and letter-writing campaigns within detention camps, and frustrating efforts to disperse Haitians outside South Florida"—they would simultaneously pressure the U.S. government to cease its support for Baby Doc and delegitimize the Haitian leader.[98] Although the United States did eventually withdraw its support for Duvalier, the timing and circumscribed nature of its policy shift in early 1986 suggests that this shift was driven less by the migrant activists' actions than by the growing strength of the rebellion on the ground in Haiti, which began the previous year. (Case 17)

Pakistan (O)—United States, c. 1980–1989 [Afghans]; *Success*

By playing on mounting U.S. fears about communist penetration within South Asia, Pakistan successfully exploited the refugees generated by the Soviet occupation of Afghanistan both to strengthen itself domestically and to raise and improve its international diplomatic stature. The Soviet invasion provoked a massive exodus across the Pakistani border, initially at a rate of 1,000 per day, which rose to 5,000 per day during the first half of 1981 as a consequence of Soviet tactics designed to empty rural areas.[99]

[96] Alex Stepick, "Unintended Consequences: Rejecting Haitian Boat People and Destabilizing Duvalier," in *Western Hemisphere Immigration and United States Foreign Policy,* ed. Christopher Mitchell (University Park: Pennsylvania State University Press, 1992), 147. See also Stepick, "The Haitian Exodus: Flight from Terror and Poverty," in *The Caribbean Exodus,* ed. Barry B. Levine (Westport, Conn.: Praeger, 1987), 148; Jorge Dominguez, "US-Latin American Relations," in *Immigration and US Foreign Policy,* ed. Robert W. Tucker, Charles B. Keely, and Linda Wrigley (Boulder: Westview Press, 1990), 158.
[97] Loescher, *Refugee Movements and International Security,* 37.
[98] Michael Teitelbaum, "Immigration, Refugees, and Foreign Policy," *International Organization* 38 (1984), 440.
[99] U.S. Memos on Afghanistan from Zbigniew Brzezinski to James E. Carter, "Reflections on Soviet Intervention in Afghanistan," December 26, 1979, www.cnn.com/SPECIALS/cold.war/episodes/20/documents/brez.carter/.

In exchange for agreeing to serve as a refuge for more than 3 million displaced Afghanis and a base of operations for Afghan insurgents, Pakistan became a major strategic ally of the United States and received a significant boost in military and economic aid. This in turn allowed Pakistani leader General Zia ul-Haq to modernize the Pakistani military and acquire an array of sophisticated weaponry.[100] Moreover—and very important to Zia—the United States was compelled to cease its criticism of the repressive policies of his regime as well as refrain from raising objections to the Pakistani nuclear program.[101] In fact, archival evidence suggests that the United States may have even materially aided Pakistani nuclear development during this period.[102] (Case 18)

Soviet Union (G)—Pakistan, 1979–1989 [Afghans]; *Failure*

Afghan insurgents (O)—Pakistan, 1979–1992 [Afghans]; *Success*

Although Pakistan benefited significantly from hosting Afghan refugees, doing so also made it susceptible to alleged attempted coercion both by the Soviets and by the refugees themselves. On one side, the Pakistani government believed the Soviets were pushing refugees out, in part to force it to seek a settlement with the Afghan regime and to convince it to stop providing military aid to the insurgents, paid for by the United States.[103] The United States supplied approximately $2 billion in military aid to the Afghan fighters between 1982 and 1992. If this was indeed the intent of the Soviets, it clearly failed.[104]

The refugees, on the other hand, were more demonstrably successful in influencing Pakistani behavior. Threats from Mujaheddin leaders—including that they would "make the refugee camps in Pakistan ungovernable if Pakistan [struck] an unacceptable peace agreement"—reportedly deterred Pakistan from signing agreements with either the Russians or successive Afghan governments. The refugees' perceived capacity to destabilize Pakistan likewise rendered futile Pakistani government attempts to persuade the rebels to sign on to the UN peace plan.[105] (Cases 19 and 20)

---

[100] Ibid. To get a sense of the largesse involved, consider that the United States offered a $400 million short-term military aid package shortly after the invasion, which was increased to $3.2 billion in 1981, and so on. Barnett Rubin, *The Fragmentation of Afghanistan* (New Haven: Yale University Press, 2002), in Terry, *Condemned to Repeat?* 59.

[101] Terry, *Condemned to Repeat?* 66. See also Frédéric Grare, "Afghan Refugees in Pakistan," in *Refugee Manipulation: War, Politics and the Abuse of Human Suffering*, ed. Stephen Stedman and Fred Tanner (Washington, D.C.: Brookings Institution, 2003), 57–94.

[102] "Draft Memo to the Secretary of Defense, Subject: Your Meeting with President Zia ul-Haq," October 1, 1986, 2, DNAS. In addition, throughout the time that it hosted the refugees, Pakistan reportedly poached the "best choice of any weapons and aid channeled through them to the resistance and the refugees." Benard, "Politics and the Refugee Experience," 623.

[103] U.S. Department of State, *Afghanistan: Eight Years of Soviet Occupation* (Washington, D.C.: U.S. Government Printing Office, 1987).

[104] Weiner, *Global Migration Crisis*, 32.

[105] Loescher, *Refugee Movements and International Security*, 51–52. See also Ahmed Rashid, "UN Presses Ahead with Afghan Peace Meeting," *Independent*, January 10, 1992; Helga

Cuba (G)—United States, 1980 [Cubans]; *at least Partial Success*

What became notoriously known as the Mariel boatlift was a mass migration from Mariel Harbor in Cuba to the state of Florida within the United States between April and October 1980. Although Fidel Castro had warned the previous month that he might open the borders of his country unless the United States was more responsive to his outstanding demands regarding the problem of hijackings in Cuba—among other things—the crisis was catalyzed by up to 10,000 economically disaffected Cubans attempting to gain asylum in the Peruvian Embassy in early April. Much as he had done fifteen years before during the Camarioca crisis, Castro announced that anyone who wanted to leave could do so, and an impromptu exodus organized by Cuban Americans (with the explicit consent of Castro) commenced in earnest. Like LBJ before him, U.S. President James E. Carter initially responded with contempt to Castro's threats, publicly announcing that the United States would welcome fleeing Cubans with "open hearts and open arms." Both Cubans and Americans took Carter at his word.

At the peak of the boatlift, about 2,800 Cubans were arriving in Key West, Florida, every day. Faced with mounting domestic opposition to the exodus—particularly once it became clear that Castro was peppering the departing boats with criminals and the mentally ill—Carter ordered the Coast Guard to prevent boats from leaving for Cuba and to seize vessels returning with refugees. Those who were undeterred (and caught) were indicted. The U.S. measures slowed the flow but did not stop it. The United States then offered to negotiate with Castro to stop the outflow. He refused, saying he would talk to the United States but "not only about refugees."[106] Castro finally halted departures on September 25, following a belated U.S. offer to accept terms proposed by the Cubans that the National Security Council had deemed too placatory the previous spring. (See chap. 2.) (Case 21)

Austria (O)—NATO member states, 1981-1982 [Poles]; *Success*

To stifle what was viewed as a worrying rise in the number of Polish refugees seeking asylum, in December 1981, Austria declared fleeing Poles "economic refugees" and closed its border to them. (The number of Poles seeking asylum had more than tripled over the previous year.) After the Polish government coincidentally declared martial law within a few days, Austria felt compelled to reverse its decision; however, it refused to bear the burden alone. In response to U.S. President Reagan's early December offer of food aid, Austrian Chancellor Bruno Kreisky retorted, "We have enough flour, sugar and rice. The Americans

Baitenmann, "NGOs and the Afghan War: The Politicization of Humanitarian Aid," *Third World Quarterly* 12 (1990): 62–85.

[106] Felix Roberto Masud-Piloto, *From Welcomed Exiles to Illegal Immigrants: Cuban Migration to the US, 1959–1995* (Lanham: Rowman and Littlefield, 1996), 85.

should take more refugees instead."[107] In the end, Austria successfully "bargained with western powers to receive substantially more assistance in exchange for the renewed open-door-to-Polish refugees policy."[108] In addition, of the 33,000 refugees subsequently admitted, nine out of ten were resettled in third countries.[109] (Case 22)

Thailand (O)—United States and France, 1982
[Vietnamese boatpeople]; *Success*

Despite the existence of earlier agreements, in 1982, Thailand again delivered "ominous warnings" that it had been "too merciful" vis-à-vis the Vietnamese boatpeople it was hosting and would not continue to "bear an endless burden" of refugees much longer.[110] Further promises of assistance from France and the United States, however, relatively quickly led the Thais to relent and allow the Indochinese to remain.[111] (Case 23)

Honduras (O)—United States, early 1980s
[Nicaraguan *Contras* and civilians]; *Success*

Taking advantage of Reagan administration concerns about the spread of communism in Latin America in the early 1980s, the Honduran government successfully leveraged its agreement to host exiled armed Nicaraguan rebels (the Contras) to boost the power of its military and significantly increase the amount of U.S.-provided military assistance and training it was receiving. In concrete terms, economic aid to Honduras doubled (from $24 million) between 1979 and 1980, and by 1982, Honduras was the second highest recipient of military aid in Latin America, receiving $31.2 million in 1982 (as opposed to the $32.5 million it received from 1946 to 1981).[112] Two years later, military aid reached $78.5 million and economic aid reached $168.7 million.

This profitable arrangement suited the Honduran leadership quite well until the U.S. Congress terminated aid to the Contras. This decision reportedly "caused shudders" in the Honduran government and military command. Honduran officials began to fear that the Contras within the refugee population—thwarted from seizing control of Nicaragua and left to fend for themselves—would

---

[107] "Austria Finds Polish Inflow a Burden," *New York Times,* January 10, 1982. See also "Polish Refugees Wait and Watch," *New York Times,* December 21, 1981.

[108] Benard, "Politics and the Refugee Experience," 621.

[109] UNHCR (Austria), "A Long Tradition of Assisting Refugees," www.unis.unvienna.org/documents/unis/25vic/25years_vic_unhcr.pdf.

[110] Leo Cherne, "Closing the Doors to People in Danger," *Washington Post,* October 21, 1982.

[111] John P. Rogge, "Thailand's Refugee Policy: Some Thoughts on Its Origin and Future Direction," in *Refuge or Asylum,* ed. Howard Adelman and C. Michael Lanphier, 150–71 (Toronto: York Lane Press, 1990).

[112] Terry, *Condemned to Repeat?* 90.

destabilize their country.[113] Thereafter, Honduran demands for aid in exchange for allowing the refugees to stay grew significantly. In early November 1984, the Honduran government requested an official security pact with the United States and a doubling of economic aid. The United States was "unenthusiastic about concluding such a treaty, fearing that singling out Honduras would devalue the security arrangements with other Latin American countries."[114] It nevertheless complied with Honduran demands both for the pact and for further aid. In exchange for continued Honduran cooperation, the United States guaranteed that it would defend Honduras in the event of an attack from Nicaragua as well as pledged to provide whatever aircraft were necessary to "maintain Honduran air superiority over Nicaragua."[115] In addition, the Reagan administration circumvented congressional obstacles by hosting joint military maneuvers—some of which required the (more or less permanent) construction of military facilities, the allocation of communications equipment (later left behind), and the expansion and improvement of Honduran airstrips.[116] Moreover, when Sandinista forces did cross the border in hot pursuit of the Contras in 1986, U.S. troops and helicopters mobilized with the Honduran military "in a large and threatening show of force."[117] (Case 24)

Bangladesh (G)—India, mid-1980s–1997
[Chittagong Hill Tribes]; *Indeterminate*

In conjunction with attempts to demographically reengineer the area in favor of their co-ethnics, throughout the 1980s and into the early 1990s, the Bangladeshi government used a variety of means to push the Chakmas (who are members of the Chittagong Hill Tribes) out of Bangladesh and into the Indian state of Tripura. Bangladesh engaged in a series of systematic expulsions, the largest of which took place in 1986. In doing so, the Bangladeshis explicitly sought to convince the Indians to stop funding the separatist Shanti Bahini insurgent group, which the Indians eventually did.[118] A peace agreement—essentially a tripartite concord among Bangladesh, the Shanti Bahini, and India—was signed in 1997.[119] Although evi-

---

[113] James Chase, "In Search of a Central American Policy," *New York Times*, November 25, 1984.

[114] Ibid.

[115] James LeMoyne, "U.S. Said to Plan a Long Presence in Honduras Bases," *New York Times*, July 13, 1986.

[116] Over 800 tons of weapons were supplied to Honduras and El Salvador in 1985 and 1986 alone. Terry, *Condemned to Repeat?* 88–89; see also Eva Gold, "Military Encirclement," in *Reagan versus the Sandinistas: The Undeclared War on Nicaragua*, ed. Thomas W. Walker (Boulder: Westview Press, 1987), 42–43.

[117] James LeMoyne, "Honduran Tells of US Pressure," *New York Times*, April 3, 1986. See also Gold, "Military Encirclement," 51.

[118] Sanjoy Hazarika, "Bangladeshi Insurgents Say India Is Supporting Them," *New York Times*, June 11, 1999.

[119] M. Rashiduzzaman, "Bangladesh's Chittagong Hill Tracts Peace Accord: Institutional Features and Strategic Concerns," *Asian Survey* 38 (1998): 653–70.

dence suggests the Chakma expulsions played some role in Indian decision making, it is unlikely to have been particularly decisive. Because this case was drawn
out over a period of several decades, other factors may have also been in play.
Therefore, we cannot reasonably ascribe too much weight to the unique power of
the migration weapon. (Case 25)

East Germany (AP)—West Germany, 1983–1986 [mixed]; *Success*

In the early 1980s, the East German (GDR) government, led by President Erich
Honecker, began placing travel services advertisements throughout the Middle
East and South Asia, promising "comfortable flights" to East Berlin and "quick
and smooth transit" into the West.[120] Under the scheme, would-be asylum seekers
from Third World nations could fly to Schoenefeld Airport in East Berlin on Soviet
bloc airlines and, once there, be granted transit visas that allowed them to enter
West Berlin unimpeded.

In short order, the number of asylum seekers in West Germany rose precipi-
tously, climbing 109 percent between 1984 and 1985. By the following year, nearly
half of all of the displaced in Western Europe sought asylum in West Germany,
and between 700 and 1,000 refugees per week were pouring into West Berlin from
the eastern sector.[121] Refugee fatigue rapidly set in. Opinion polls showed growing
disaffection with handling of the issue, and mobilization among those opposed to
admission steadily grew. The inflow also divided the sitting center-right coalition,
with the centrist Free Democrats resisting demands from some of then Chancellor
Helmut Kohl's Christian Democrats for legislation that would soften the right to
political asylum enshrined in the Constitution.[122] The more conservative members
of Kohl's coalition, especially the Christian Social Party of Bavaria, demanded that
the Constitution be amended to eliminate the right to refuge.

Following a series of high-level meetings, in September 1986, East Germany
agreed to bring the crisis to an end in exchange for hundreds of millions of dollars of additional aid and a variety of other concessions, including a substantial
increase in interest-free credit for trade between Bonn and East Berlin.[123] The West
Germans also approved two agreements East Germany had "insistently sought"
for some time: an accord on environmental aid, under which Bonn agreed to help
pay to clean up East German industrial pollution, and a technology transfer agreement, which resulted in long-desired technical and scientific cooperation. It has

[120] Leslie Collitt, "Surge of Refugees Alarms West Berlin," *Financial Times,* January 18, 1986.
See also Elizabeth Pond, "Asylum-seekers Flock to West Germany," *Christian Science Monitor,*
July 31, 1986.
[121] "Refugee Rebuke by Kohl—West German Chancellor says East Germany Encouraging
Third World Citizens to Flood West Berlin," *Guardian,* August 4, 1986.
[122] "Bonn, Feeling Pressure of Voters, Is Trying to Curb Refugee Influx," *New York Times,*
August 24, 1986.
[123] John Tagliabue, "East Germans to Help Bonn Stem Flood of Third-World Immigrants,"
New York Times, September 19, 1986.

also been argued that East Germany may have successfully used the crisis to gain leverage in its diplomatic relations with Moscow.[124] (Case 26)

East Germany (AP)—Sweden, c. 1984–1985
[mixed, largely South Asian]; *Success*

In the fall of 1985, East Germany successfully used the facilitated "travel to the West" strategy to extract financial aid from Sweden. For normative as much as legal reasons, the Swedish government felt compelled to offer asylum status to a large number of the South Asians (mostly Sri Lankan Tamils) who had managed— with East German help—to reach the country. Having fled from a country at war, these asylum seekers were more difficult to cast as economic migrants, even if that was what many of them were. Consequently, the Swedes were eager to staunch the influx. In exchange for an undisclosed amount of aid, East Germany stopped the transit of asylum seekers.[125] (Case 27)

Libya (G)—Tunisia, Egypt, and Mauritania, 1985
[North African guestworkers]; *Indeterminate*

In September 1985, Libya expelled about 100,000 immigrant workers to neighboring Tunisia and Egypt. At the time, observers believed that Libyan leader Muammar Gaddafi was "using economic necessity to make a political point." Although Libya was in the midst of a serious economic decline (with oil revenues down from US$22 billion per year in 1981 to $8–10 billion in 1985[126]) and thus facing a broad-based labor surplus, he singled out for expulsion foreign workers from countries then at odds with his own—particularly, Tunisians, Egyptians and Mauritanians.[127] At the time, Gaddafi explicitly said he was unhappy about being excluded from the treaty of mutual respect among Tunisia, Algeria, and Mauritania, and he also suggested that Egypt rethink its ties with the United States.[128]

---

[124] Milan Svec, "A New Use for the Line between East and West," *Christian Science Monitor,* October 8, 1986.

[125] Loescher, *Refugee Movements and International Security.* Some sources suggest that the Swedes and Danes both "reached understandings on restrictions with East Germany." James M. Markham, "Europe Seeks to Dam a Flood of Third World Refugees," *New York Times,* May 10, 1987.

[126] This was made worse by U.S.-imposed sanctions and trade bans; see John Haldane, "Qaddafi's Quagmire," *Washington Report on Middle East Affairs* (Washington, D.C.: American Educational Trust, December 30, 1985).

[127] Ibrahim Fawat, "Libya: Economic Crisis, Political Expulsions," *AfricAsia* 22 (October 1985): 32–43.

[128] The Treaty of Fraternity and Concord that reportedly so exercised Gaddafi originated in 1983 as a bilateral agreement between Tunisia and Algeria. The treaty pledged each nation to respect the other's territorial sovereignty, to refrain from supporting insurgent groups in the other country, and to refrain from the use of force in resolving diplomatic conflicts. the accession of Mauritania to the treaty motivated the conclusion of a corresponding bilateral agreement between Libya and Morocco, the Treaty of Oujda in August 1984.

Although the evidence is suggestive, it is insufficient to declare this a bona fide case of attempted coercion because the expulsions continued and expanded to include foreign workers from a broader array of countries well into the following year. It is nevertheless worth noting that just a few years later Libya was invited to join an economic and political union that included all five Mahgreb nations, the Union of the Arab Maghreb (Union du Maghreb Arabe, UMA).[129] (Case 28)

Hong Kong, ASEAN (O)—especially the United States, United Kingdom, and France, 1989–1990
[Vietnamese boatpeople; other Indochinese]; *Success*

In the late 1980s, a new outflow of Vietnamese commenced, this time from the north of the country, which had been under communist control since 1954. In response, Hong Kong threatened to revoke first-asylum status and begin summary repatriation of all Vietnamese on its soil. This plan was abandoned, however, when the United States made an unexpected offer to directly resettle half the refugees that found themselves in Hong Kong. Although the acting refugee official at the U.S. Consulate claimed at the time that this shift did not in fact represent any change in U.S. policy, other officials acknowledged otherwise.[130]

ASEAN member states soon followed Hong Kong's lead and again threatened to push back/push out the Indochinese or end asylum altogether. It quickly became evident that bilateral emergency actions—such as the one offered by the United States to Hong Kong—would neither be domestically sustainable nor solve the growing problem.[131] So, as had been the case approximately a decade before, an international conference was convened, which resulted this time around in the first UNHCR-brokered package deal, the Comprehensive Plan of Action (CPA). Under the CPA, those fleeing would no longer automatically be considered prima facie refugees but only asylum seekers, who would have to apply individually for refugee status. Recognized refugees would receive resettlement opportunities in third countries. Those denied refugee status would be returned to their countries of origin, principally Vietnam and Laos. The UNHCR—through donor-country funding—covered the costs of the asylum seekers and provided further assistance to countries of first asylum.

Financial assistance was likewise provided to those who were repatriated and to the communities that agreed to take them back. (In the decade that followed, UNHCR spent more than US$70 million in Vietnam.) The program largely succeeded, and the remaining camps for Indochinese were closed in May 1996. By the end of May 1998, approximately 110,000 boatpeople had returned to Vietnam from the camps and detention centers in the ASEAN countries, Hong Kong,

[129] Edmund Jan Osmanczyk, *Encyclopedia of the United Nations and International Agreements* (London: Taylor and Francis, 2002), 1321.
[130] The change was made in part to stave off criticism of U.S. opposition to mandatory repatriation. See Robinson, *Terms of Refuge*, chap. 8.
[131] UNHCR, *State of the World's Refugees 2000*, chap. 4.

and Japan.[132] The first-asylum countries not only relieved themselves of a long-festering problem, but also derived further financial benefits for their trouble.[133] (Case 29)

Vietnam (O)—United Nations Security Council/United States, late 1980s (especially 1989) [Vietnamese boatpeople]; *Success*

In the midst of the 1989–1990 crisis (case 29), the Vietnamese government took advantage of the extant vulnerability exhibited by the United States and its allies to extract a variety of economic and diplomatic benefits for itself. Vietnam explicitly and successfully conditioned its cooperation vis-à-vis the CPA (see case 29) and the organized repatriation scheme on the willingness of the West to effect the integration of Vietnam back into the world economy to provide access to international credit, and to extend diplomatic recognition, especially by the United States.[134] The International Monetary Fund (IMF) resumed lending to Vietnam in October 1993, and the World Bank and the Asian Development Bank soon followed suit. In 1995, the United States lifted its twenty-year embargo on trade and later that year normalized diplomatic relations. Vietnam was welcomed into ASEAN that same year.[135] A credit and community development program, funded primarily by the European Union, was also established, with the purpose of anchoring would-be exiles in their own communities and promoting the reintegration of those who returned from first-asylum countries. At the same time, more than half a million people were able to emigrate from Vietnam in a legal manner.[136] With these outcomes in mind, Vietnam was arguably the biggest beneficiary of the 1989 crisis. (Case 30)

Saudi Arabia (G)—Yemen, 1990 [Yemeni guestworkers]; *Failure*

On September 19, 1990, after Yemen refused to support the Saudi Arabian decision to host foreign troops in the wake of Saddam Hussein's invasion of Kuwait, the Saudis announced that all Yemeni guestworkers had two months to find a sponsor or face expulsion. The Yemeni government was reportedly caught by surprise and stunned by the strength of the Saudi response. By the November deadline, somewhere between 650,000 and 800,000 Yemenis were pushed out, swelling the

[132] UNHCR, "The United Nations High Commissioner for Refugees," http://www.un.org.vn/unag/unhcr1/unhcr.htm.

[133] Robinson, *Terms of Refuge*, chap. 8.

[134] Vaughn Robinson, "Security, Migration and Refugees," in *Migration and Public Policy*, ed. Vaughan Robinson (Cheltenham, UK: Edward Elgar, 1999), 85.

[135] Steve Crawshaw, "Pressure Mounts on Boat People to Go Home," *Independent*, January 31, 1996.

[136] UNHCR, "Vietnamese Boat People: The End of the Story," in *State of the World's Refugees, 1995* (Geneva: UNHCR, 1995), 208–9.

population of Yemen by more than 5 percent and drying up the lucrative remittances (~$2 billion per year) on which many poorer Yemenis had relied.[137]

It was widely understood in Yemeni government—as well as reported in the non-U.S. press—that the Saudis had issued their demand with the expectation that Yemen would reverse its position, support the Saudi decision, and later join the coalition against Saddam. But not only did the Saudi expulsions fail to achieve these objectives, they also created antipathy toward Saudi Arabia and King Fahd and created localized labor shortages within the Saudi kingdom. One reason the gambit foundered may be the fact that some Yemenis believed the Saudis had an additional, and still less acceptable, objective—to force Yemenis to sign a treaty resolving a border dispute over a region where more than 1 billion barrels of new oil reserves had just been discovered. This demand too went unheeded.[138] (Case 32)

Israel (AP/O)—Palestinians, 1990s [Soviet Jews]; *Failure as of this writing*

United States (O)—Israel, 1991–1992 [Soviet Jews]; *Partial, Short-term Success*

In a clear case of dispossessive engineered migration—which appears concomitantly to be a coercive case—throughout the 1990s, Israel agreed to accept and integrate Jews who wished to emigrate from the (former) Soviet Union. The new arrivals were moved into disputed territories or into strategically important locations in Jerusalem where they would alter the demographic balance between Arabs and Jews. At least some Israelis viewed this move as an explicit method of deterring or undermining Arab designs on the city. As the mayor of Jerusalem put it, "The solution is to bring as many immigrants to the city as possible and make it an overwhelmingly Jewish city, so that they will get it out of their heads that Jerusalem will not be Israel's capital."[139] The influx of Soviet Jews thus reportedly became critical to the "expansion and affirmation" of Israeli territorial hegemony; they were even termed by some "settlement fodder."[140] As of this writing, however, Palestinian claims on Jerusalem have not ceased.

In the context of this same influx, the United States sought to use its financial leverage over Israel to counteract these activities, arguing that Israeli refugee settlement policy was damaging Middle East peace negotiations. (This case is somewhat unusual in that the United States threatened to withhold money to indirectly make the situation worse rather than more directly affecting it.) In March

[137] Patrick Cockburn, "Crisis in the Gulf: Immigrant Yemenis Incur Saudis' Wrath," *Independent*, November 24, 1990; Ray Jureidini, "Middle East Guestworkers," in *Immigration and Asylum from 1900 to the Present*, ed. Matthew Gibney and Randall Hansen (Oxford: ABC-CLIO, 2005), 205.

[138] William Drozdiak, "UN Force Resolution Dangerous, Yemen Says; Bush Urged to Send Envoy to Meet Iraqis," *Washington Post*, November 26, 1990.

[139] Quoted in Joost Hiltermann, "Settling for War: Soviet Emigration and Israel's Settlement Policy in East Jerusalem," *Journal of Palestine Studies* 20 (1991): 82.

[140] Robinson, "Security, Migration and Refugees," 85–86.

1990, U.S. Secretary of State James Baker threatened to withhold $400 million in housing loans to settle the Soviet refugees unless Israel promised not to use the funds to locate them in any of the territories acquired during the 1967 War. After an escalation of tensions, however, the Bush administration backed down, and on November 2, 1990, agreed to release the funds.[141]

The stakes were raised the following year—and the outcome was quite different—when Bush refused an Israeli request for $10 billion in bank loans, to be used to settle Soviet refugees in the West Bank. In fact, the Labor Party's public opposition to the proposed settlements and the implication that their suspension would lead the United States to change its position may even have been a factor in the Labor victory over Likud in June 1992.[142] Government-sanctioned settlements were suspended after Labor assumed power, although settlers continued to build "unauthorized outposts."[143] (Cases 33 and 34)

Albania (G)—Italy, 1990–91 [Albanians]; *Success*

Italy/European Community, August 1991 [Albanians]; *Success*

In March 1990, a mass exodus from Albania to Italian Adriatic ports commenced. Although those fleeing were initially viewed with some sympathy by the government and the Italian people, this sentiment quickly evaporated.[144] The Italians initially tried to persuade Albanians without employment to return home in exchange for US$40, a new pair of pants, and a T-shirt. When that failed, the government declared the fleeing Albanians to be migrants (rather than refugees) and commenced repatriation.[145] This proved embarrassing and politically damaging, however, when "scenes of the flight of Albanians, their arrival, and their forcible repatriation were dramatically captured by European television."[146] Desperate to end the crisis after an influx of approximately 20,000 people, the following month the Italians cut a deal. Albanian President Ramiz Alia agreed to enforce stricter departure controls against his own people in exchange for Italian food aid and credits to shore up the Albanian economy. In August 1991, however, after concluding that Italy was moving too slowly in providing the promised assistance, Albanian authorities facilitated another mass departure. Italy and its EC partners responded with a sweeter and speedier economic aid package, and the crisis was brought to a close.[147] This is not to suggest that the entire outflow was engineered—many Albanians left of their own accord. Nevertheless, when the

---

[141] Hiltermann, "Settling for War."

[142] David Bar-Ilan, "Why Likud Lost—and Who Won," *Commentary* 94 (1992): 28.

[143] Greg Myre, "Israel Pledges to Dismantle 24 West Bank Settlements," *New York Times*, March 13, 2005.

[144] Jessika ter Wal, "Racism and Cultural Diversity in the Mass Media," 2002, 250–51, http://eumc.eu.int/eumc/material/pub/media_report/MR-CH4-8-Italy.pdf.

[145] Ankica Kosic and Anna Triandafyllidou, "Albanian Immigrants in Italy: Migration Plans, Coping Strategies and Identity Issues," *Journal of Ethnic and Migration Studies* 29 (2003), 999.

[146] Weiner, *Global Migration Crisis*, 60.

[147] Loescher, *Refugee Movements and International Security*, 33.

government in Tirana cracked down on the departures, the crisis abated and then ended. (Cases 35 and 36)

Albania (G)—Greece, 1991–1994 [Albanians]; *Success*

Concomitant with the outflow of Albanians across the Adriatic Sea (cases 35–36), Greece faced growing numbers of Albanians crossing its mountainous land border. In response, Greece separately agreed to pour substantial aid into its neighbor; this included food aid and economic credits. The program, known as the Mini-Marshall Plan, targeted specifically, but not exclusively, ethnic Greeks. In 1993 alone, Greek investments in Albania totaled approximately US$44 million, second only to the Italian investment of $72 million.[148] In exchange, the Albanian government promised to exercise stricter immigration controls and keep Albanians at home and out of Greece. (Case 37)

Poland (G)—United States/European Community, spring 1991 [Poles]; *Indeterminate*

In the midst of the first Italian-Albanian crisis (case 35), Polish President Lech Walesa warned of an Albanian-like exodus from his country if Poland failed to receive sufficient economic assistance and debt relief from the West.[149] The following week, President George H. W. Bush announced that the United States would forgive 70 percent of the Polish debt to the United States, reducing it from $3.8 billion to $1.14 billion. At the same time, Bush publicly encouraged the Paris Club of industrialized countries to go beyond the 50 percent reductions already approved.[150] Finally, President Bush also proposed a $45 million private-sector initiative over two years to facilitate investment in Eastern and central Europe.

At this point, it cannot be said with certainty that Bush's decision was driven by Walesa's threat. But the timing and nature of the U.S. offers are suggestive. It is also clear that Walesa benefited politically at home from the outcome at a time when Poles were facing another round of harsh austerity programs designed to curb rising inflation.[151] (Case 38)

Ethiopia (reverse G)—Israel, 1991 [Falashas]; *Success*

In May 1991, in the midst of the U.S.-sponsored peace negotiations between rebels and the Ethiopian government following the fall of President Mengistu Haile

---

[148] Nicholas Glytsos, "Problems and Policies Regarding the Socio-economic Integration of Returnees and Foreign Workers in Greece," in *Migration and Public Policy* 33, no. 2 (1995): 155.
[149] Loescher, *Refugee Movements and International Security*, 33.
[150] The Paris Club is an informal group of official creditors whose role is to find coordinated and sustainable solutions to the payment difficulties experienced by debtor nations.
[151] Bailey Morris, "Time to Put the West's Money Where Its Mouth Is," *Independent*, March 24, 1991.

Mariam, the Ethiopians demanded, and received, more than $36 million before it would permit 16,000 Falashan Jews to emigrate to Israel and before the peace process could move forward. In essence, "the future of 45 million people hung in the balance," while the migration crisis was being settled.[152] (Case 39)

Turkey (O)—United States, 1991 [mostly Iraqi Kurds]; *Success*

The Shiite and Kurdish uprisings in Iraq immediately following the end of the First Gulf War triggered a crackdown that sent some 350,000–500,000 Kurds fleeing toward Turkey. At the time, the Turks asserted that the Kurdish mass migration was not simply a consequence of Iraqi counterinsurgency operations but, rather, a deliberate policy of retribution by the Iraqi leader for their having sided with the U.S.-led coalition during the war.[153] Regardless of Iraqi leader Saddam Hussein's intent, after several hundred thousand Kurds crossed the border into Turkey, the Turks—who were having problems with their own Kurdish minority—closed the border and demanded that their ally, the United States, assume responsibility for the refugees.

The Bush administration initially rejected Turkish demands and agreed to provide only basic humanitarian assistance (largely via airdrops), hoping that the problem would resolve itself (i.e., that Kurds would return home). The Kurds, who feared further Iraqi retaliation, did not oblige. As the numbers of displaced mounted and reported deaths approached 1,000 per day along the sealed border—a fact that received worldwide media coverage—the United States reversed its position.[154] Despite opposition both from Iraq and from the Pentagon, the U.S. government (in conjunction with the United Kingdom) announced that it would spearhead an unprecedented humanitarian intervention, establishing a safe haven (and, subsequently, a no-fly zone) within northern Iraq. The safe haven—authorized by UN Resolution 688—was a path-breaking initiative; it marked the first time that the Security Council authorized UN action in an humanitarian crisis and deviated markedly from its traditional unwillingness to violate the sovereignty of a member state.

In the end, the Turks got exactly what they demanded, although their demands were arguably more modest than they should have been, given the size and scope of the Kurdish-based insurgency that the Turks found themselves fighting for much of the decade that followed.[155] As for the Kurds, the intervention permitted an

---

[152] Richard Dowden, "Addis Ababa Tricked into a 'Soft Landing'; The People of Ethiopia's Capital Feel Betrayed by the US Decision to Back the Rebel Advance on the City," *Independent*, May 31, 1991; see also Paul Boyle, Keith Halfacress, and Vaughn Robinson, *Exploring Contemporary Migration* (New York: Prentice-Hall, 1998).

[153] Clyde Haberman, "After the War; Turks Say Hussein Plotted to Drive Out the Kurds," *New York Times*, April 12, 1991.

[154] John Cassidy and Margaret Driscoll, "New Hope for Kurds as US Troops Fly In," *Times*, April 14, 1991.

[155] Marvin Lipton, "Kurds Create Diplomatic Dilemma," *Toronto Star*, April 22, 1991.

estimated 1.5 million who had fled to Turkey (and Iran) to return and allowed them to form their own government and protected quasi-state within Iraq. (Case 40)

Jean-Bertrand Aristide of Haiti (AP)—United States, 1992–1994 [Haitians]; *Success*

In the period between December 1992 and September 1994, exiled Haitian President Jean-Bertrand Aristide twice successfully exploited the threat of mass migrations from Haiti to the United States to extract political concessions from President William Jefferson Clinton. Because Clinton had promised to reverse the U.S. policy of summary repatriation of Haitian migrants if he was elected, on the eve of his 1992 inauguration, it appeared that an influx of as many as 150,000 Haitians was imminent. Eager to avoid such a politically problematic outcome, Clinton promised Aristide that he would aggressively intervene diplomatically to see Aristide returned to power in exchange for Aristide's assistance in forestalling the outflow. Aristide agreed, and through assistance from his supporters on the ground in Haiti and direct appeals to Haitians to stay at home, the crisis was averted.

However, when more than a year had passed, and there were few signs that Aristide was any closer to regaining power, he went on the offensive. With assistance from a variety of public and political figures, he forced the Clinton administration to undertake a variety of policy shifts, which resulted in a new spate of boat building on the ground in Haiti and portents of a new crisis. By the summer 1994, another mass migration appeared imminent. Clinton again appealed to Aristide for assistance, but this time Aristide refused; in fact, he encouraged Haitians to take to the seas. More than 30,000 did exactly that before the Clinton administration launched a military operation to reinstall Aristide in power in Port-au-Prince in September 1994. This coercive attempt took longer than Aristide had hoped and expected, but it was, in the end, a clear success. (See chap. 4.) (Case 41)

Bosnians (G/AP)—United Nations Security Council, 1992–1995 (especially 1993–1994) [Bosnians]; *Partial Success*

Throughout the 1992–1995 Bosnian War, Bosnian Muslim (Bosniak) forces routinely exploited their own displaced populations in attempts to force NATO and/or UN forces to take stronger action against the Serbs.[156] Refugee-related actions took two forms: outmigration-generating actions designed to generate anxiety within

---

[156] Such assertions—and examples of these attempts—were commonplace in my interviews with French, American, British, and German UN, UNHCR, and NATO officials, 1997–2001. Manipulation of refugees and noncombatants was not limited to the Bosnians; however, it was widely asserted that they engaged in it most frequently. This is not especially surprising. First, the Bosnians were widely viewed as the greatest victims of this war, so they were the most likely to succeed at generating international sympathy and corresponding action. Second, they were the weakest group and therefore the most likely to feel the need to resort to this unconventional weapon.

Western Europe about mounting numbers of asylum seekers and outmigration-prohibiting actions designed to generate international outrage and calls to act as a result of the humanitarian consequences of forcing would-be refugees to stay. Such actions were reportedly undertaken "even to the extent of launching offensives that would delay aid convoys to starving enclaves, on the grounds that this would place even greater pressure on the UN mandate and increase the demands for more robust international intervention."[157] Moreover, secure in their position as the victims in this war, Bosnian forces even broke ceasefires and launched attacks, confident that blame would be ascribed to another faction.[158]

In terms of actions that specifically involved the movement of people, reports have surfaced that Bosniak forces did not defend the safe area of Gorazde, for instance, in the expectation that the humanitarian consequences (read more casualties and refugees) would increase pressure on NATO to take more aggressive action.[159] Likewise, in April 1993, government officials in Srebrenica reportedly held their own people hostage, refusing point-blank to allow civilians to be evacuated without a UN agreement to deploy troops in Srebrenica and to evacuate all wounded from the area by air—including military as well as civilian casualties.[160] In the end, NATO did intervene; however, the wait was a long and costly one, and only partially driven by the migration-related crises/catastrophes to which the Bosnians found themselves subjected.[161] (Case 42)

Poland (O)—Germany, 1994 [Poles]; *Success*

The German government acquiesced to a demand by Poland for $76.4 million in compensation in exchange for agreeing to take back rejected Polish asylum seekers.[162] (Case 43)

Cuba (G)—United States, 1994 [Cubans]; *Success*

In August 1994, in the wake of some of the worst civil unrest that Cuba had witnessed in decades, President Fidel Castro reversed the long-standing Cuban policy

---

[157] William Shawcross, *Deliver Us from Evil* (New York: Simon & Schuster, 2001), 97–98.

[158] Miles Hudson and John Stanier, *War and the Media: A Random Searchlight* (Bodmin, UK: Sutton Publishing, 1997), 292. General Sir Michael Rose, who commanded UN troops in Bosnia-Herzegovina during the war, echoed these claims, asserting that the Bosniaks were trying to "create images of war for the world, to get us to respond with air power." Quoted in Steven L. Burg and Paul Shoup, *The War in Bosnia-Herzegovina: Ethnic Conflict and International Intervention* (Armonk, N.Y.: M. E. Sharpe, 1999), 153.

[159] See, for instance, Oliver Ramsbotham and Tom Woodhouse, *Humanitarian Intervention in Contemporary Conflict: A Reconceptualization* (Cambridge, UK: Polity, 1996), 186; Terry, *Condemned to Repeat?* chap. 1.

[160] "Stalemate," *McNeil-Lehrer News Hour*, April 6, 1993, transcript #4600.

[161] See, for instance, Warren Bass, "The Triage of Dayton," *Foreign Affairs* 77 (1998): 95–108, on the role of Op-Plan 40410 in forcing the U.S. government's hand and precipitating greater NATO involvement.

[162] Robinson, "Security, Migration, and Refugees," 85.

of arresting anyone who tried to escape from the island by sea. Castro laid the blame for Cuba's domestic unrest on the United States, claiming that the riots were caused by rumors of a U.S.-sponsored boatlift to Miami. Castro then demanded "either the US take serious measures to guard their coasts, or we will stop putting obstacles in the way of people who want to leave the country, and we will stop putting obstacles in the way of people in the US who want to come and look for their relatives here."[163] This invitation, coupled with a threat, marked the beginning of a major, albeit brief, refugee crisis, during which tens of thousands fled the island and headed toward the coast of Florida.

The crisis ended after about a month, following the announcement of an unprecedented immigration accord between the United States and the Caribbean island nation. This accord marked the beginning of the end of the three-decade-long U.S. policy of welcoming all Cubans as de facto refugees and the start of their being treated (at least on paper) like other groups trying to gain entry to the United States; a follow-up accord eight months later solidified this policy shift, although its implementation was complicated by myriad other U.S.-Cuban diplomatic issues (e.g., the Brothers to the Rescue shoot-down in 1996; see chap. 2) (Case 44).

Zaire (O)—Western great powers (especially the United States, United Kingdom, France, and Belgium), mid-1990s [Rwandan Hutus]; *Success*

In the wake of the 1994 Rwandan genocide and the accession to power of the Tutsi-led Rwandan Patriotic Front, well over 1 million Hutus fled to neighboring Zaire. Zairean President Mobutu Sese Seko made clear that his willingness to host the refugees was conditioned on his successful acquisition of a variety of political and financial concessions. As a result, sheltering the refugees provided him with not only a lever to attempt to destabilize the new Tutsi-dominated government in Rwanda but also an opportunity to extract political and financial concessions from the international community, particularly France, Belgium, and the United States, states which, among other things, quietly dropped their ongoing pressure for Mobutu to surrender power.[164]

In the years leading up to the crisis, France, Belgium, and the United States had been pushing Mobutu to concede power to the opposition and hold free elections. In the wake of the riots that had swept the country in 1991, France had suspended aid and even refused Mobutu a visa. The United States too had been pressing hard—using "diplomatic iciness and suspension of aid to prod Mobutu toward reform—but this changed with the emergence of the crisis."[165]

[163] Fidel Castro, "La Razon Es Nuestra: Comparencia de Fidel Castro en la TV Cubana y las Ondas Internacionales de Radio Habana Cuba," televised speech, Editora Politica, 1994. See also Masud-Piloto, *From Welcomed Exiles to Illegal Immigrants*, chap. 9, esp. 137–44.

[164] Chris McGreal, "Escalating Ethnic Conflict Threatens to Destroy Zaire: Africa's Grisly Harvest of Death," *Observer*, October 27, 1996.

[165] Chris McGreal, "World Pays New Respect To Zairean Leader after Favours over Refugees," *Guardian*, August 10, 1994.

The crisis also offered Mobutu an opportunity to "restore his international credibility" by demanding renewed attention and deference from vulnerable world leaders. As one Western diplomat in Zaire said, it was all music to Mr. Mobutu's ears: "Mobutu really cares about turning his image around. He wants to restore his international credibility.... This is a golden opportunity for him."[166]

After about a year, in August 1995, Zairean troops marched into several refugee camps, forced families on to buses and trucks, and dumped them across the Rwandan border. Over the course of a week, approximately 15,000 people were forcibly repatriated. The UN Security Council was swift to condemn the action, and Mobutu quickly called what observers viewed as simply a diplomatic stunt to a halt. Had Mobutu been serious about closing down the camps, however, he likely would have targeted the Hutu militia leaders in the camps, who, in keeping the refugees in fearful thrall, were known to be most responsible for preventing repatriation. He also probably would have ordered a larger and more comprehensive repatriation operation. Hence, most concluded these limited expulsions were simply a ploy to squeeze more money from donor nations and to sow panic in Rwanda.[167] This was not a new strategy for Mobutu, who had, throughout the Cold War, held Washington hostage to his demands and tried to "shake [the United States] down" for more aid and favors.[168] It had worked before, and it worked again.

Nevertheless, it is possible that Mobutu may have envisioned a somewhat larger outflow than the "token" 15,000 pushed out because, although the international community was outraged at the expulsion, Zaireans were overjoyed by it. Exasperated by a year of environmental degradation, dramatic increases in food prices, and a crime wave all blamed on the refugees, Zaireans fully supported the move to repatriate the Rwandans by force if necessary.[169] A lack of discipline among Zairean troops, however, meant that many spent more time looting and drinking during the expulsion than rounding up Rwandans.[170] In any case, the 15,000 were sufficient to stimulate the desired international response. They also strengthened the Rwandan government resolve to see Mobutu removed from power. They were instrumental in supporting the subsequent rebellion led by Laurent Kabila, which swept Mobutu from power and also catalyzed a protracted internationalized civil war.[171] (Case 45)

[166] Quoted in ibid.

[167] "He is raising the stakes, getting attention and demanding more resources. Then he will try to calm things down," one diplomat said. Quoted in Robert Block, "Mobutu 'Raising the Stakes in Search of Aid,'" *Globe and Mail*, August 24, 1995.

[168] Lynn Duke, "An Ally in Africa, but at What Price? From the Start, Mobutu Has Been Both Solution and Problem for His Foreign Patrons," *Washington Post*, April 1, 1997.

[169] Ibid.

[170] James C. McKinley Jr., "Zaire's Gamble: Persuading Refugees to Leave, or Else," *New York Times*, February 12, 1996.

[171] A key aim of the rebels—beyond unseating Mobutu after thirty-one years of authoritarian rule—was to "solve" the refugee crisis once and for all. Andrew Maykuth, "Camp Crisis: The Hutu Refugee Problem Was Long Feared," *Philadelphia Inquirer*, November 10, 1996.

Libya (G)—Egypt/Arab League, 1995 [Palestinians]; *Failure*

After three months of threatening to do so, in September 1995, Libyan President Muammar al-Gaddafi expelled and stranded more than 5,000 Palestinians on the Libyan-Egyptian border. Gaddafi claimed to have generated the crisis to express his displeasure with—and to encourage a redrafting of—the proposed Israeli–Palestinian Liberation Organization (PLO) peace accords. At the time, however, some diplomats argued that Libya may have also been "using the deportations to win leverage on other issues," including, but not limited to, lifting what was widely seen to be a crippling economic embargo.[172] (See the 2004 Libya, case 62, for further details.) Whatever the true objectives, the gambit failed. The governments of Egypt and Israel refused to accept the Palestinians, who were eventually forcibly moved to another location by Libyan police and military in April 1997.[173] (Case 46)

North Korea (tacit/reluctant G)—China, mid- to late 1990s [North Koreans]; *Success*

Already reeling from the economic consequences of the decline and collapse of the Soviet Union, in the mid-1990s, North Korea was ravaged by a series of major floods and poor harvests. Pyongyang found itself with a crippled economy, unable to feed its 24 million people. As economic and humanitarian conditions deteriorated, concerns in neighboring countries about the consequences of a possible regime collapse quickly mounted. Fears were sufficiently acute that talks were reportedly held between U.S. diplomatic and military planners and South Korea, Japan, and China about how to cope if large numbers of hungry refugees began pouring out of the country.[174]

Throughout the crisis period, North Korean leader Kim Jong Il was able to successfully leverage the mass migration–related fears of his neighbors—and especially China—to extract food and other economic aid.[175] Specific threats to unleash an outflow were not necessary, although it has been repeatedly asserted that Kim did indeed make some.[176] The uncertainties associated with the fact that "no one

[172] Sunni Khalid, "Qaddafi Expels Palestinians, Arab League May Step In," *All Things Considered*, NPR, September 13, 1995, transcript #1969–3.

[173] Anthony Cordesman, *A Tragedy of Arms: Military and Security Developments in the Maghreb* (Santa Barbara: Greenwood Publishing, 2002), 191.

[174] Thomas E. Ricks, "US Gears Up for North Korean Collapse," *Wall Street Journal*, June 26, 1997.

[175] U.S. CIA Office of Asian Pacific and Latin American Analysis, "Exploring the Implications of Alternative North Korean Endgames: Results From a Discussion Panel on Continuing Coexistence between North and South Korea," January 21, 1998, 3, www.gwu.edu/~nsarchiv/NSAEBB/NSAEBB205/Document%20No%2014.pdf.

[176] "Their message is not only that others should feed their people but that others should also confirm their authority; otherwise they may unleash either floods of desperate refugees or the forces of their well-fed army." "Engaging North Korea," *Washington Post*, August 9, 1997. This message was echoed in my interviews with government officials and NGO representatives.

kn[ew] what a cutoff of aid would lead to because the North retain[ed] the lever-age to provoke a variety of crises" meant that China was committed to provid-ing whatever resources were necessary to maintain North Korea's existence "as a separate but weak state."[177] During the 1990s, Chinese assistance was principally financial (food and fuel); however, it blossomed into something rather more sig-nificant (i.e., into a diplomatic counterweight to the United States on the nuclear question) in the years that followed.[178]

China was not alone in providing aid to North Korea. Indeed, an estimated $2 billion was provided between 1994 and 1998, $650 million of which came from the United States. But China was particularly vulnerable/exposed and thus par-ticularly willing to provide aid—along with other assistance, it provided nearly 800,000 tons of grain in 1997 alone. (Case 47)

Albania (G)—European Union/Italy, 1997 [Albanians]; *Success*

In early 1997, in the wake of widespread chaos in Albania following the collapse of pyramid savings schemes, President Sali Berisha called for an EU military in-tervention to bring order to his country and forestall another major outflow of Al-banians.[179] In response—speaking for the European Union—German Chancellor Helmut Kohl insisted that the Albanian upheaval was largely an internal political problem and that sending in outside forces would not quash the domestic chaos.[180]

But as the number of asylum seekers crossing the Adriatic passed 10,000, Italy panicked and broke ranks with the rest of the European Union. On March 19, the government declared a state of emergency to cope with the influx. On March 25, after the number of displaced Albanians on Italian soil reportedly topped 18,000, Italy announced that not only would it not accept any more Albanians but also, with the acquiescence of Albanian Prime Minister Bahkim Fino, it would deploy special forces troops (from the San Macro Brigade—the Italian equivalent of the Special Air Service, SAS) to stop the influx and repatriate undesirables back to Tirana.[181]

In short, although the European Union as a whole had rejected Albanian de-mands, Italy unilaterally conceded to them and undertook its own intervention—sanctioned by the UN, but managed by the Italians.[182] The mission had two major

---

[177] U.S. CIA Office of Asian Pacific and Latin American Analysis, "Exploring the Impli-cations," 8.

[178] See, for instance, Elizabeth Rosenthal, "The Korean Breakthrough; China Hopes to Ben-efit from Korean Talks," *New York Times*, June 16, 2000.

[179] The Albanian government had been duped into encouraging its nationals to invest in a pyramid scheme. When the original sponsors fled with all of the money, widespread rioting and raids on government facilities ensued.

[180] William Drozdiak, "Europeans Reject Call for Help in Albania; NATO Reluctant to In-tervene Despite Threat," *Washington Post*, March 15, 1997.

[181] Richard Owen, "Italy Declares State of Emergency over Albanian Refugees," *Times*, March 20, 1997.

[182] Shortly after an announcement by Italian Foreign Minister Lamberto Dini that the exo-dus posed "a threat to the whole of Europe," the UN Security Council adopted a resolution

objectives: the distribution of humanitarian aid and assistance to the Albanian government to help it "regain control of flashpoints and to get state institutions working again."[183] In elections held in June and July, Berisha and his party were voted out of office, and foreign forces left Albania in early August. So although Berisha achieved his stated objectives, he still lost power. Nonetheless, he was resuscitated relatively quickly. He was reelected Socialist Party leader in October 1997 and resumed leadership of the country in 2005. (Case 48)

Turkey (G)—Italy, 1998 [Kurds]; *Indeterminate*

The arrival of 1,200 Kurdish refugees in Italy in early 1998 was alleged by some to have been engineered (or, at least, tacitly permitted) by Turkey to try to persuade Italy to shift its negative stance on Turkish accession to the European Union. Others claim the Turks facilitated the outmigration to punish Italy for its lack of support during the period leading up to the outflow. At the same time, some German officials claimed that their country was the real target of the outmigration from Turkey because most of the refugees expressed their intent to transit immediately from Italy to Germany.[184] However, if coercion (by Turkey) of either Italy or Germany (regarding EU membership) was the intent, it failed; however, the available evidence is at best inconclusive.[185] (Case 49)

Kosovo Liberation Army (KLA) (AP)—NATO/United Nations Security Council, 1998–1999 [Kosovar Albanians]; *Success*

After watching the nonviolent resistance movement of Ibrahim Rugova, Kosovar Albanian leader, stall while, next door, Bosnia gained independence through the strategic use of violence and victimhood, the rebel KLA stepped up its attacks on their Serb oppressors and especially on members of the military and police forces. The KLA rightly surmised these attacks would lead the Serbs to crack down brutally and disproportionately on Kosovar civilians.[186] After several false

---

drafted by Italy that planted a stamp of international legitimacy on a plan to dispatch a "temporary and limited multinational force to facilitate the safe and prompt delivery of humanitarian assistance." Andrew Gumbel, "Italy Ready for Mission Impossible," *Independent*, April 7, 1997.

[183] Piero Fassino, Italian deputy foreign minister, in ibid.

[184] John Schmid, "Bonn Hails 8-Nation European Pact to Slow Flood of Kurdish Refugees," *International Herald Tribune*, January 10, 1998. See also Boyle, Halfacress, and Robinson, *Exploring Contemporary Migration*.

[185] Rupert Cornwell, "A Good Time Not to Say 'I Told You So,'" *Independent*, January 8, 1998.

[186] As Veton Surroi, Kosovo Albanian political leader, put it, "There [was] a message...being sent to the Kosovars—if you want to draw international attention you have to fight for it. That is exactly it. You need to use violence to achieve your goals." Quoted in British Broadcasting Company (BBC2) documentary, *Moral Combat: NATO at War*, broadcast on March 12, 2000, transcript available at http://news.bbc.co.uk/hi/english/static/events/panorama/transcripts/transcript_12_03_00.txt.

starts, the KLA was successful in drawing NATO into its fight for autonomy and, eventually, independence. Before the NATO campaign commenced, there were approximately 70,000 Kosovar refugees living abroad. The bombing campaign catalyzed a still more brutal and systematic crackdown by the Serbs, which engendered an outflow of over 800,000 Kosovar Albanians. The televised horrors associated with the massive outflow, and both the fears and compassion it engendered, galvanized public support for continuing the bombing campaign until the ethnic cleansing could be reversed and the Serb forces driven out of the province. The conflict ended with a negotiated settlement in June 1999, and after a series of protests, a good deal of diplomatic wrangling, and several regime changes in Serbia, Kosovo became independent in February 2008. (See chap. 3.) (Case 50)

Federal Republic of Yugoslavia (G)—NATO, 1998–1999 [Kosovar Albanians]; *Failure*

After the 1992–1995 war in Bosnia-Herzegovina, which had created more than 2 million refugees, the prospect of another outflow from the Balkans was viewed with grave concern and more than a little hostility by most Western European states. Evidence suggests Federal Republic of Yugoslavia (FRY) President Slobodan Milosevic gambled that public and leadership-level anxieties surrounding the possibility of another massive refugee flow from the Balkans, and disagreements over whether bombing was an appropriate response, would undermine NATO unity and keep the alliance from attacking him in response to his brutal counterinsurgency operations in Kosovo.[187] After deterrence failed, and the threatened NATO bombing campaign began in earnest, Milosevic and his leadership cadre set their sights on the possibility that NATO would fracture under the political pressures associated with a massive refugee outmigration and a sustained bombing campaign.[188] Thus, what had been a trickle of an outflow in the lead up to and first days of NATO bombing quickly blossomed into a full-scale humanitarian disaster that sent more than 800,000 Kosovar Albanians from their homes in a matter of weeks. Although the NATO alliance was placed under great strain as a result of the crisis—and for a time it appeared that it was in danger of fracturing—in the end the alliance held fast.[189] Moreover, the massive size and scale of the outflow itself, coupled with the existence of a deft NATO propaganda campaign designed to recall the horrors of the Holocaust and the fact that relatively few of the displaced actually made it to western European soil, meant that support for

[187] Ibid.; Tim Judah, *Kosovo: War and Revenge* (New Haven: Yale University Press, 2002), chap. 8; Brian C. Rathbun, *Partisan Interventions: European Party Politics and Peace Enforcement in the Balkans* (Ithaca, N.Y.: Cornell University Press, 2004); Rosa Balfour, Roberto Menotti, and Ghita Micieli de Biase, "Italy's Crisis Diplomacy in Kosovo, March–June 1999," *International Spectator* 36 (1999): 67–81.

[188] *Moral Combat*; Judah, *Kosovo*; Rathbun, *Partisan Interventions*.

[189] As British Prime Minister Tony Blair put it, "The bottom line was we couldn't lose. If we lost, it's not just that we would have failed in our strategic objective; failed in terms of the moral purpose—we would have dealt a devastating blow to the credibility of NATO and the world would have been less safe as a result of that." Quoted in *Moral Combat*.

the operation and for Kosovar Albanian refugees actually grew over time, rather than declined.[190] Milosevic's gambit consequently failed. (See chap. 3.) (Case 51)

Macedonia (O)—NATO, April 1999 [Kosovar Albanians]; *Success*

Macedonia (O)—NATO, May 1999 [Kosovar Albanians]; *Success*

The Macedonian decision to align itself with NATO during its spring 1999 war with the FRY entailed obvious risks from the outset. Once the resulting refugee crisis increased the cost of cooperation, key figures within the Macedonian leadership threatened to close the border against further inflows, to publicly criticize NATO airstrikes, and to demand that NATO forces leave the country. (To be fair, Macedonian media and politicians had been warning for years that their border would be closed in the event of a massive exodus from Kosovo;[191] however, this threat was not incorporated into UNHCR or NATO planning since it was widely believed that the right of refuge in the country of first asylum would nevertheless be upheld.) As the numbers of Kosovars bottled up at the Blace field on the Macedonian border began to grow exponentially—and pictures were broadcast worldwide—strong incentives to find an acceptable solution were created. NATO was particularly susceptible for two reasons. First, the timing of the refugee flight (during the NATO bombing campaign expressly undertaken on behalf of Kosovar Albanians) led to a presumption of NATO responsibility for the refugees. In addition, it became increasingly clear that, at least in the short term, the air campaign had resulted in more rather than less violence against them. Second, the Kosovar Albanian refugees resisted a UNHCR proposal to transfer them from Macedonia to Albania, which would have eliminated any opportunity for evacuation from the region. In short, NATO was seen as "responsible" for the crisis, a problem that was not going to conveniently resolve itself.[192]

Within days, the United States took the lead in promising economic assistance, help to build refugee camps and care for the displaced, and refugee burden-sharing with initially resistant Western European countries. The World Bank also offered an initial installment of a massive aid program of $40 million dollars.[193] Macedonia reopened its border; a larger crisis was averted.

About a month later, however, on May 5, after accepting about 350,000 refugees—which represented close to 20 percent of its own population and seriously threatened the ethnic balance of the country—Macedonia closed its border again.[194] This move generated outrage within human rights organizations. At the

---

[190] "Kosovo: The Untold Story; How the War Was Won," *Observer*, July 18, 1999.
[191] Michael Barutciski and Astri Suhrke, "Lessons from the Kosovo Refugee Crisis: Innovations in Protection and Burden-Sharing," *Journal of Refugee Studies* 14 (2001), 96.
[192] U.S. Committee on Refugees (USCR), *World Refugee Survey 2000* (Washington, D.C.: USCR, 2000), 255.
[193] Barutciski and Suhrke, "Lessons from the Kosovo Refugee Crisis"; Jeremy Harding, "Europe's War," *London Review of Books*, April 29, 1999, www.lrb.co.uk/v21/n09/hard01_.html.
[194] Barutciski and Suhrke, "Lessons from the Kosovo Refugee Crisis", 96.

time, Amnesty International released a statement, declaring, "the authorities in Macedonia are effectively holding to ransom those refugees waiting on its borders to enter....Frequent closures of the border by the Macedonian authorities seem to be used to prompt quicker action in evacuating refugees."[195] It also generated great anger and consternation within NATO. Nevertheless, evacuations to parts of Western Europe were stepped up in response. Then, on May 13—the very same day that Macedonia agreed to reopen its border[196]—the World Bank approved $50 million in credit, which permitted Macedonia to address a number of domestic problems, not all of which were tied to the Kosovar refugee crisis, including "shortfalls in export revenues, rising balance of payment pressures, and exceptional demands on public expenditures."[197]

By the end of 1999, the number of refugees in Macedonia had fallen from the previously stated high of approximately 300,000–350,000 to approximately 17,000. The number of NATO troops likewise fell from approximately 30,000 to 7,000. Foreign Minister Aleksandr Dimitrov called on the international community to "live up to its promises by assisting Macedonia in addressing economic problems associated with its cooperation during the war for Kosovo." The subsequent lack of progress on this front "suggests that, with the refugee numbers dwindling and few new asylum seekers coming, Macedonia had less leverage than before."[198]

Early on in the crisis, Albania too made noises suggesting it might be forced to block or stop the refugee exodus from Kosovo, but it reached an agreement with NATO without having to follow through on its threats.[199] (Cases 52 and 53)

Nauru (O)—Australia, 2001–2003 [mixed, mostly Afghanis and Kurds]; *Success*

In what appears to have commenced as a purely opportunistic gesture that expanded to full-scale and repeated financial coercion over time, in fall 2001 the tiny island nation of Nauru (population 11,000) agreed to host several hundred Afghan and Kurdish asylum seekers who had been intercepted in Australian territorial waters. Australia would pay all costs for room and board and provide Nauru with $10 million in development aid. Although the original package was for $10 million, over the course of the next several years Nauru leveraged a series

---

[195] Amnesty International, "Kosovo: Playing Politics with Refugees in Macedonia," May 1999, www.amnesty.org/en/library/info/EUR70/071/1999.

[196] "Reopened Macedonian Border Draws Few Refugees," CNN, May 13, 1999.

[197] John H. P. Williams and Lester A. Zeager, "Macedonian Border Closings in the Kosovo Refugee Crisis: A Game-Theoretic Perspective," *Conflict Management and Peace Science* 21 (2004): 135.

[198] Ibid. See also Foreign Broadcast Information Service (FBIS), "The Internal Conflicts Could Be Crucial for Macedonia," *Skopje Utrinski Vesnik*, July 7–18, 1999 [translated text]; *FBIS Publications* (Washington, D.C.: U.S. Central Intelligence Agency, July–September 1999), CD-ROM disc no. 3.

[199] It has also been argued that Albania could not exercise the same leverage over NATO because the refugees were their co-ethnics. See Williams and Zeager, "Macedonian Border Closings."

of threatened (proto-)crises into a payout of more than $40 million in aid under the so-called Pacific Solution. Australia was able to warehouse the vast majority of its would-be asylum seekers offshore and essentially make the problem relatively invisible to its domestic audiences—although not the international community— and Nauru staved off bankruptcy. Given the fact that the Australian public was deeply divided about how to deal with the asylum seekers, it may have seemed like a small price to pay.[200] (See also Nauru 2004, case 59.) (Case 54)

Belarus (AP)—European Union, 2002 [mixed]; *Failure*

On November 13, 2002, Belarussian President Aleksandr Lukashenko threatened to flood the European Union with illegal immigrants after being told he would likely be refused entry to the NATO summit in Prague later that month.[201] Belarus was in a position to carry out its threats because it had at the time approximately 150,000 would-be emigrants, including refugees from Chechnya, within its territory. But Lukashenko did not follow through on his threats, despite eventual exclusion from the summit and ongoing EU admission discussions.[202] (Case 55)

Network of Activists and NGOs—China, South Korea 2002–2005 [North Koreans]; *Failures*

In 1989, Hungary opened its barbed-wire border with Austria and allowed thousands of East Germans vacationing in Hungary to escape communism. This tide of refugees turned into a flood, hastening not only the collapse of East Germany, but also the fall of the Iron Curtain. From early 2002–2005, a loose network of at least seven international human rights NGOs sought to replicate the eastern European experience in northeast Asia. The network targeted China and South Korea. Its immediate goals were to persuade China to offer protection to North Koreans seeking refuge instead of repatriating them and to persuade South Korea to take in more North Koreans. The underlying premise in both cases was that more welcoming environments in potential host countries would incite a flood of North Korean refugees who, in escaping political oppression en masse, would stimulate the same type of regime collapse in North Korea that had occurred in East Germany.[203] The activists tried to pressure both governments by staging well-publicized embassy crashings. When these publicity stunts failed to change target behavior, the activists tried instead to replicate the Vietnamese boatpeople crisis, putting North

[200] Peter Mares, *Borderline: Australia's Response to Refugees and Asylum Seekers in the Wake of the Tampa* (Sydney: University of New South Wales Press, 2002), chap. 5.

[201] President Lukashenko, quoted in Robin Shepherd, "Belarus Issues Threat to EU over Summit," *Times*, November 14, 2002.

[202] "Will Belarus Flood Poland with 50,000 Migrants by Christmas?" *Wprost*, December 15, 2002; RFE/RL Newsline, October 2, 2002.

[203] Brad Glosserman and Scott Snyder, "Borders and Boundaries: The North Korean Refugee Crisis," *PacNet Newsletter* 21 (2002), www.csis.org/pacfor/pac0221.htm.

Koreans out to sea in the hope that they would be rescued and offered asylum. These attempts too failed to generate the desired responses and, in the end, neither China nor South Korea conceded to the demands of the activists.

Whatever the expected reputational costs associated with failing to be more receptive, the anticipated economic costs and potential political dangers of concession were deemed to be higher. As Dr. Kim Kihwan, South Korean ambassador-at-large for economic affairs, put it, a "flood of refugees will cause enormous social and economic difficulties, so we have to avoid the implosion scenario by all means."[204] Moreover, not only did coercion fail to generate the desired effect, it actually backfired. Whereas previously Chinese authorities had turned a blind eye to the vast majority of North Koreans who had managed to reach China and had allowed inconspicuous NGOs to help some of them gain asylum abroad, the high-profile escapes and associated publicity compelled China to shut down what was in essence a functioning underground railroad. Hence, prospects for most would-be North Korean refugees actually worsened as a consequence of the activists' actions. (See chap. 5.) (Cases 56 and 57)

North Korea (G)—China, 2002-2005 and beyond (North Koreans); *Success*

Throughout the period that the NGO network was pressuring China and South Korea—and indirectly trying to bring down the North Korean regime (cases 56–57)—Kim Jong Il was simultaneously exploiting Chinese (and South Korean) fears of implosion to extract aid and continued diplomatic support. As in the 1990s, Kim issued threats to get more assistance. In addition, he actively leveraged Chinese fears on the refugee front and motivated their resistance to U.S. demands that Kim end his nuclear program. As was the case in the 1990s, this was—and continues to be—a delicate game for the North Korean regime. A massive outflow could well be highly damaging to China, but it is even more likely to spell the end for Kim's regime. Ironically, therefore, to paraphrase Otto von Bismarck, Kim Jong Il has essentially been threatening to commit suicide in order to avoid death. (Case 58)

Nauru (O)—Australia, 2004 [mixed groups, South and Southwest Asians, including Afghanis, Kurds, Iraqis, Sri Lankans, and Burmese]; *Success*

In early January 2004, Australian Immigration Minister Phillip Ruddock alleged that Nauru was—consistent with its behavior in previous years (case 54)—using the plight of a small number of asylum-seeking hunger strikers to extract money from Australia. As he put it, "One of the things that of course regularly does happen with Nauru is that it seeks to get the best deal it can from being involved these arrangements, and one has to, I think, look at the sorts of comments that

---

[204] Robert Garran, "North Korean Famine Threatens Leaders," *Australian*, May 28, 1997.

are made from time to time as to whether or not they are part of a wider negotiating position."[205] Nauru vehemently denied the allegations. Yet, in exchange for extending the life of the controversial Australian-funded refugee detention center on the island until June 2005, Australia agreed to provide another $26 million in development aid and to send Australian officials to run the Nauruan finance department and police force.

Australia eventually (and summarily) ended its vulnerability to coercion by Nauru. In December 2007, newly elected Prime Minister Kevin Rudd announced that Australia would grant the last remaining Burmese and Sri Lankan detainees on Nauru (there were fewer than one hundred) residency rights and would put an immediate end to the Pacific Solution.[206] This was probably a wise move. When all was said and done, to house and process fewer than 1,700 asylum seekers, the Pacific Solution had cost Australia more than $1 billion over five years, or more than $500,000 per asylum seeker.[207] (Case 59)

Haiti (G)—United States, 2004 [Haitians]; *Failure*

In the period leading up to President Aristide's hasty departure from Haiti in February 2004, the French were actively calling for Aristide to step down, whereas the United States had adopted a more ambiguous stance. Although blaming Aristide for contributing to ongoing violence on the ground, Secretary of State Colin Powell declared that the United States could not "buy into a proposition that says the elected president must be forced out of office by thugs and those who do not respect law and are bringing terrible violence to the Haitian people."[208] Washington also publicly supported a plan that would have allowed Aristide to serve out his term, albeit with substantially reduced powers, but refused to commit U.S. troops to protect him during his remaining time in power.

The relatively supportive U.S. position shifted abruptly, however, in the face of growing violence in Haiti and fast on the heels of an assertion by Aristide that, absent the insertion of previously requested armed international assistance, another Haitian migration crisis was likely to follow. At a press conference in English, Creole, French and Spanish, Aristide declared, "We need the presence of the international community as soon as possible. Unfortunately many brothers and sisters in Port-de-Paix will not come down to Port-au-Prince; they will take to the sea, they will become boat people. How many will die before reaching Florida? I don't know."[209] Irrespective of whether Aristide meant his statement to be taken as a coercive threat, it appears to have been received as one.

[205] Matt Brown, "Nauru Seeking Financial Gain over Asylum Seekers: Ruddock," ABC News, January 7, 2004, www.abc.net.au/pm/content/2003/s1021840.htm; See also *Courier Mail* (Queensland), January 8, 2004.
[206] "Australia Ends 'Pacific Solution,'" BBC News, February 8, 2008.
[207] Connie Levett, "Pacific Solution Cost $1 Billion," *Sydney Morning Herald*, August 25, 2007.
[208] "France Ponders Haiti Peace Force," BBC News, February 18, 2004.
[209] Carol J. Williams, "Aristide Appeals to World for Aid," *Los Angeles Times*, February 25, 2004.

Within twenty-four hours, President George W. Bush warned Haitians against trying to escape the violence and turmoil by sailing to the United States, saying that any Haitians caught doing so would be turned back." U.S. officials, including Secretary Powell, also announced that an Aristide resignation was an "increasing possibility" and "more a feature of the [ongoing] discussions than it was before."[210] Just two days later, the United States sent an aircraft to Port-au-Prince to help Aristide decamp for renewed exile, this time in the Central African Republic. (See chap. 4.) (Case 60)

Belarus (AP)—European Union, 2004 [mixed]; *Failure*

On May 26, 2004, President Lukashenko of Belarus demanded millions of euros from Brussels to stop refugees flooding into the European Union and warned that the consequences could be dire for Europe if EU members failed to deliver the required cash. EU leaders did not concede to Lukashenko's demands. However, they did agreed to spend upward of a half billion euros to increase security at the outermost borders of the European Union. They likewise created a new agency devoted to the protection of the outer frontier. It was noted at the time that Belarus played "a particular role in EU plans."[211] (Case 61)

Libya (AP)—European Union, 2004 [mixed, mostly North Africans]; *Success*

In October 2004, EU foreign ministers agreed to lift all remaining sanctions on Libya in exchange for a Libyan promise to stop outflows of illegal immigrants from Libyan ports to Western Europe, and, especially, to the Italian island of Lampedusa. The migrants in question were mostly North Africans, but some came from as far away as Sri Lanka and Bangladesh; in any case, their arrival was unwelcome. The decision to end sanctions came after months of pressure from Italy—on whose shores over 9,700 migrants had arrived in 2004 alone—and which had threatened to lift sanctions unilaterally if the European Union failed to agree to do so unanimously.[212] For its part, Libya—which had explicitly stated that it could "no longer act as Europe's coast guard" if sanctions were not lifted—also

---

[210] "Boatpeople Fleeing Haitian Crisis; U.N. Security Council to Address Situation Thursday," CNN, February 26, 2004.

[211] "EU Asked for Payment to Stop Refugees," *Irish Times*, May 27, 2004; "Radioactive Refuge: Offering Asylum in Chernobyl's No Man's Land," *Der Spiegel On-Line*, October 14, 2005, http://www.spiegel.de/international/0,1518,379727,00.html.

[212] Indeed, Italy concluded a separate bilateral deal with Libya in August of the same year. The details of this bilateral agreement remain unknown; Italy has refused to make it public despite public requests from the European Parliament; the UN Human Rights Committee; and NGOs, including Human Rights Watch. See, for instance, Human Rights Watch (HRW), *Stemming the Flow: Abuses against Migrants, Asylum Seekers and Refugees, publication 18, 2006,* chap. 10, http://www.hrw.org/en/reports/2006/09/12/stemming-flow.

received promises of annual financial assistance from the European Commission in exchange for its cooperation on the immigration issue.[213] (Case 62)

Chad (G)—United Nations Security Council/international community, 2006 [Darfurians]; *Indeterminate*

In April 2006, Chadian President Idriss Déby threatened to expel 200,000 Sudanese refugees sheltering in the east of the country after repeating accusations that Sudan was supporting the Chadian rebels who had launched a new offensive to oust him that week. Déby asserted that "the international community" (essentially, the UN Security Council) had until June 2006 to resolve the Darfur crisis. If it failed, he would expel the refugees.[214] Following closed-door talks with UN officials, Déby agreed not to follow through on the threat.[215] Although it is not clear what, if anything, Chad received in exchange for backing down, in the weeks that followed the threat, efforts to end the conflict were (temporarily) stepped up. (The UN Security Council announced plans to do so the very same day Déby made his threat, so attributing direct causality to the threat would be a stretch.) U.S. officials, including U.S. Deputy Secretary of State Robert Zoellick, traveled to the region in early May, and a peace accord was successfully concluded between the major rebel factions and the Sudanese government (although fighting would continue for some time thereafter). Chad and Sudan also signed an agreement to stop hosting one another's rebel groups on their respective territories in July 2006, although little changed materially on the ground. (Case 63)

Libya (AP)—European Union (especially Italy), 2006 [mixed, largely North Africans]; *Partial Success*

In August 2006, the number of migrants—both drowned and intercepted—between Libya and Italy again mounted. Italy expressed suspicions that Gaddafi was encouraging the outflow to extract further financial concessions either from Italy specifically or from the European Union more generally. Consistently with this assertion, the following month Gaddafi announced at a meeting of the African Union that "we will ask Europe to pay 10 billion euros per year if it really wants to stop migration toward Europe." "Europeans who do not want to take the immigrants in should either emigrate to America or pay Libya to keep its borders closed."[216]

[213] "EU Set to Lift Arms Embargo on Libya," *Middle East On-line*, September 22, 2004, www.swissinfo.org/eng/index.html?siteSect=143&sid=5231206.

[214] "Chad Threatens to Expel Sudanese Refugees," *New York Times*, April 14, 2006; Marc Lacey, "After Battle in Capital, Chad Threatens to Expel Sudanese," *New York Times*, April 15, 2006.

[215] "Chad: President Retracts Refugee Threat, Closes Sudan Border," IRIN, April 17, 2006; "Chad Won't Expel Refugees, U.N. Official Says," CNN, April 17, 2006.

[216] "African Immigrants: Gaddafi's Price Has Gone Up," *Brussels Journal*, September 13, 2006. When asked whether Libya would countenance outsourcing and asylum-processing

Theretofore, EU payouts to Libya had been rather more modest; for example,, in 2005 the EU Commission reportedly paid Libya 2 billion euros to contain the outflow from North Africa. Gaddafi was at least somewhat successful, however, in extracting additional funds.[217] Moreover, the payoff he received appears disproportionate to the actual threat. A 2006 study conducted by Italian police, for instance, concluded that cross-Mediterranean migration accounted for only 4 percent of the migrants who arrived illegally in Italy in 2004.[218] (Case 64)

---

camps on its territory, Shukri Ghanim, then Libyan general secretary of the General People's Congress, replied, "Why should we. We don't want to be the trashcan for Europe." Quoted in HRW, *Stemming the Flow*, 99.

[217] "African Immigrants."

[218] "Sunk: More Boats, More Drownings—and Suspicions about Libya's Role," *Economist*, August 24, 2006; Sara Hamood, "EU-Libya Cooperation on Migration: A Raw Deal for Refugees and Migrants?" *Journal of Refugee Studies* 21 (2008): 19–42. (As of this writing, the issue of engineered migrations between North Africa and the European Union has not been decisively resolved, but rather, like the Mediterranean itself, continues to ebb and flow.)

Index

Note: Page numbers in *italics* indicate figures; those with a *t* indicate tables.

www.ingramcontent.com/pod-product-compliance
Lightning Source LLC
Chambersburg PA
CBHW030637270326
41929CB00007B/108